PRAISE FOR GA
THIRD ARC O

Major Spoilers
"I would be very surprised if this book doesn't end up on a best of list for 2015."

SciFiPulse
"This is the perfect team for Sonja's exploits as they show in this issue... Sonja continues to dazzle and terrify with this creative team."

The Fandom Post
"As always, the writing, the art, the color, and the letters are excellent and combine to make a comic that is full of action, adventure, humor, and thought."

Comic Bastards
"There are few titles that have captured my love month in and month out. There are even fewer that can maintain it for so long. Red Sonja for Simone and Geovani's run has been one such title."

Comicosity
"The perfect completion to Gail Simones time on the Red Devil."

ComicWow!
"Simone does high-concept as well as anyone in the business. At the same time, she does small stories with a poignancy and a sense of subtle, nuanced dialogue (both internal and external) that are matched only by a talented few."

Spartan Town
"Red Sonja in general is a phenominal character for her humor, wit, tenacity and confidence. Under Simone, Sonja continually is growing and developing."

Unleash the Fanboy
"Red Sonja continues to be one of Dynamite's best current series, with this current arc being truly captivating."

Nerds Unchained
"This may just be a masterpiece in the making."

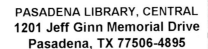

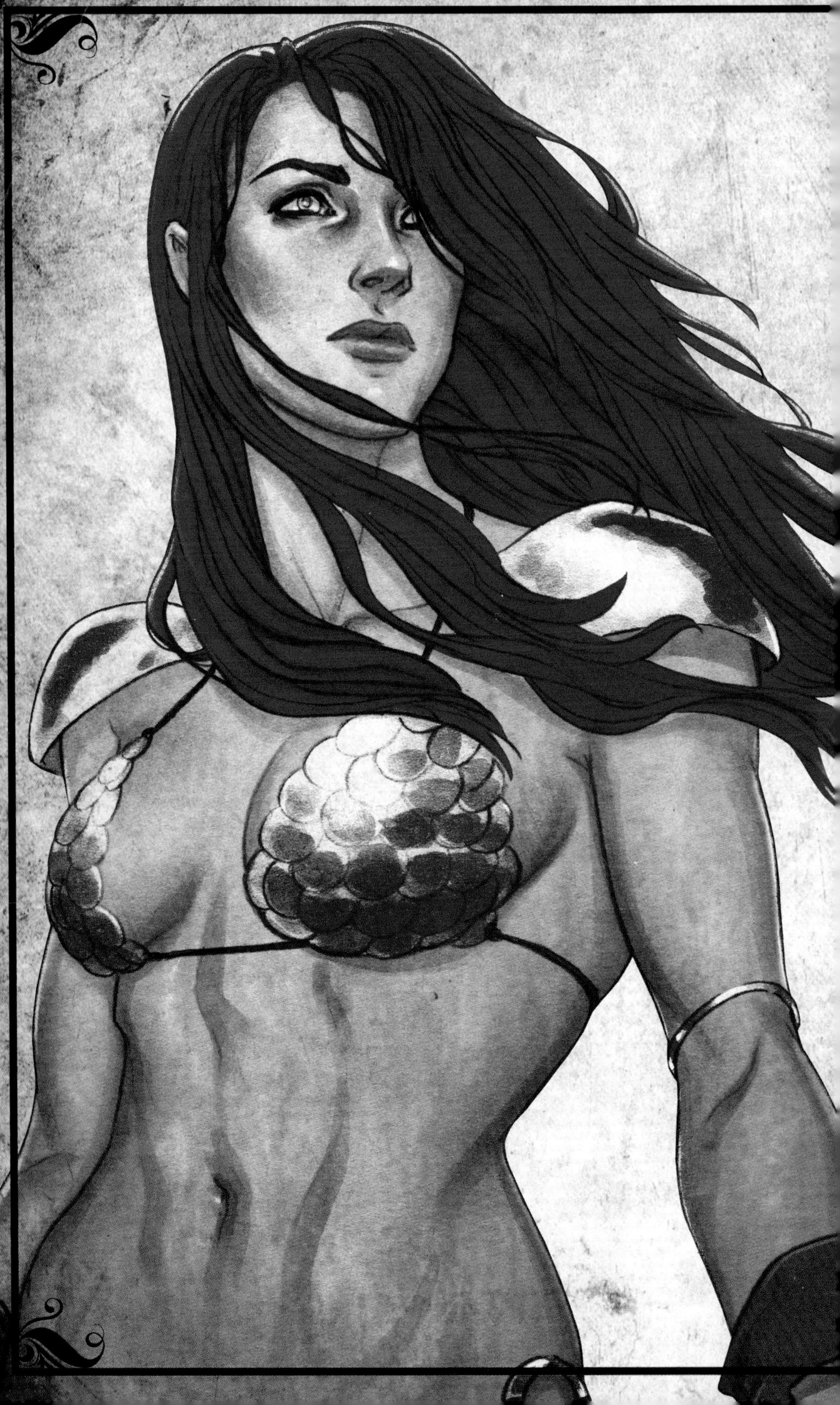

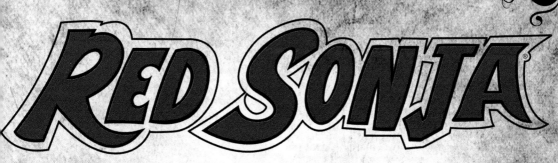

RED SONJA®

VOLUME THREE:
THE FORGIVING OF MONSTERS

written by **GAIL SIMONE**

illustrated by **WALTER GEOVANI**

colored by **ADRIANO LUCAS, ALEX GUIMARÃES, MARCO LESKO, and VINICIUS ANDRADE**

lettered by **SIMON BOWLAND**

series editor **JOSEPH RYBANDT**

collection design by **JASON ULLMEYER**

based on the heroine created by **ROBERT E. HOWARD**

executive editor - Red Sonja **LUKE LIEBERMAN**

in memory of **ARTHUR LIEBERMAN**

DYNAMITE®

Nick Barrucci, CEO / Publisher
Juan Collado, President / COO

Joe Rybandt, Senior Editor
Rachel Pinnelas, Associate Editor

Jason Ullmeyer, Design Director
Geoff Harkins, Graphic Designer
Chris Caniano, Digital Associate
Rachel Kilbury, Digital Assistant

Brandon Dante Primavera, Dir. of IT/Operations
Rich Young, Dir. of Business Development

Keith Davidsen, Marketing Manager
Kevin Pearl, Sales Associate

Visit us online at **www.DYNAMITE.com**
Follow us on Twitter **@dynamitecomics**
Like us on Facebook **/Dynamitecomics**
Watch us on YouTube **/Dynamitecomics**

First Printing
ISBN-10: 1-60690-601-1
ISBN-13: 978-1-60690-601-9
10 9 8 7 6 5 4 3 2 1

RED SONJA®, VOL. 3: THE FORGIVING OF MONSTERS. First printing. This volume collects material originally published in Red Sonja ® volume 2 #13-18. Published by Dynamite Entertainment. 113 Gaither Dr., STE 205, Mt. Laurel, NJ 08054.

Printed in Canada.

For media rights, foreign rights, promotions, licensing, and advertising: marketing@dynamite.com

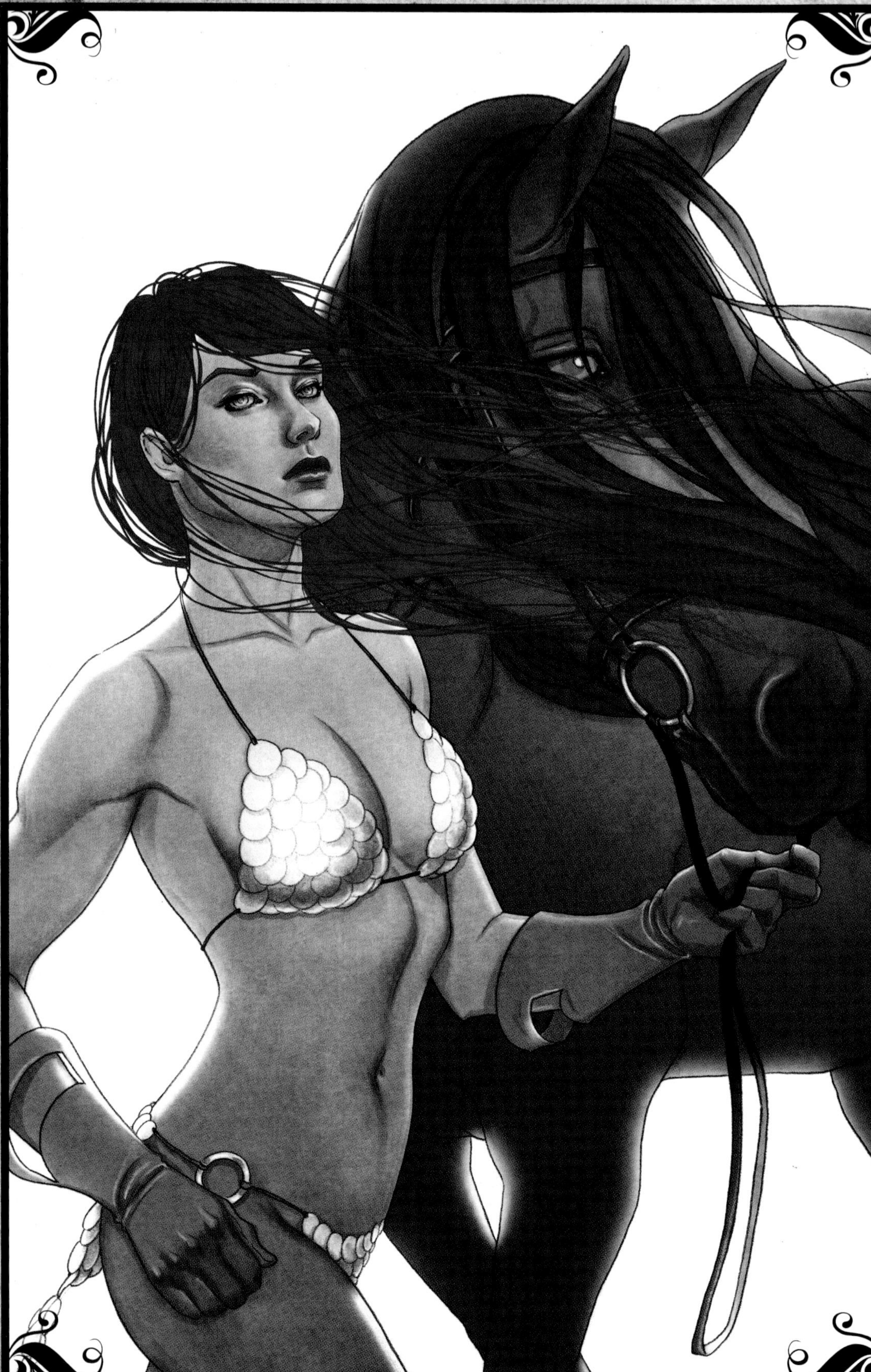

ISSUE THIRTEEN
cover by JENNY FRISON

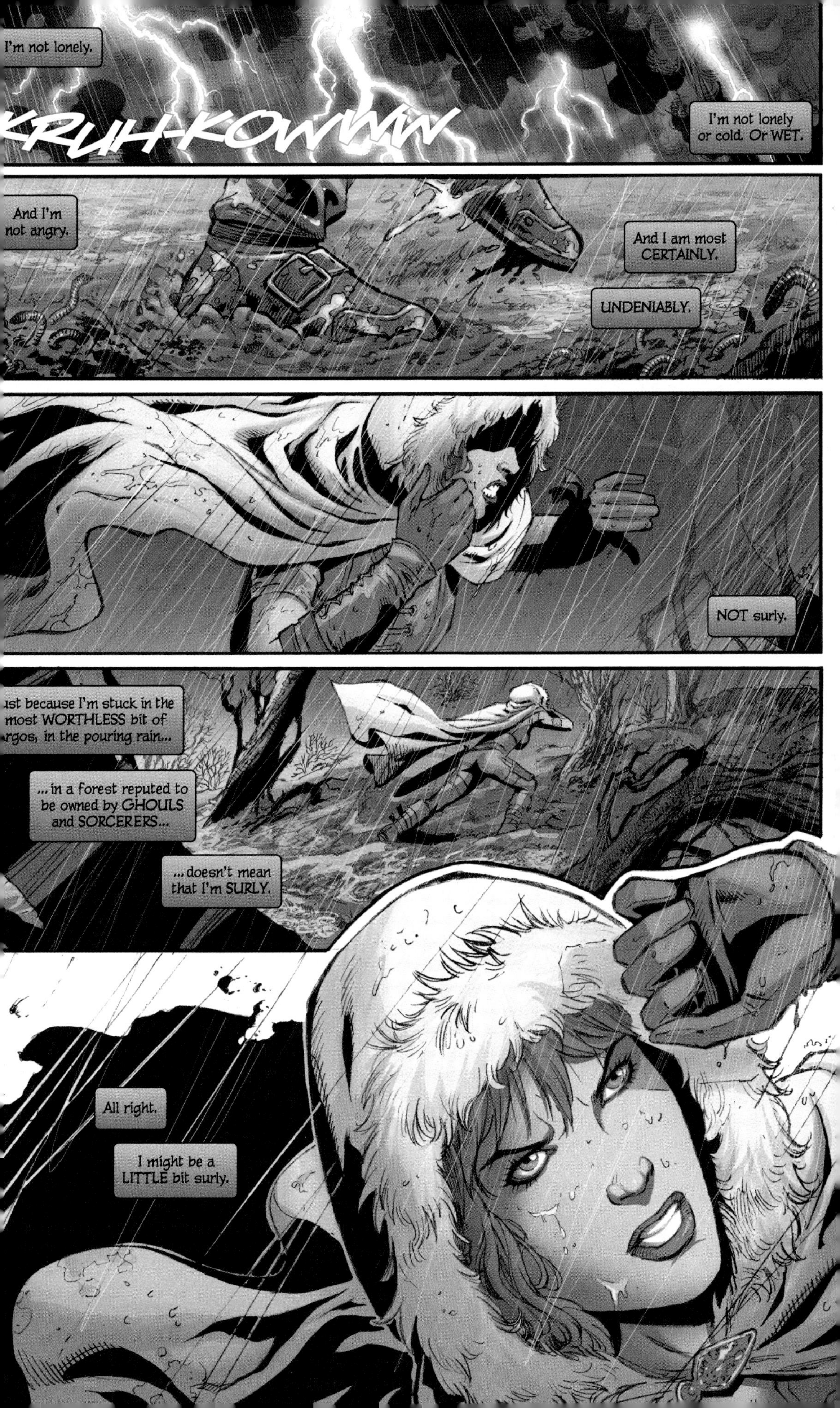
I'm not lonely.
KRUH-KOWWW
I'm not lonely or cold. Or WET.
And I'm not angry.
And I am most CERTAINLY.
UNDENIABLY.
NOT surly.
ust because I'm stuck in the most WORTHLESS bit of rgos, in the pouring rain...
...in a forest reputed to be owned by GHOULS and SORCERERS...
...doesn't mean that I'm SURLY.
All right.
I might be a LITTLE bit surly.

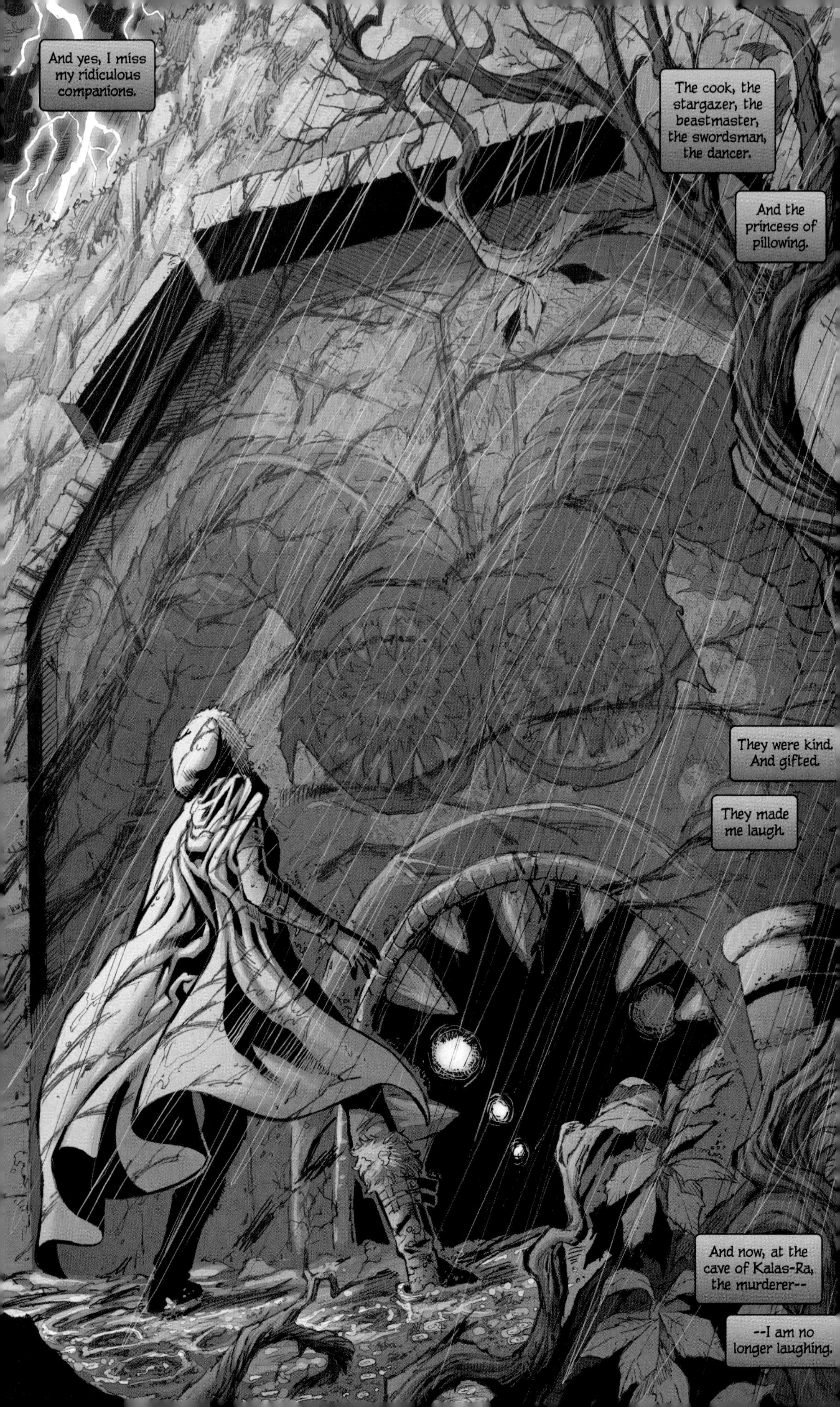

And yes, I miss my ridiculous companions.
The cook, the stargazer, the beastmaster, the swordsman, the dancer.
And the princess of pillowing.
They were kind. And gifted.
They made me laugh.
And now, at the cave of Kalas-Ra, the murderer--
--I am no longer laughing.

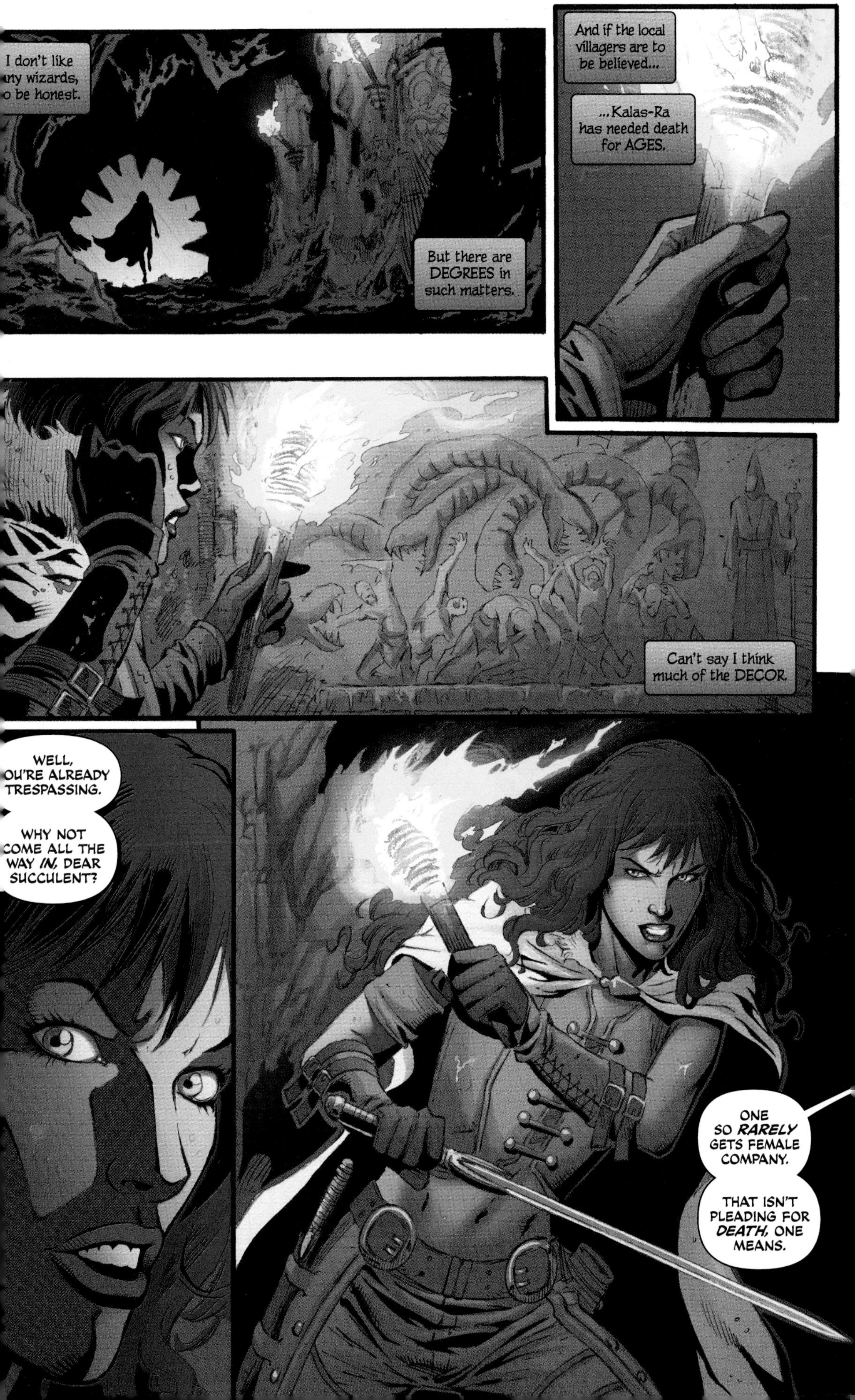
I don't like
ny wizards,
o be honest.
But there are DEGREES in such matters.
And if the local villagers are to be believed...
...Kalas-Ra has needed death for AGES.
Can't say I think much of the DECOR.
WELL, OU'RE ALREADY TRESPASSING.
WHY NOT COME ALL THE WAY *IN,* DEAR SUCCULENT?
ONE SO *RARELY* GETS FEMALE COMPANY.
THAT ISN'T PLEADING FOR *DEATH,* ONE MEANS.

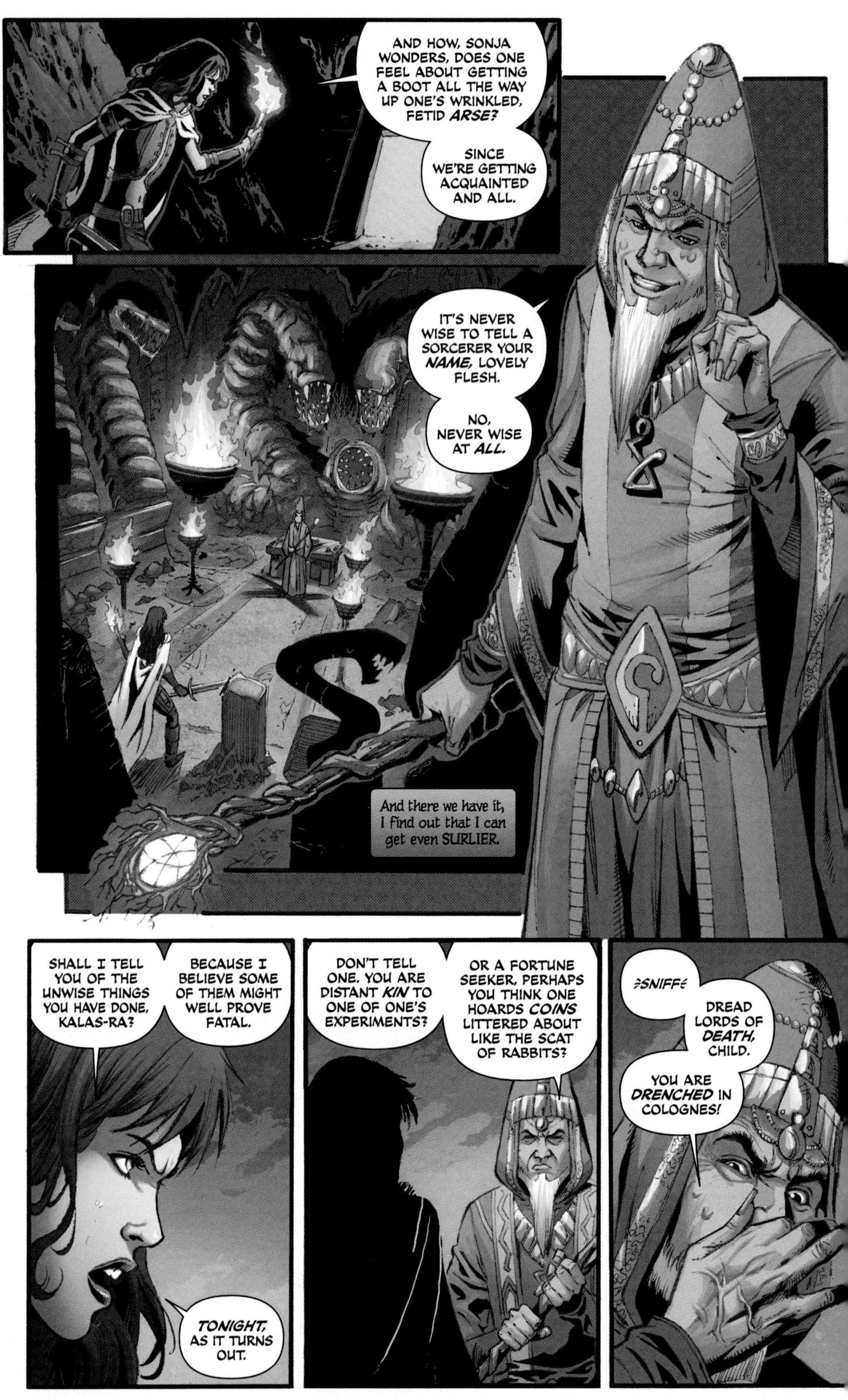
AND HOW, SONJA WONDERS, DOES ONE FEEL ABOUT GETTING A BOOT ALL THE WAY UP ONE'S WRINKLED, FETID ARSE?
SINCE WE'RE GETTING ACQUAINTED AND ALL.
IT'S NEVER WISE TO TELL A SORCERER YOUR NAME, LOVELY FLESH.
NO, NEVER WISE AT ALL.
And there we have it, I find out that I can get even SURLIER.
SHALL I TELL YOU OF THE UNWISE THINGS YOU HAVE DONE, KALAS-RA?
BECAUSE I BELIEVE SOME OF THEM MIGHT WELL PROVE FATAL.
TONIGHT, AS IT TURNS OUT.
DON'T TELL ONE. YOU ARE DISTANT KIN TO ONE OF ONE'S EXPERIMENTS?
OR A FORTUNE SEEKER, PERHAPS YOU THINK ONE HOARDS COINS LITTERED ABOUT LIKE THE SCAT OF RABBITS?
SNIFF
DREAD LORDS OF DEATH, CHILD.
YOU ARE DRENCHED IN COLOGNES!

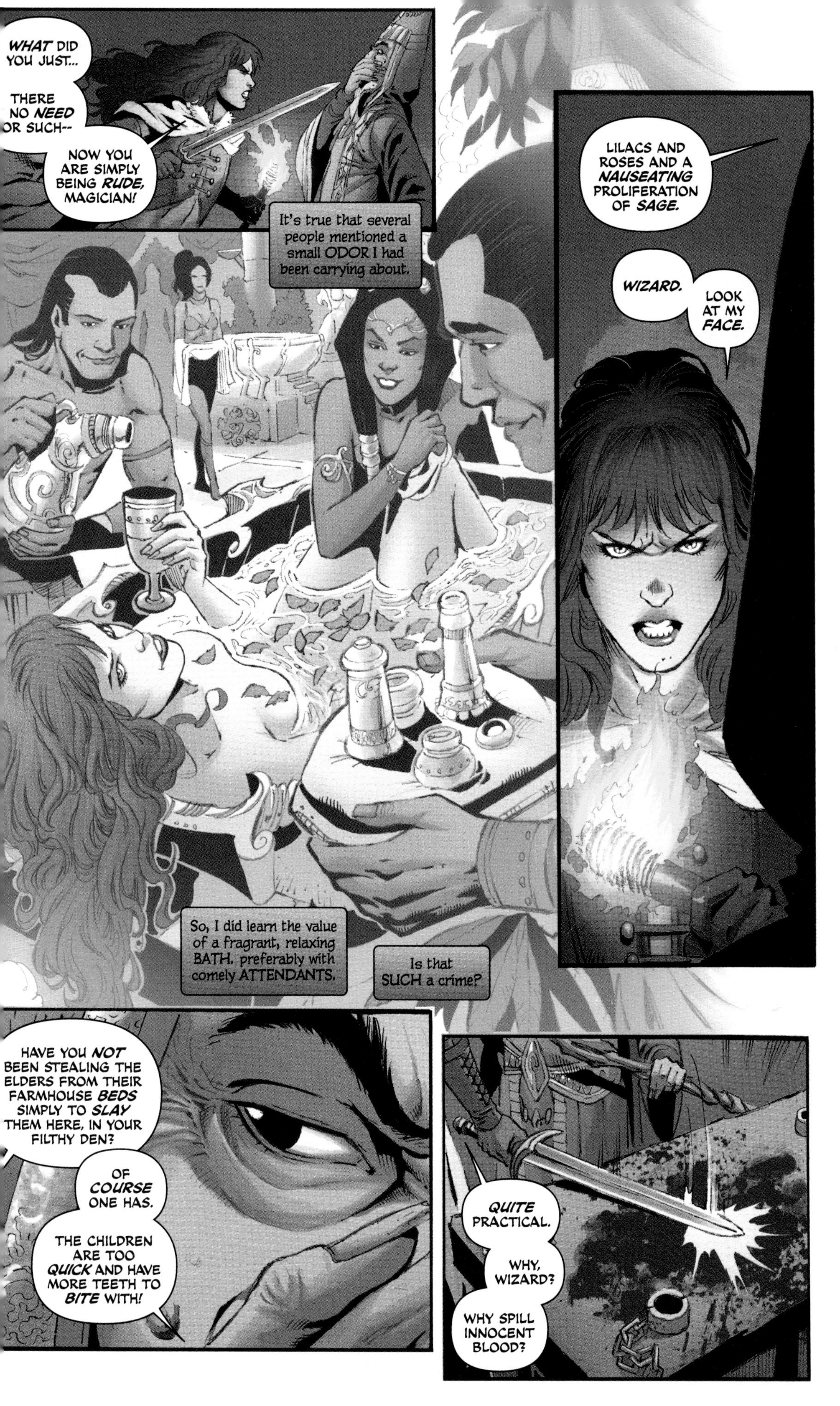
WHAT DID YOU JUST...
THERE NO NEED OR SUCH--
NOW YOU ARE SIMPLY BEING RUDE, MAGICIAN!
LILACS AND ROSES AND A NAUSEATING PROLIFERATION OF SAGE.
It's true that several people mentioned a small ODOR I had been carrying about.
WIZARD.
LOOK AT MY FACE.
So, I did learn the value of a fragrant, relaxing BATH. preferably with comely ATTENDANTS.
Is that SUCH a crime?
HAVE YOU NOT BEEN STEALING THE ELDERS FROM THEIR FARMHOUSE BEDS SIMPLY TO SLAY THEM HERE, IN YOUR FILTHY DEN?
OF COURSE ONE HAS.
THE CHILDREN ARE TOO QUICK AND HAVE MORE TEETH TO BITE WITH!
QUITE PRACTICAL.
WHY, WIZARD?
WHY SPILL INNOCENT BLOOD?

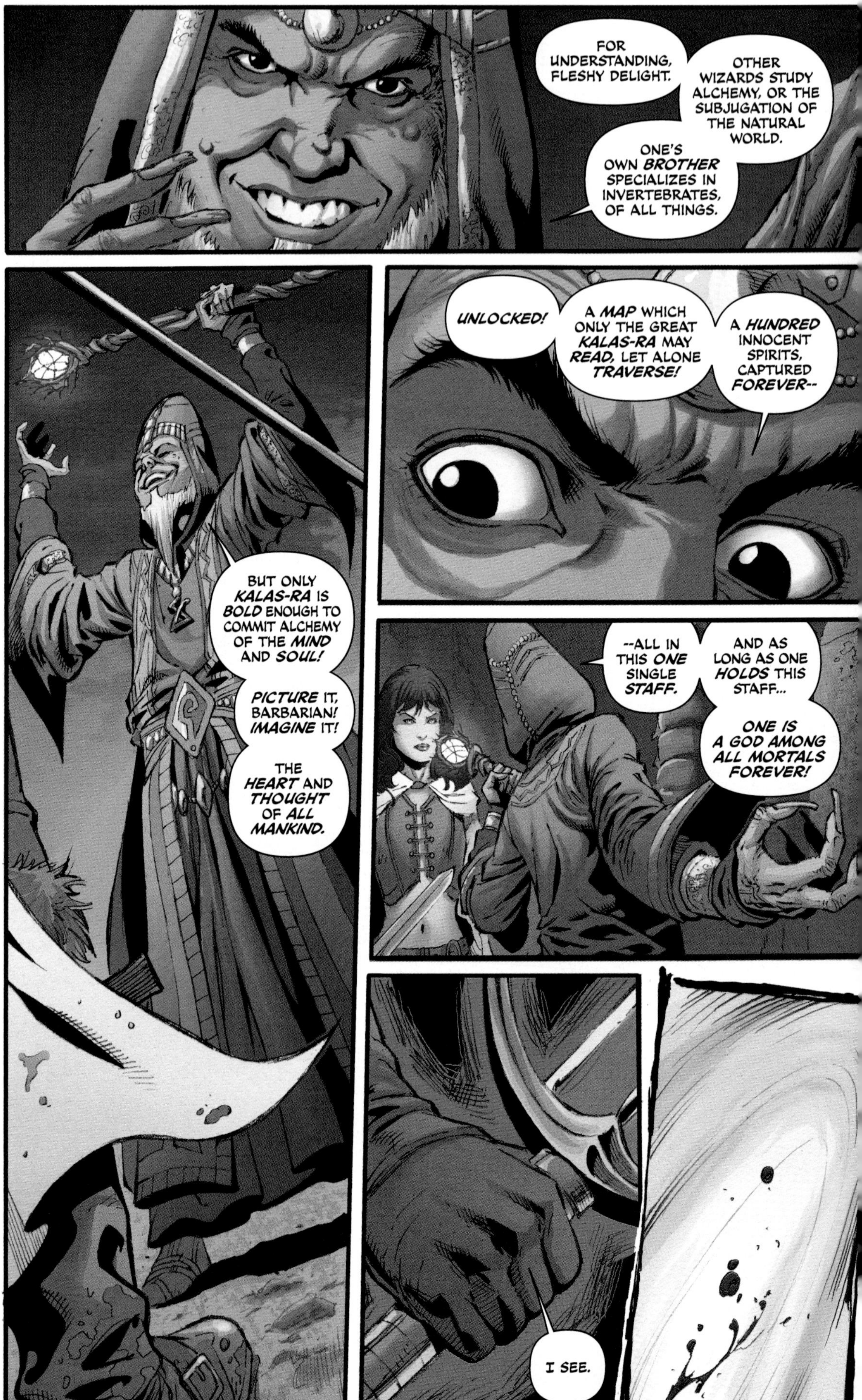
FOR UNDERSTANDING, FLESHY DELIGHT.
OTHER WIZARDS STUDY ALCHEMY, OR THE SUBJUGATION OF THE NATURAL WORLD.
ONE'S OWN BROTHER SPECIALIZES IN INVERTEBRATES, OF ALL THINGS.
BUT ONLY KALAS-RA IS BOLD ENOUGH TO COMMIT ALCHEMY OF THE MIND AND SOUL!
PICTURE IT, BARBARIAN! IMAGINE IT!
THE HEART AND THOUGHT OF ALL MANKIND.
UNLOCKED!
A MAP WHICH ONLY THE GREAT KALAS-RA MAY READ, LET ALONE TRAVERSE!
A HUNDRED INNOCENT SPIRITS, CAPTURED FOREVER--
--ALL IN THIS ONE SINGLE STAFF.
AND AS LONG AS ONE HOLDS THIS STAFF...
ONE IS A GOD AMONG ALL MORTALS FOREVER!
I SEE.

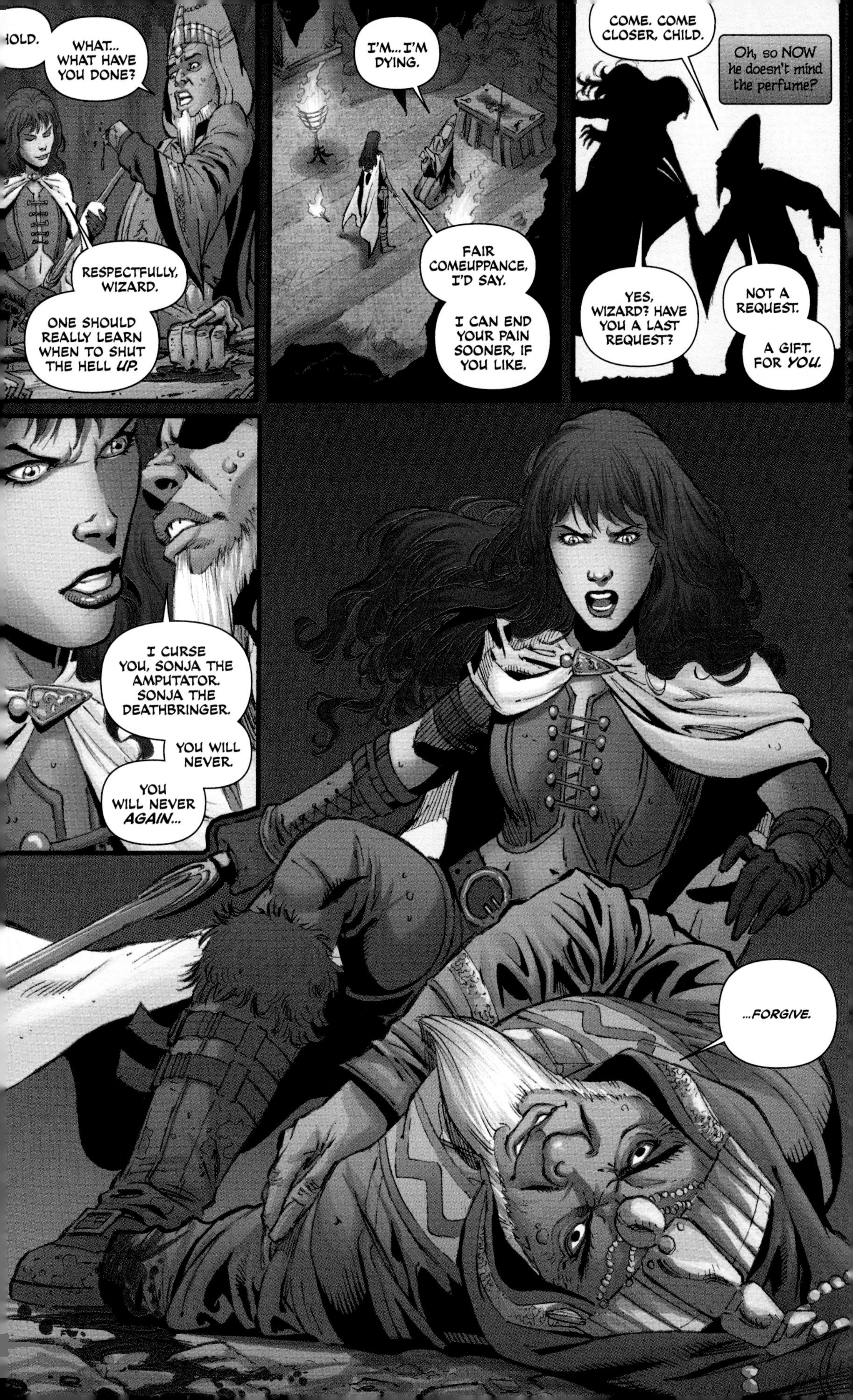

HOLD.
WHAT... WHAT HAVE YOU DONE?
RESPECTFULLY, WIZARD.
ONE SHOULD REALLY LEARN WHEN TO SHUT THE HELL *UP*.
I'M... I'M DYING.
FAIR COMEUPPANCE, I'D SAY.
I CAN END YOUR PAIN SOONER, IF YOU LIKE.
COME. COME CLOSER, CHILD.
Oh, so NOW he doesn't mind the perfume?
YES, WIZARD? HAVE YOU A LAST REQUEST?
NOT A REQUEST.
A GIFT. FOR *YOU*.
I CURSE YOU, SONJA THE AMPUTATOR. SONJA THE DEATHBRINGER.
YOU WILL NEVER.
YOU WILL NEVER *AGAIN*...
...FORGIVE.

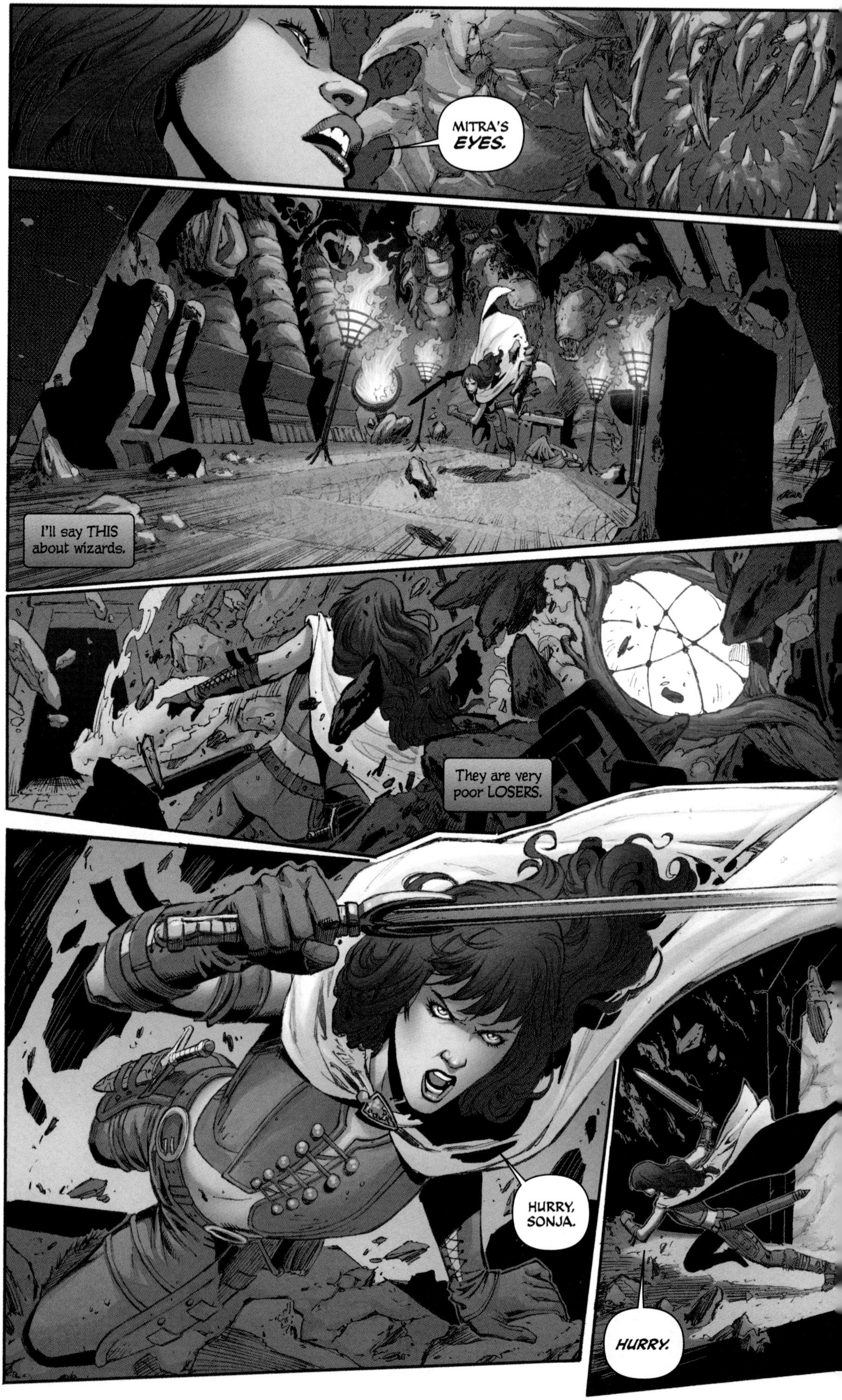
MITRA'S EYES.
I'll say THIS about wizards.
They are very poor LOSERS.
HURRY, SONJA.
HURRY.

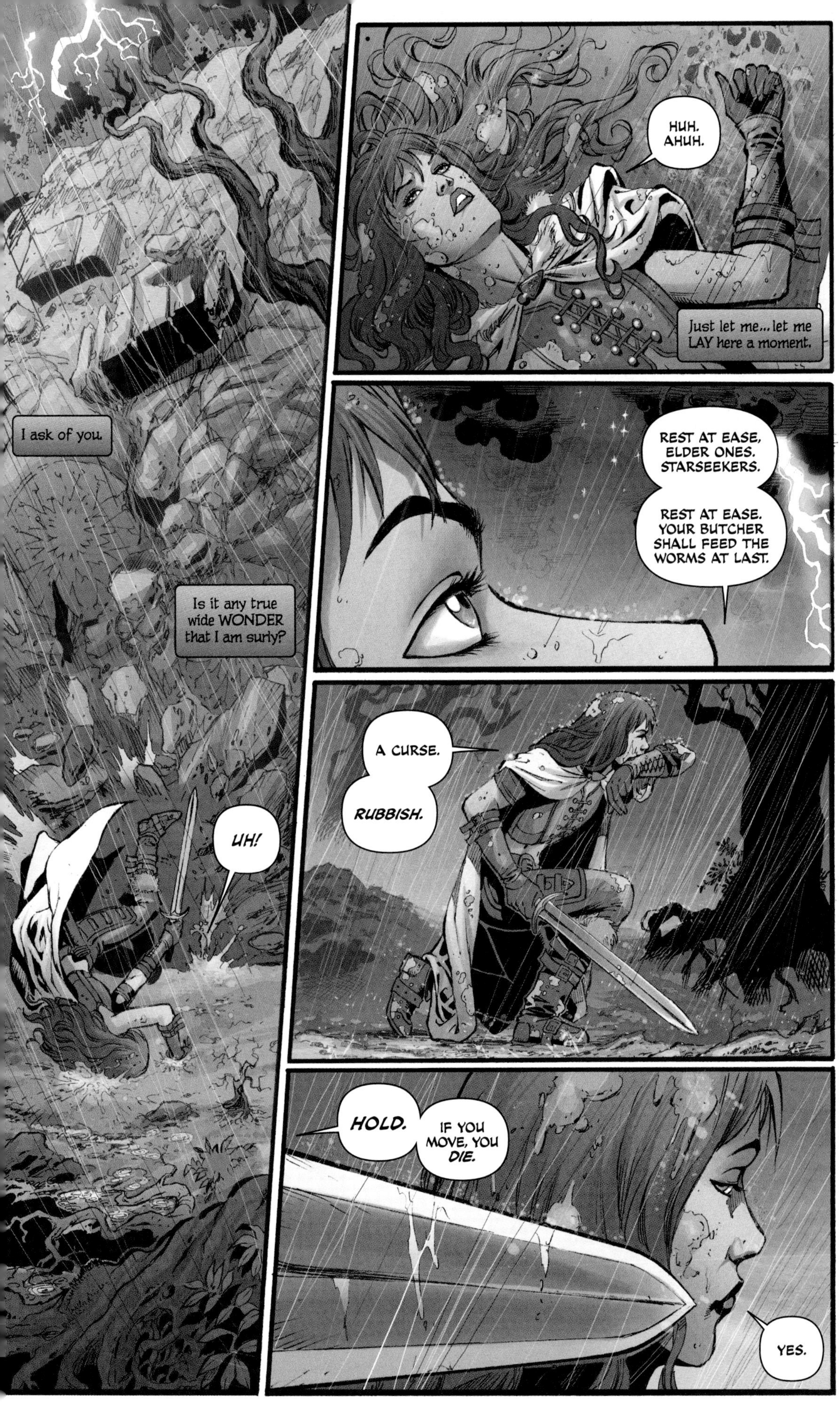
I ask of you.
Is it any true wide WONDER that I am surly?
UH!
HUH. AHUH.
Just let me... let me LAY here a moment.
REST AT EASE, ELDER ONES. STARSEEKERS.
REST AT EASE. YOUR BUTCHER SHALL FEED THE WORMS AT LAST.
A CURSE.
RUBBISH.
HOLD.
IF YOU MOVE, YOU DIE.
YES.

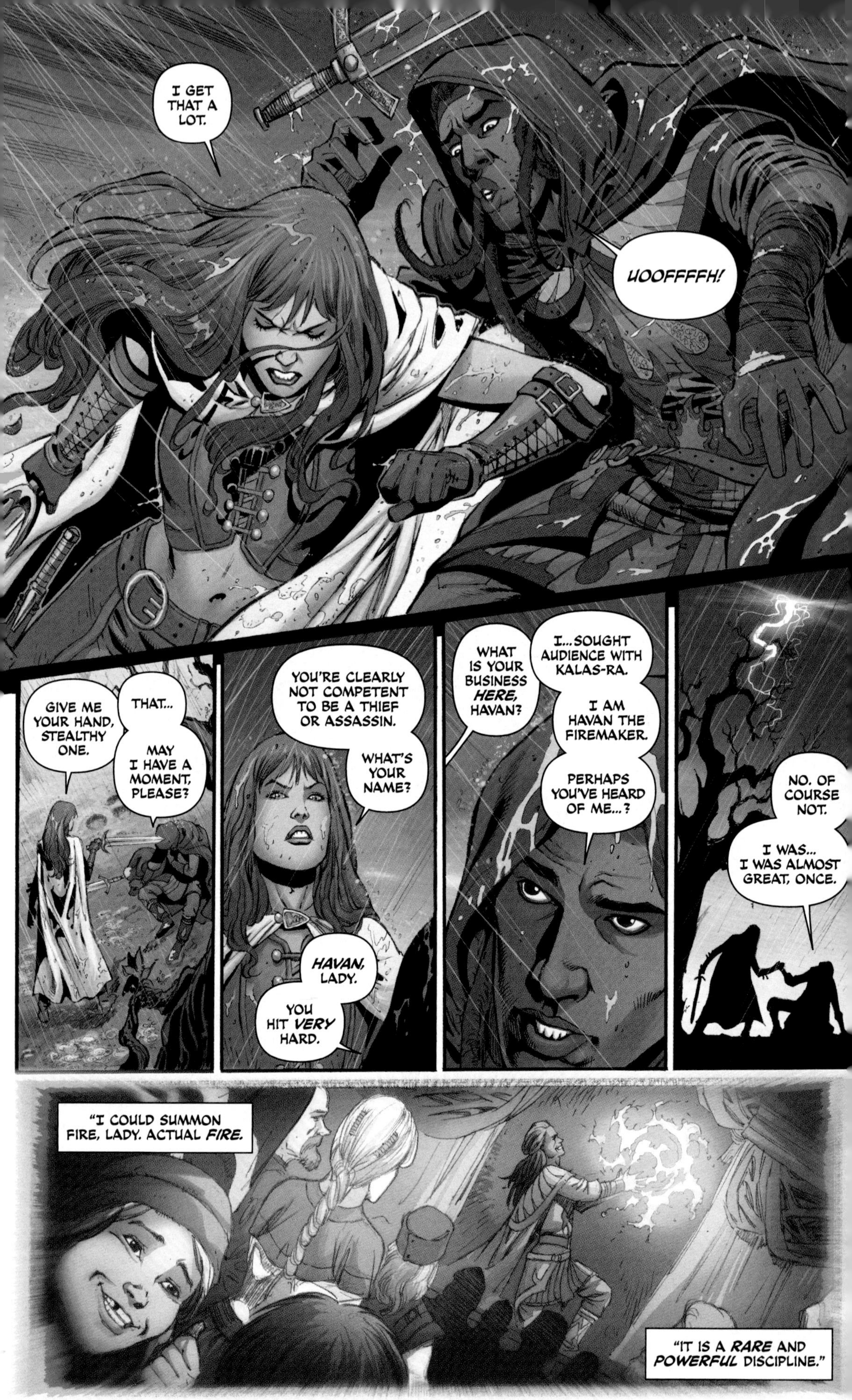
I GET THAT A LOT.
UOOFFFFH!
GIVE ME YOUR HAND, STEALTHY ONE.
THAT...
MAY I HAVE A MOMENT, PLEASE?
YOU'RE CLEARLY NOT COMPETENT TO BE A THIEF OR ASSASSIN.
WHAT'S YOUR NAME?
HAVAN, LADY.
YOU HIT *VERY* HARD.
WHAT IS YOUR BUSINESS *HERE,* HAVAN?
I...SOUGHT AUDIENCE WITH KALAS-RA.
I AM HAVAN THE FIREMAKER.
PERHAPS YOU'VE HEARD OF ME...?
NO. OF COURSE NOT.
I WAS... I WAS ALMOST GREAT, ONCE.
"I COULD SUMMON FIRE, LADY. ACTUAL *FIRE.*
"IT IS A *RARE* AND *POWERFUL* DISCIPLINE."

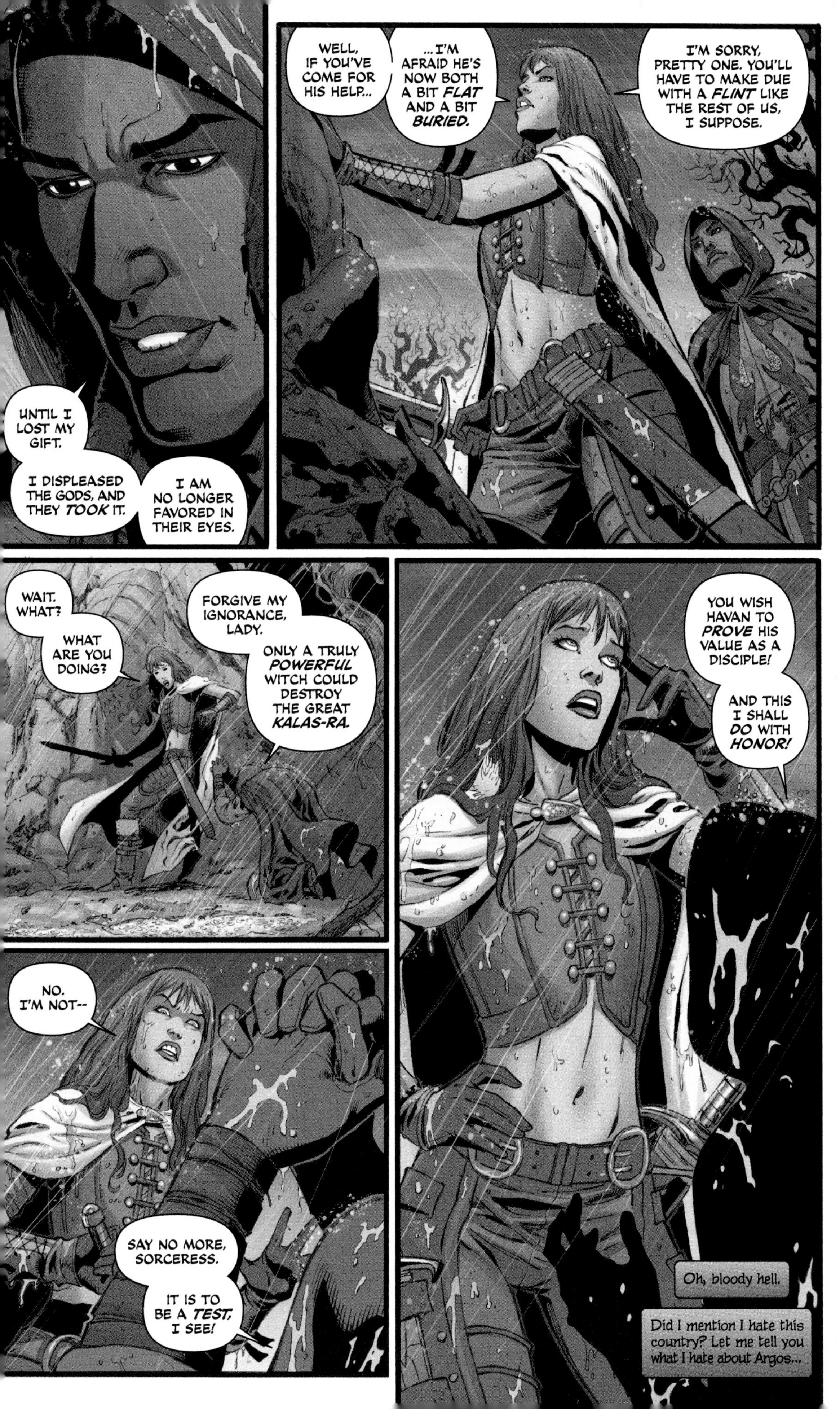
UNTIL I LOST MY GIFT.
I DISPLEASED THE GODS, AND THEY TOOK IT.
I AM NO LONGER FAVORED IN THEIR EYES.
WELL, IF YOU'VE COME FOR HIS HELP...
...I'M AFRAID HE'S NOW BOTH A BIT FLAT AND A BIT BURIED.
I'M SORRY, PRETTY ONE. YOU'LL HAVE TO MAKE DUE WITH A FLINT LIKE THE REST OF US, I SUPPOSE.
WAIT. WHAT?
WHAT ARE YOU DOING?
FORGIVE MY IGNORANCE, LADY.
ONLY A TRULY POWERFUL WITCH COULD DESTROY THE GREAT KALAS-RA.
NO. I'M NOT--
SAY NO MORE, SORCERESS.
IT IS TO BE A TEST, I SEE!
YOU WISH HAVAN TO PROVE HIS VALUE AS A DISCIPLE!
AND THIS I SHALL DO WITH HONOR!
Oh, bloody hell.
Did I mention I hate this country? Let me tell you what I hate about Argos...

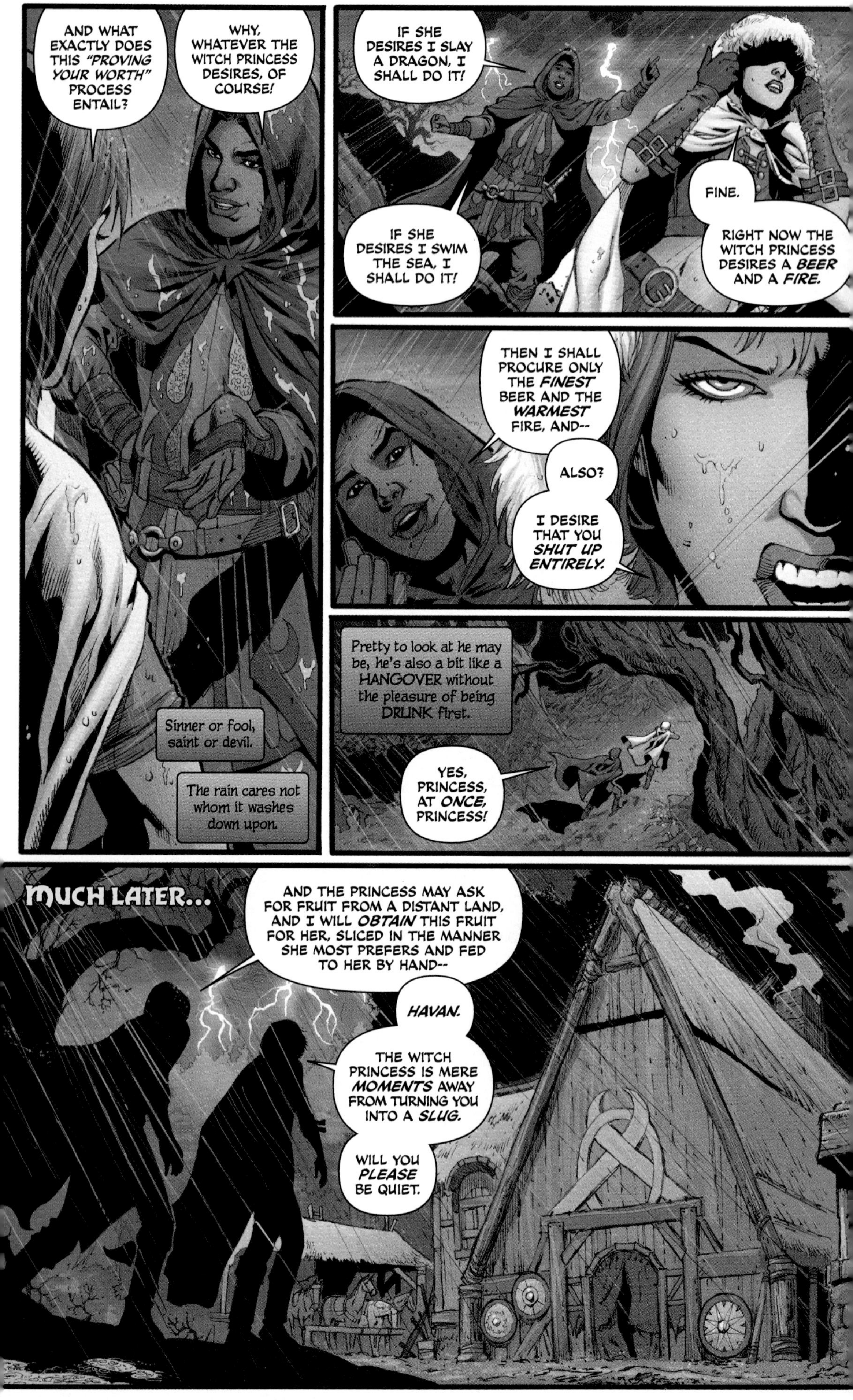
AND WHAT EXACTLY DOES THIS "PROVING YOUR WORTH" PROCESS ENTAIL?
WHY, WHATEVER THE WITCH PRINCESS DESIRES, OF COURSE!
Sinner or fool, saint or devil.
The rain cares not whom it washes down upon.
IF SHE DESIRES I SLAY A DRAGON, I SHALL DO IT!
IF SHE DESIRES I SWIM THE SEA, I SHALL DO IT!
FINE.
RIGHT NOW THE WITCH PRINCESS DESIRES A BEER AND A FIRE.
THEN I SHALL PROCURE ONLY THE FINEST BEER AND THE WARMEST FIRE, AND--
ALSO?
I DESIRE THAT YOU SHUT UP ENTIRELY.
Pretty to look at he may be, he's also a bit like a HANGOVER without the pleasure of being DRUNK first.
YES, PRINCESS, AT ONCE, PRINCESS!
MUCH LATER...
AND THE PRINCESS MAY ASK FOR FRUIT FROM A DISTANT LAND, AND I WILL OBTAIN THIS FRUIT FOR HER, SLICED IN THE MANNER SHE MOST PREFERS AND FED TO HER BY HAND--
HAVAN.
THE WITCH PRINCESS IS MERE MOMENTS AWAY FROM TURNING YOU INTO A SLUG.
WILL YOU PLEASE BE QUIET.

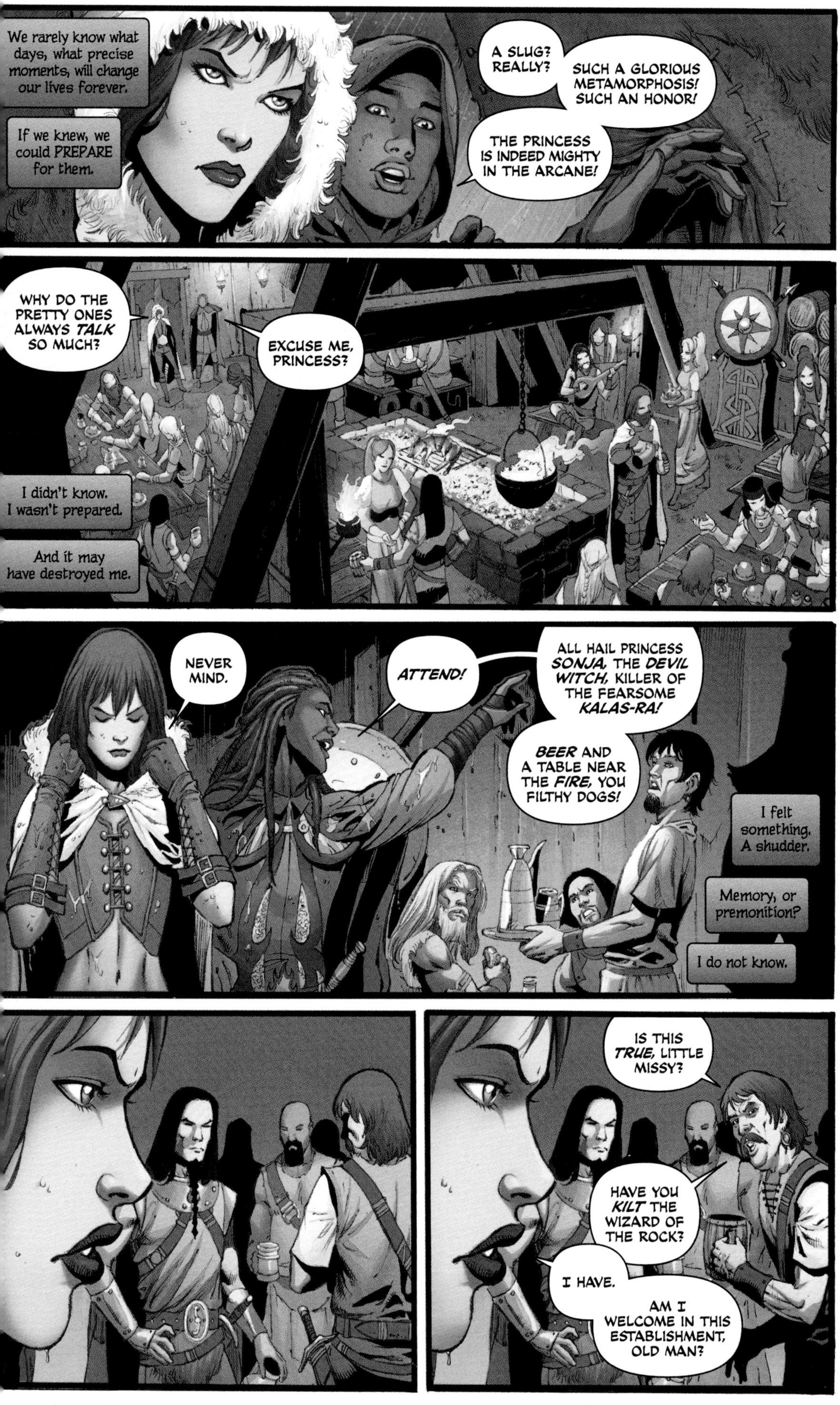

We rarely know what days, what precise moments, will change our lives forever.
If we knew, we could PREPARE for them.
A SLUG? REALLY?
SUCH A GLORIOUS METAMORPHOSIS! SUCH AN HONOR!
THE PRINCESS IS INDEED MIGHTY IN THE ARCANE!
WHY DO THE PRETTY ONES ALWAYS *TALK* SO MUCH?
EXCUSE ME, PRINCESS?
I didn't know. I wasn't prepared.
And it may have destroyed me.
NEVER MIND.
ATTEND!
ALL HAIL PRINCESS *SONJA*, THE *DEVIL WITCH*, KILLER OF THE FEARSOME *KALAS-RA!*
BEER AND A TABLE NEAR THE *FIRE*, YOU FILTHY DOGS!
I felt something. A shudder.
Memory, or premonition?
I do not know.
IS THIS *TRUE*, LITTLE MISSY?
HAVE YOU *KILT* THE WIZARD OF THE ROCK?
I HAVE.
AM I WELCOME IN THIS ESTABLISHMENT, OLD MAN?

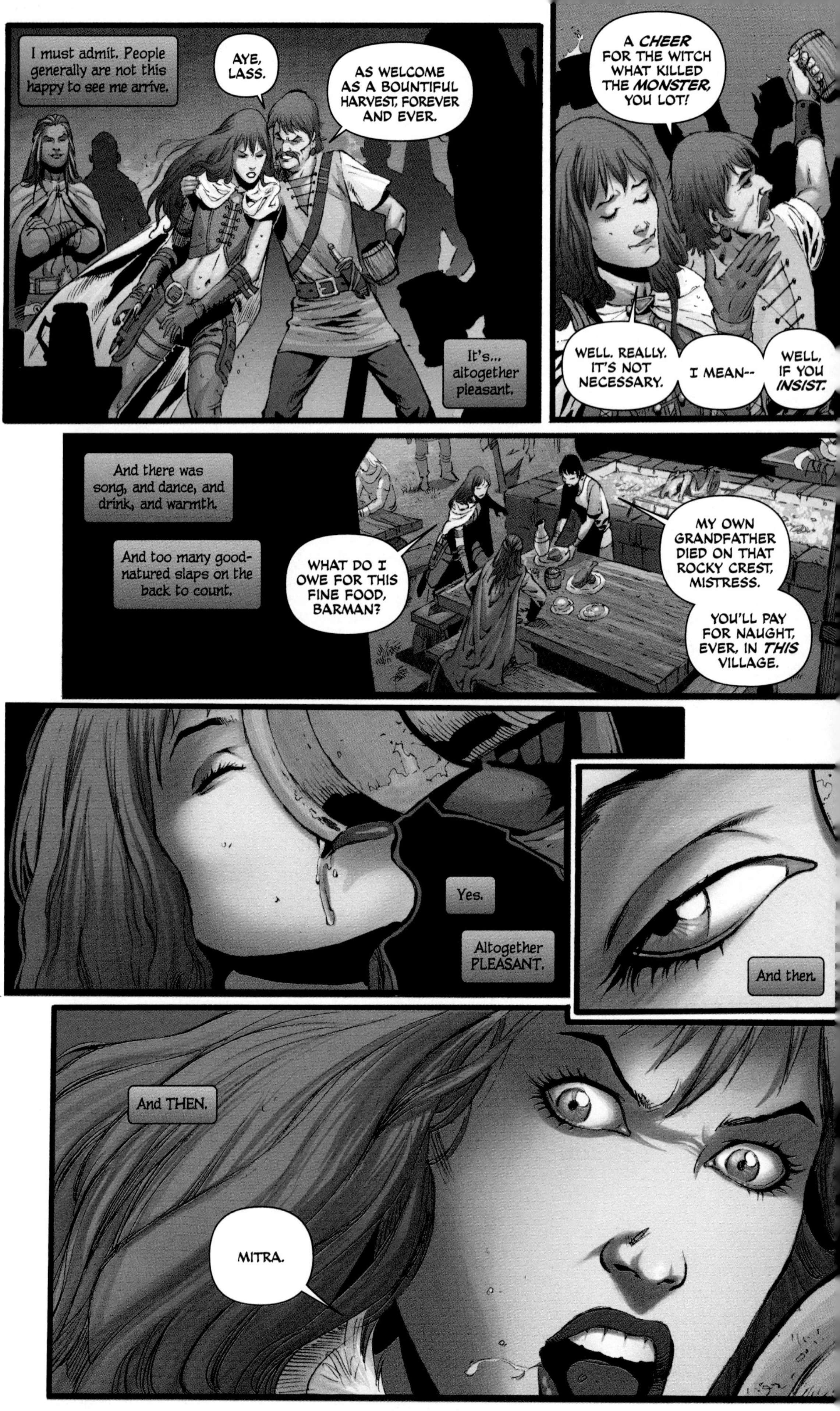
I must admit. People generally are not this happy to see me arrive.
AYE, LASS.
AS WELCOME AS A BOUNTIFUL HARVEST, FOREVER AND EVER.
It's... altogether pleasant.
A *CHEER* FOR THE WITCH WHAT KILLED THE *MONSTER*, YOU LOT!
WELL. REALLY. IT'S NOT NECESSARY.
I MEAN--
WELL, IF YOU *INSIST.*
And there was song, and dance, and drink, and warmth.
And too many good-natured slaps on the back to count.
WHAT DO I OWE FOR THIS FINE FOOD, BARMAN?
MY OWN GRANDFATHER DIED ON THAT ROCKY CREST, MISTRESS.
YOU'LL PAY FOR NAUGHT, EVER, IN *THIS* VILLAGE.
Yes.
Altogether PLEASANT.
And then.
And THEN.
MITRA.

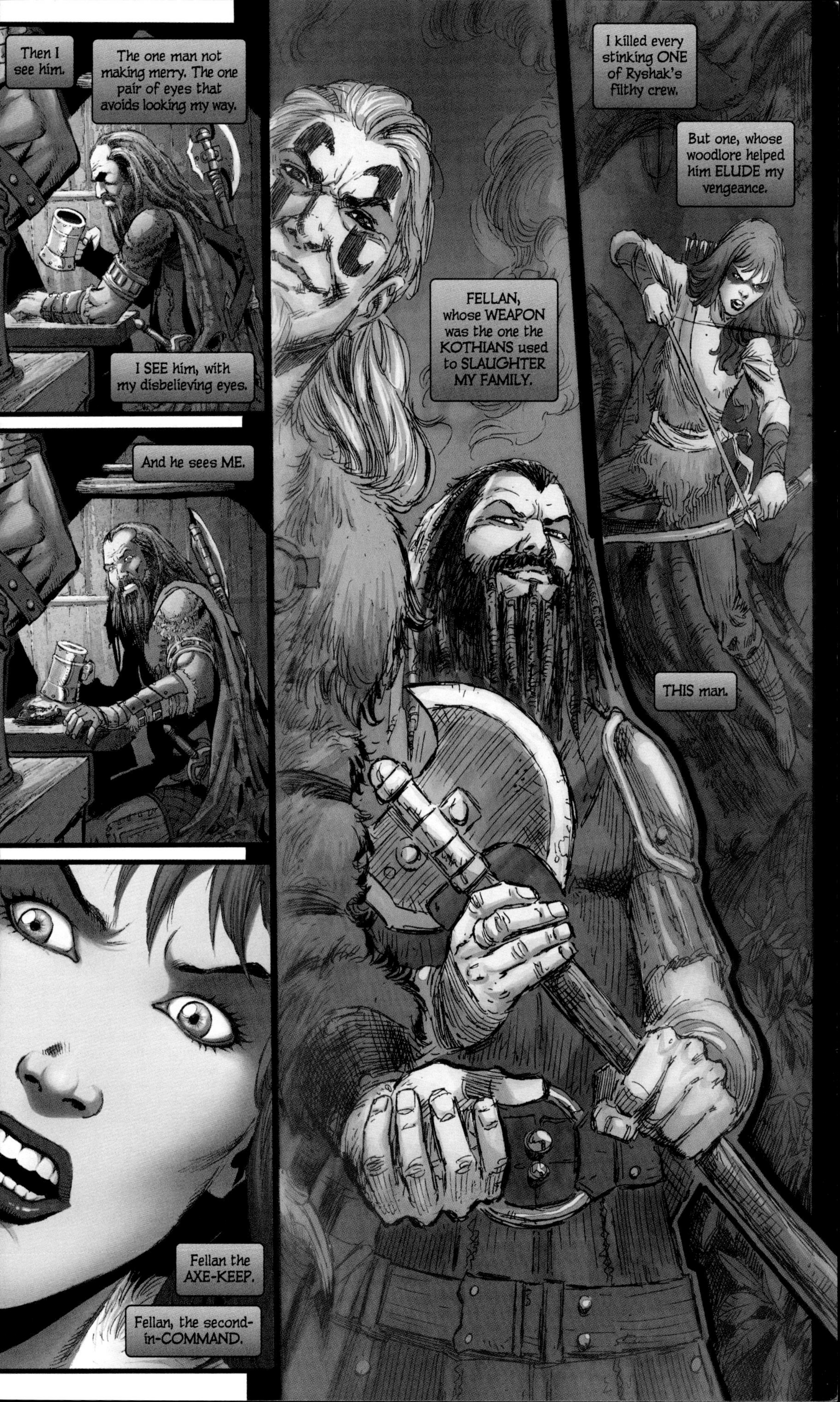
Then I see him.
The one man not making merry. The one pair of eyes that avoids looking my way.
I SEE him, with my disbelieving eyes.
And he sees ME.
Fellan the AXE-KEEP.
Fellan, the second-in-COMMAND.
FELLAN, whose WEAPON was the one the KOTHIANS used to SLAUGHTER MY FAMILY.
I killed every stinking ONE of Ryshak's filthy crew.
But one, whose woodlore helped him ELUDE my vengeance.
THIS man.

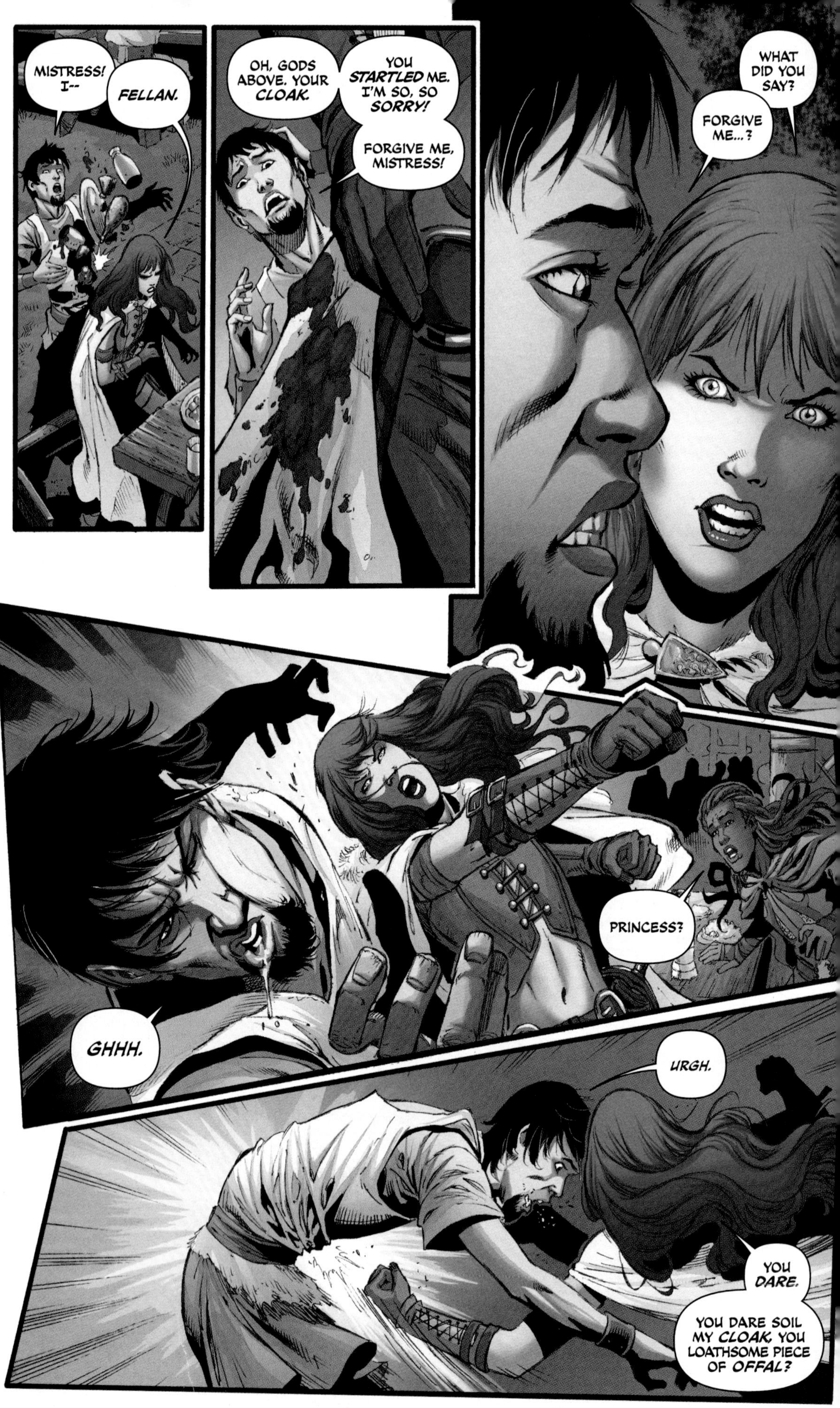
MISTRESS! I--
FELLAN.
OH, GODS ABOVE. YOUR CLOAK.
YOU STARTLED ME. I'M SO, SO SORRY!
FORGIVE ME, MISTRESS!
WHAT DID YOU SAY?
FORGIVE ME...?
PRINCESS?
GHHH.
URGH.
YOU DARE.
YOU DARE SOIL MY CLOAK, YOU LOATHSOME PIECE OF OFFAL?

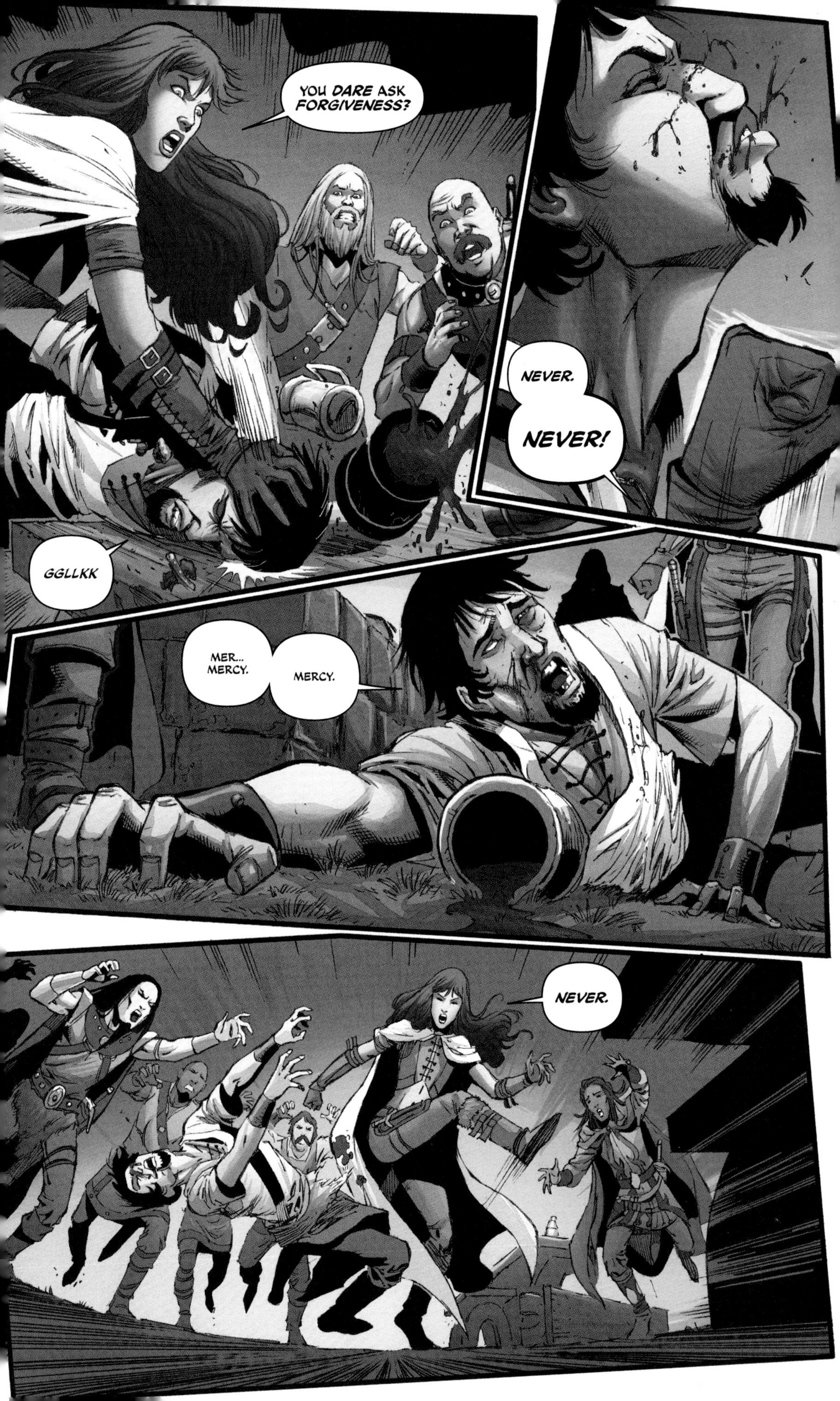
YOU DARE ASK FORGIVENESS?
NEVER.
NEVER!
GGLLKK
MER... MERCY.
MERCY.
NEVER.

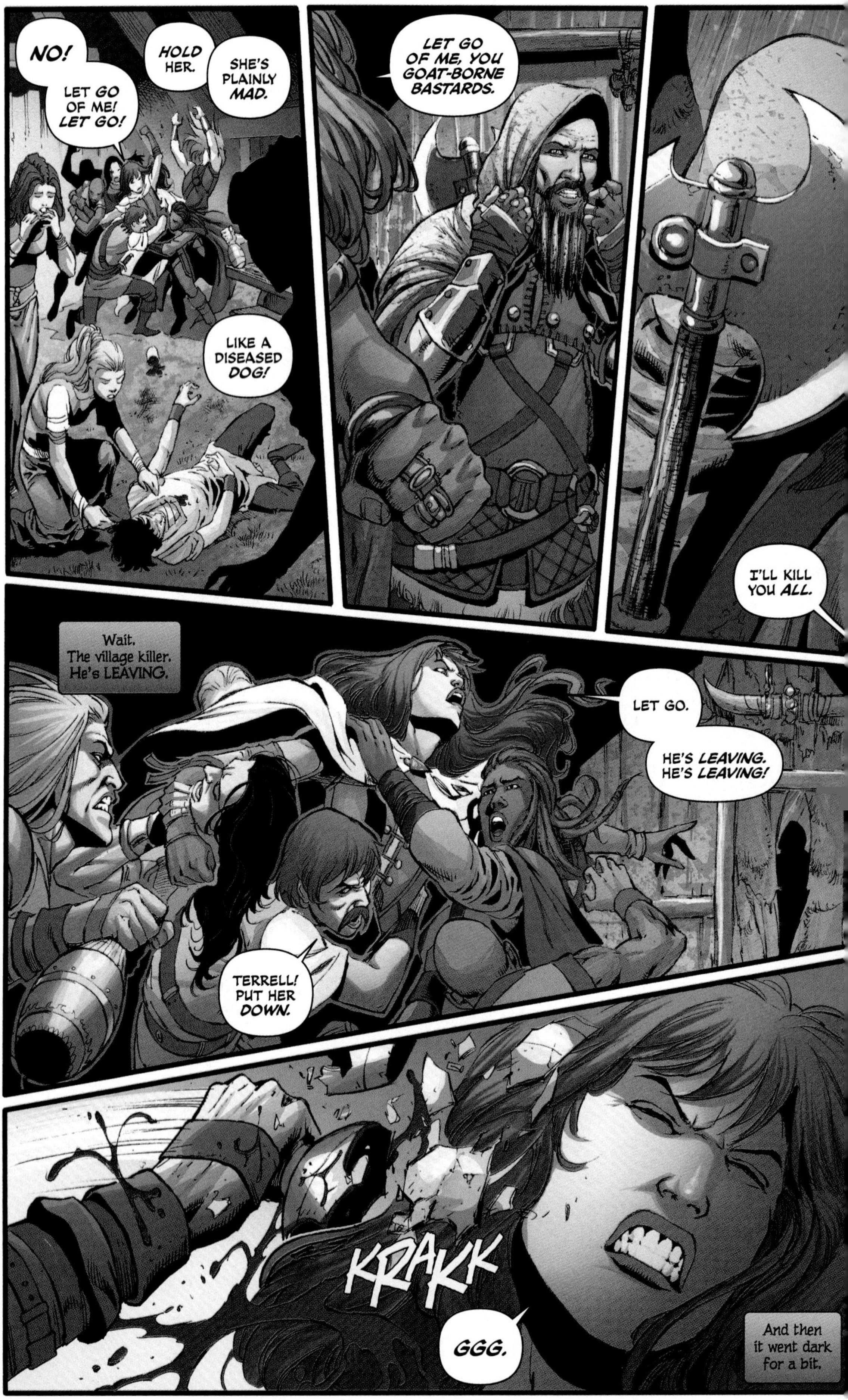
NO!
LET GO OF ME! LET GO!
HOLD HER.
SHE'S PLAINLY MAD.
LIKE A DISEASED DOG!
LET GO OF ME, YOU GOAT-BORNE BASTARDS.
I'LL KILL YOU ALL.
Wait. The village killer. He's LEAVING.
LET GO.
HE'S LEAVING. HE'S LEAVING!
TERRELL! PUT HER DOWN.
KRAKK
GGG.
And then it went dark for a bit.

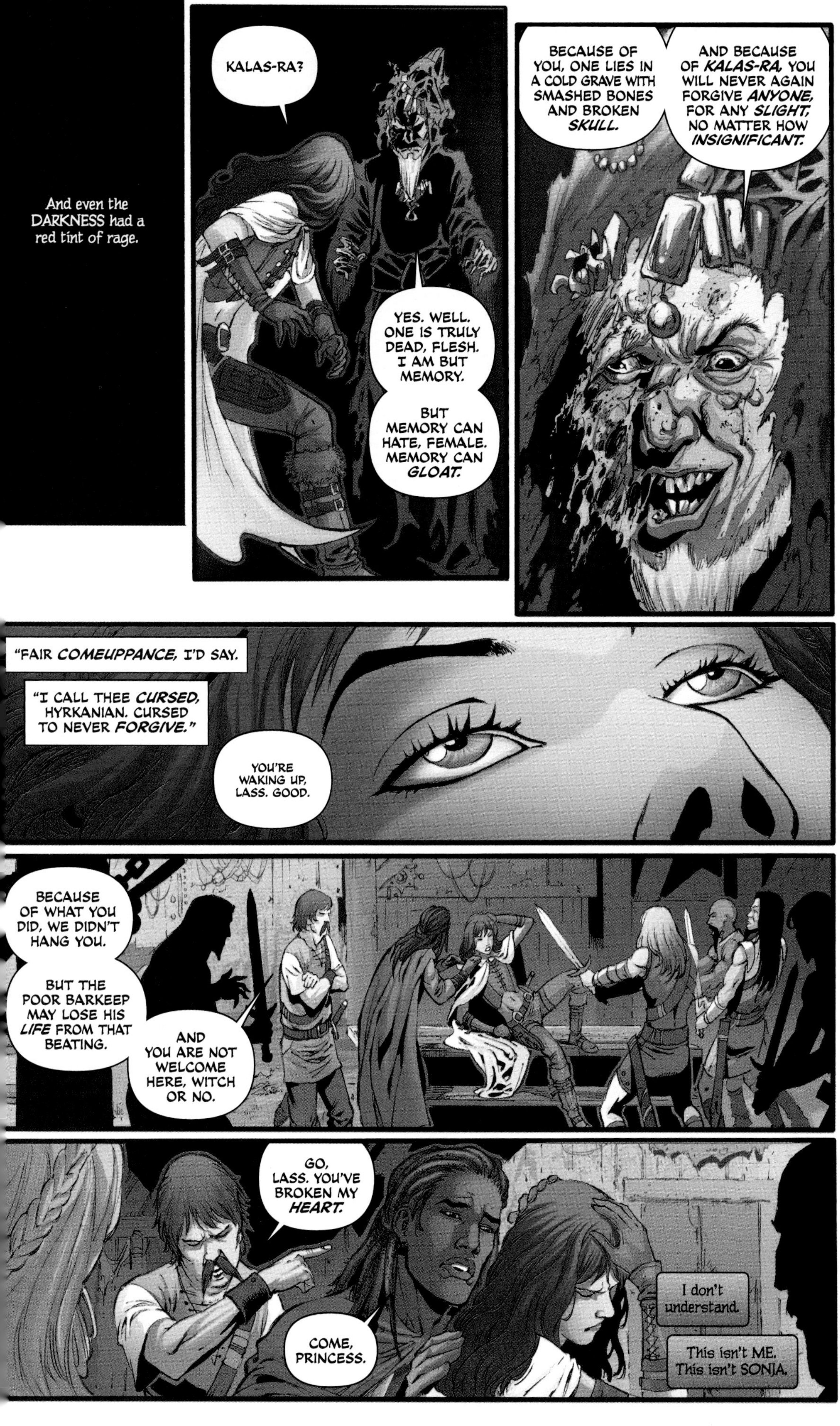
And even the DARKNESS had a red tint of rage.
KALAS-RA?
YES. WELL. ONE IS TRULY DEAD, FLESH. I AM BUT MEMORY.
BUT MEMORY CAN HATE, FEMALE. MEMORY CAN GLOAT.
BECAUSE OF YOU, ONE LIES IN A COLD GRAVE WITH SMASHED BONES AND BROKEN SKULL.
AND BECAUSE OF KALAS-RA, YOU WILL NEVER AGAIN FORGIVE ANYONE, FOR ANY SLIGHT, NO MATTER HOW INSIGNIFICANT.
"FAIR COMEUPPANCE, I'D SAY.
"I CALL THEE CURSED, HYRKANIAN. CURSED TO NEVER FORGIVE."
YOU'RE WAKING UP, LASS. GOOD.
BECAUSE OF WHAT YOU DID, WE DIDN'T HANG YOU.
BUT THE POOR BARKEEP MAY LOSE HIS LIFE FROM THAT BEATING.
AND YOU ARE NOT WELCOME HERE, WITCH OR NO.
GO, LASS. YOU'VE BROKEN MY HEART.
COME, PRINCESS.
I don't understand.
This isn't ME. This isn't SONJA.

WAIT. *WAIT.*

DO YOU *KNOW* OF HIM?

Cursed or NOT... I saw what I saw!

THERE WAS A *MAN.* IN THAT *CORNER.*

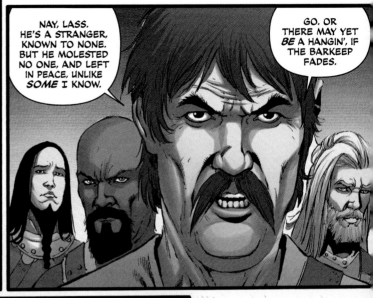

NAY, LASS. HE'S A STRANGER, KNOWN TO NONE. BUT HE MOLESTED NO ONE, AND LEFT IN PEACE, UNLIKE *SOME I KNOW.*

GO. OR THERE MAY YET *BE* A HANGIN', IF THE BARKEEP FADES.

COME. THERE MAY YET BE *TIME!*

...?

TIME FOR *WHAT,* VIOLENT ONE?

SONJA IS A DRUNKARD AND A WARRIOR, NOVICE.

BUT BEFORE ALL *THAT...*

...SHE WAS A *TRACKER.*

NO.

THE *RAIN.*

Please. A print. A piece of cloth.

IT'S DESTROYED THE *TRAIL.*

THERE'S NO MARK, NOT EVEN A *SCENT* LEFT BEHIND!

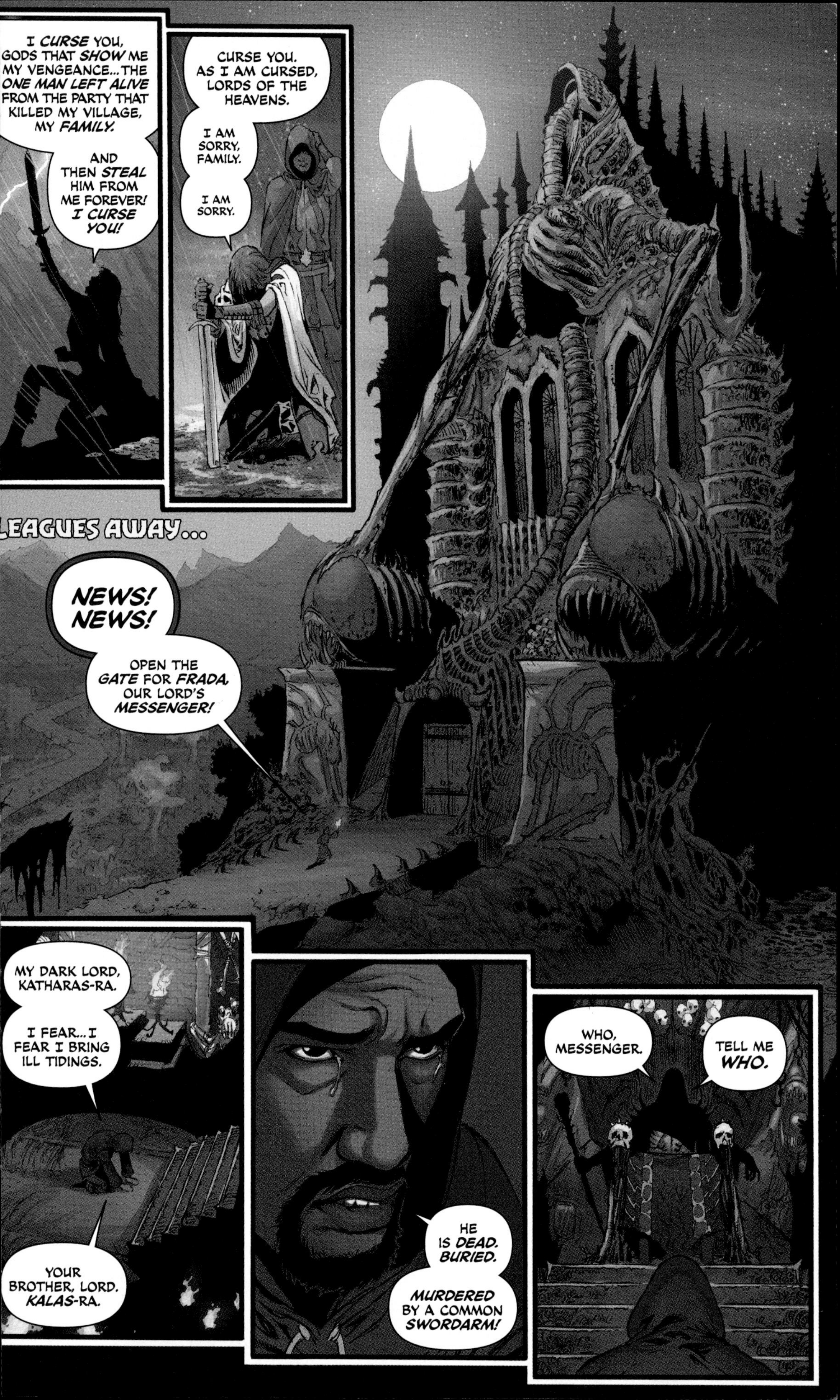
I CURSE YOU, GODS THAT SHOW ME MY VENGEANCE...THE ONE MAN LEFT ALIVE FROM THE PARTY THAT KILLED MY VILLAGE, MY FAMILY.
AND THEN STEAL HIM FROM ME FOREVER! I CURSE YOU!
CURSE YOU. AS I AM CURSED, LORDS OF THE HEAVENS.
I AM SORRY, FAMILY.
I AM SORRY.
LEAGUES AWAY...
NEWS! NEWS!
OPEN THE GATE FOR FRADA, OUR LORD'S MESSENGER!
MY DARK LORD, KATHARAS-RA.
I FEAR...I FEAR I BRING ILL TIDINGS.
YOUR BROTHER, LORD. KALAS-RA.
HE IS DEAD. BURIED.
MURDERED BY A COMMON SWORDARM!
WHO, MESSENGER.
TELL ME WHO.

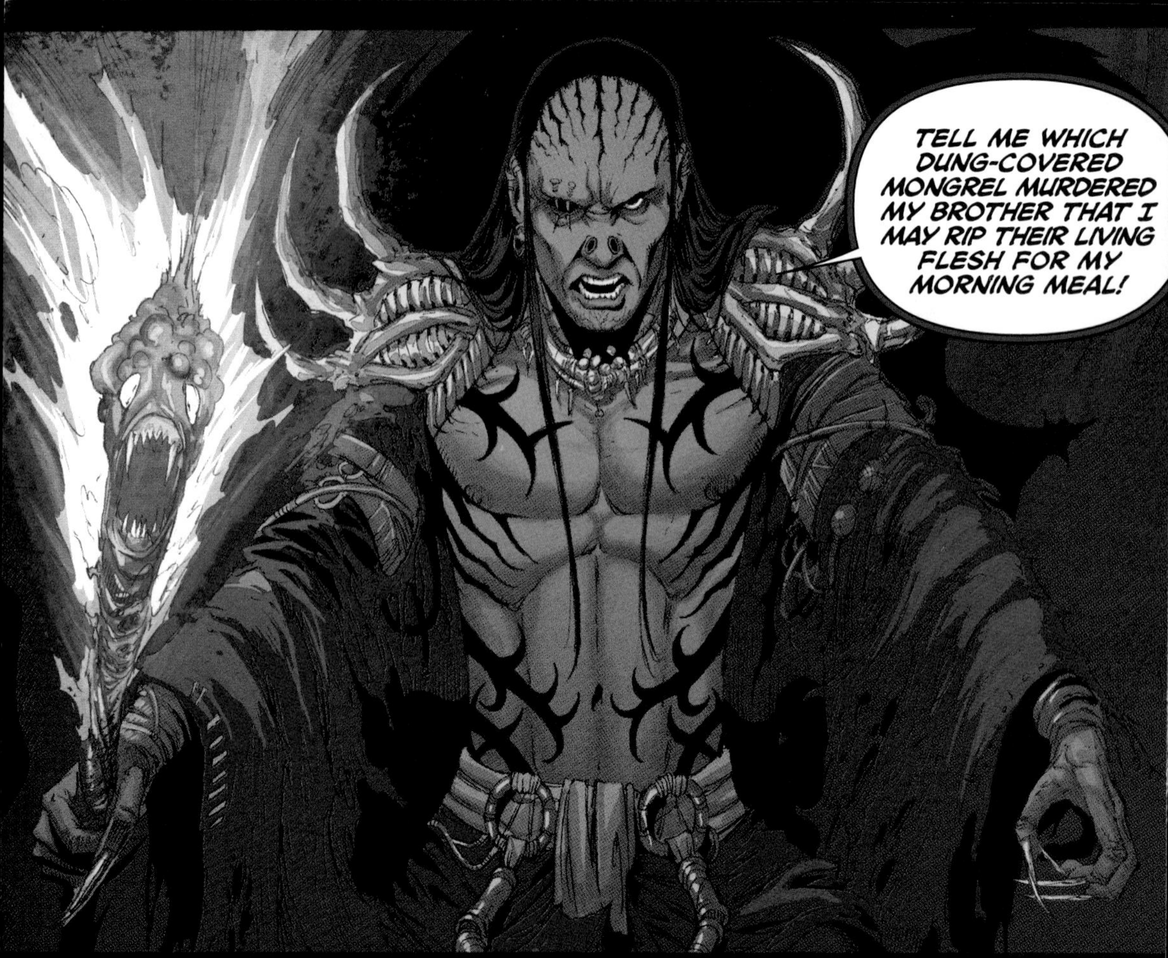
TELL ME WHICH DUNG-COVERED MONGREL MURDERED MY BROTHER THAT I MAY RIP THEIR LIVING FLESH FOR MY MORNING MEAL!

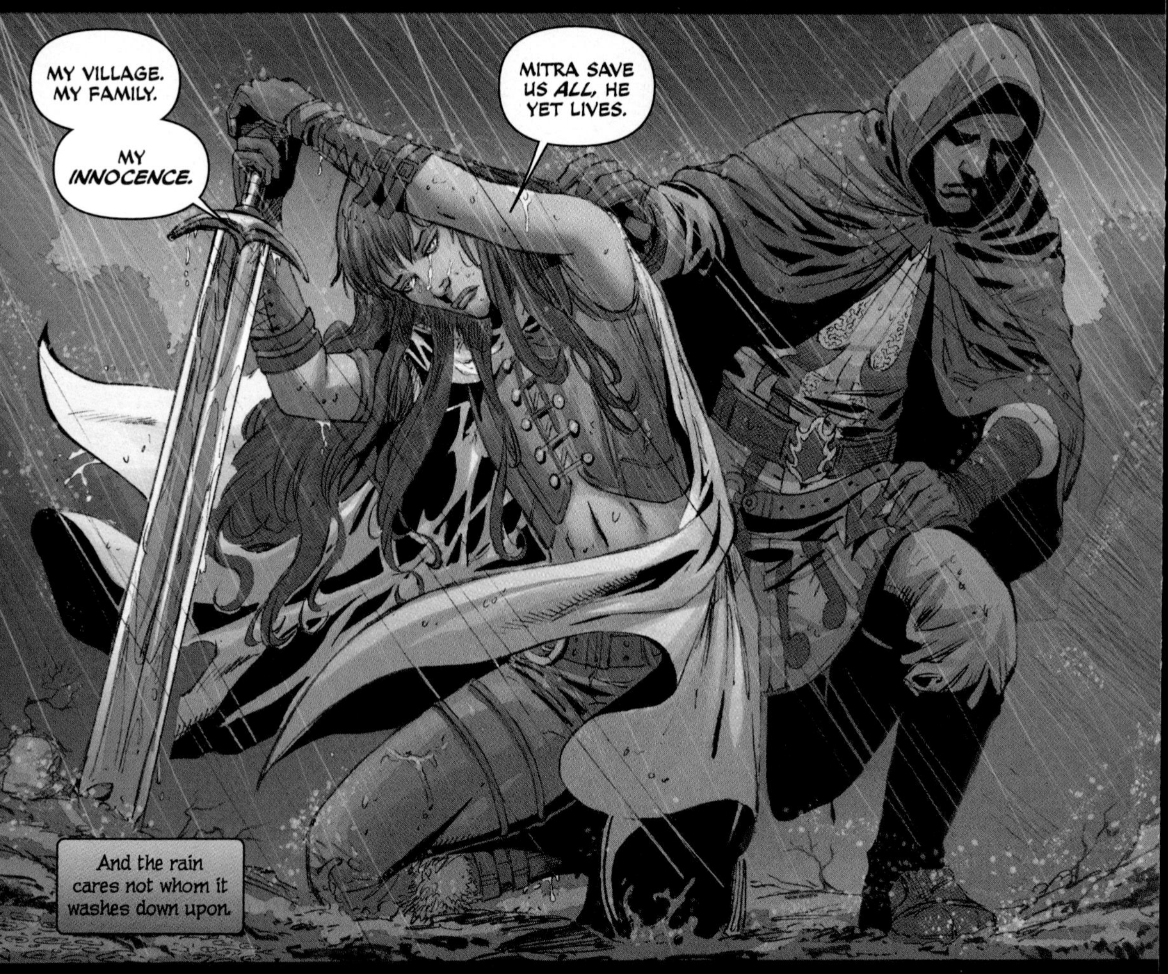
MY VILLAGE. MY FAMILY.
MY *INNOCENCE.*
MITRA SAVE US *ALL*, HE YET LIVES.
And the rain cares not whom it washes down upon.

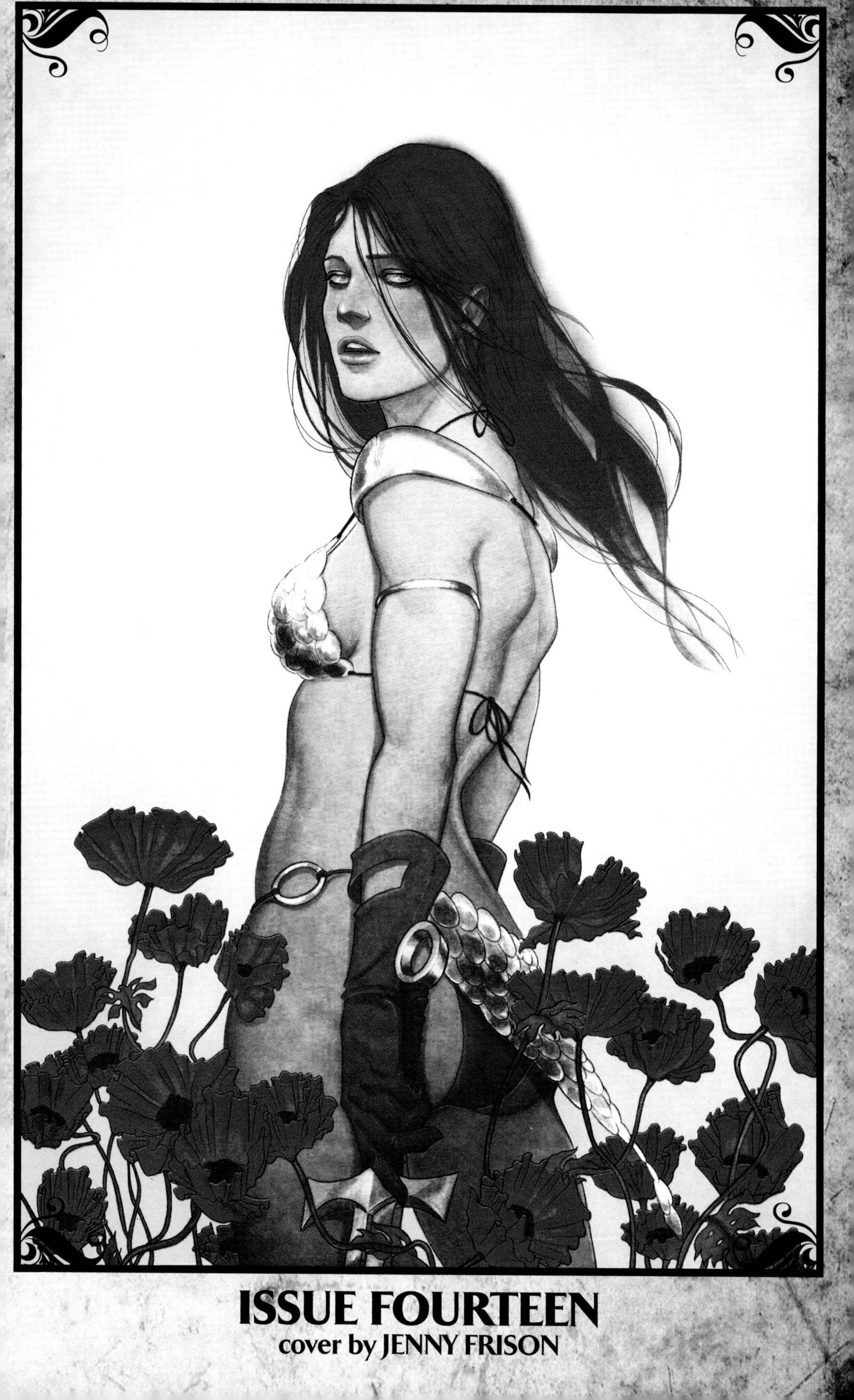

ISSUE FOURTEEN

cover by JENNY FRISON

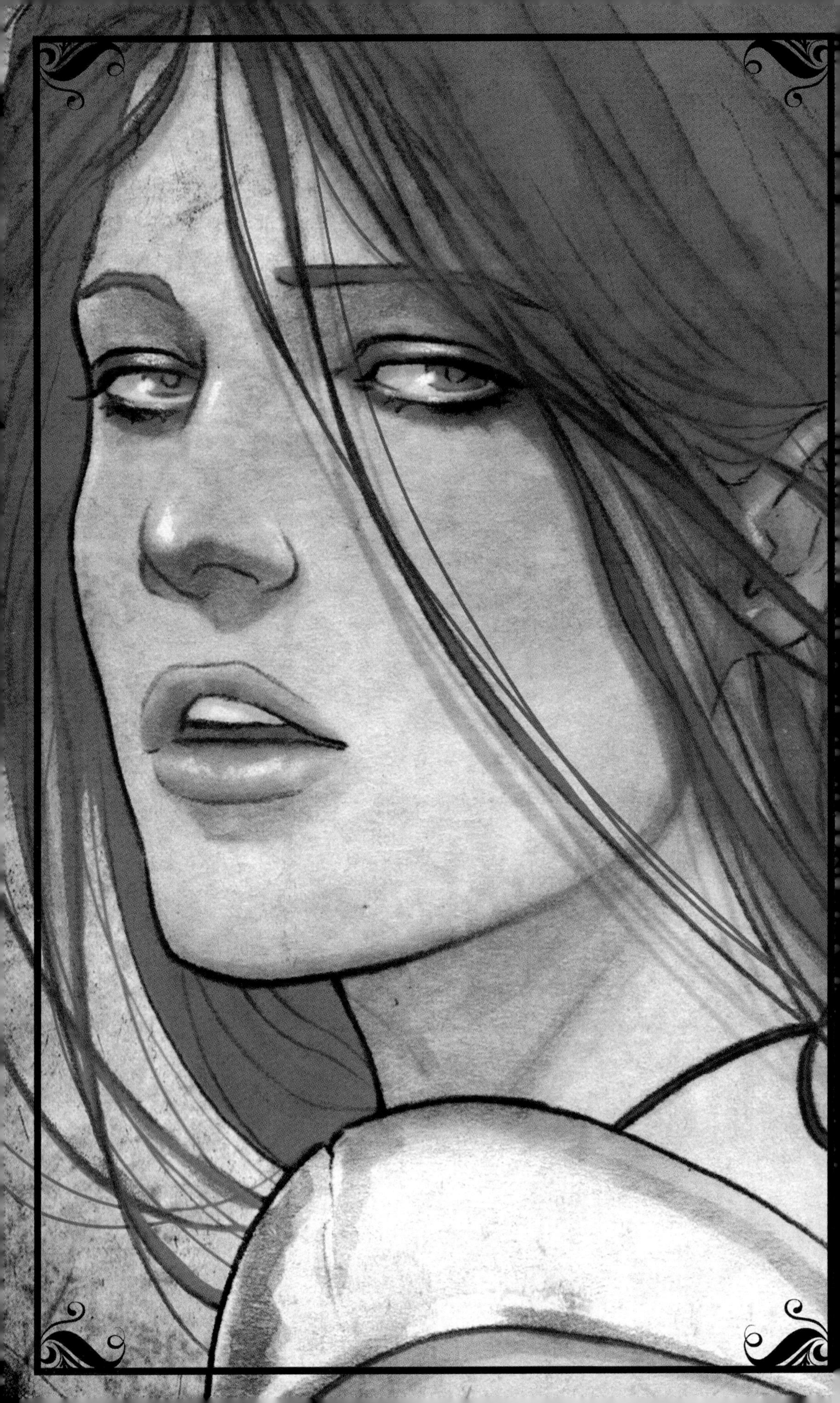

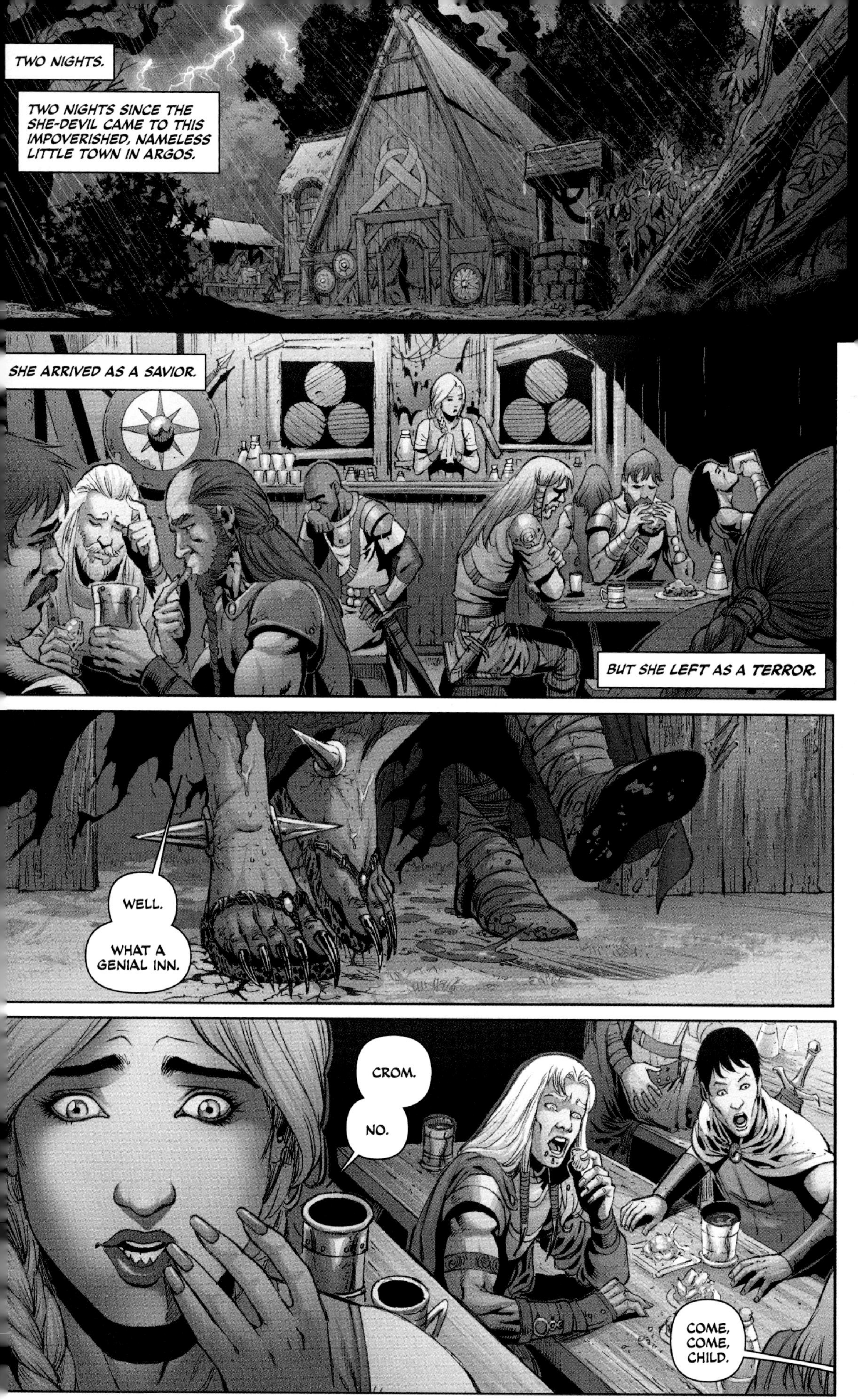
TWO NIGHTS.
TWO NIGHTS SINCE THE SHE-DEVIL CAME TO THIS IMPOVERISHED, NAMELESS LITTLE TOWN IN ARGOS.
SHE ARRIVED AS A SAVIOR.
BUT SHE LEFT AS A TERROR.
WELL.
WHAT A GENIAL INN.
CROM.
NO.
COME, COME, CHILD.

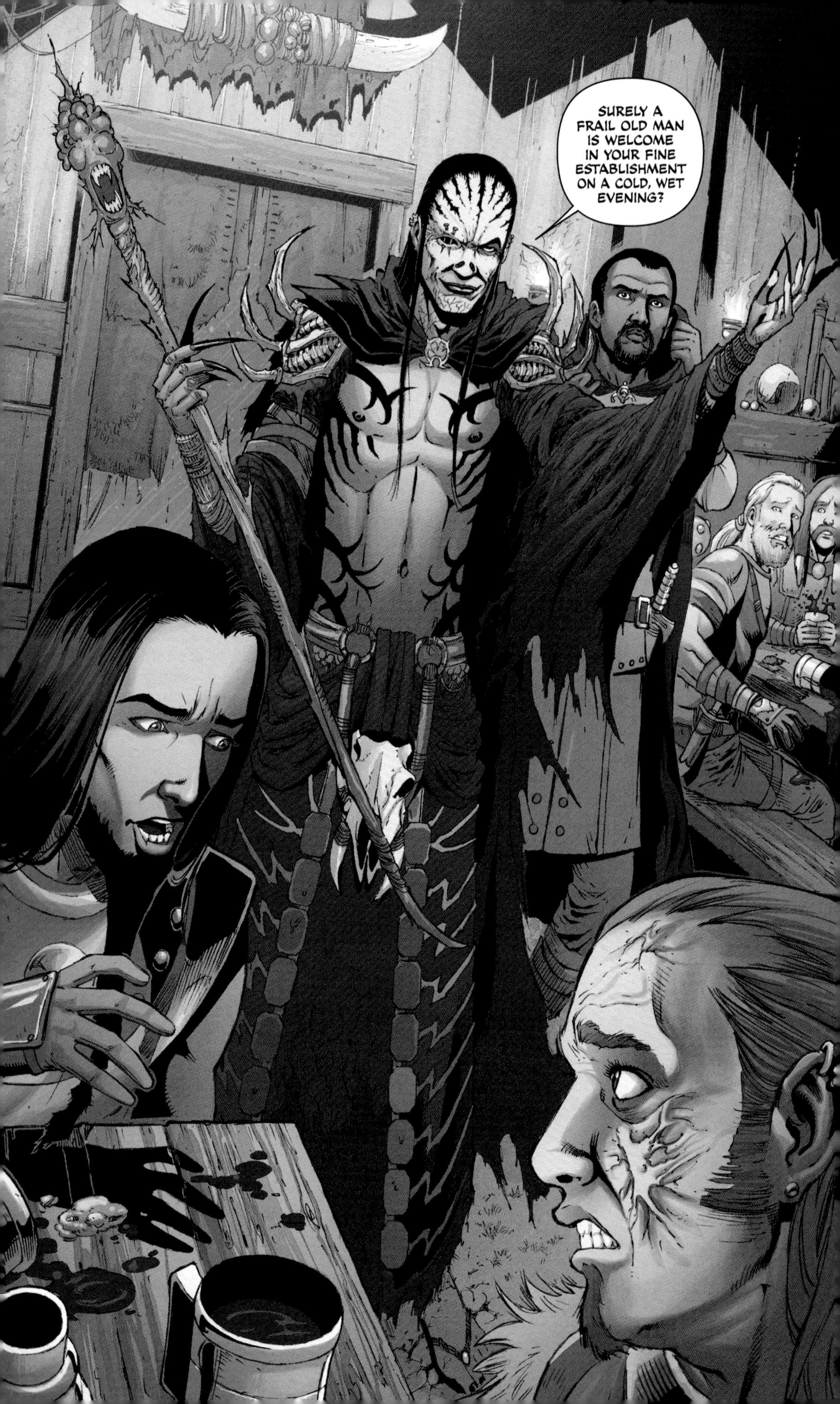
SURELY A FRAIL OLD MAN IS WELCOME IN YOUR FINE ESTABLISHMENT ON A COLD, WET EVENING?

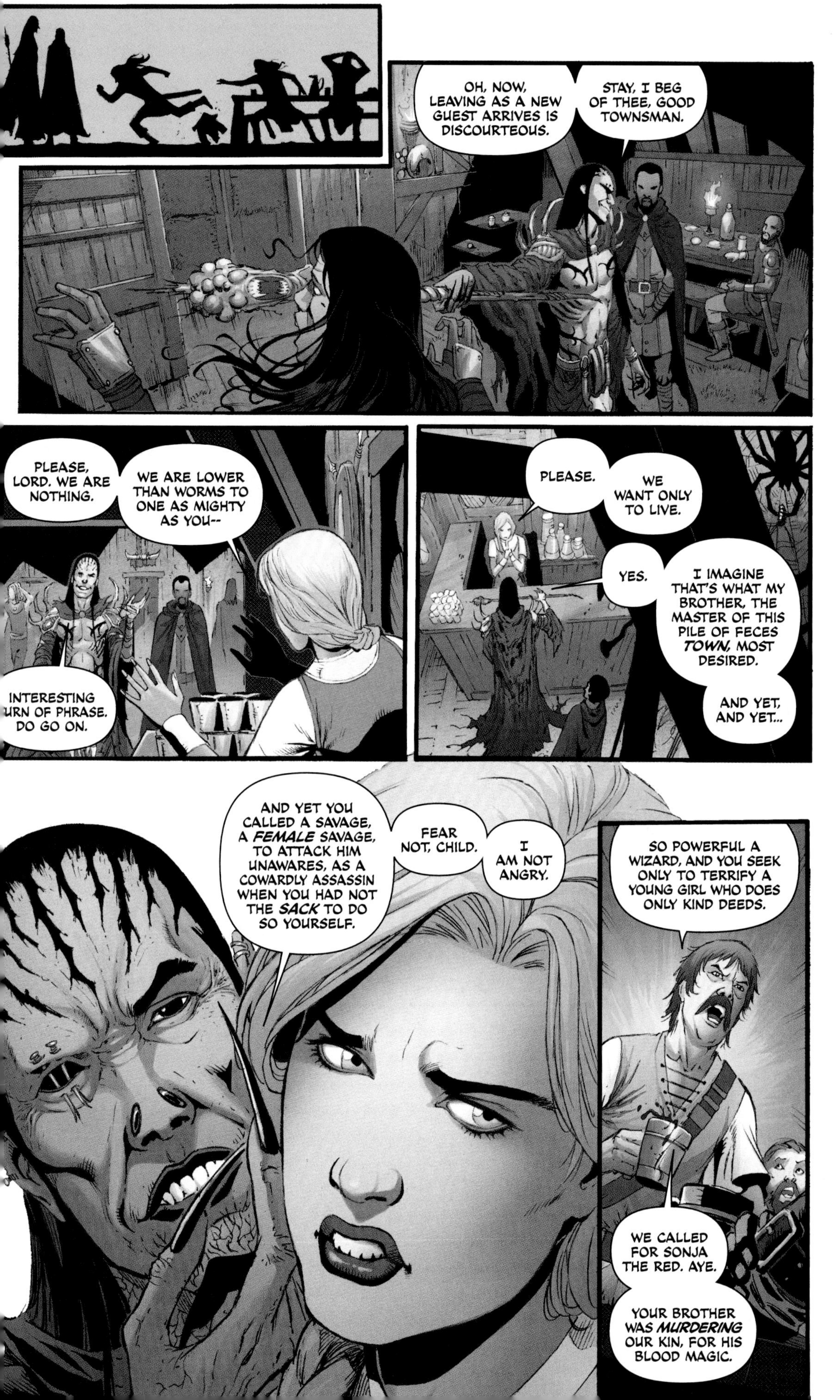
OH, NOW, LEAVING AS A NEW GUEST ARRIVES IS DISCOURTEOUS.
STAY, I BEG OF THEE, GOOD TOWNSMAN.
PLEASE, LORD. WE ARE NOTHING.
WE ARE LOWER THAN WORMS TO ONE AS MIGHTY AS YOU--
INTERESTING URN OF PHRASE. DO GO ON.
PLEASE.
WE WANT ONLY TO LIVE.
YES.
I IMAGINE THAT'S WHAT MY BROTHER, THE MASTER OF THIS PILE OF FECES *TOWN*, MOST DESIRED.
AND YET, AND YET...
AND YET YOU CALLED A SAVAGE, A *FEMALE* SAVAGE, TO ATTACK HIM UNAWARES, AS A COWARDLY ASSASSIN WHEN YOU HAD NOT THE *SACK* TO DO SO YOURSELF.
FEAR NOT, CHILD.
I AM NOT ANGRY.
SO POWERFUL A WIZARD, AND YOU SEEK ONLY TO TERRIFY A YOUNG GIRL WHO DOES ONLY KIND DEEDS.
WE CALLED FOR SONJA THE RED. AYE.
YOUR BROTHER WAS *MURDERING* OUR KIN, FOR HIS BLOOD MAGIC.

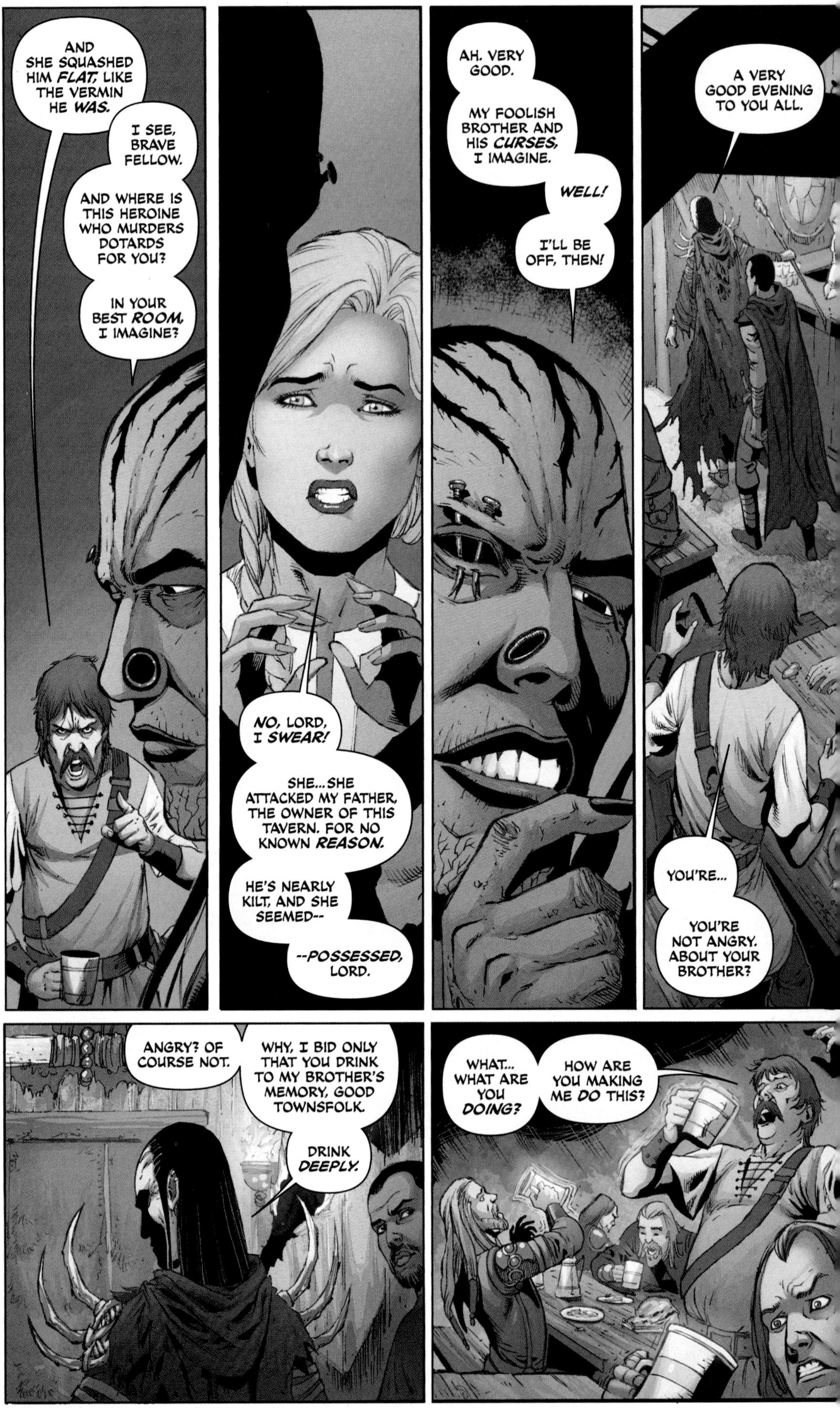
AND SHE SQUASHED HIM FLAT, LIKE THE VERMIN HE WAS.
I SEE, BRAVE FELLOW.
AND WHERE IS THIS HEROINE WHO MURDERS DOTARDS FOR YOU?
IN YOUR BEST ROOM, I IMAGINE?
NO, LORD, I SWEAR!
SHE...SHE ATTACKED MY FATHER, THE OWNER OF THIS TAVERN. FOR NO KNOWN REASON.
HE'S NEARLY KILT, AND SHE SEEMED--
--POSSESSED, LORD.
AH. VERY GOOD.
MY FOOLISH BROTHER AND HIS CURSES, I IMAGINE.
WELL!
I'LL BE OFF, THEN!
A VERY GOOD EVENING TO YOU ALL.
YOU'RE...
YOU'RE NOT ANGRY. ABOUT YOUR BROTHER?
ANGRY? OF COURSE NOT.
WHY, I BID ONLY THAT YOU DRINK TO MY BROTHER'S MEMORY, GOOD TOWNSFOLK.
DRINK DEEPLY.
WHAT... WHAT ARE YOU DOING?
HOW ARE YOU MAKING ME DO THIS?

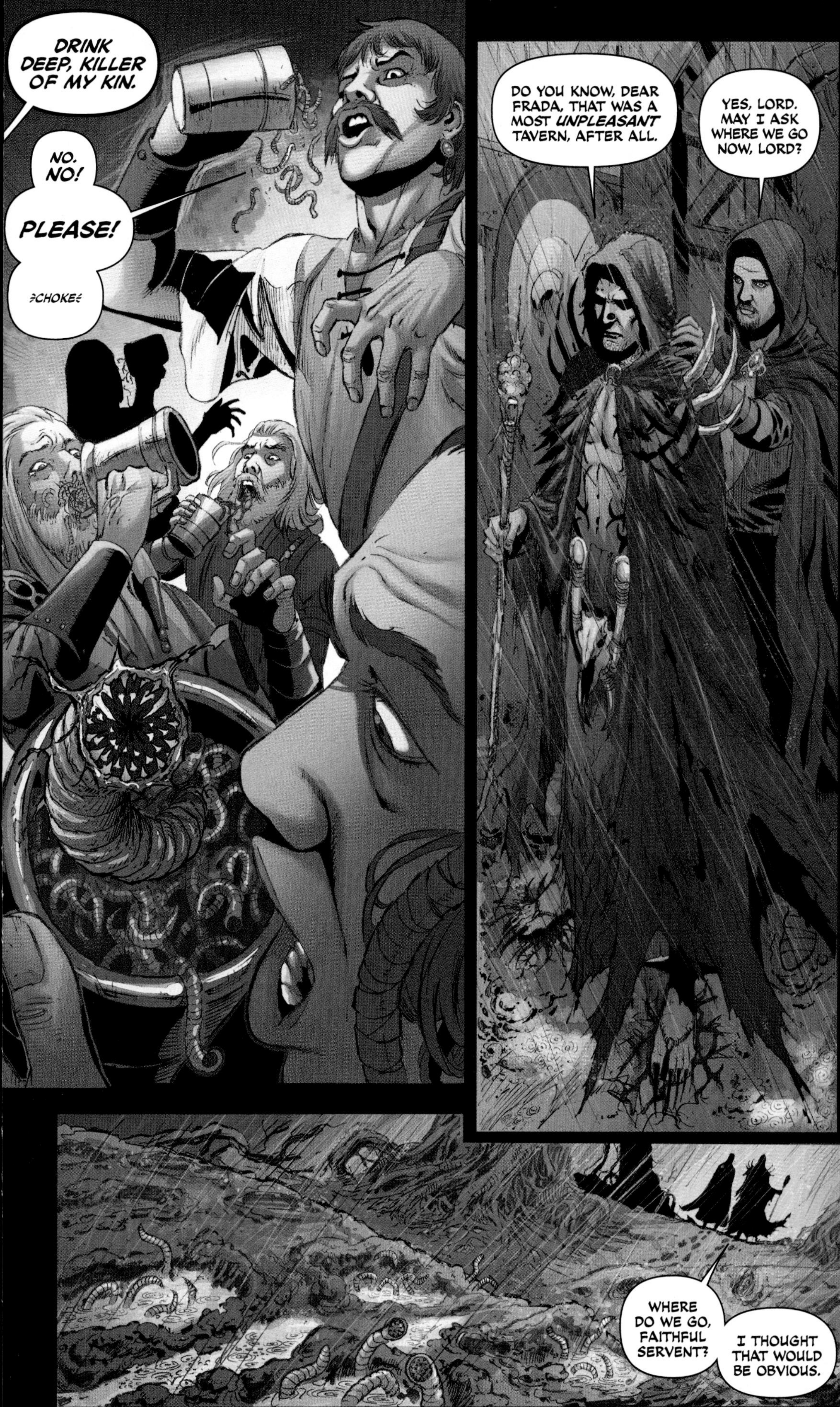
DRINK DEEP, KILLER OF MY KIN.
NO. NO!
PLEASE!
CHOKE
DO YOU KNOW, DEAR FRADA, THAT WAS A MOST UNPLEASANT TAVERN, AFTER ALL.
YES, LORD. MAY I ASK WHERE WE GO NOW, LORD?
WHERE DO WE GO, FAITHFUL SERVENT?
I THOUGHT THAT WOULD BE OBVIOUS.

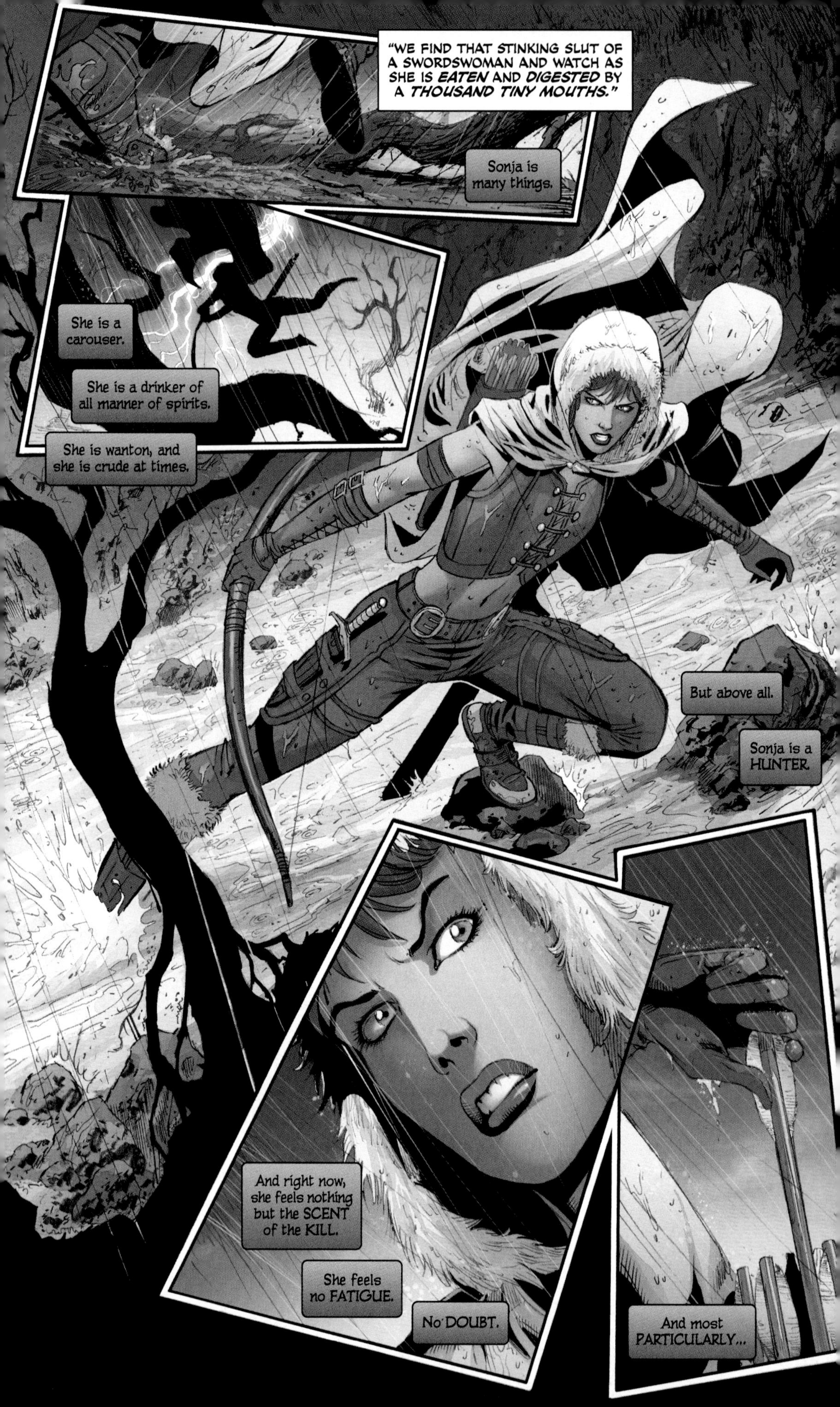
"WE FIND THAT STINKING SLUT OF A SWORDSWOMAN AND WATCH AS SHE IS *EATEN* AND *DIGESTED* BY A *THOUSAND TINY MOUTHS.*"
Sonja is many things.
She is a carouser.
She is a drinker of all manner of spirits.
She is wanton, and she is crude at times.
But above all.
Sonja is a HUNTER.
And right now, she feels nothing but the SCENT of the KILL.
She feels no FATIGUE.
No DOUBT.
And most PARTICULARLY...

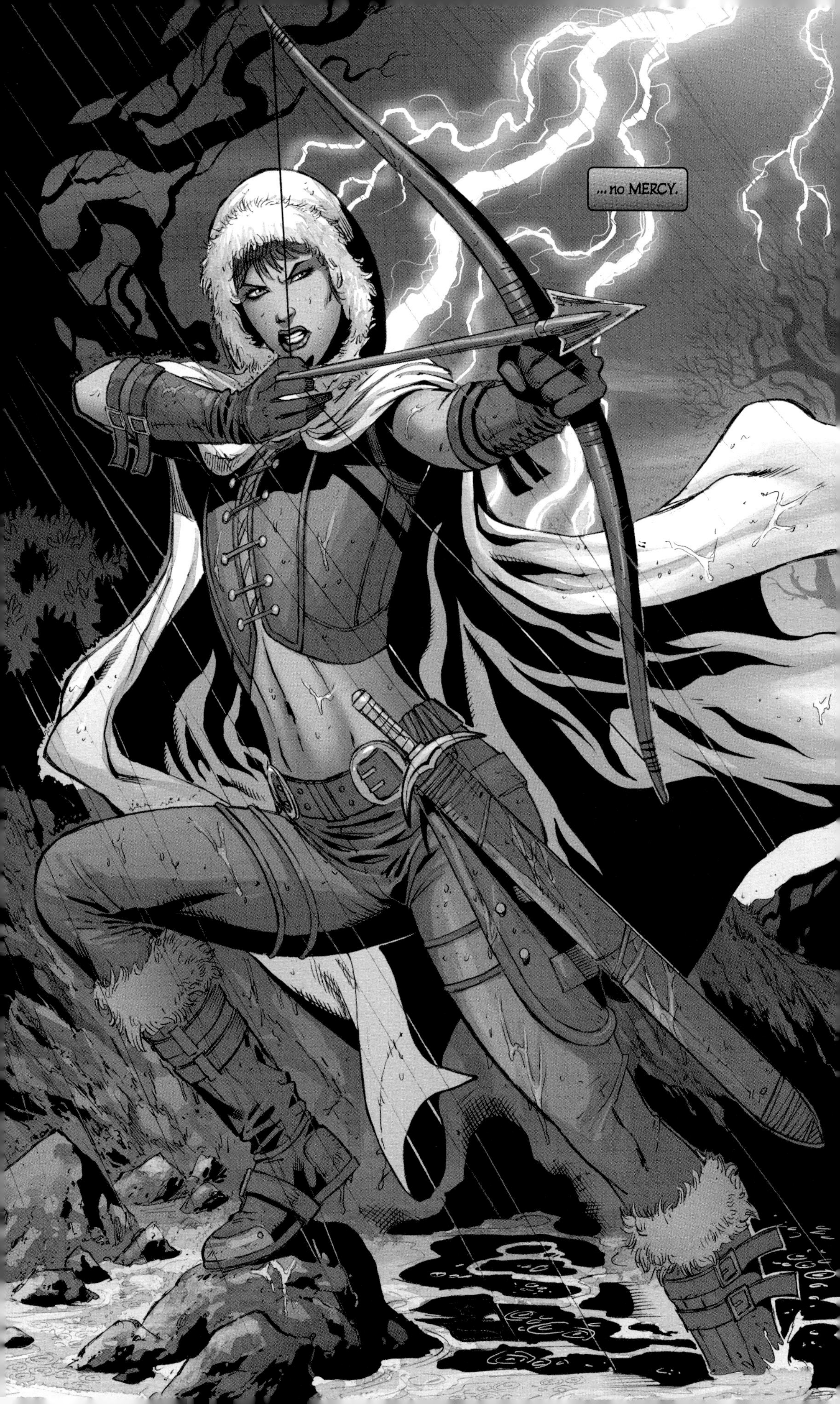
...no MERCY.

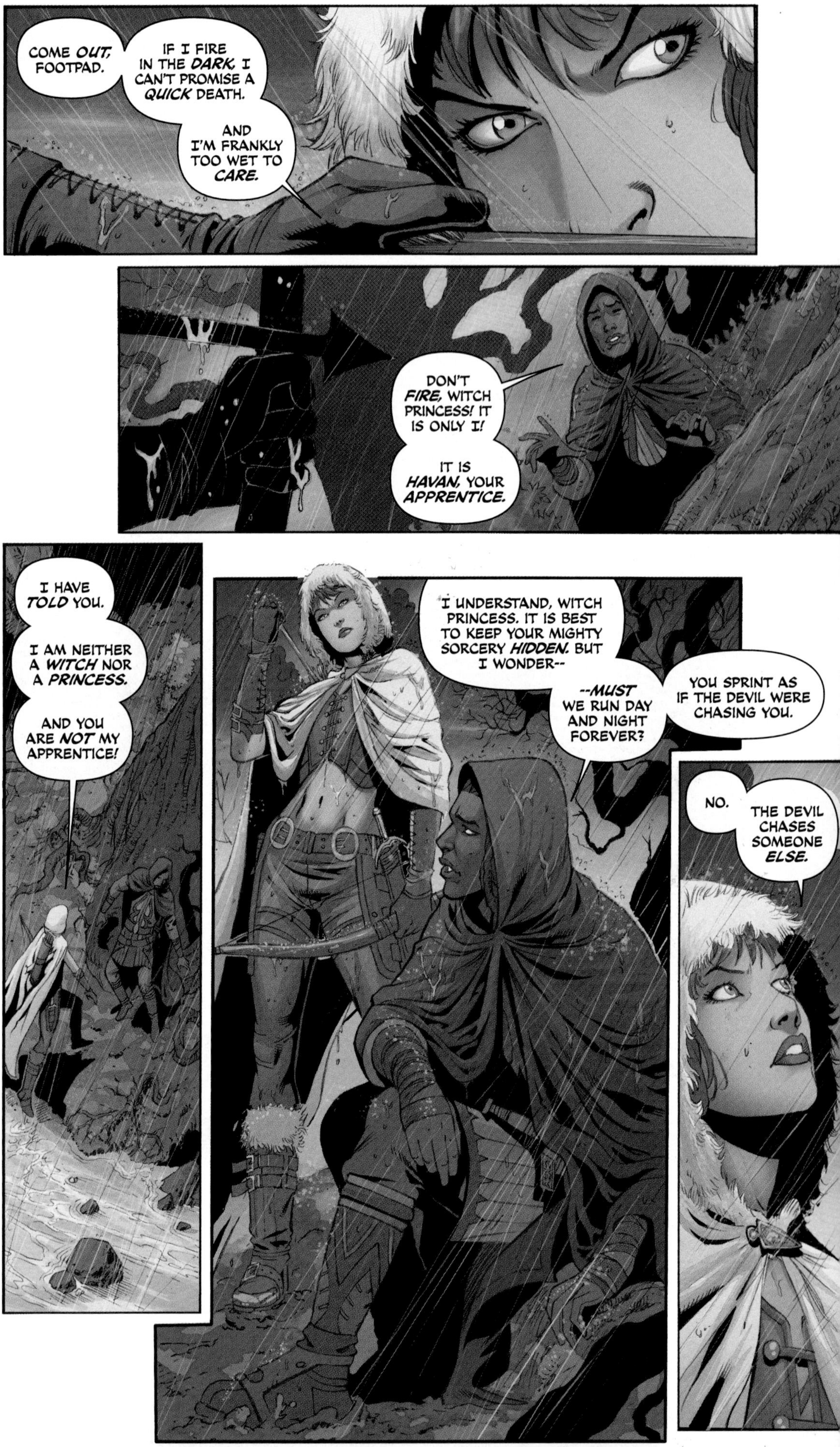
COME OUT, FOOTPAD.
IF I FIRE IN THE DARK, I CAN'T PROMISE A QUICK DEATH.
AND I'M FRANKLY TOO WET TO CARE.
DON'T FIRE, WITCH PRINCESS! IT IS ONLY I!
IT IS HAVAN, YOUR APPRENTICE.
I HAVE TOLD YOU.
I AM NEITHER A WITCH NOR A PRINCESS.
AND YOU ARE NOT MY APPRENTICE!
I UNDERSTAND, WITCH PRINCESS. IT IS BEST TO KEEP YOUR MIGHTY SORCERY HIDDEN. BUT I WONDER--
--MUST WE RUN DAY AND NIGHT FOREVER?
YOU SPRINT AS IF THE DEVIL WERE CHASING YOU.
NO.
THE DEVIL CHASES SOMEONE ELSE.

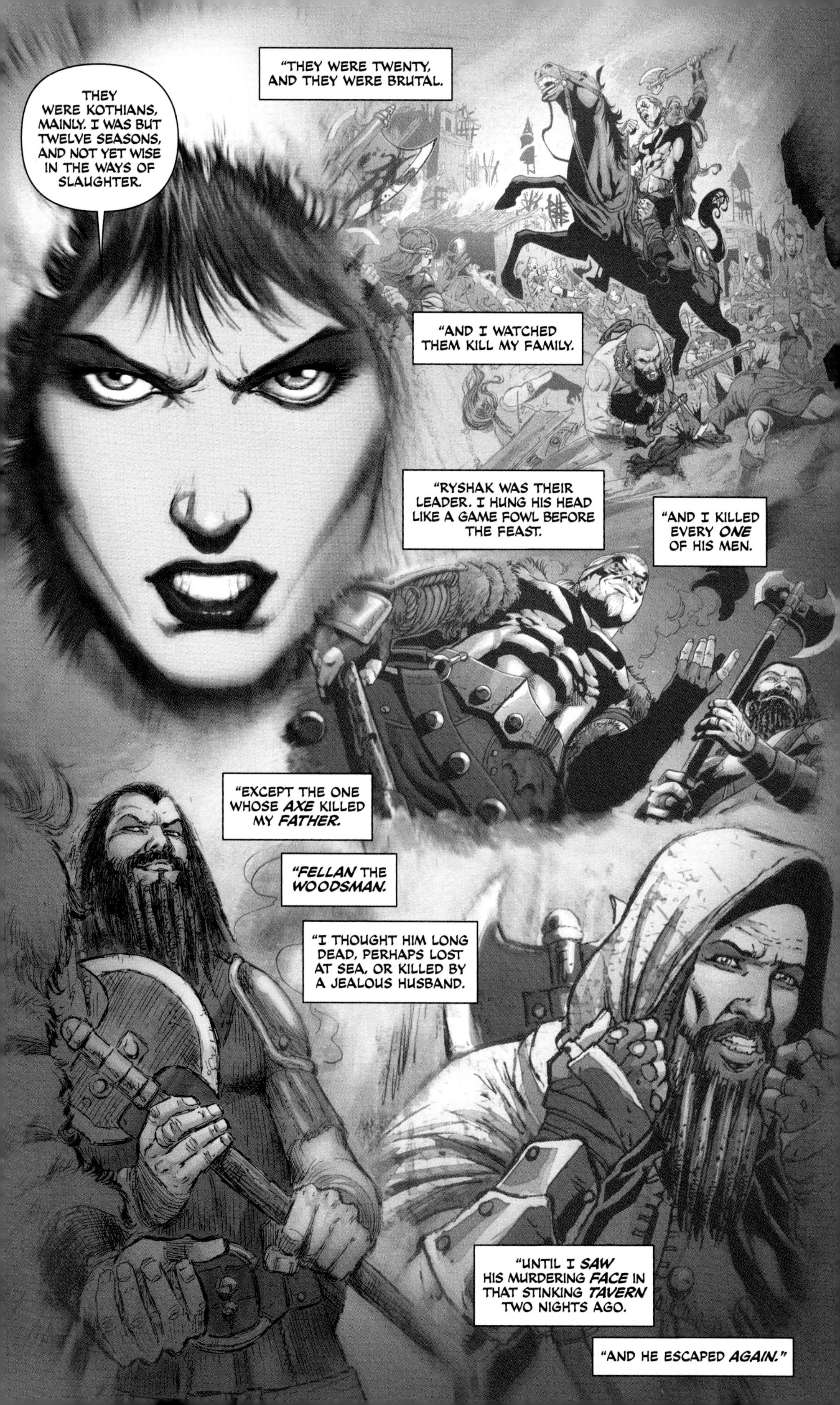
THEY WERE KOTHIANS, MAINLY. I WAS BUT TWELVE SEASONS, AND NOT YET WISE IN THE WAYS OF SLAUGHTER.
"THEY WERE TWENTY, AND THEY WERE BRUTAL.
"AND I WATCHED THEM KILL MY FAMILY.
"RYSHAK WAS THEIR LEADER. I HUNG HIS HEAD LIKE A GAME FOWL BEFORE THE FEAST.
"AND I KILLED EVERY *ONE* OF HIS MEN.
"EXCEPT THE ONE WHOSE *AXE* KILLED MY *FATHER.*
"*FELLAN* THE *WOODSMAN.*
"I THOUGHT HIM LONG DEAD, PERHAPS LOST AT SEA, OR KILLED BY A JEALOUS HUSBAND.
"UNTIL I *SAW* HIS MURDERING *FACE* IN THAT STINKING *TAVERN* TWO NIGHTS AGO.
"AND HE ESCAPED *AGAIN.*"

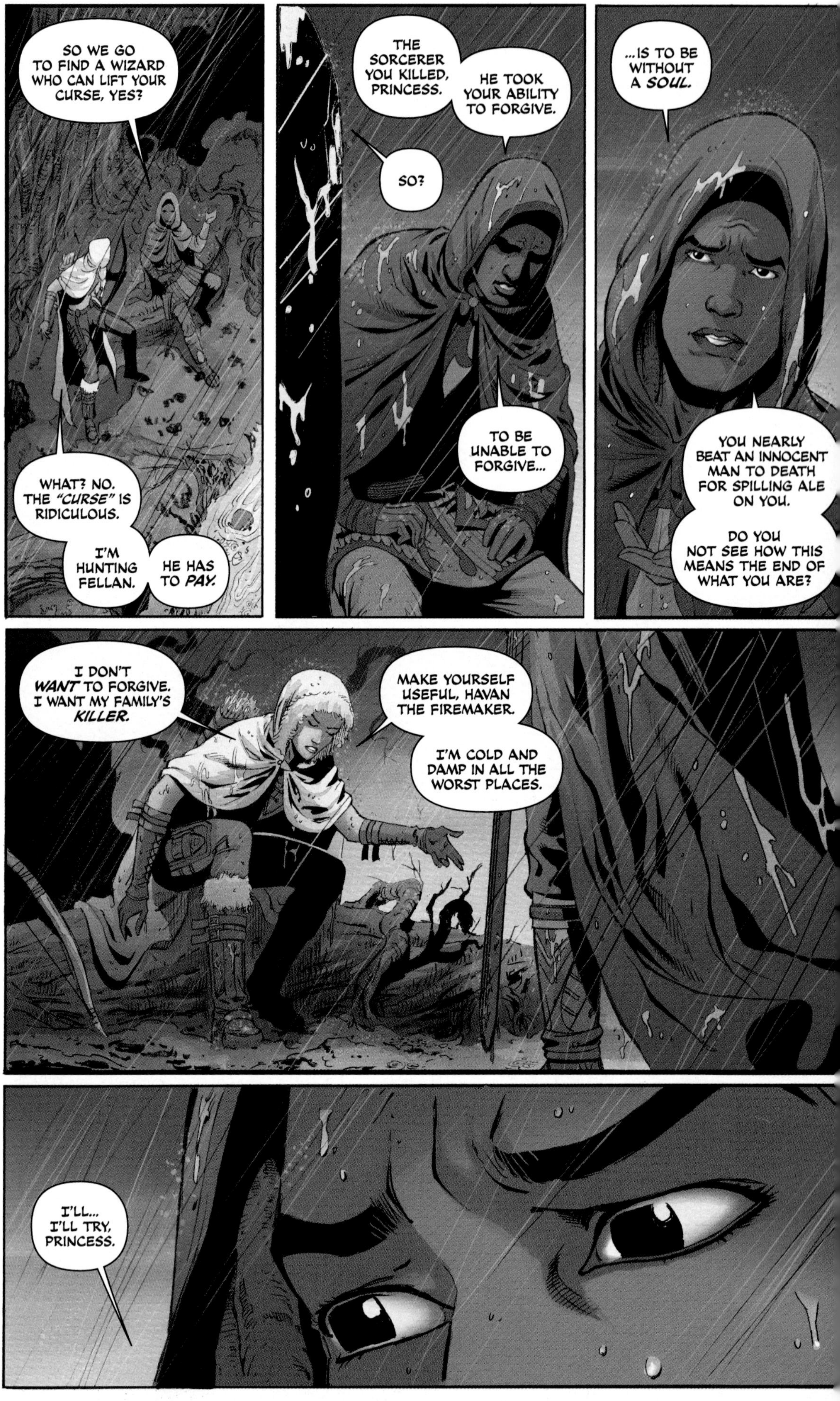
SO WE GO TO FIND A WIZARD WHO CAN LIFT YOUR CURSE, YES?
WHAT? NO. THE "CURSE" IS RIDICULOUS.
I'M HUNTING FELLAN.
HE HAS TO PAY.
THE SORCERER YOU KILLED, PRINCESS.
HE TOOK YOUR ABILITY TO FORGIVE.
SO?
TO BE UNABLE TO FORGIVE...
...IS TO BE WITHOUT A SOUL.
YOU NEARLY BEAT AN INNOCENT MAN TO DEATH FOR SPILLING ALE ON YOU.
DO YOU NOT SEE HOW THIS MEANS THE END OF WHAT YOU ARE?
I DON'T WANT TO FORGIVE. I WANT MY FAMILY'S KILLER.
MAKE YOURSELF USEFUL, HAVAN THE FIREMAKER.
I'M COLD AND DAMP IN ALL THE WORST PLACES.
I'LL... I'LL TRY, PRINCESS.

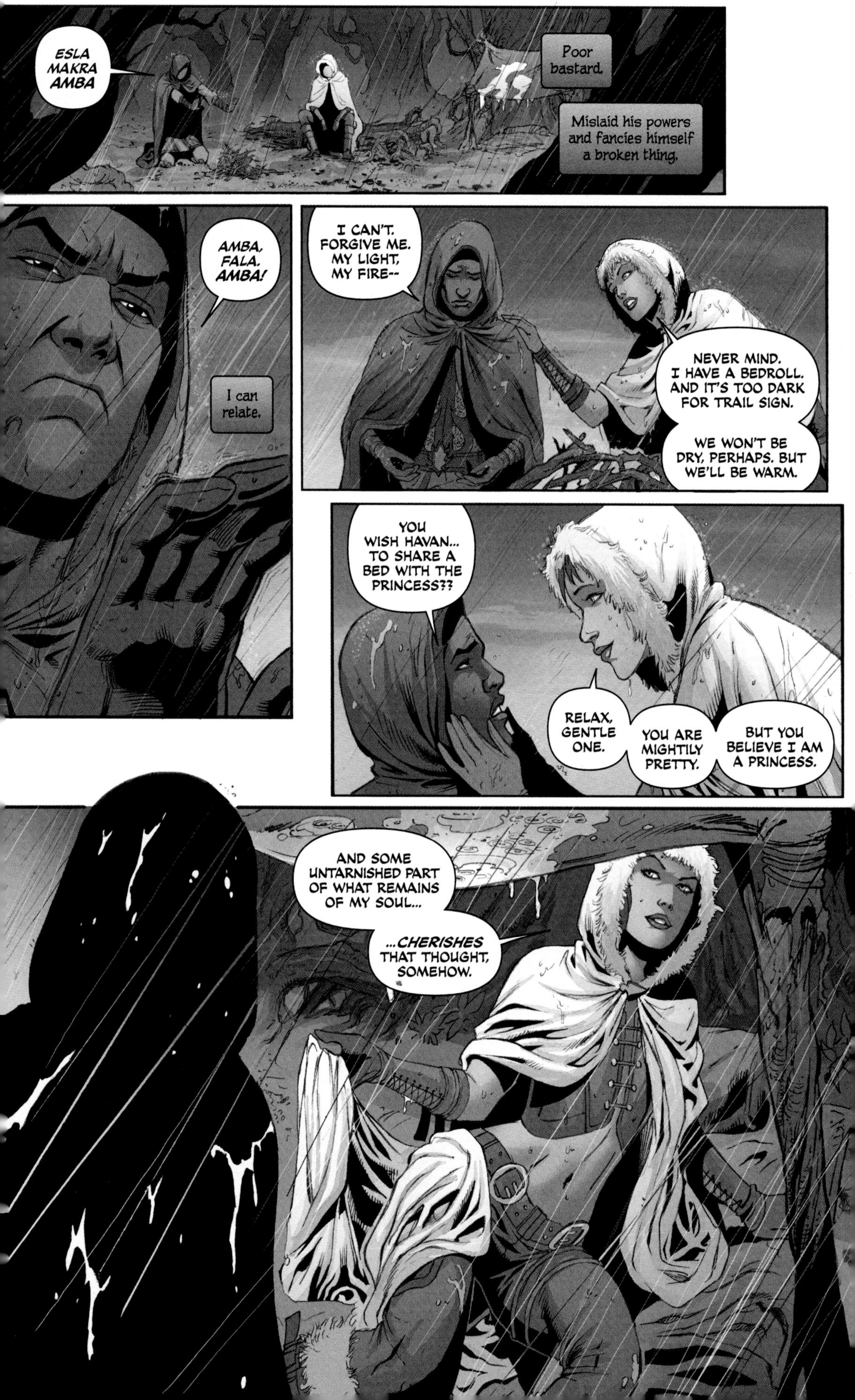
ESLA MAKRA AMBA
Poor bastard.
Mislaid his powers and fancies himself a broken thing.
AMBA, FALA. AMBA!
I can relate.
I CAN'T. FORGIVE ME. MY LIGHT, MY FIRE--
NEVER MIND. I HAVE A BEDROLL. AND IT'S TOO DARK FOR TRAIL SIGN.
WE WON'T BE DRY, PERHAPS. BUT WE'LL BE WARM.
YOU WISH HAVAN... TO SHARE A BED WITH THE PRINCESS??
RELAX, GENTLE ONE.
YOU ARE MIGHTILY PRETTY.
BUT YOU BELIEVE I AM A PRINCESS.
AND SOME UNTARNISHED PART OF WHAT REMAINS OF MY SOUL...
...*CHERISHES* THAT THOUGHT, SOMEHOW.

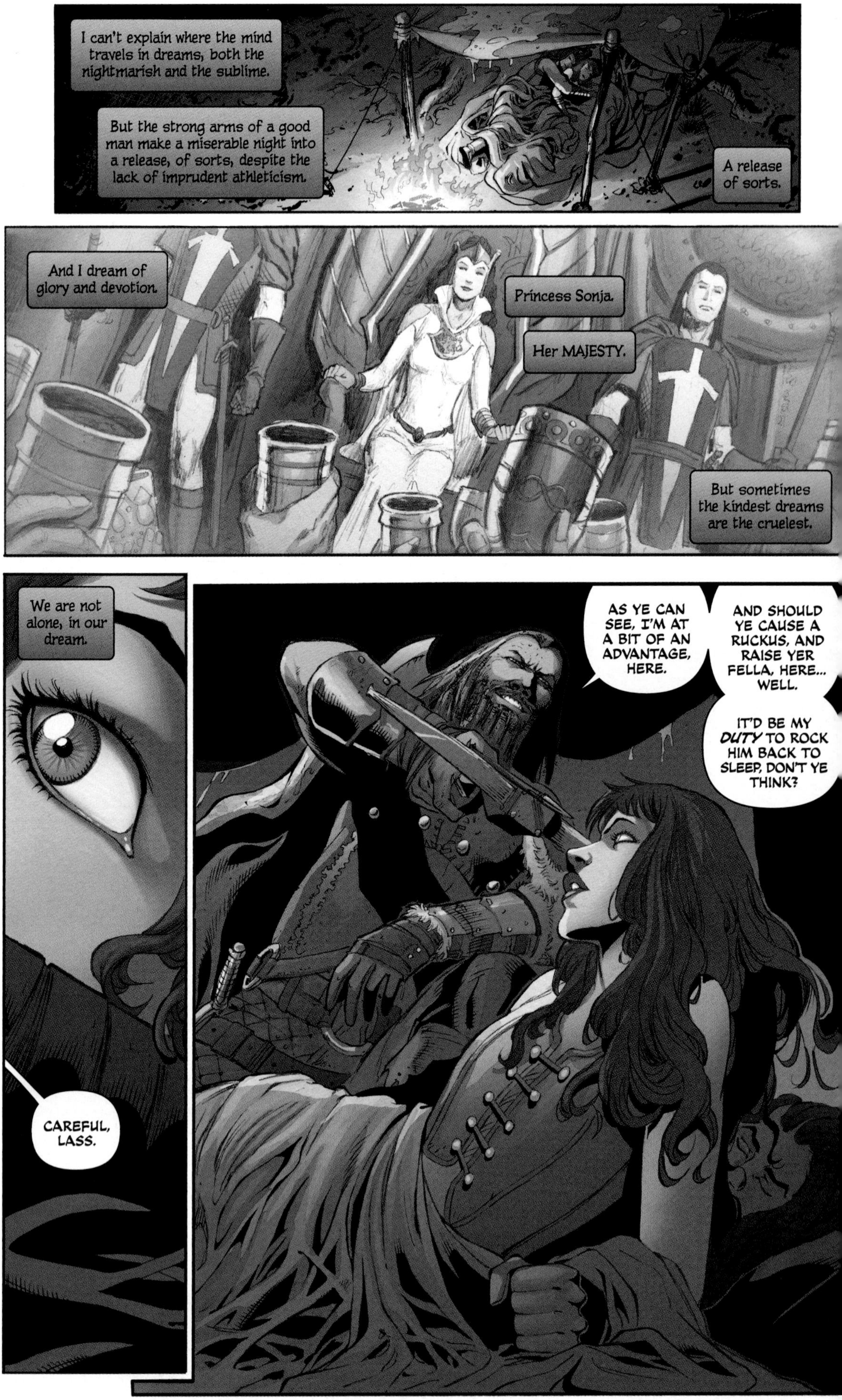

I can't explain where the mind travels in dreams, both the nightmarish and the sublime.
But the strong arms of a good man make a miserable night into a release, of sorts, despite the lack of imprudent athleticism.
A release of sorts.
And I dream of glory and devotion.
Princess Sonja.
Her MAJESTY.
But sometimes the kindest dreams are the cruelest.
We are not alone, in our dream.
CAREFUL, LASS.
AS YE CAN SEE, I'M AT A BIT OF AN ADVANTAGE, HERE.
AND SHOULD YE CAUSE A RUCKUS, AND RAISE YER FELLA, HERE... WELL.
IT'D BE MY *DUTY* TO ROCK HIM BACK TO SLEEP, DON'T YE THINK?

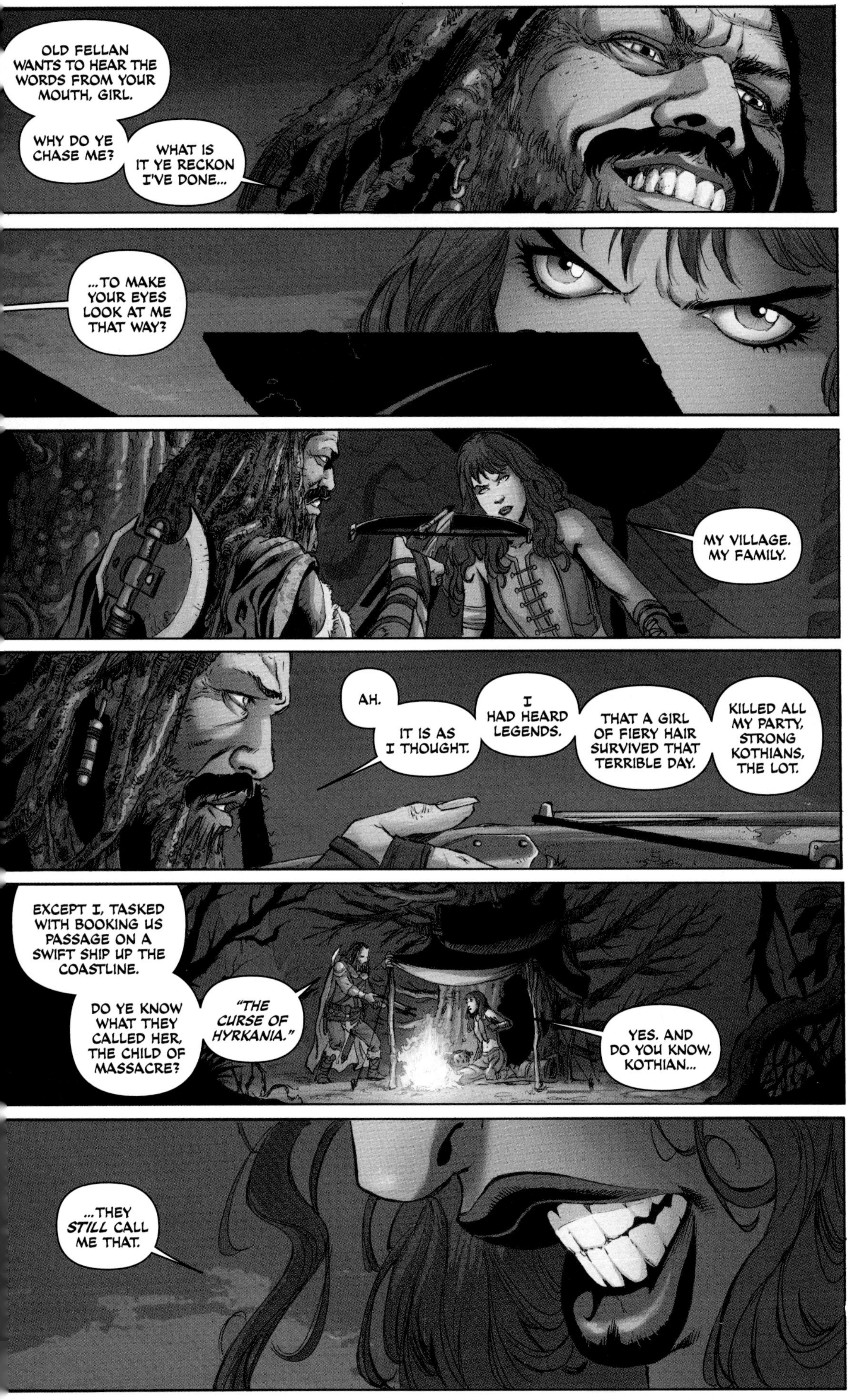
OLD FELLAN WANTS TO HEAR THE WORDS FROM YOUR MOUTH, GIRL.
WHY DO YE CHASE ME?
WHAT IS IT YE RECKON I'VE DONE...
...TO MAKE YOUR EYES LOOK AT ME THAT WAY?
MY VILLAGE. MY FAMILY.
AH.
IT IS AS I THOUGHT.
I HAD HEARD LEGENDS.
THAT A GIRL OF FIERY HAIR SURVIVED THAT TERRIBLE DAY.
KILLED ALL MY PARTY, STRONG KOTHIANS, THE LOT.
EXCEPT I, TASKED WITH BOOKING US PASSAGE ON A SWIFT SHIP UP THE COASTLINE.
DO YE KNOW WHAT THEY CALLED HER, THE CHILD OF MASSACRE?
"THE CURSE OF HYRKANIA."
YES. AND DO YOU KNOW, KOTHIAN...
...THEY *STILL* CALL ME THAT.

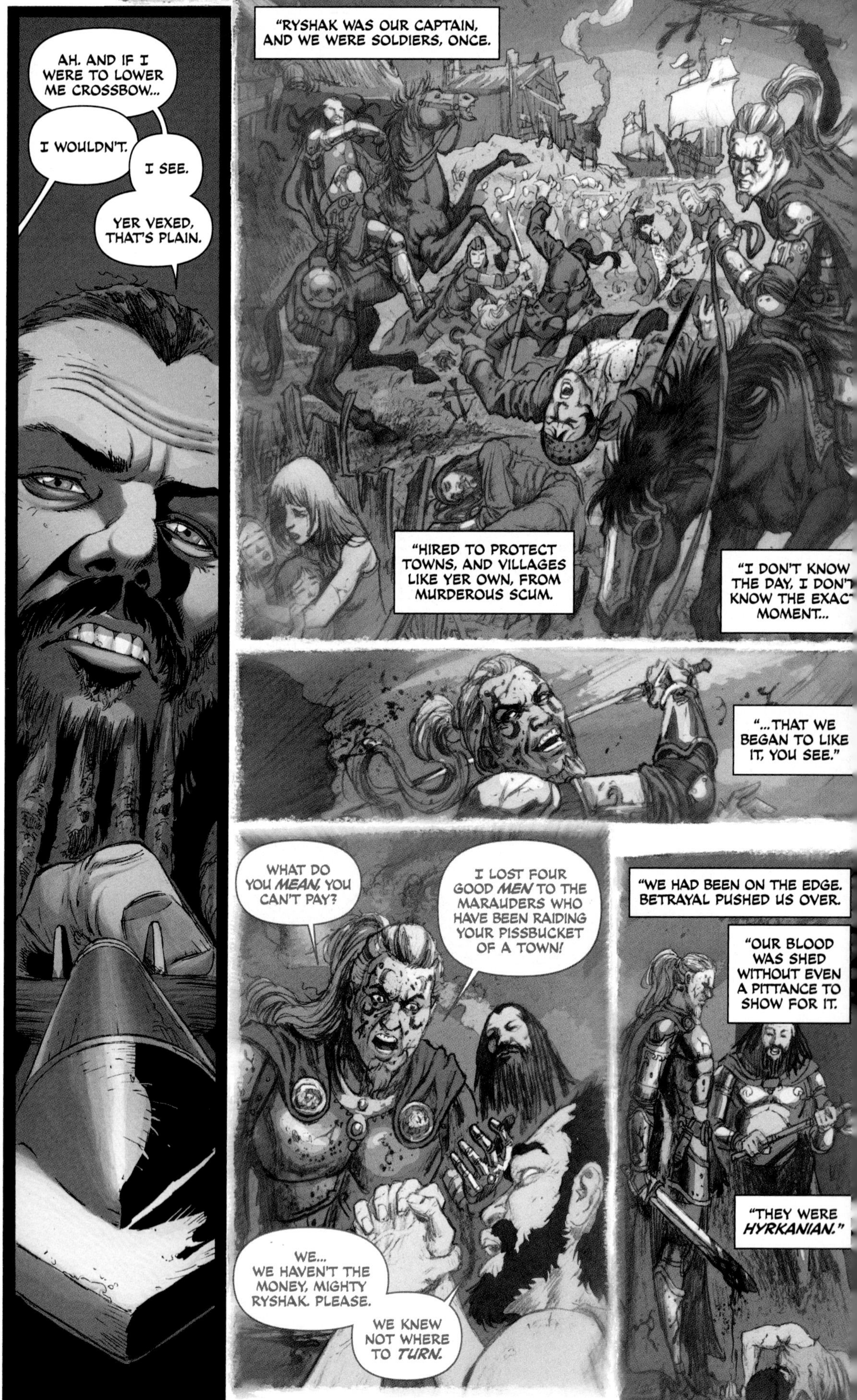

AH. AND IF I WERE TO LOWER ME CROSSBOW...
I WOULDN'T.
I SEE.
YER VEXED, THAT'S PLAIN.
"RYSHAK WAS OUR CAPTAIN, AND WE WERE SOLDIERS, ONCE.
"HIRED TO PROTECT TOWNS, AND VILLAGES LIKE YER OWN, FROM MURDEROUS SCUM.
"I DON'T KNOW THE DAY, I DON'T KNOW THE EXACT MOMENT...
"...THAT WE BEGAN TO LIKE IT, YOU SEE."
WHAT DO YOU *MEAN*, YOU CAN'T PAY?
I LOST FOUR GOOD *MEN* TO THE MARAUDERS WHO HAVE BEEN RAIDING YOUR PISSBUCKET OF A TOWN!
WE... WE HAVEN'T THE MONEY, MIGHTY RYSHAK. PLEASE.
WE KNEW NOT WHERE TO *TURN*.
"WE HAD BEEN ON THE EDGE. BETRAYAL PUSHED US OVER.
"OUR BLOOD WAS SHED WITHOUT EVEN A PITTANCE TO SHOW FOR IT.
"THEY WERE *HYRKANIAN*."

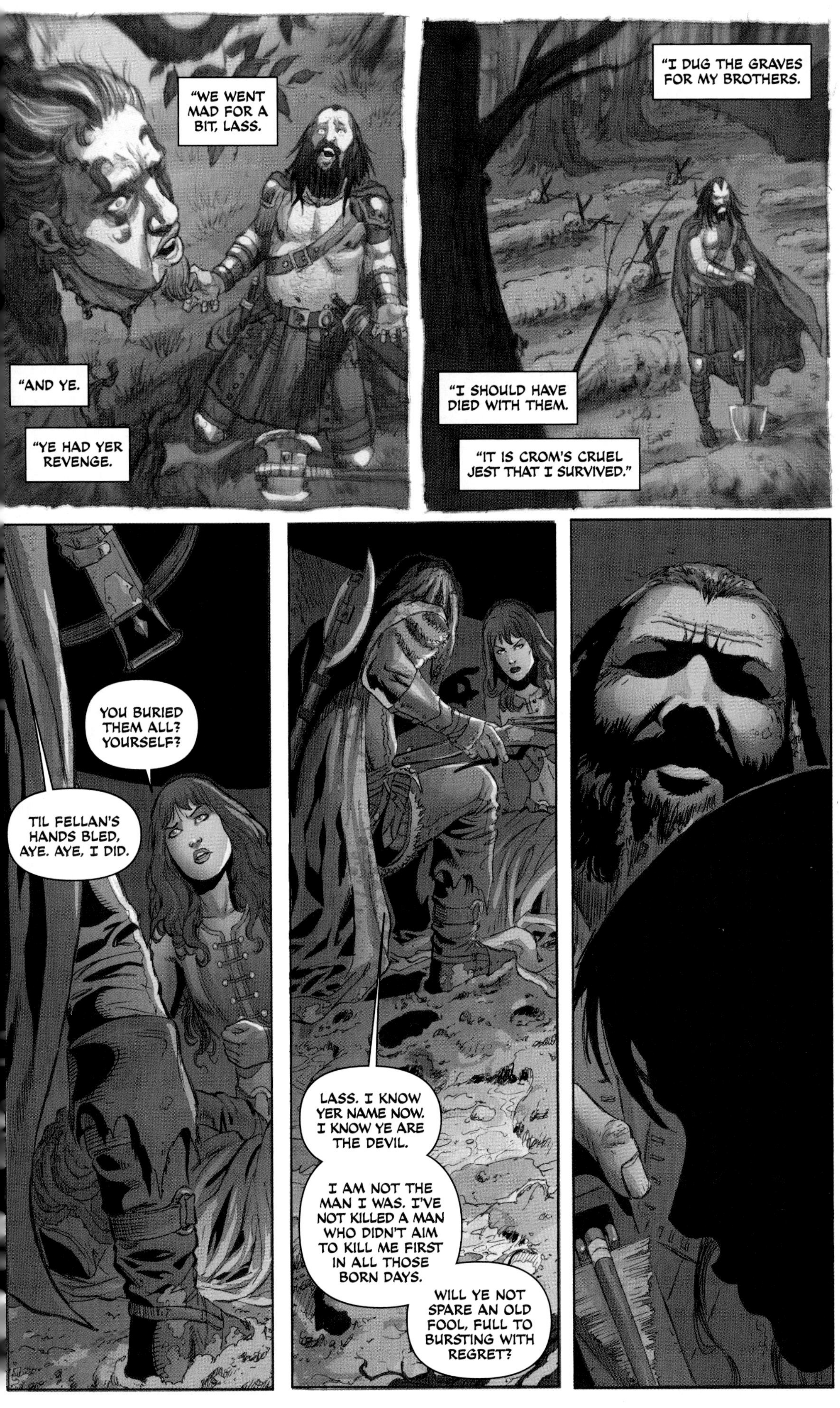
"WE WENT MAD FOR A BIT, LASS.
"AND YE.
"YE HAD YER REVENGE.
"I DUG THE GRAVES FOR MY BROTHERS.
"I SHOULD HAVE DIED WITH THEM.
"IT IS CROM'S CRUEL JEST THAT I SURVIVED."
YOU BURIED THEM ALL? YOURSELF?
TIL FELLAN'S HANDS BLED, AYE. AYE, I DID.
LASS. I KNOW YER NAME NOW. I KNOW YE ARE THE DEVIL.
I AM NOT THE MAN I WAS. I'VE NOT KILLED A MAN WHO DIDN'T AIM TO KILL ME FIRST IN ALL THOSE BORN DAYS.
WILL YE NOT SPARE AN OLD FOOL, FULL TO BURSTING WITH REGRET?

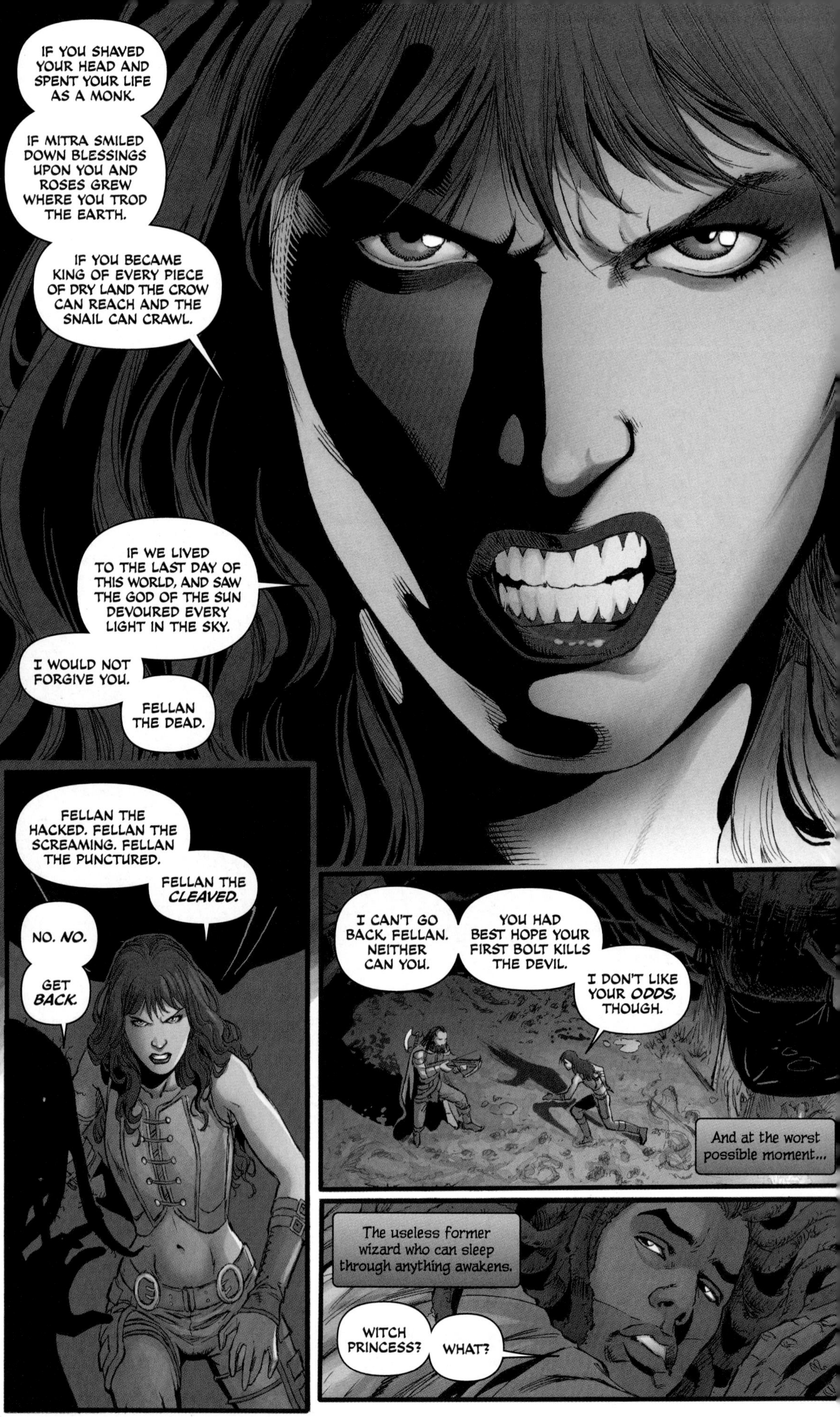
IF YOU SHAVED YOUR HEAD AND SPENT YOUR LIFE AS A MONK.
IF MITRA SMILED DOWN BLESSINGS UPON YOU AND ROSES GREW WHERE YOU TROD THE EARTH.
IF YOU BECAME KING OF EVERY PIECE OF DRY LAND THE CROW CAN REACH AND THE SNAIL CAN CRAWL.
IF WE LIVED TO THE LAST DAY OF THIS WORLD, AND SAW THE GOD OF THE SUN DEVOURED EVERY LIGHT IN THE SKY.
I WOULD NOT FORGIVE YOU.
FELLAN THE DEAD.
FELLAN THE HACKED. FELLAN THE SCREAMING. FELLAN THE PUNCTURED.
FELLAN THE *CLEAVED.*
NO. *NO.*
GET *BACK.*
I CAN'T GO BACK, FELLAN. NEITHER CAN YOU.
YOU HAD BEST HOPE YOUR FIRST BOLT KILLS THE DEVIL.
I DON'T LIKE YOUR *ODDS,* THOUGH.
And at the worst possible moment...
The useless former wizard who can sleep through anything awakens.
WITCH PRINCESS?
WHAT?

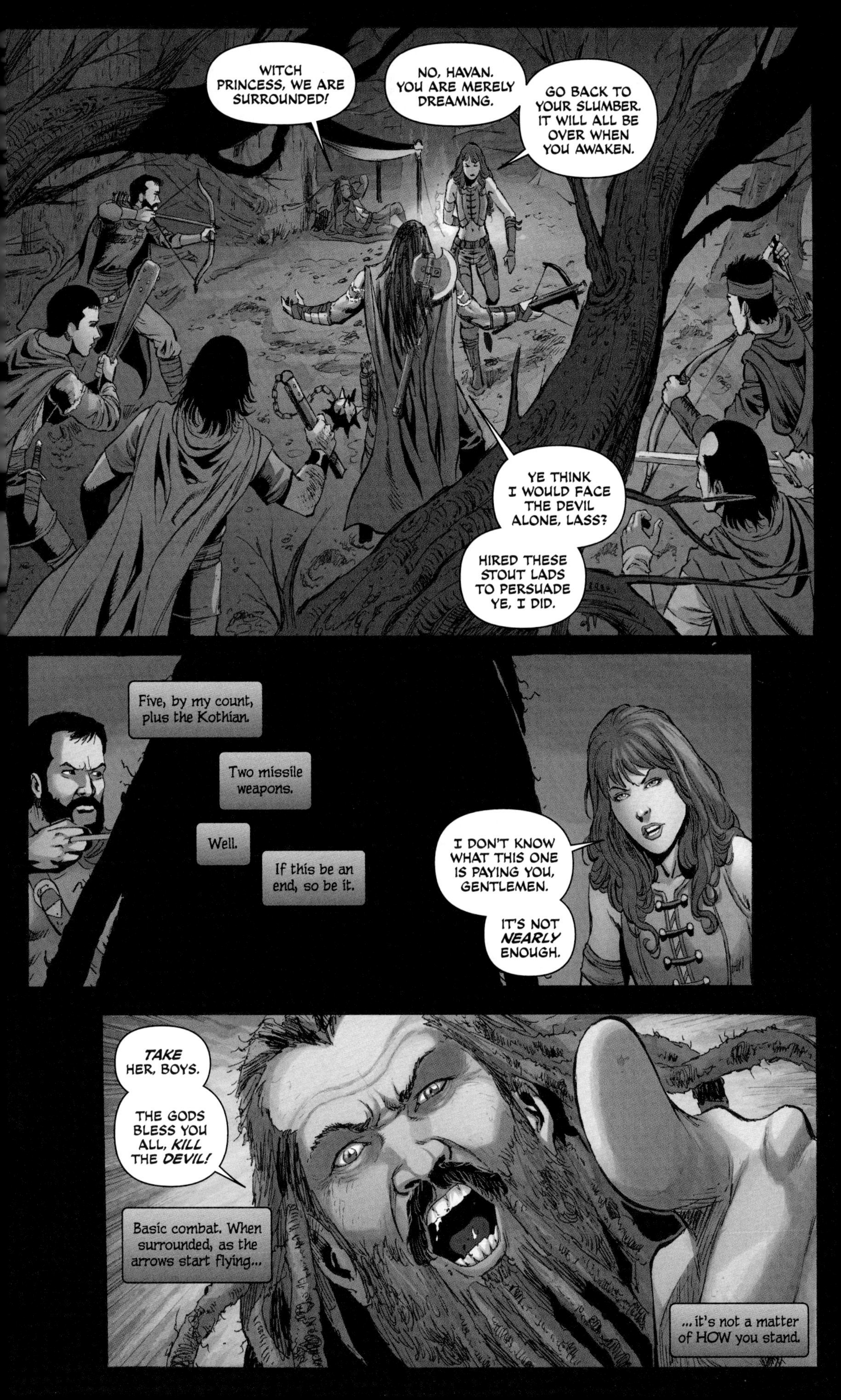
WITCH PRINCESS, WE ARE SURROUNDED!
NO, HAVAN. YOU ARE MERELY DREAMING.
GO BACK TO YOUR SLUMBER. IT WILL ALL BE OVER WHEN YOU AWAKEN.
YE THINK I WOULD FACE THE DEVIL ALONE, LASS?
HIRED THESE STOUT LADS TO PERSUADE YE, I DID.
Five, by my count, plus the Kothian.
Two missile weapons.
Well.
If this be an end, so be it.
I DON'T KNOW WHAT THIS ONE IS PAYING YOU, GENTLEMEN.
IT'S NOT *NEARLY* ENOUGH.
TAKE HER, BOYS.
THE GODS BLESS YOU ALL, ***KILL*** THE ***DEVIL!***
Basic combat. When surrounded, as the arrows start flying...
...it's not a matter of HOW you stand.

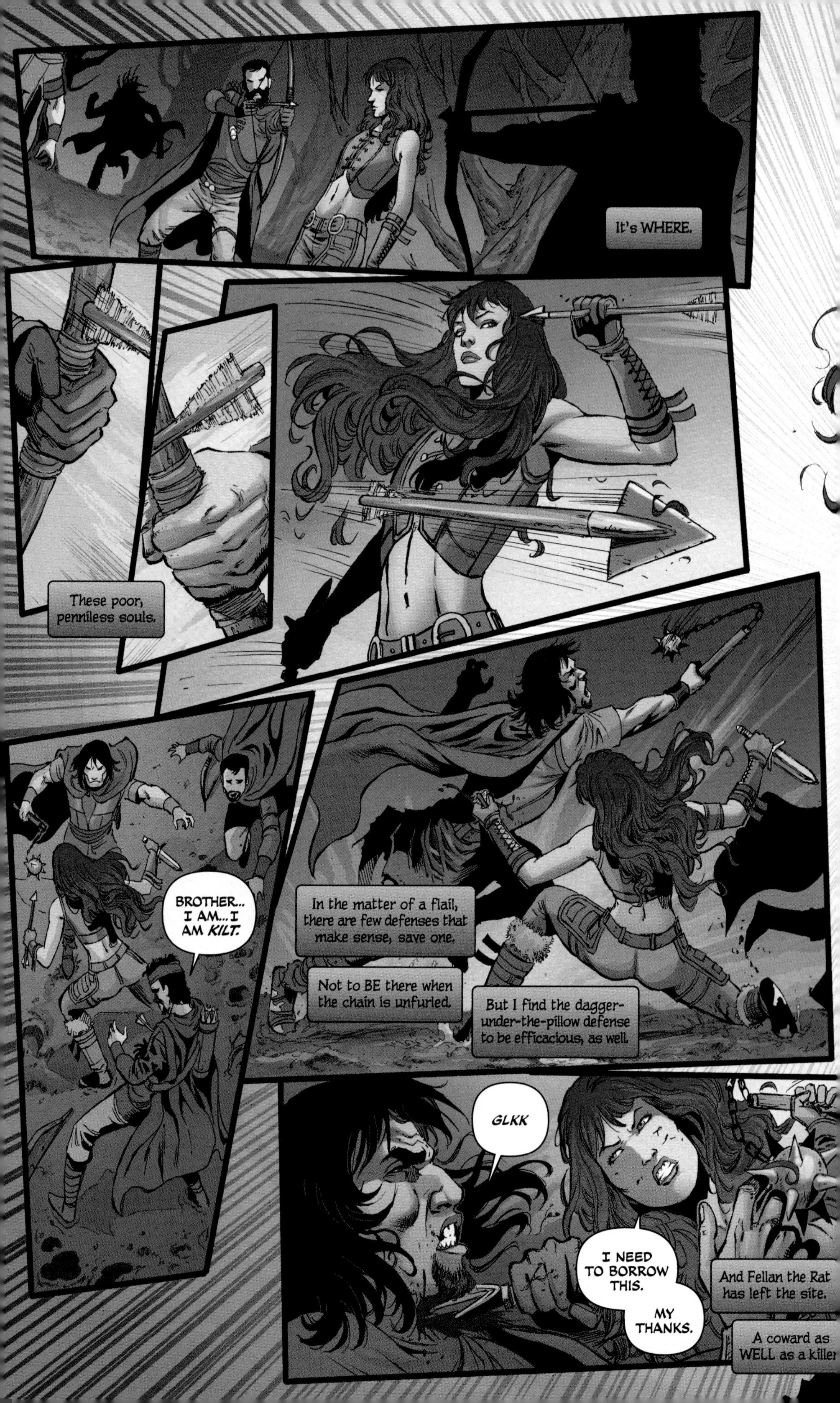
It's WHERE.
These poor, penniless souls.
BROTHER... I AM... I AM *KILT.*
In the matter of a flail, there are few defenses that make sense, save one.
Not to BE there when the chain is unfurled.
But I find the dagger-under-the-pillow defense to be efficacious, as well.
GLKK
I NEED TO BORROW THIS.
MY THANKS.
And Fellan the Rat has left the site.
A coward as WELL as a killer

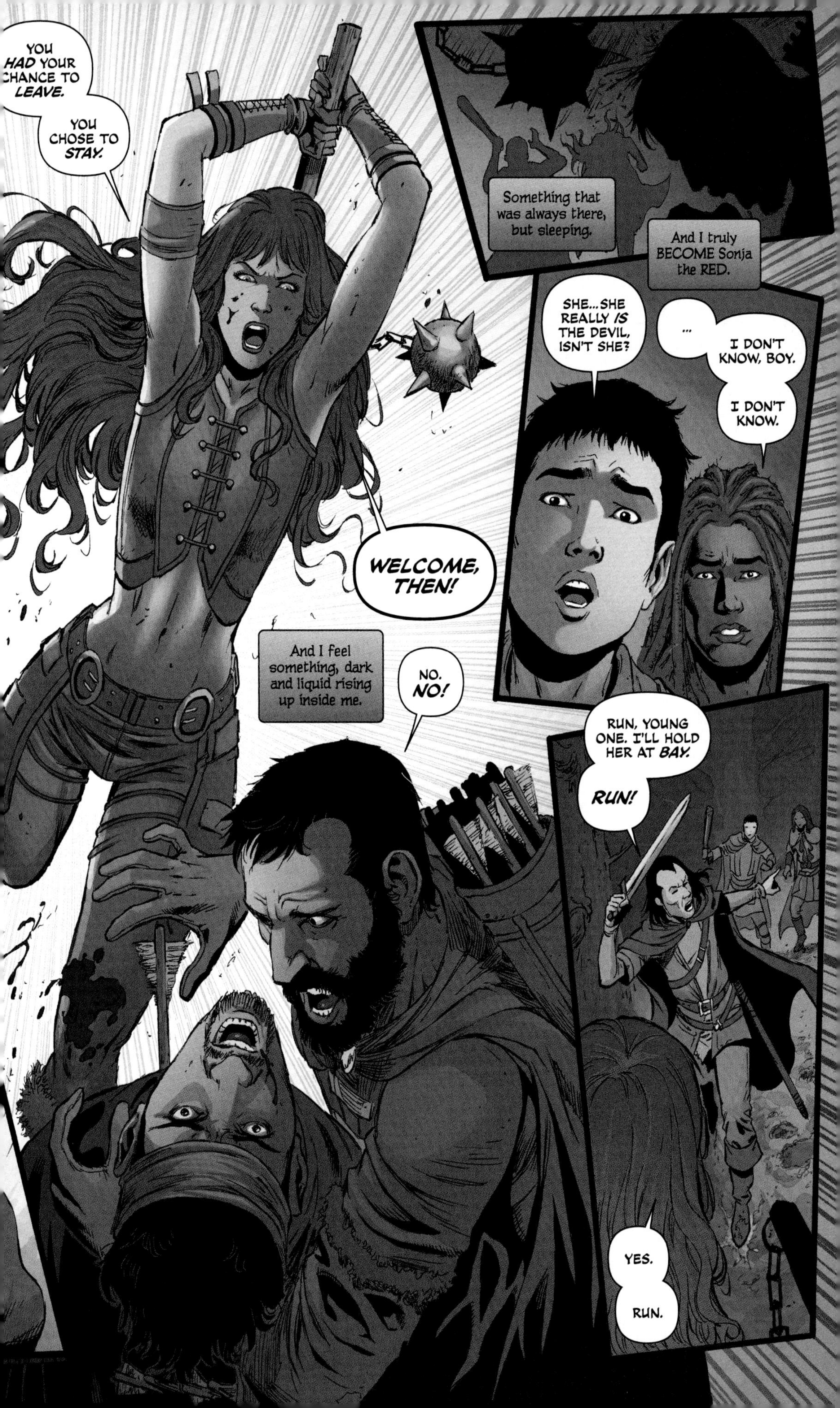

YOU HAD YOUR CHANCE TO LEAVE.
YOU CHOSE TO STAY.
Something that was always there, but sleeping.
And I truly BECOME Sonja the RED.
SHE...SHE REALLY IS THE DEVIL, ISN'T SHE?
...
I DON'T KNOW, BOY.
I DON'T KNOW.
WELCOME, THEN!
And I feel something, dark and liquid rising up inside me.
NO. NO!
RUN, YOUNG ONE. I'LL HOLD HER AT BAY.
RUN!
YES.
RUN.

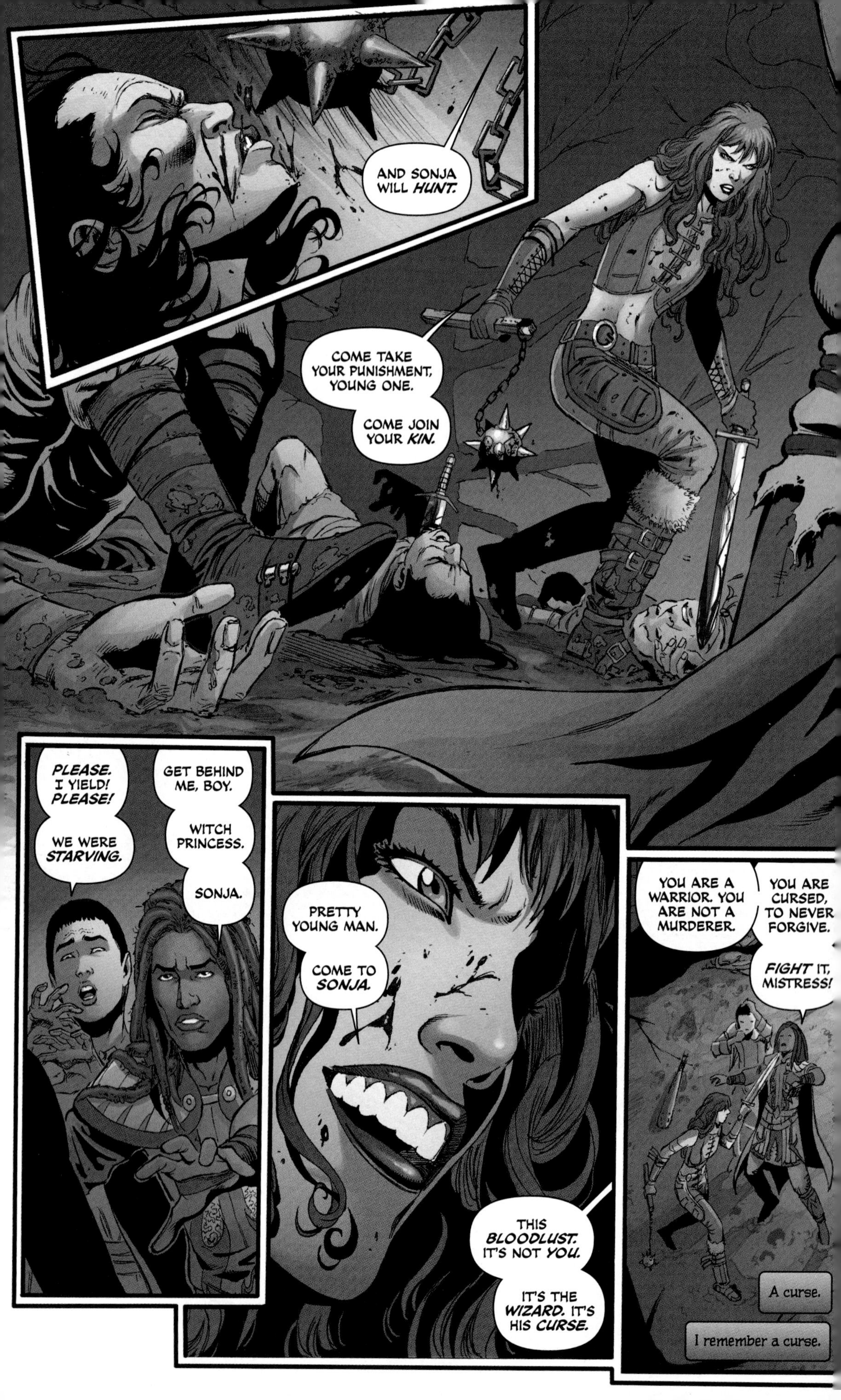
AND SONJA WILL *HUNT.*
COME TAKE YOUR PUNISHMENT, YOUNG ONE.
COME JOIN YOUR *KIN.*
PLEASE. I YIELD! *PLEASE!*
WE WERE *STARVING.*
GET BEHIND ME, BOY.
WITCH PRINCESS.
SONJA.
PRETTY YOUNG MAN.
COME TO *SONJA.*
THIS *BLOODLUST.* IT'S NOT *YOU.*
IT'S THE *WIZARD.* IT'S HIS *CURSE.*
YOU ARE A WARRIOR. YOU ARE NOT A MURDERER.
YOU ARE CURSED, TO NEVER FORGIVE.
FIGHT IT, MISTRESS!
A curse.
I remember a curse.

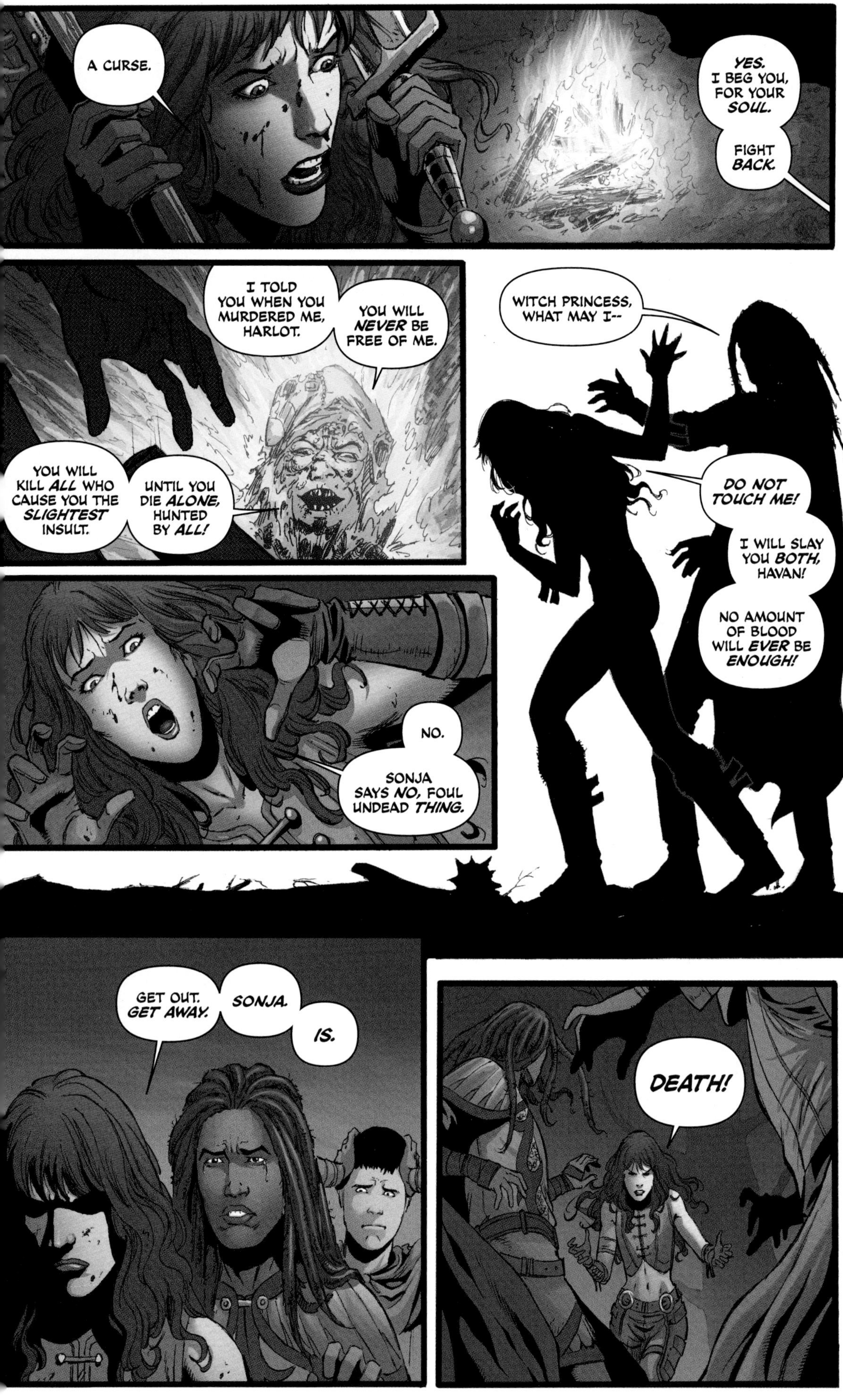
A CURSE.
YES. I BEG YOU, FOR YOUR SOUL.
FIGHT BACK.
I TOLD YOU WHEN YOU MURDERED ME, HARLOT.
YOU WILL NEVER BE FREE OF ME.
YOU WILL KILL ALL WHO CAUSE YOU THE SLIGHTEST INSULT.
UNTIL YOU DIE ALONE, HUNTED BY ALL!
NO.
SONJA SAYS NO, FOUL UNDEAD THING.
WITCH PRINCESS, WHAT MAY I--
DO NOT TOUCH ME!
I WILL SLAY YOU BOTH, HAVAN!
NO AMOUNT OF BLOOD WILL EVER BE ENOUGH!
GET OUT. GET AWAY.
SONJA.
IS.
DEATH!

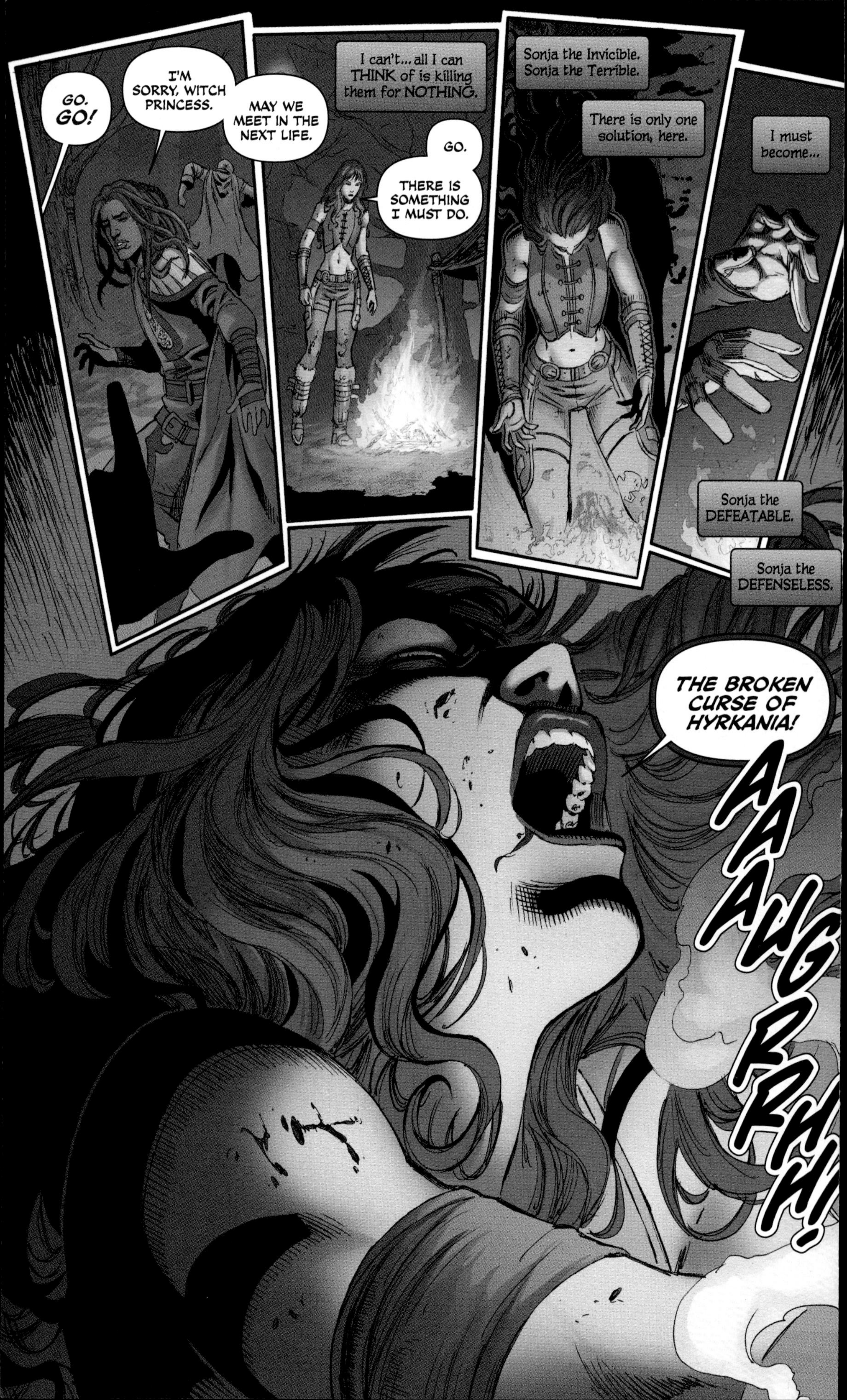
GO. GO!
I'M SORRY, WITCH PRINCESS.
MAY WE MEET IN THE NEXT LIFE.
I can't... all I can THINK of is killing them for NOTHING.
GO.
THERE IS SOMETHING I MUST DO.
Sonja the Invicible. Sonja the Terrible.
There is only one solution, here.
I must become...
Sonja the DEFEATABLE.
Sonja the DEFENSELESS.
THE BROKEN CURSE OF HYRKANIA!
AAAUGRHH!

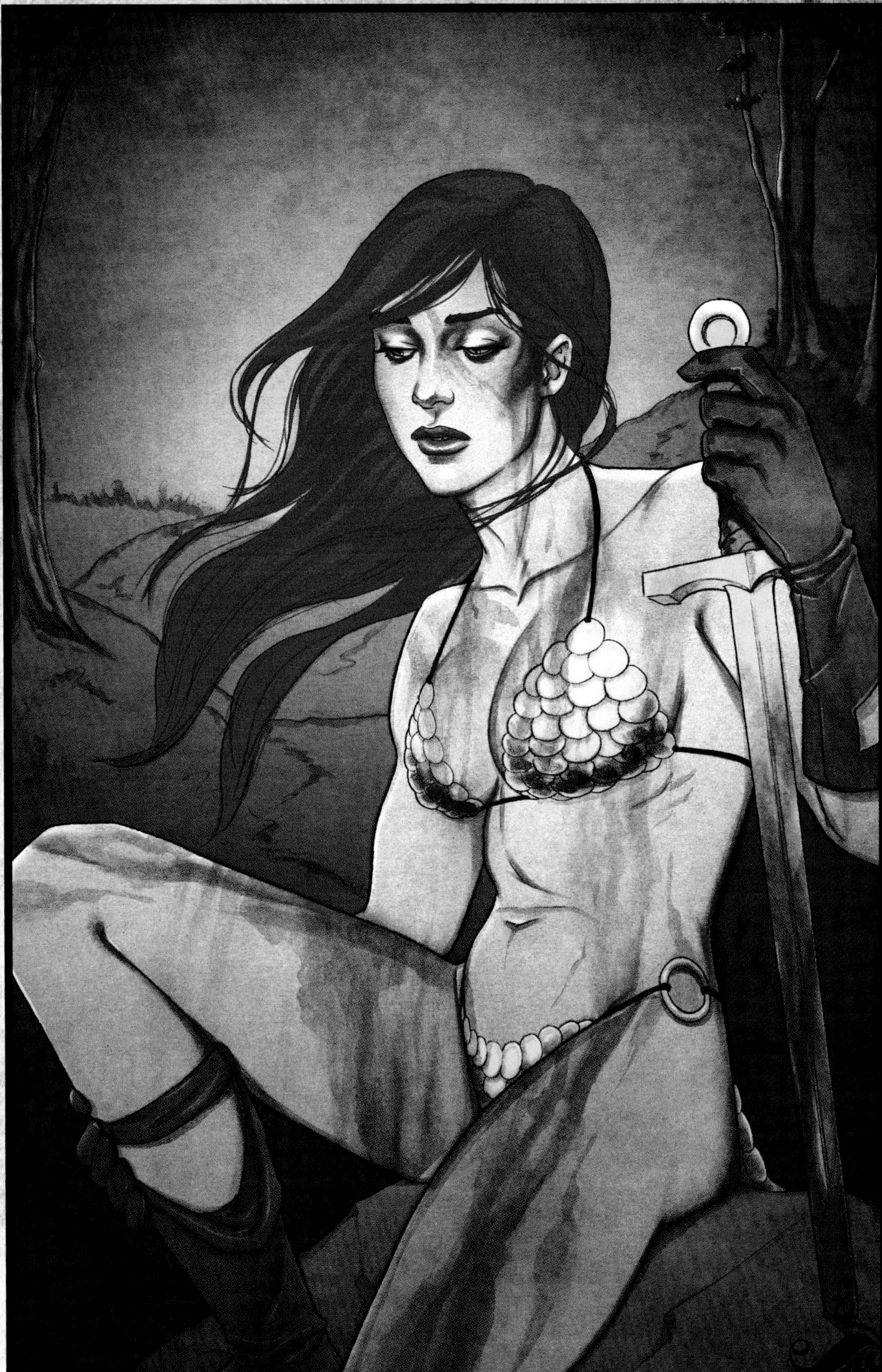

ISSUE FIFTEEN
cover by JENNY FRISON

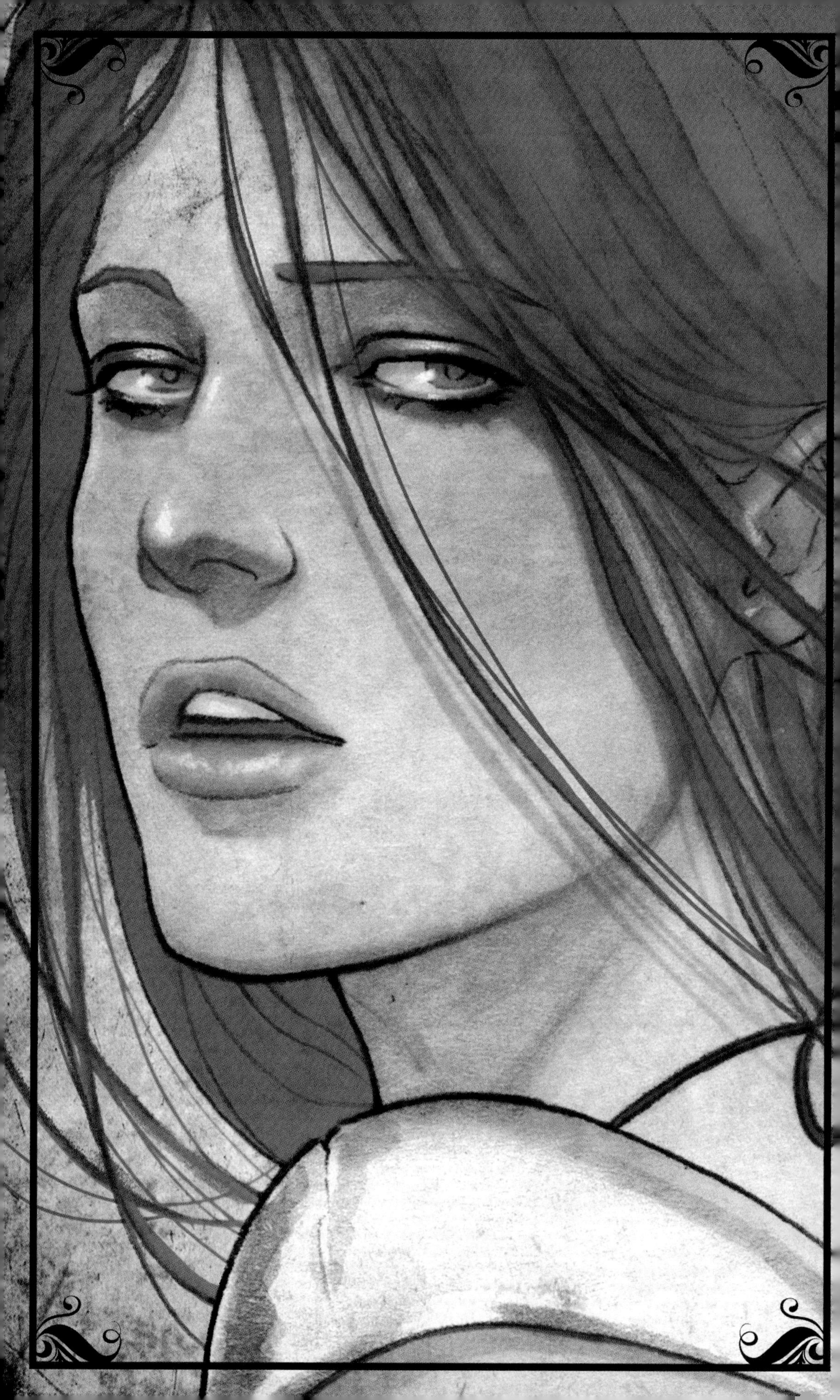

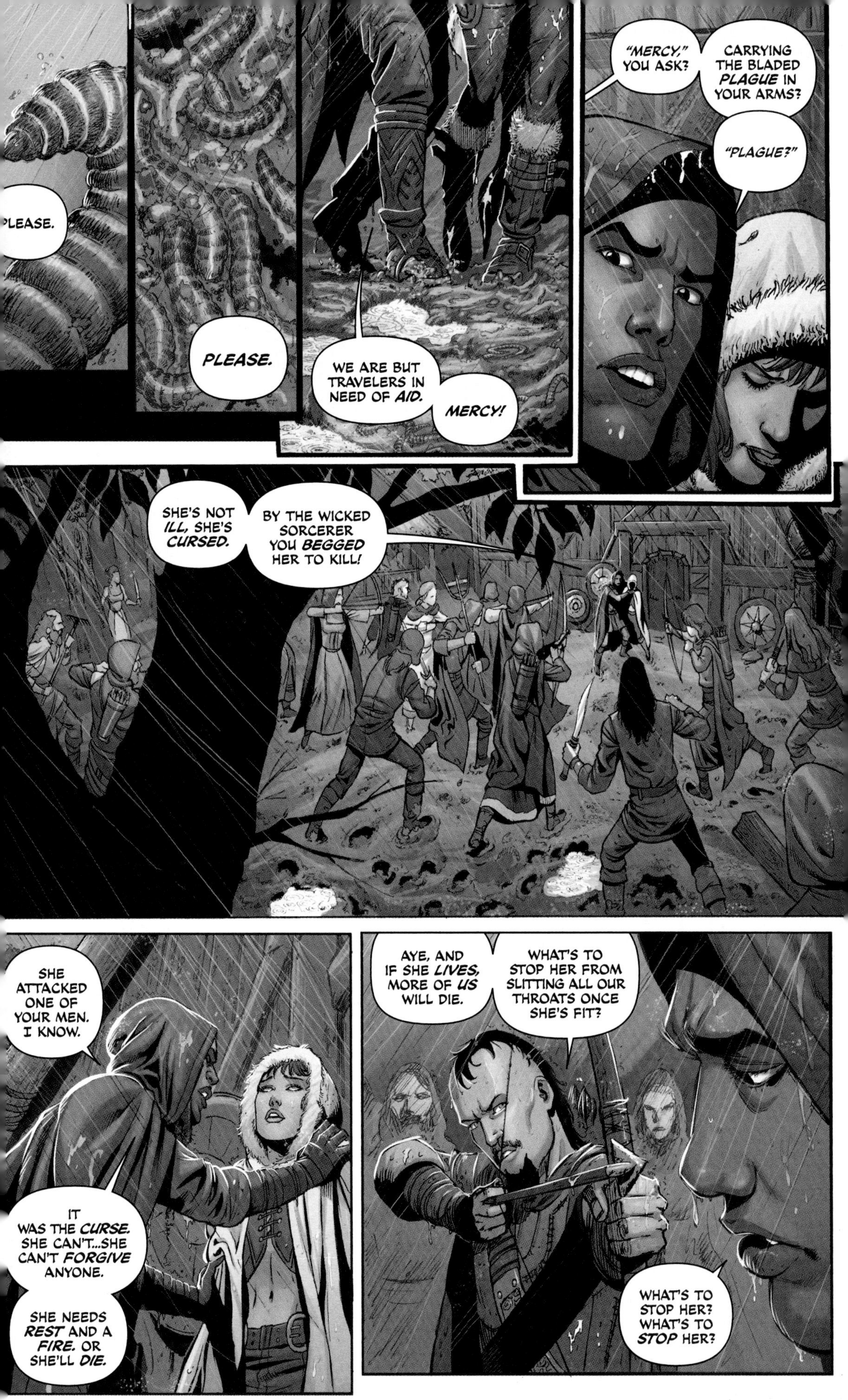
PLEASE.
PLEASE.
WE ARE BUT TRAVELERS IN NEED OF AID.
MERCY!
"MERCY," YOU ASK?
CARRYING THE BLADED PLAGUE IN YOUR ARMS?
"PLAGUE?"
SHE'S NOT ILL, SHE'S CURSED.
BY THE WICKED SORCERER YOU BEGGED HER TO KILL!
SHE ATTACKED ONE OF YOUR MEN. I KNOW.
IT WAS THE CURSE. SHE CAN'T...SHE CAN'T FORGIVE ANYONE.
SHE NEEDS REST AND A FIRE. OR SHE'LL DIE.
AYE, AND IF SHE LIVES, MORE OF US WILL DIE.
WHAT'S TO STOP HER FROM SLITTING ALL OUR THROATS ONCE SHE'S FIT?
WHAT'S TO STOP HER? WHAT'S TO STOP HER?

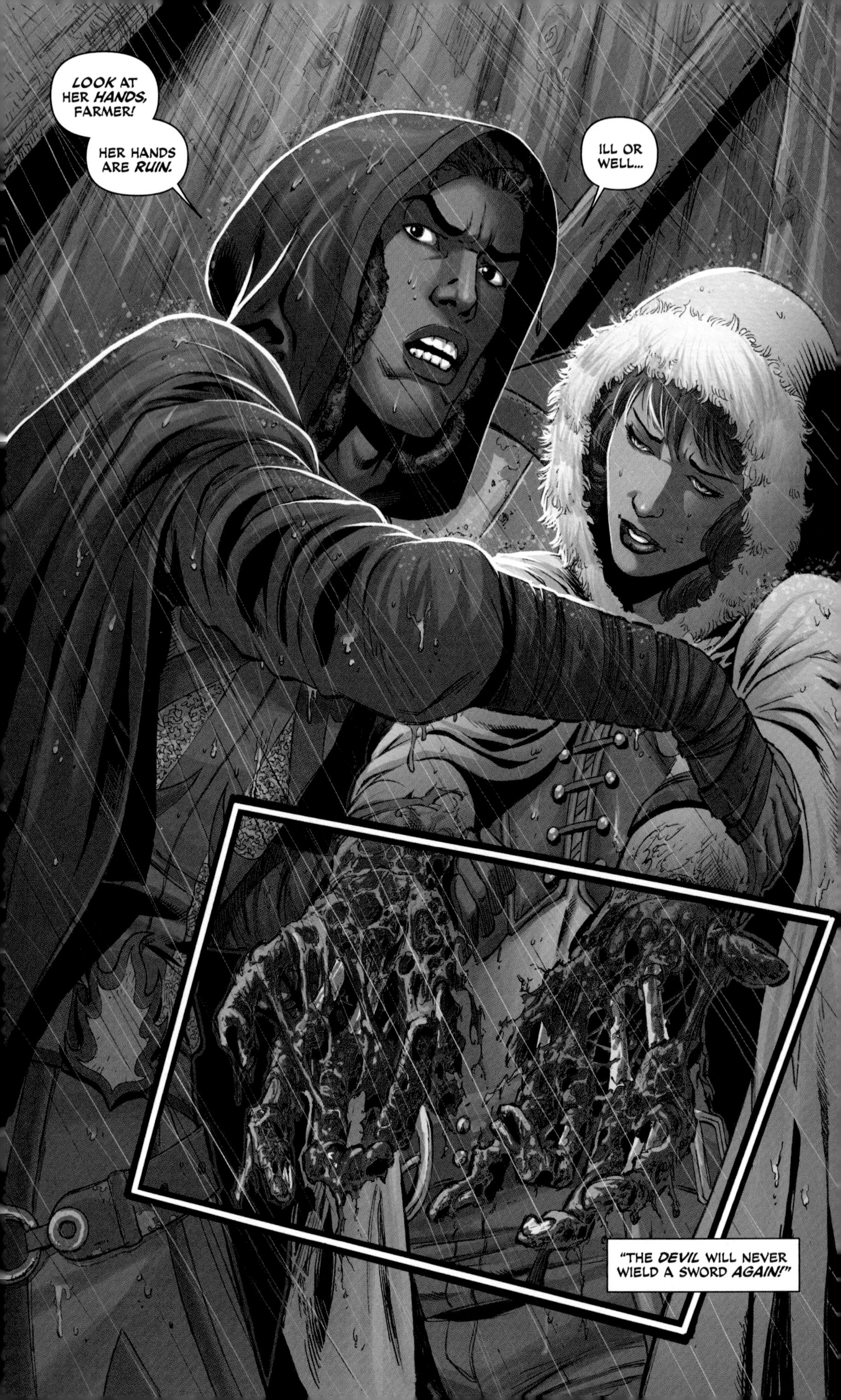
LOOK AT HER HANDS, FARMER!
HER HANDS ARE RUIN.
ILL OR WELL...
"THE DEVIL WILL NEVER WIELD A SWORD AGAIN!"

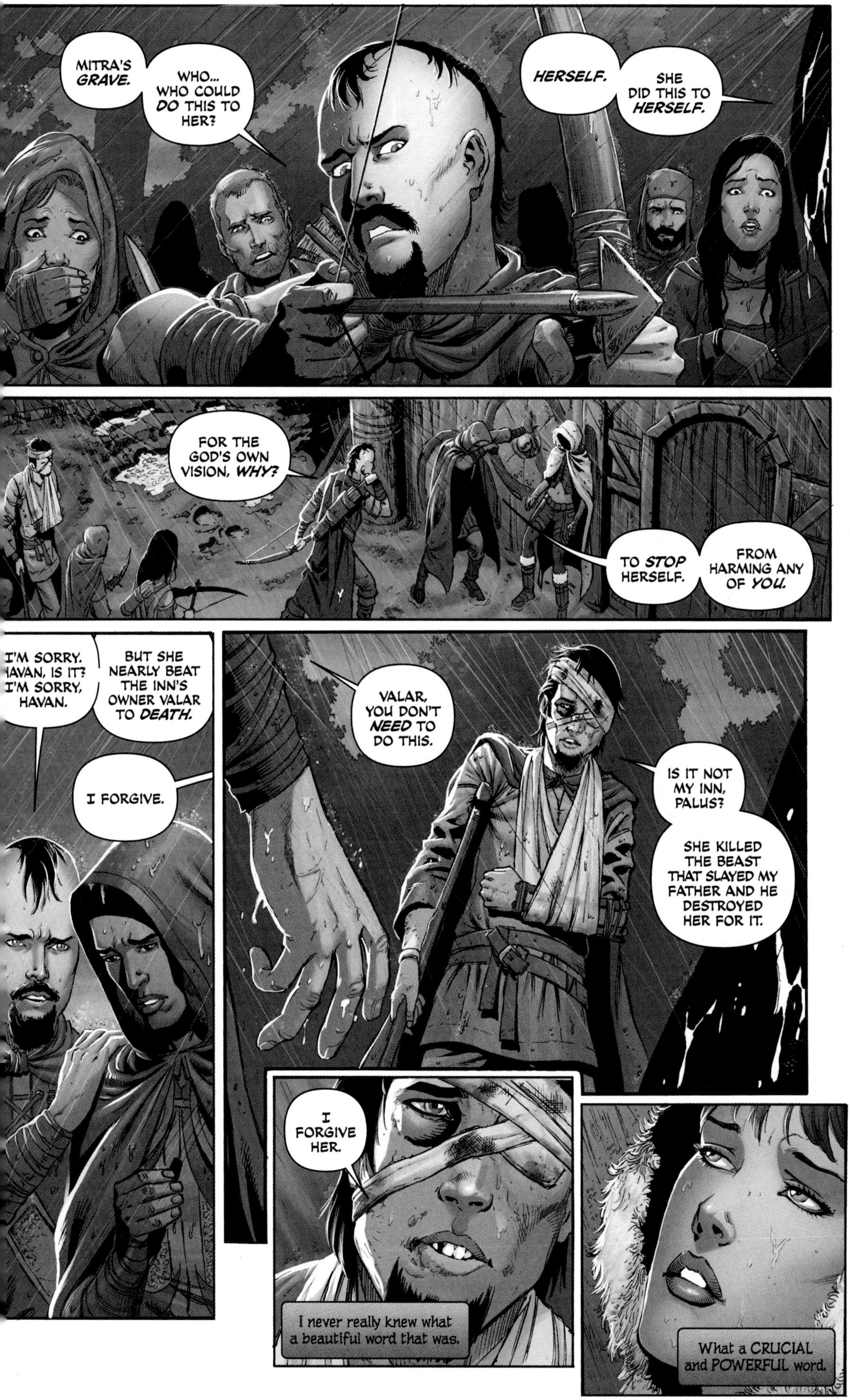
MITRA'S GRAVE.
WHO... WHO COULD DO THIS TO HER?
HERSELF.
SHE DID THIS TO HERSELF.
FOR THE GOD'S OWN VISION, WHY?
TO STOP HERSELF.
FROM HARMING ANY OF YOU.
I'M SORRY. HAVAN, IS IT? I'M SORRY, HAVAN.
BUT SHE NEARLY BEAT THE INN'S OWNER VALAR TO DEATH.
I FORGIVE.
VALAR, YOU DON'T NEED TO DO THIS.
IS IT NOT MY INN, PALUS?
SHE KILLED THE BEAST THAT SLAYED MY FATHER AND HE DESTROYED HER FOR IT.
I FORGIVE HER.
I never really knew what a beautiful word that was.
What a CRUCIAL and POWERFUL word.

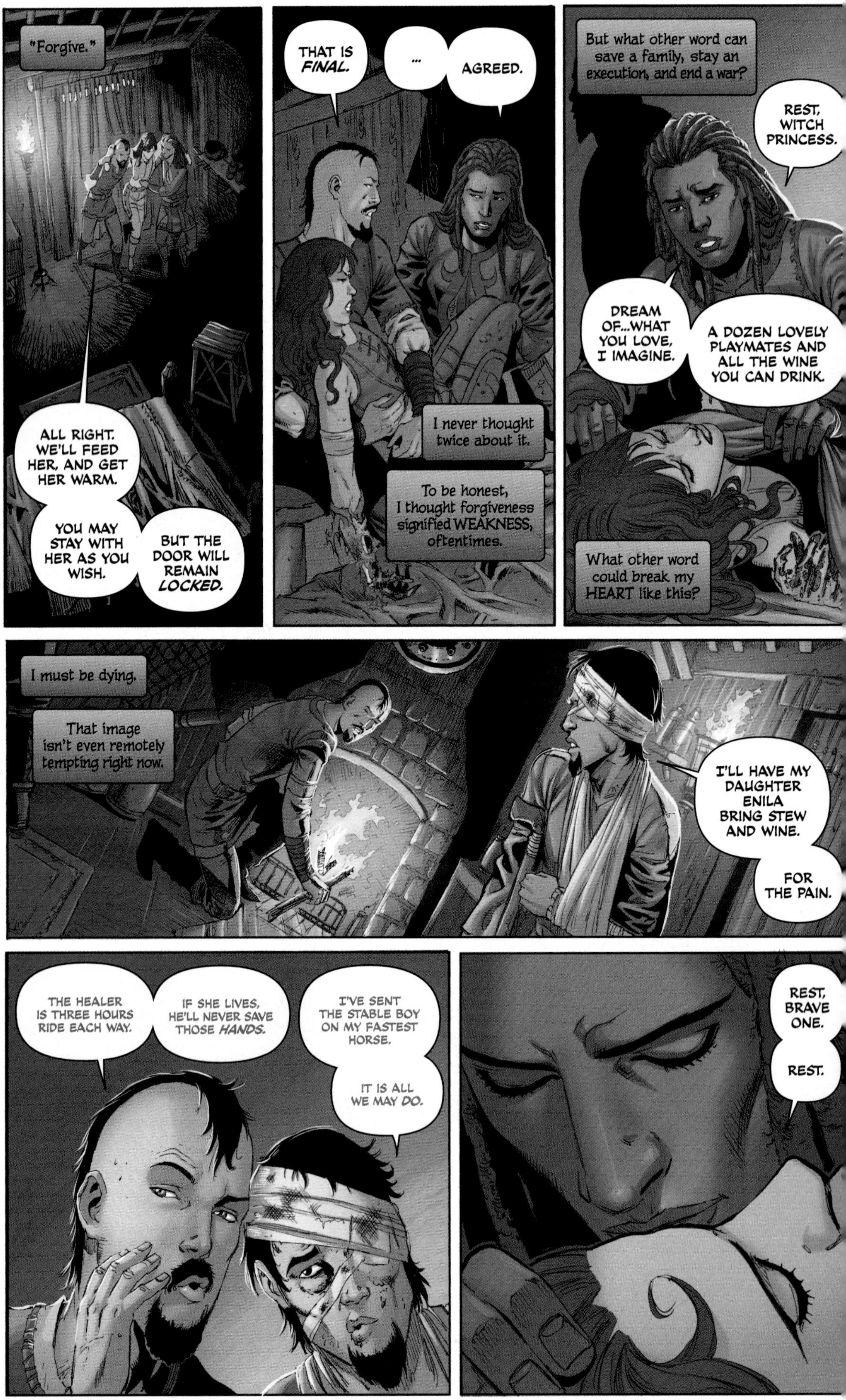
"Forgive."
ALL RIGHT. WE'LL FEED HER, AND GET HER WARM.
YOU MAY STAY WITH HER AS YOU WISH.
BUT THE DOOR WILL REMAIN LOCKED.
THAT IS FINAL.
...
AGREED.
I never thought twice about it.
To be honest, I thought forgiveness signified WEAKNESS, oftentimes.
But what other word can save a family, stay an execution, and end a war?
REST, WITCH PRINCESS.
DREAM OF...WHAT YOU LOVE, I IMAGINE.
A DOZEN LOVELY PLAYMATES AND ALL THE WINE YOU CAN DRINK.
What other word could break my HEART like this?
I must be dying.
That image isn't even remotely tempting right now.
I'LL HAVE MY DAUGHTER ENILA BRING STEW AND WINE.
FOR THE PAIN.
THE HEALER IS THREE HOURS RIDE EACH WAY.
IF SHE LIVES, HE'LL NEVER SAVE THOSE HANDS.
I'VE SENT THE STABLE BOY ON MY FASTEST HORSE.
IT IS ALL WE MAY DO.
REST, BRAVE ONE.
REST.

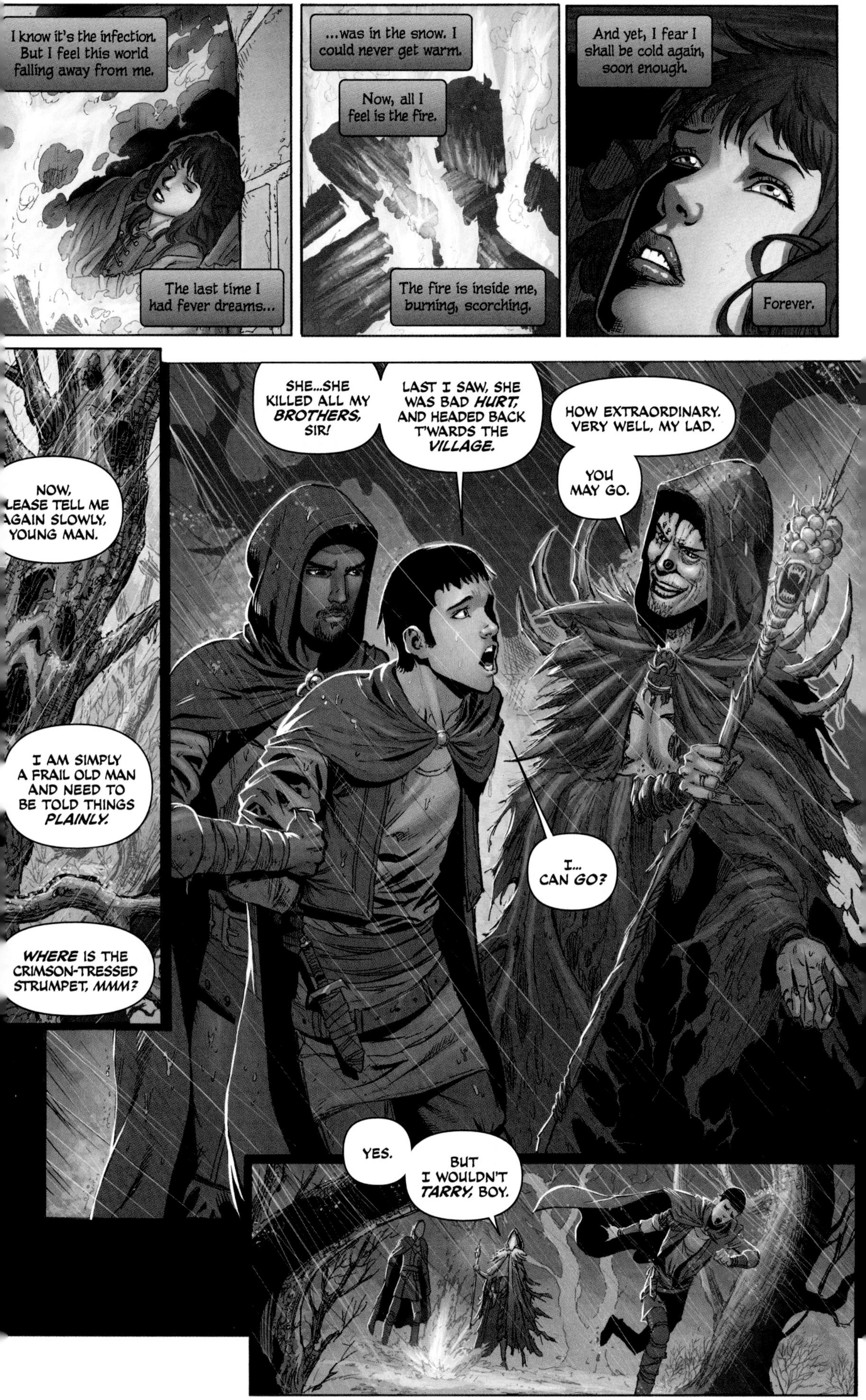
I know it's the infection. But I feel this world falling away from me.
The last time I had fever dreams...
...was in the snow. I could never get warm.
Now, all I feel is the fire.
The fire is inside me, burning, scorching.
And yet, I fear I shall be cold again, soon enough.
Forever.
NOW, LEASE TELL ME AGAIN SLOWLY, YOUNG MAN.
I AM SIMPLY A FRAIL OLD MAN AND NEED TO BE TOLD THINGS PLAINLY.
WHERE IS THE CRIMSON-TRESSED STRUMPET, MMM?
SHE...SHE KILLED ALL MY BROTHERS, SIR!
LAST I SAW, SHE WAS BAD HURT, AND HEADED BACK T'WARDS THE VILLAGE.
HOW EXTRAORDINARY. VERY WELL, MY LAD.
YOU MAY GO.
I... CAN GO?
YES.
BUT I WOULDN'T TARRY, BOY.

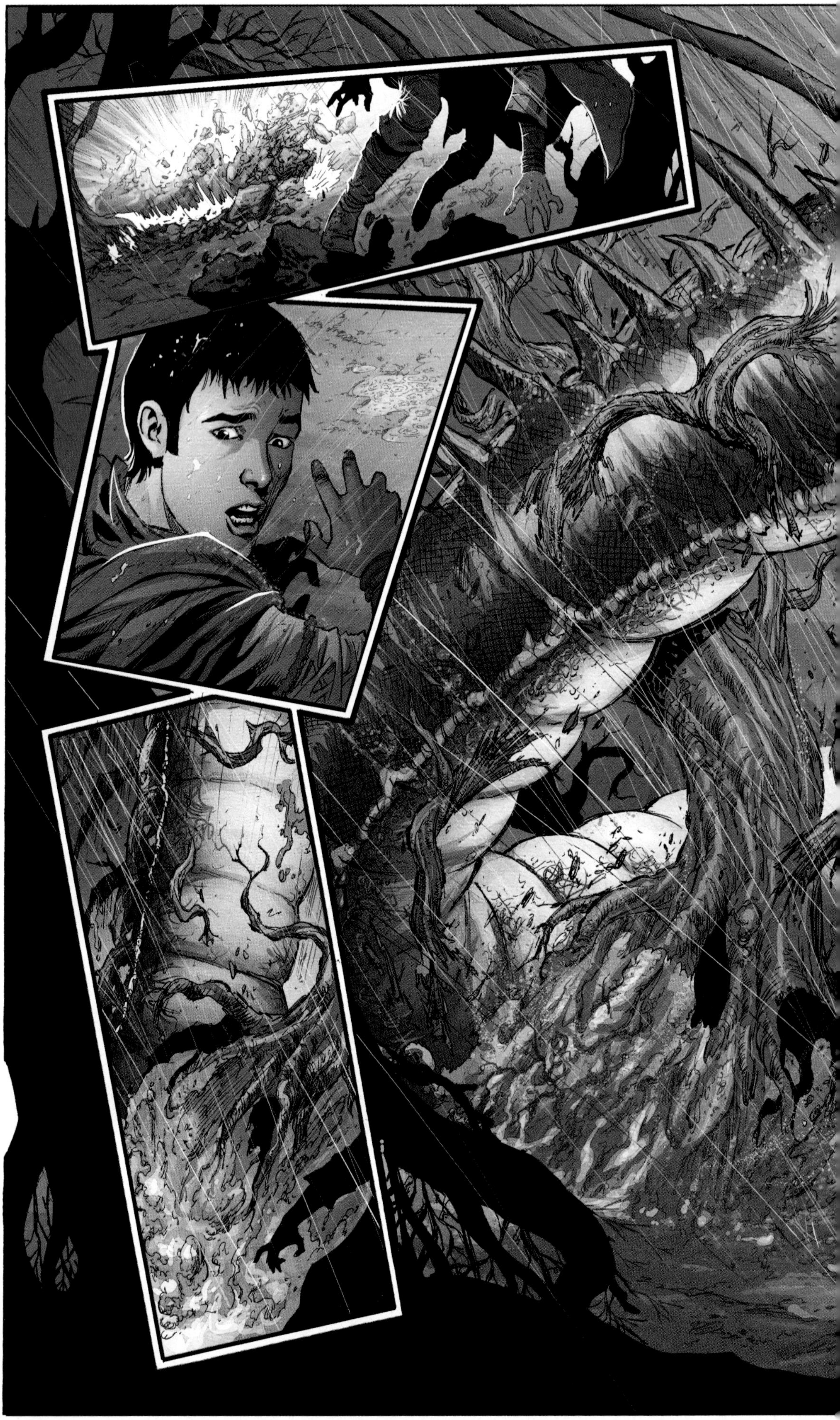

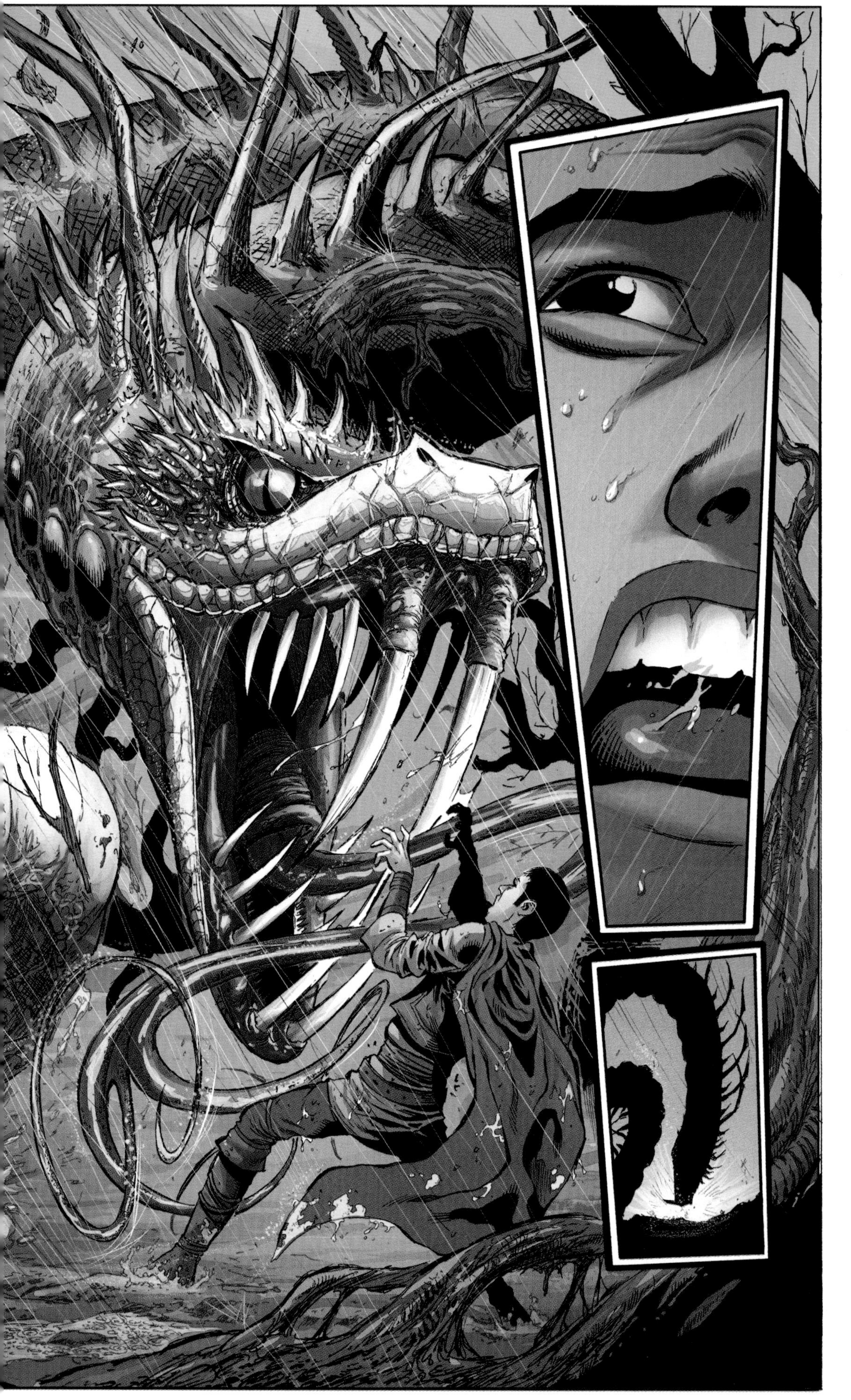

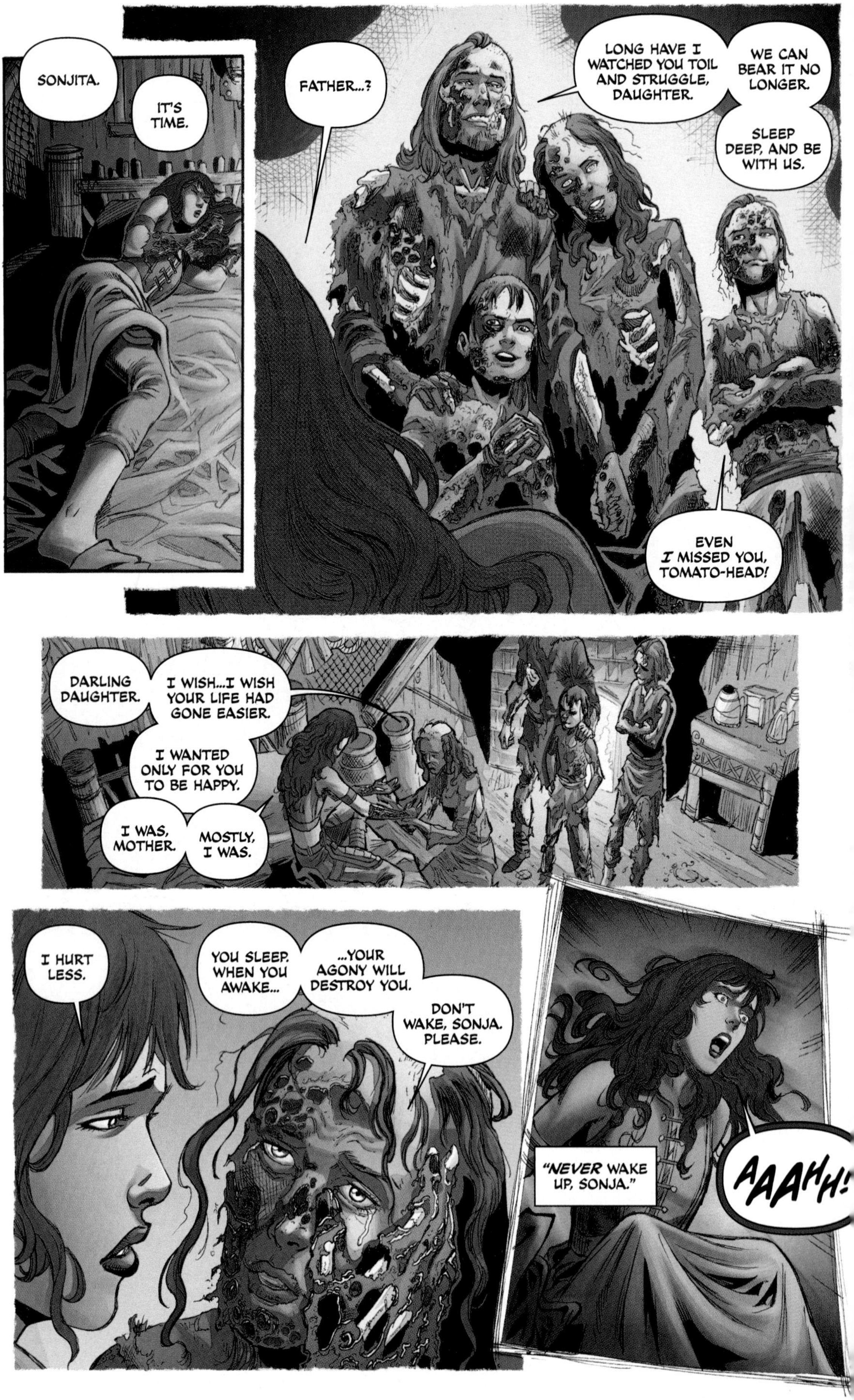
SONJITA.
IT'S TIME.
FATHER...?
LONG HAVE I WATCHED YOU TOIL AND STRUGGLE, DAUGHTER.
WE CAN BEAR IT NO LONGER.
SLEEP DEEP, AND BE WITH US.
EVEN *I* MISSED YOU, TOMATO-HEAD!
DARLING DAUGHTER.
I WISH...I WISH YOUR LIFE HAD GONE EASIER.
I WANTED ONLY FOR YOU TO BE HAPPY.
I WAS, MOTHER.
MOSTLY, I WAS.
I HURT LESS.
YOU SLEEP. WHEN YOU AWAKE...
...YOUR AGONY WILL DESTROY YOU.
DON'T WAKE, SONJA. PLEASE.
"*NEVER* WAKE UP, SONJA."
AAAHH!

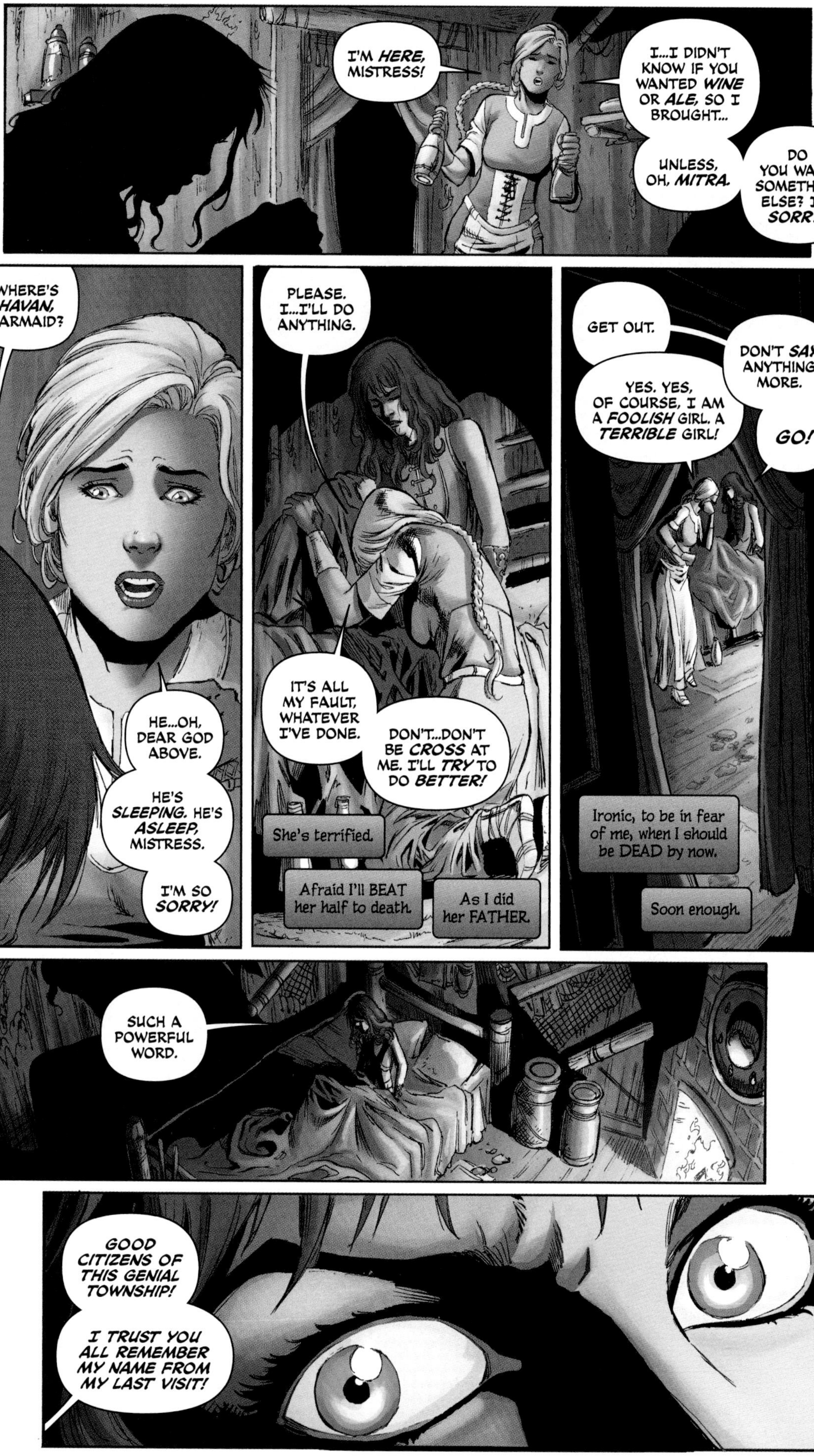
I'M HERE, MISTRESS!
I...I DIDN'T KNOW IF YOU WANTED WINE OR ALE, SO I BROUGHT...
UNLESS, OH, MITRA.
DO YOU WANT SOMETHING ELSE? I'M SORRY!
WHERE'S HAVAN, BARMAID?
HE...OH, DEAR GOD ABOVE.
HE'S SLEEPING. HE'S ASLEEP, MISTRESS.
I'M SO SORRY!
PLEASE. I...I'LL DO ANYTHING.
IT'S ALL MY FAULT, WHATEVER I'VE DONE.
DON'T...DON'T BE CROSS AT ME. I'LL TRY TO DO BETTER!
She's terrified.
Afraid I'll BEAT her half to death.
As I did her FATHER.
GET OUT.
DON'T SAY ANYTHING MORE.
YES. YES, OF COURSE, I AM A FOOLISH GIRL. A TERRIBLE GIRL!
GO!
Ironic, to be in fear of me, when I should be DEAD by now.
Soon enough.
SUCH A POWERFUL WORD.
GOOD CITIZENS OF THIS GENIAL TOWNSHIP!
I TRUST YOU ALL REMEMBER MY NAME FROM MY LAST VISIT!

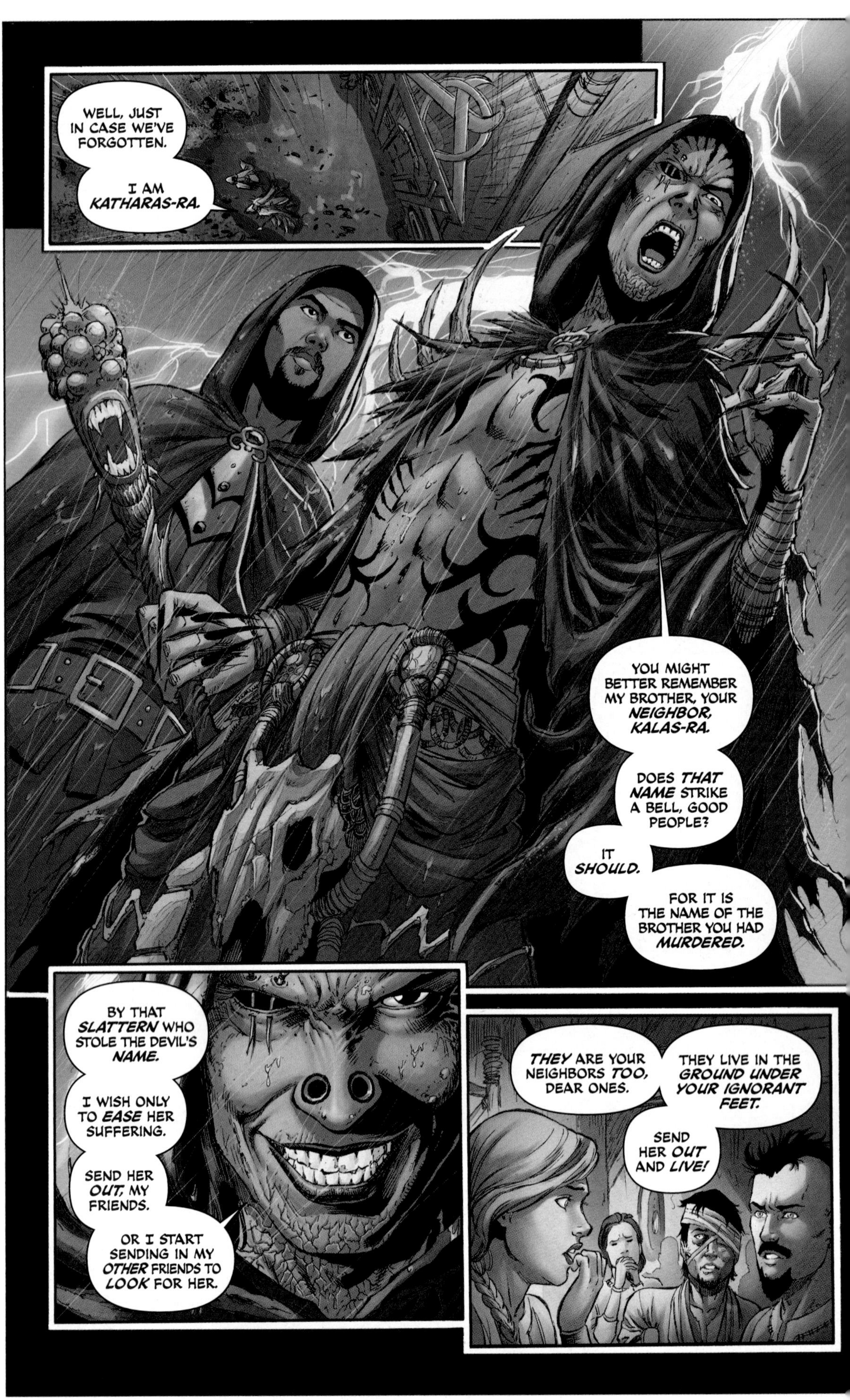
WELL, JUST IN CASE WE'VE FORGOTTEN.
I AM *KATHARAS-RA.*
YOU MIGHT BETTER REMEMBER MY BROTHER, YOUR *NEIGHBOR, KALAS-RA.*
DOES *THAT NAME* STRIKE A BELL, GOOD PEOPLE?
IT *SHOULD.*
FOR IT IS THE NAME OF THE BROTHER YOU HAD *MURDERED.*
BY THAT *SLATTERN* WHO STOLE THE DEVIL'S *NAME.*
I WISH ONLY TO *EASE* HER SUFFERING.
SEND HER *OUT,* MY FRIENDS.
OR I START SENDING IN MY *OTHER* FRIENDS TO *LOOK* FOR HER.
THEY ARE YOUR NEIGHBORS *TOO,* DEAR ONES.
THEY LIVE IN THE *GROUND UNDER YOUR IGNORANT FEET.*
SEND HER *OUT* AND *LIVE!*

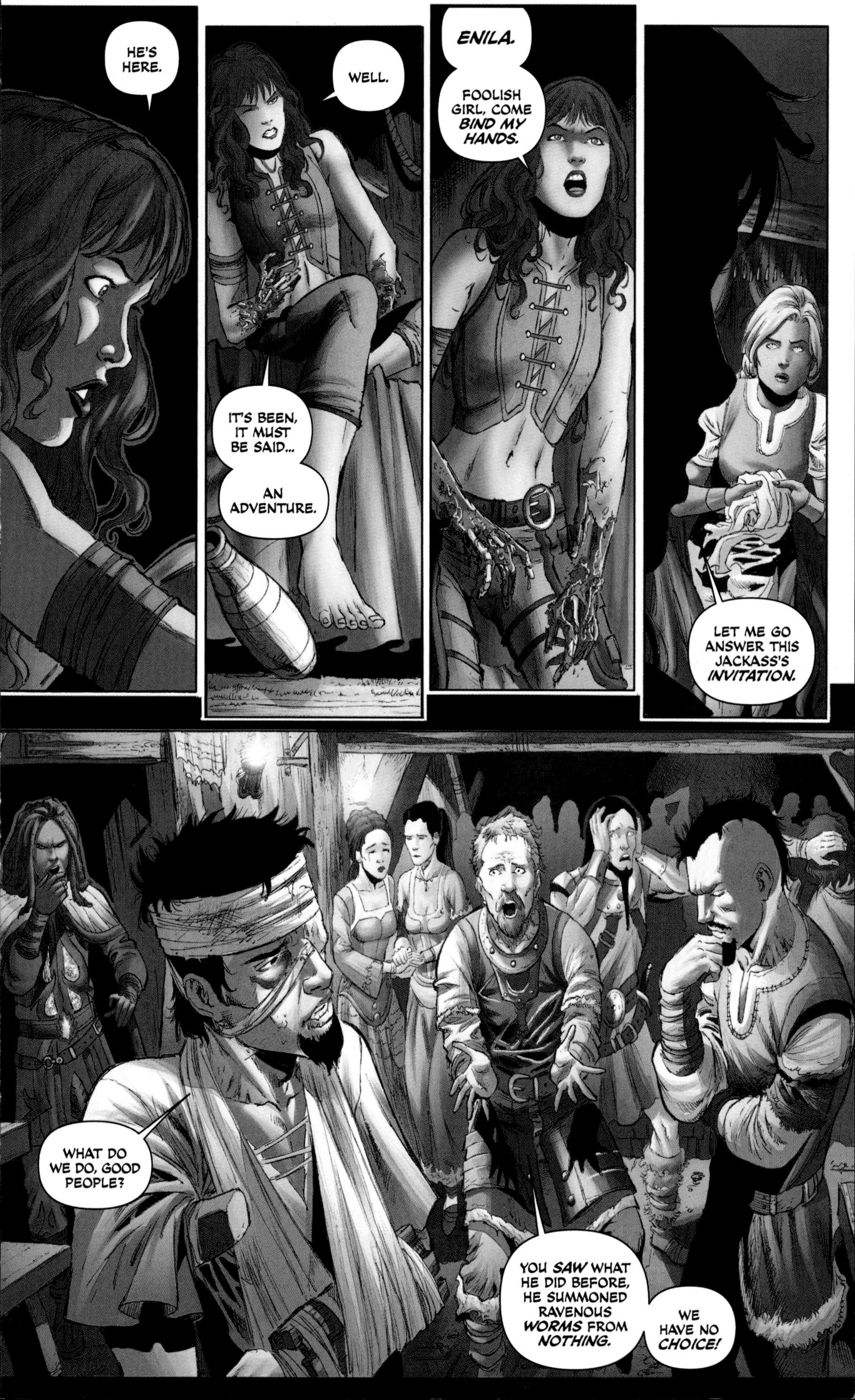
HE'S HERE.
WELL.
IT'S BEEN, IT MUST BE SAID...
AN ADVENTURE.
ENILA.
FOOLISH GIRL, COME BIND MY HANDS.
LET ME GO ANSWER THIS JACKASS'S INVITATION.
WHAT DO WE DO, GOOD PEOPLE?
YOU SAW WHAT HE DID BEFORE, HE SUMMONED RAVENOUS WORMS FROM NOTHING.
WE HAVE NO CHOICE!

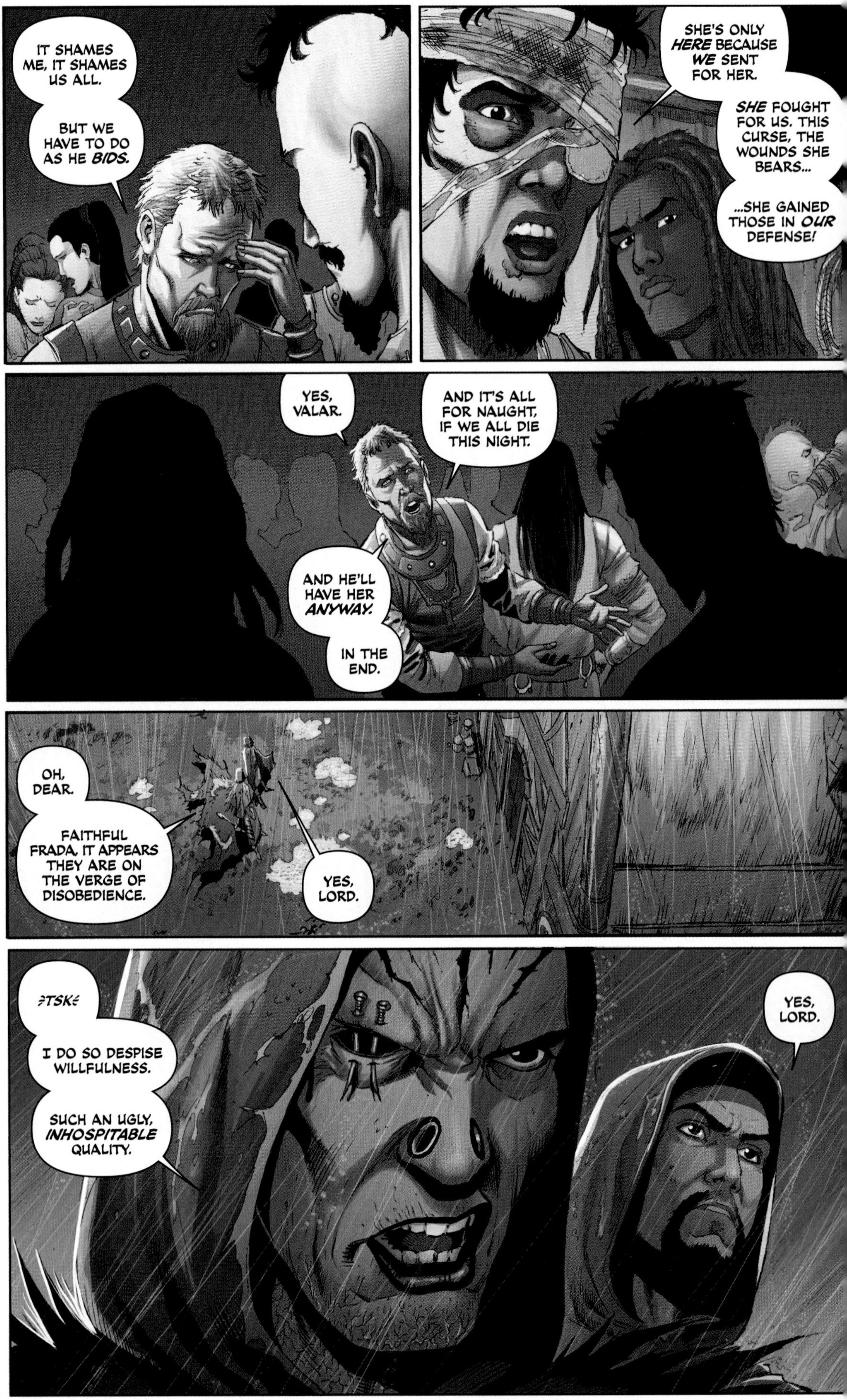
IT SHAMES ME, IT SHAMES US ALL.
BUT WE HAVE TO DO AS HE *BIDS.*
SHE'S ONLY *HERE* BECAUSE *WE* SENT FOR HER.
SHE FOUGHT FOR US. THIS CURSE, THE WOUNDS SHE BEARS...
...SHE GAINED THOSE IN *OUR* DEFENSE!
YES, VALAR.
AND IT'S ALL FOR NAUGHT, IF WE ALL DIE THIS NIGHT.
AND HE'LL HAVE HER *ANYWAY.*
IN THE END.
OH, DEAR.
FAITHFUL FRADA, IT APPEARS THEY ARE ON THE VERGE OF DISOBEDIENCE.
YES, LORD.
TSK
I DO SO DESPISE WILLFULNESS.
SUCH AN UGLY, *INHOSPITABLE* QUALITY.
YES, LORD.

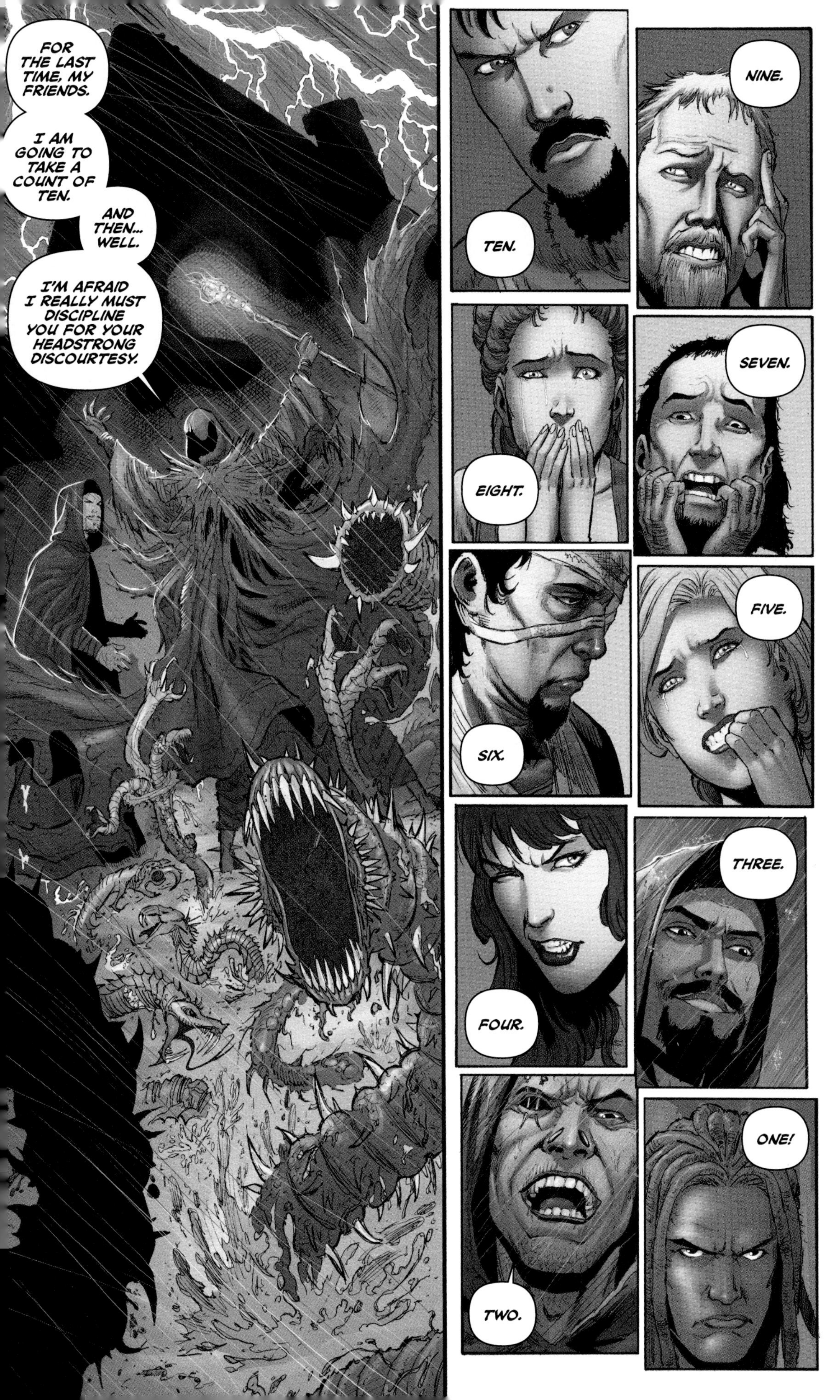

FOR THE LAST TIME, MY FRIENDS.
I AM GOING TO TAKE A COUNT OF TEN.
AND THEN... WELL.
I'M AFRAID I REALLY MUST DISCIPLINE YOU FOR YOUR HEADSTRONG DISCOURTESY.
TEN.
NINE.
EIGHT.
SEVEN.
SIX.
FIVE.
FOUR.
THREE.
TWO.
ONE!

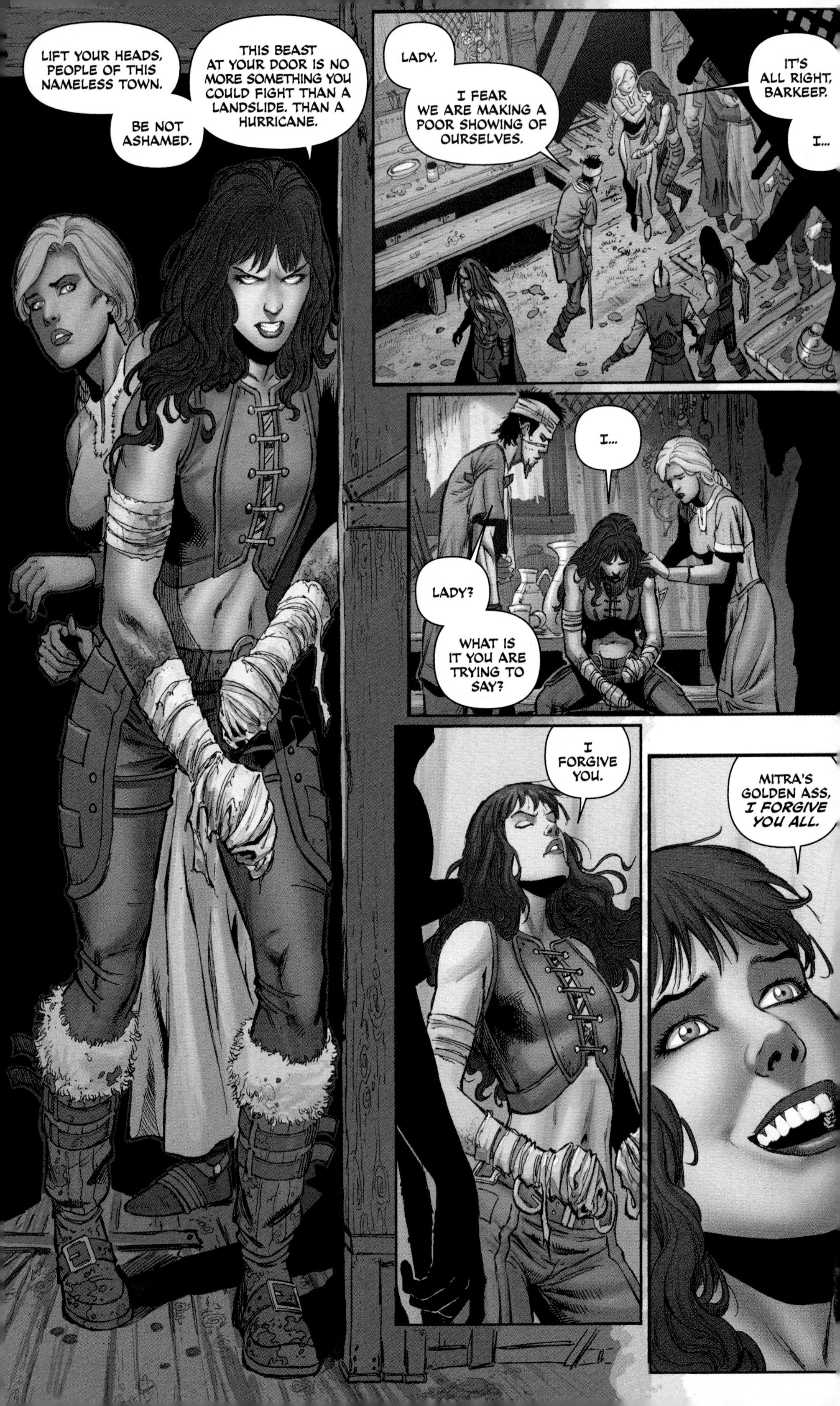
LIFT YOUR HEADS, PEOPLE OF THIS NAMELESS TOWN.
BE NOT ASHAMED.
THIS BEAST AT YOUR DOOR IS NO MORE SOMETHING YOU COULD FIGHT THAN A LANDSLIDE. THAN A HURRICANE.
LADY.
I FEAR WE ARE MAKING A POOR SHOWING OF OURSELVES.
IT'S ALL RIGHT, BARKEEP.
I...
I...
LADY?
WHAT IS IT YOU ARE TRYING TO SAY?
I FORGIVE YOU.
MITRA'S GOLDEN ASS, *I FORGIVE YOU ALL.*

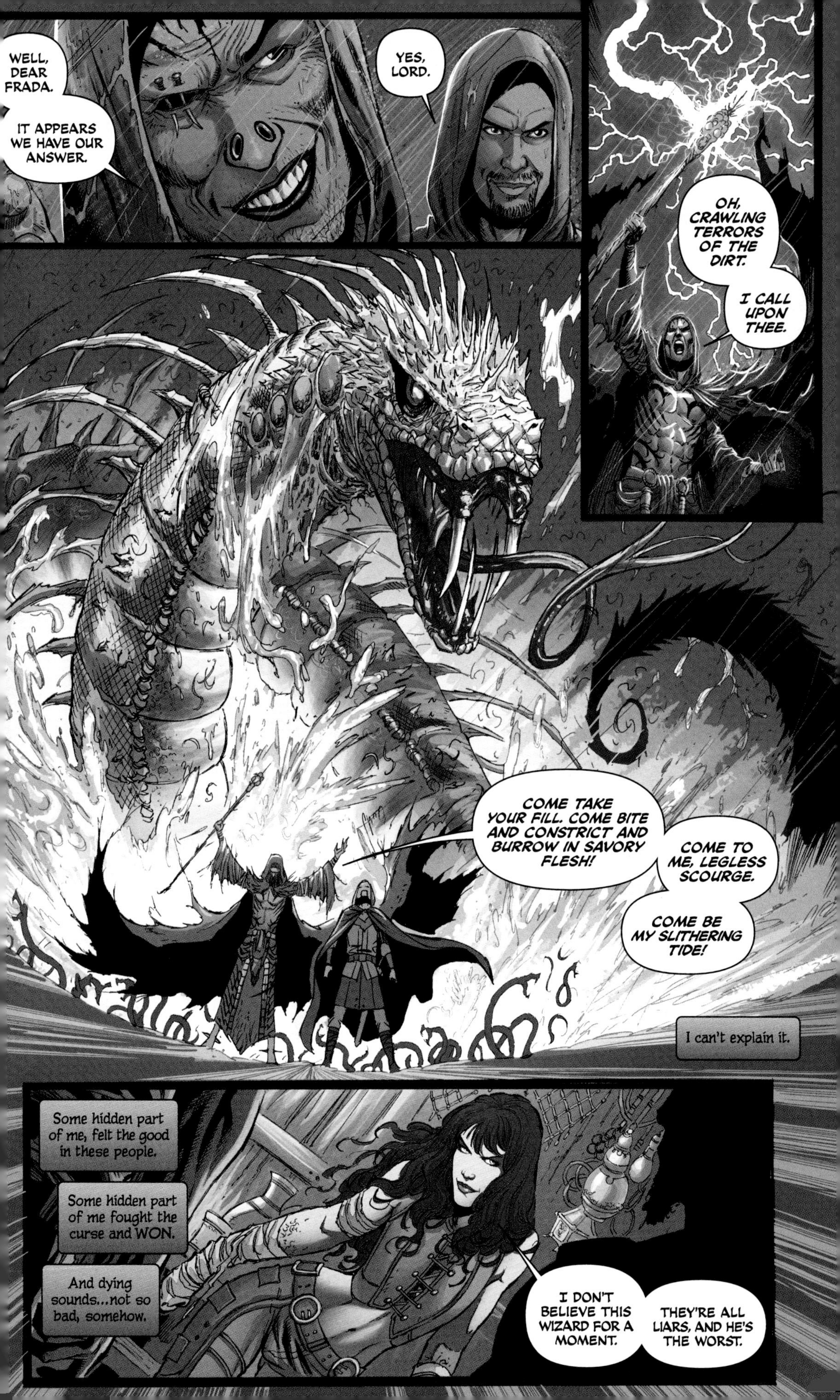
WELL, DEAR FRADA.
IT APPEARS WE HAVE OUR ANSWER.
YES, LORD.
OH, CRAWLING TERRORS OF THE DIRT.
I CALL UPON THEE.
COME TAKE YOUR FILL. COME BITE AND CONSTRICT AND BURROW IN SAVORY FLESH!
COME TO ME, LEGLESS SCOURGE.
COME BE MY SLITHERING TIDE!
I can't explain it.
Some hidden part of me, felt the good in these people.
Some hidden part of me fought the curse and WON.
And dying sounds...not so bad, somehow.
I DON'T BELIEVE THIS WIZARD FOR A MOMENT.
THEY'RE ALL LIARS, AND HE'S THE WORST.

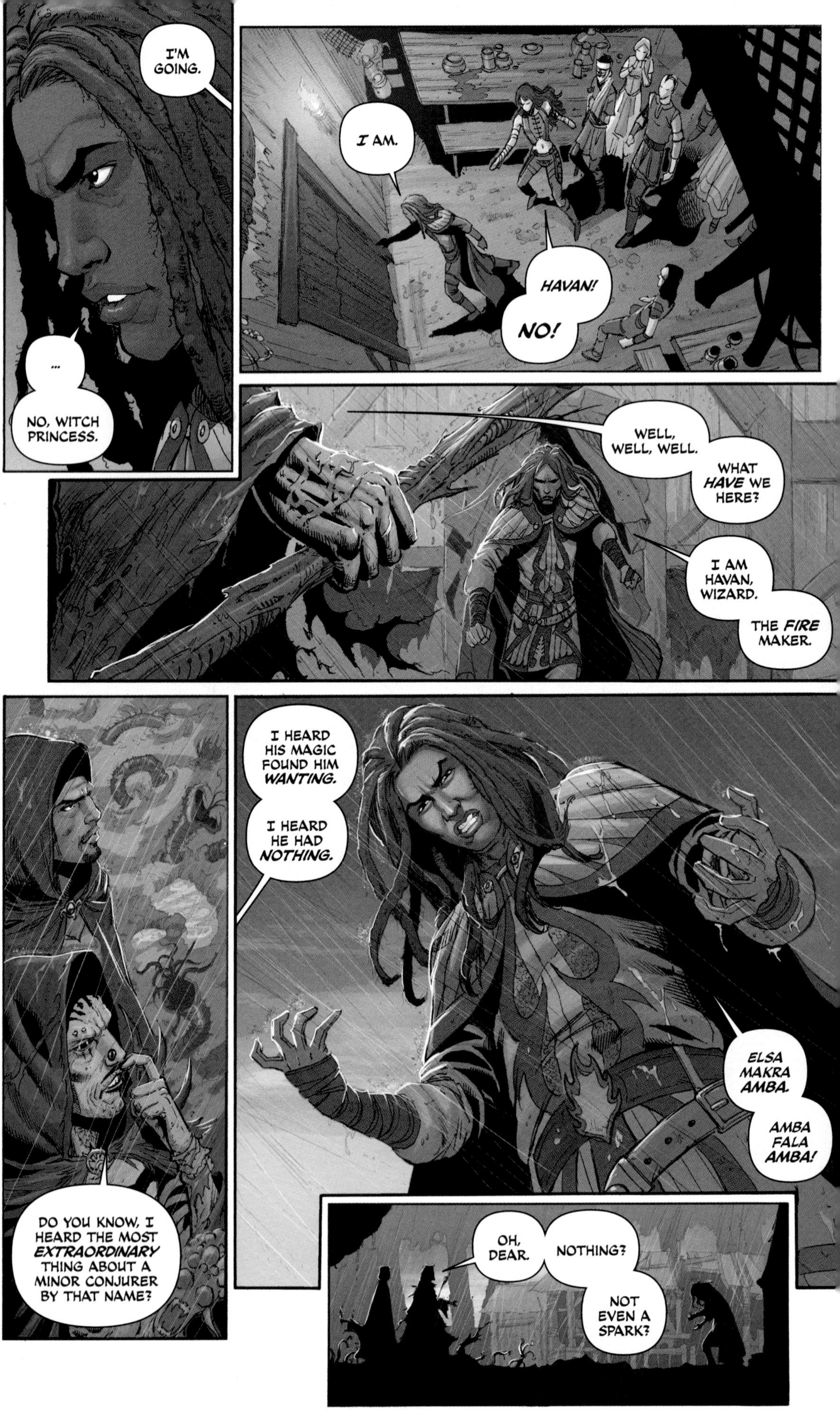
I'M GOING.
...
NO, WITCH PRINCESS.
I AM.
HAVAN!
NO!
WELL, WELL, WELL.
WHAT *HAVE* WE HERE?
I AM HAVAN, WIZARD.
THE *FIRE* MAKER.
DO YOU KNOW, I HEARD THE MOST *EXTRAORDINARY* THING ABOUT A MINOR CONJURER BY THAT NAME?
I HEARD HIS MAGIC FOUND HIM *WANTING.*
I HEARD HE HAD *NOTHING.*
ELSA MAKRA AMBA.
AMBA FALA AMBA!
OH, DEAR.
NOTHING?
NOT EVEN A SPARK?

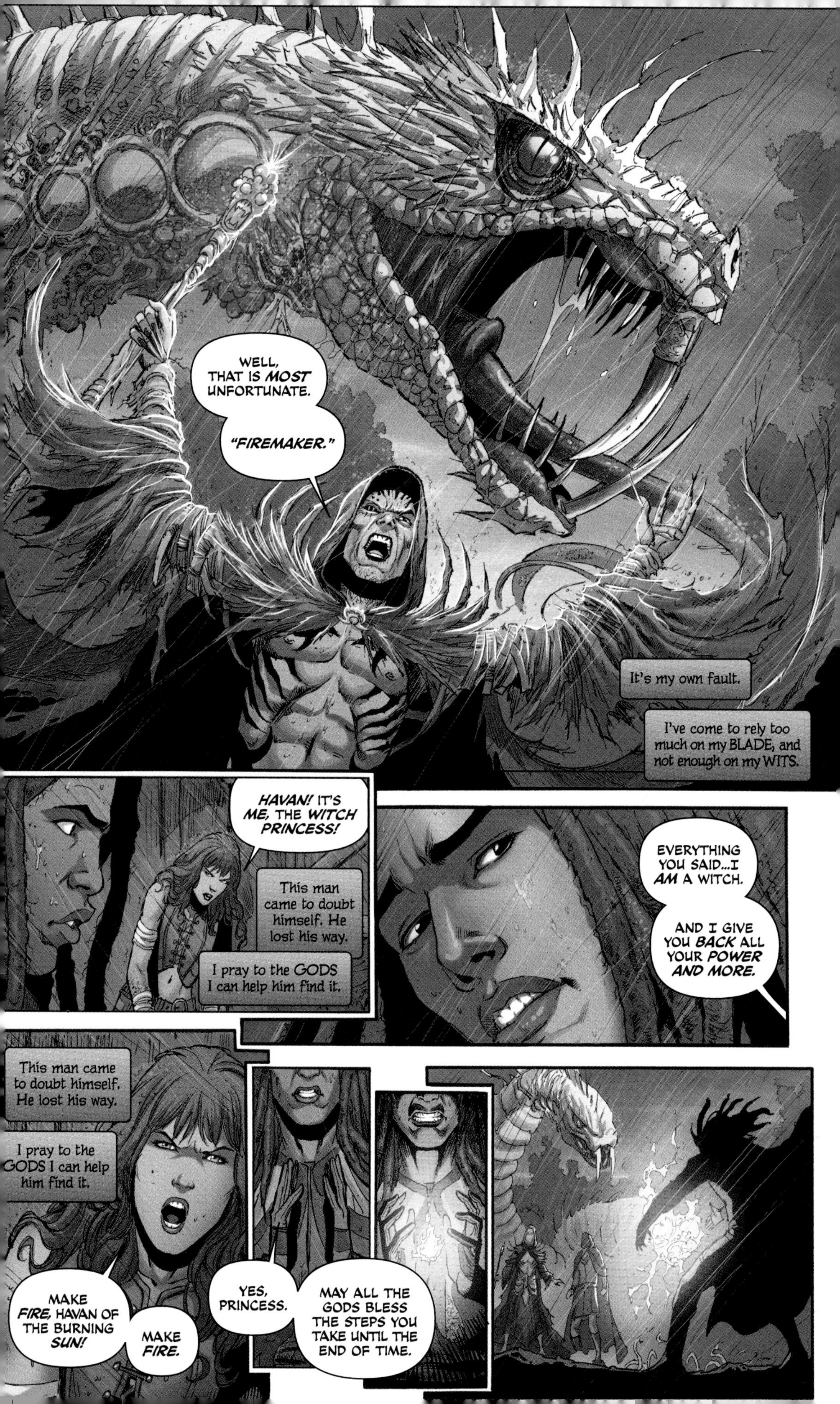
WELL, THAT IS *MOST* UNFORTUNATE.
"FIREMAKER."
It's my own fault.
I've come to rely too much on my BLADE, and not enough on my WITS.
HAVAN! IT'S *ME,* THE *WITCH PRINCESS!*
This man came to doubt himself. He lost his way.
I pray to the GODS I can help him find it.
EVERYTHING YOU SAID...I *AM* A WITCH.
AND I GIVE YOU *BACK* ALL YOUR *POWER AND MORE.*
This man came to doubt himself. He lost his way.
I pray to the GODS I can help him find it.
MAKE *FIRE,* HAVAN OF THE BURNING *SUN!*
MAKE *FIRE.*
YES, PRINCESS.
MAY ALL THE GODS BLESS THE STEPS YOU TAKE UNTIL THE END OF TIME.

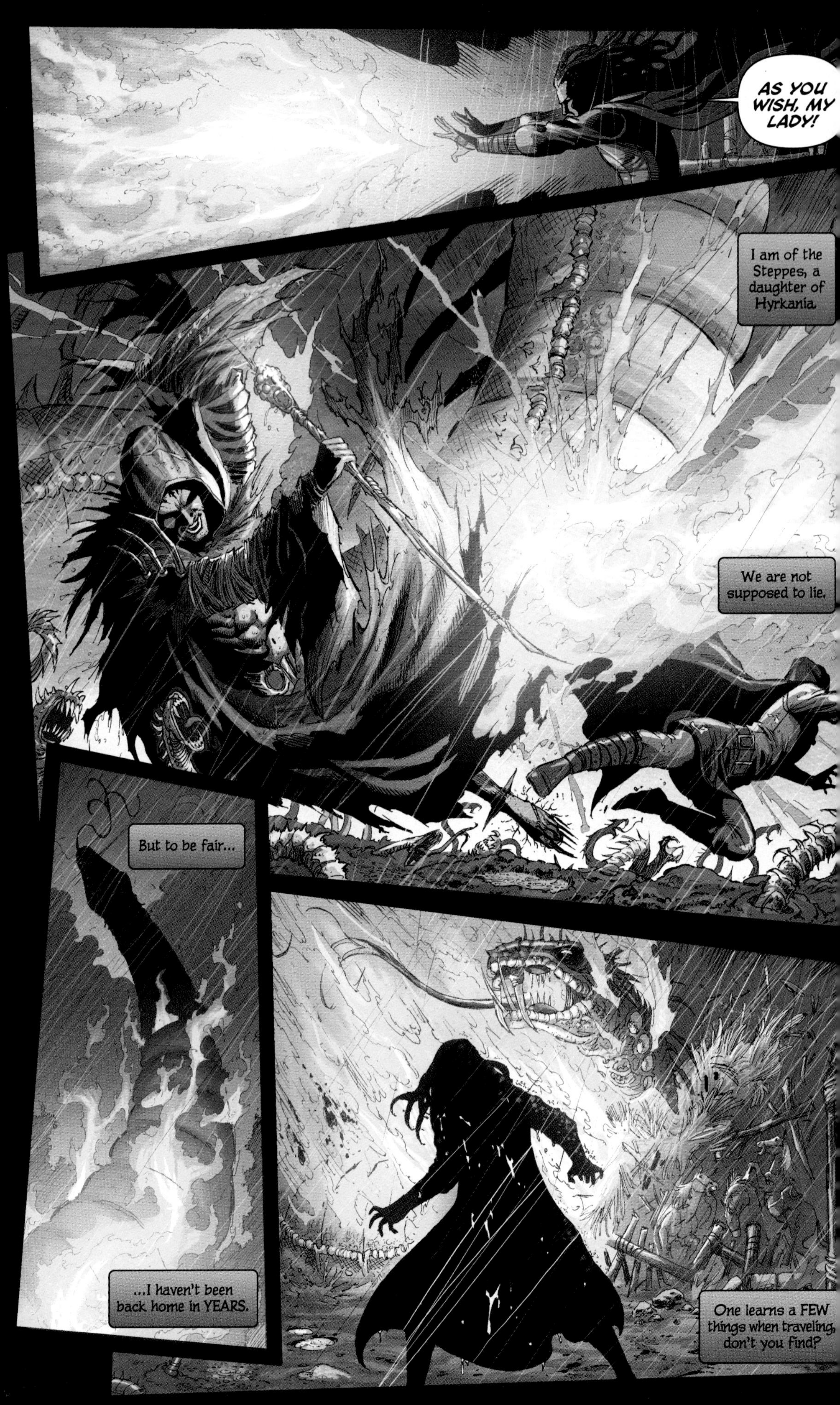
AS YOU WISH, MY LADY!
I am of the Steppes, a daughter of Hyrkania.
We are not supposed to lie.
But to be fair...
...I haven't been back home in YEARS.
One learns a FEW things when traveling, don't you find?

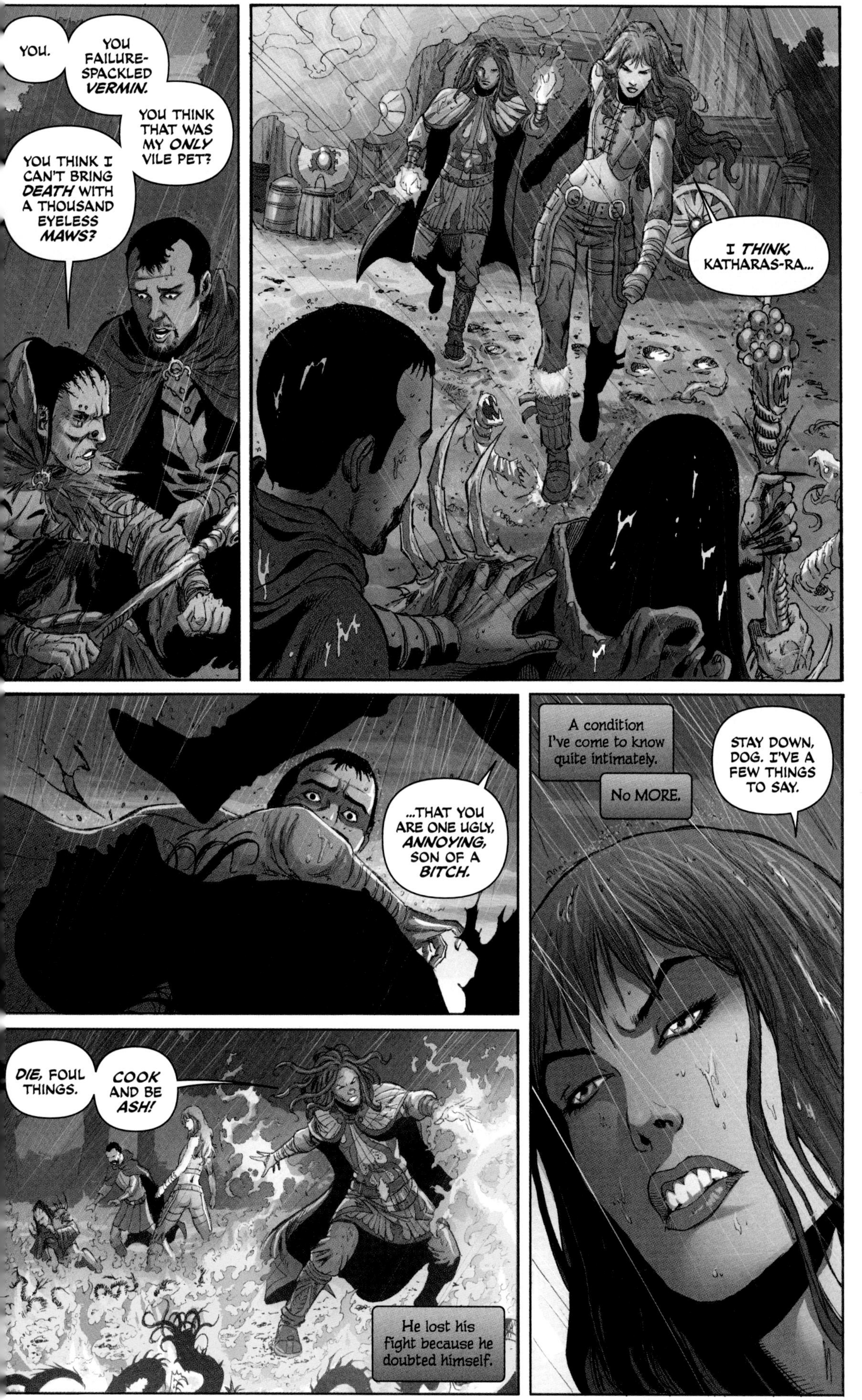

YOU.
YOU FAILURE-SPACKLED VERMIN.
YOU THINK THAT WAS MY ONLY VILE PET?
YOU THINK I CAN'T BRING DEATH WITH A THOUSAND EYELESS MAWS?
I THINK, KATHARAS-RA...
...THAT YOU ARE ONE UGLY, ANNOYING, SON OF A BITCH.
A condition I've come to know quite intimately.
No MORE.
STAY DOWN, DOG. I'VE A FEW THINGS TO SAY.
DIE, FOUL THINGS.
COOK AND BE ASH!
He lost his fight because he doubted himself.

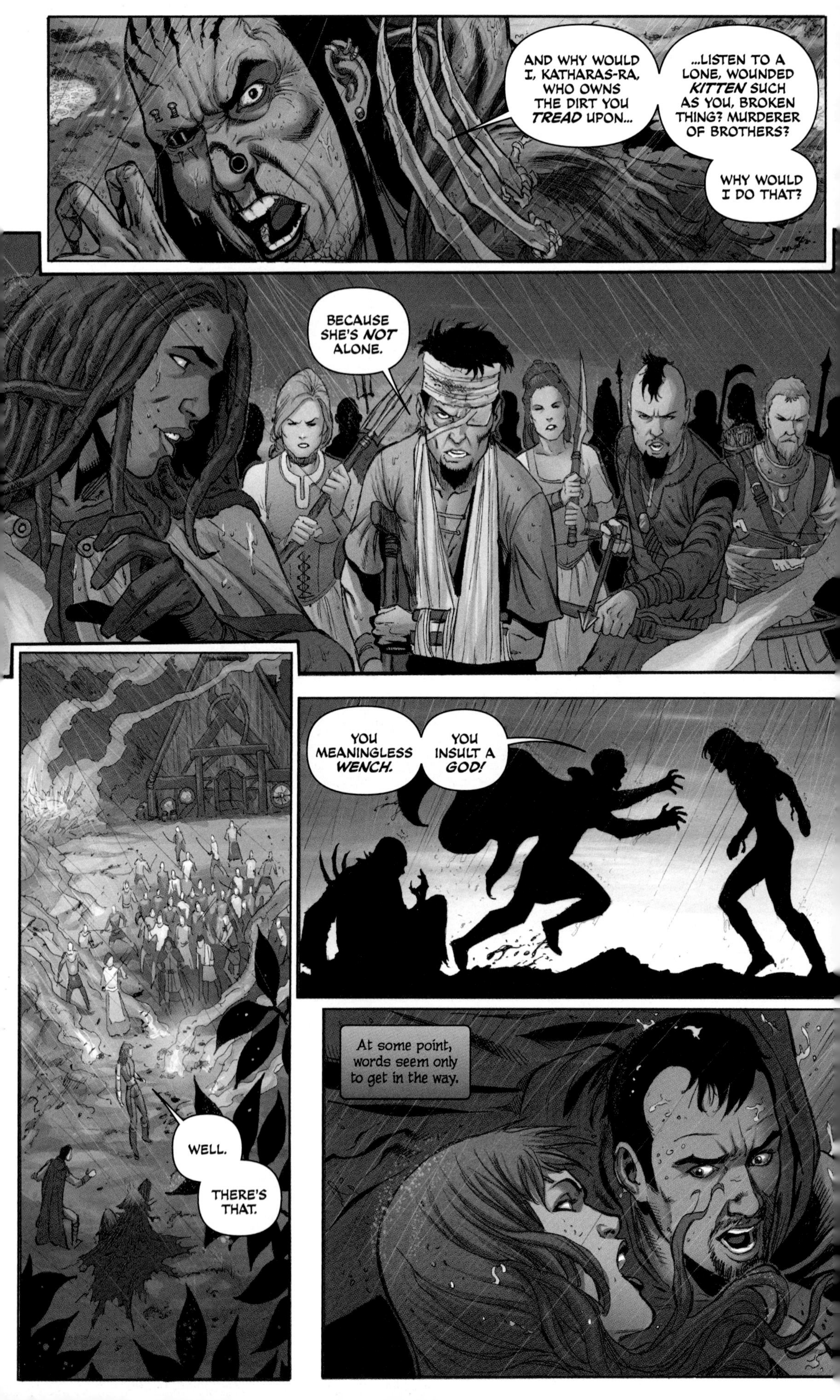
AND WHY WOULD I, KATHARAS-RA, WHO OWNS THE DIRT YOU *TREAD* UPON...
...LISTEN TO A LONE, WOUNDED *KITTEN* SUCH AS YOU, BROKEN THING? MURDERER OF BROTHERS?
WHY WOULD I DO THAT?
BECAUSE SHE'S *NOT* ALONE.
WELL.
THERE'S THAT.
YOU MEANINGLESS *WENCH.*
YOU INSULT A *GOD!*
At some point, words seem only to get in the way.

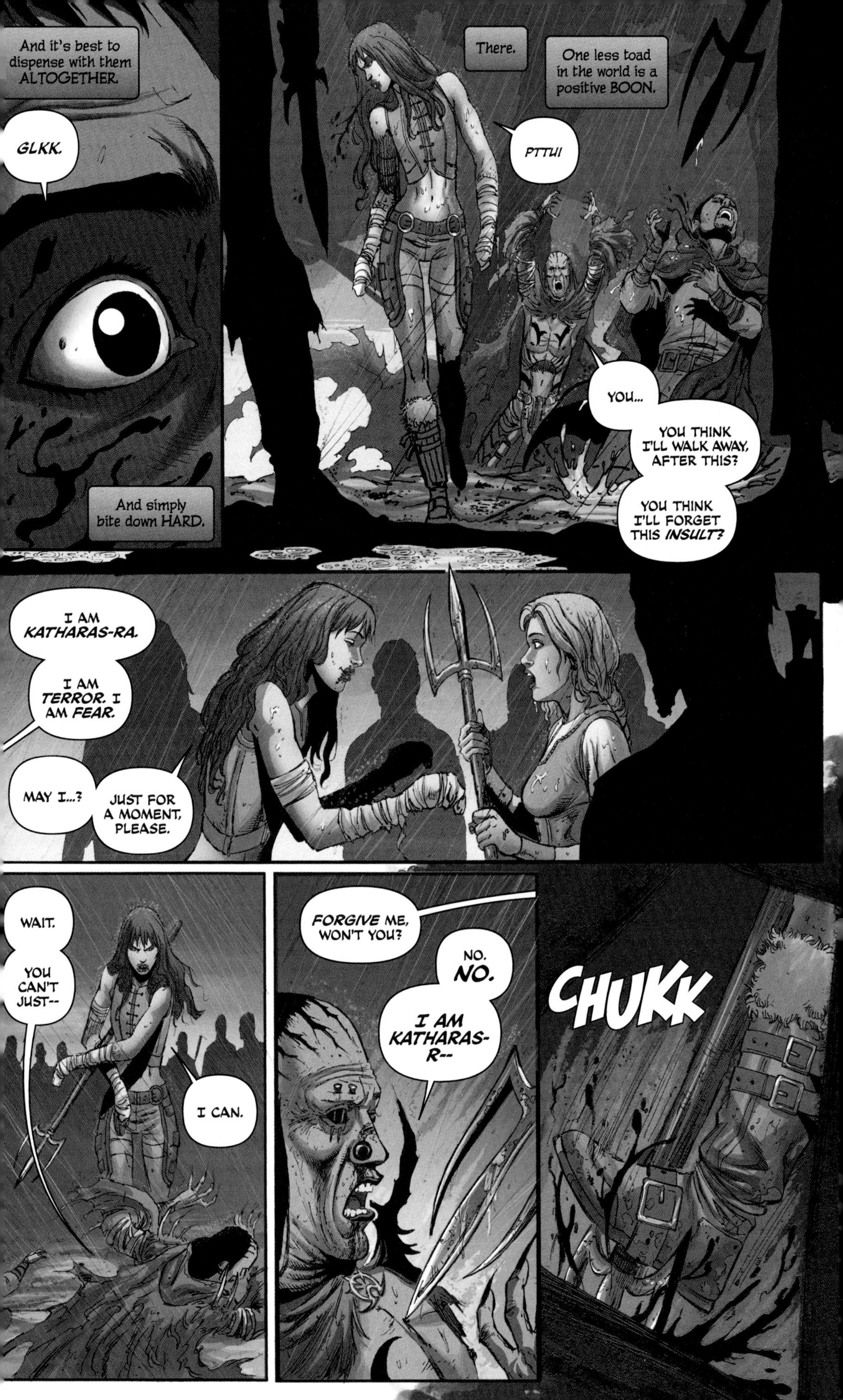
And it's best to dispense with them ALTOGETHER.
GLKK.
And simply bite down HARD.
There.
One less toad in the world is a positive BOON.
PTTUI
YOU...
YOU THINK I'LL WALK AWAY, AFTER THIS?
YOU THINK I'LL FORGET THIS INSULT?
I AM KATHARAS-RA.
I AM TERROR. I AM FEAR.
MAY I...?
JUST FOR A MOMENT, PLEASE.
WAIT.
YOU CAN'T JUST--
I CAN.
FORGIVE ME, WON'T YOU?
NO. NO.
I AM KATHARAS-R--
CHUKK

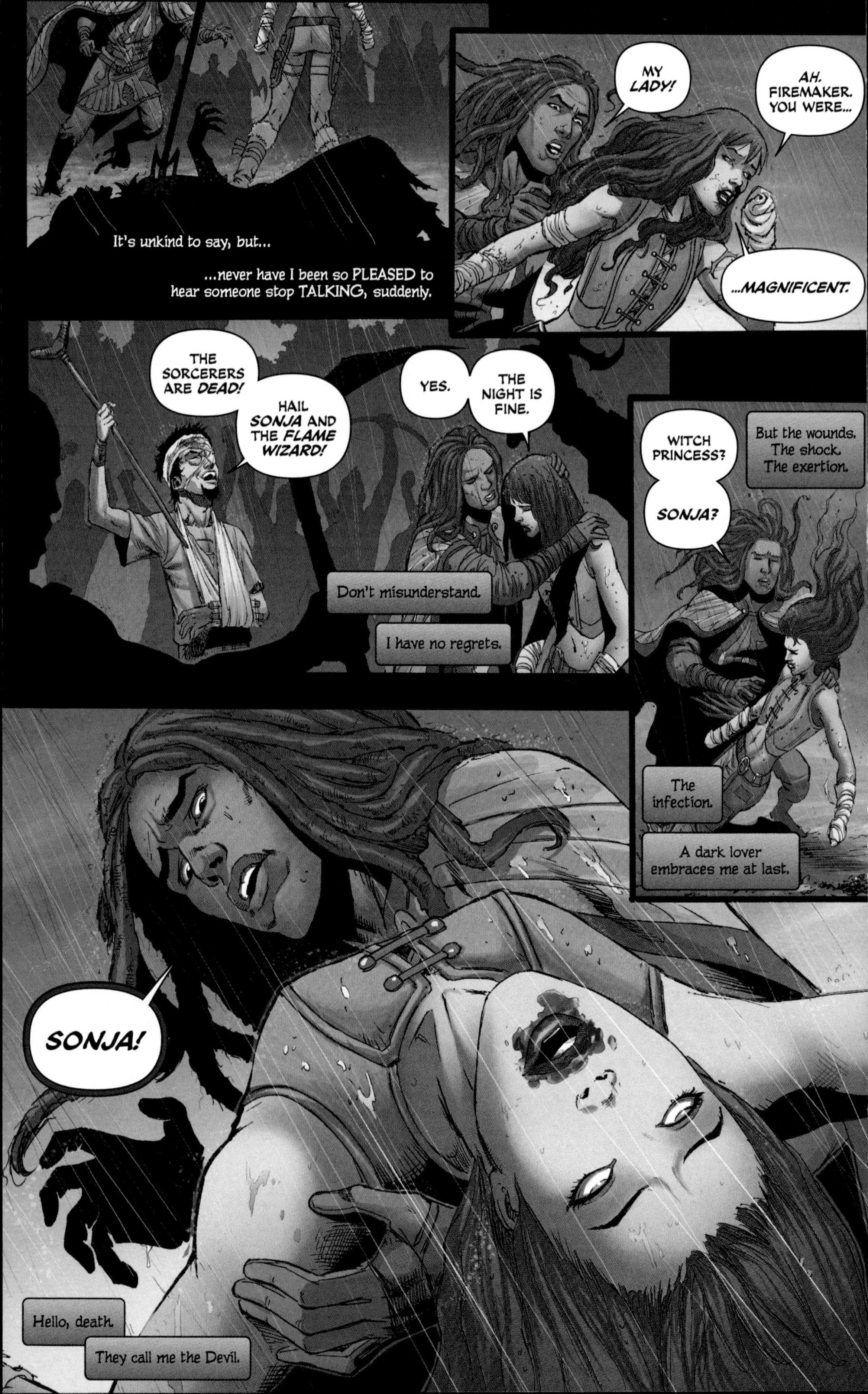

It's unkind to say, but...
...never have I been so PLEASED to hear someone stop TALKING, suddenly.
MY LADY!
AH. FIREMAKER. YOU WERE...
...MAGNIFICENT.
THE SORCERERS ARE DEAD!
HAIL SONJA AND THE FLAME WIZARD!
YES.
THE NIGHT IS FINE.
Don't misunderstand.
I have no regrets.
WITCH PRINCESS?
SONJA?
But the wounds. The shock. The exertion.
The infection.
A dark lover embraces me at last.
SONJA!
Hello, death.
They call me the Devil.

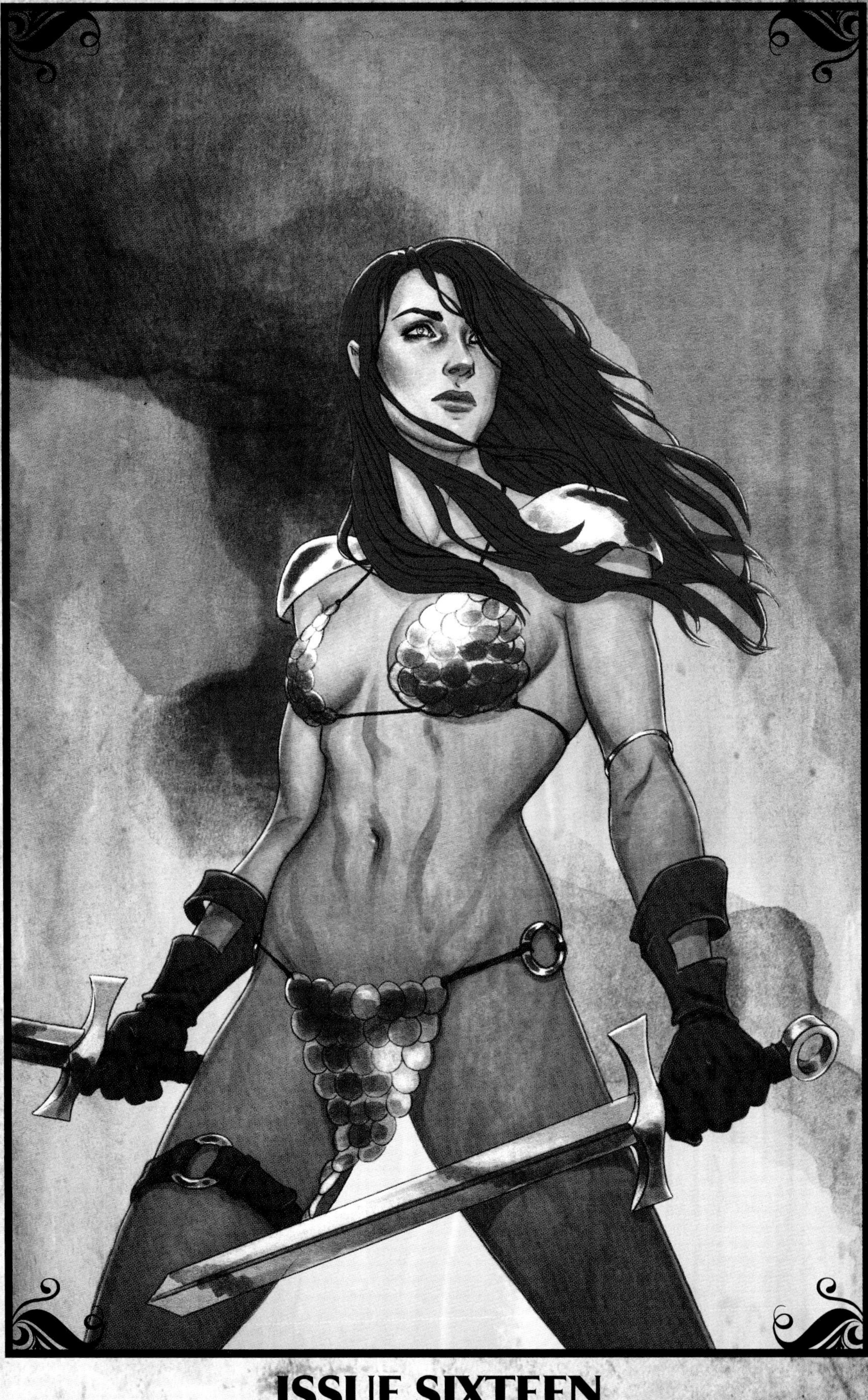

ISSUE SIXTEEN
cover by JENNY FRISON

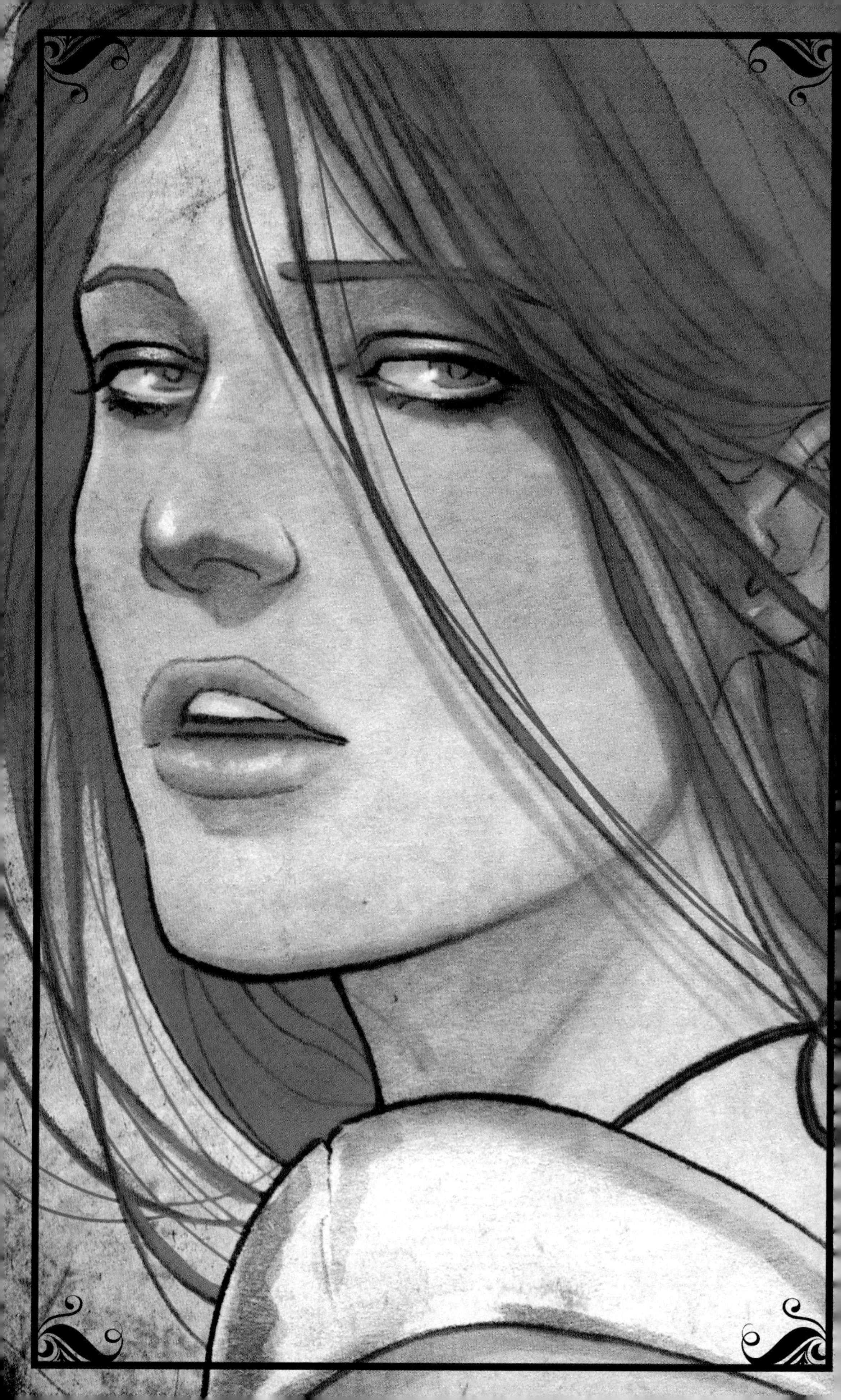

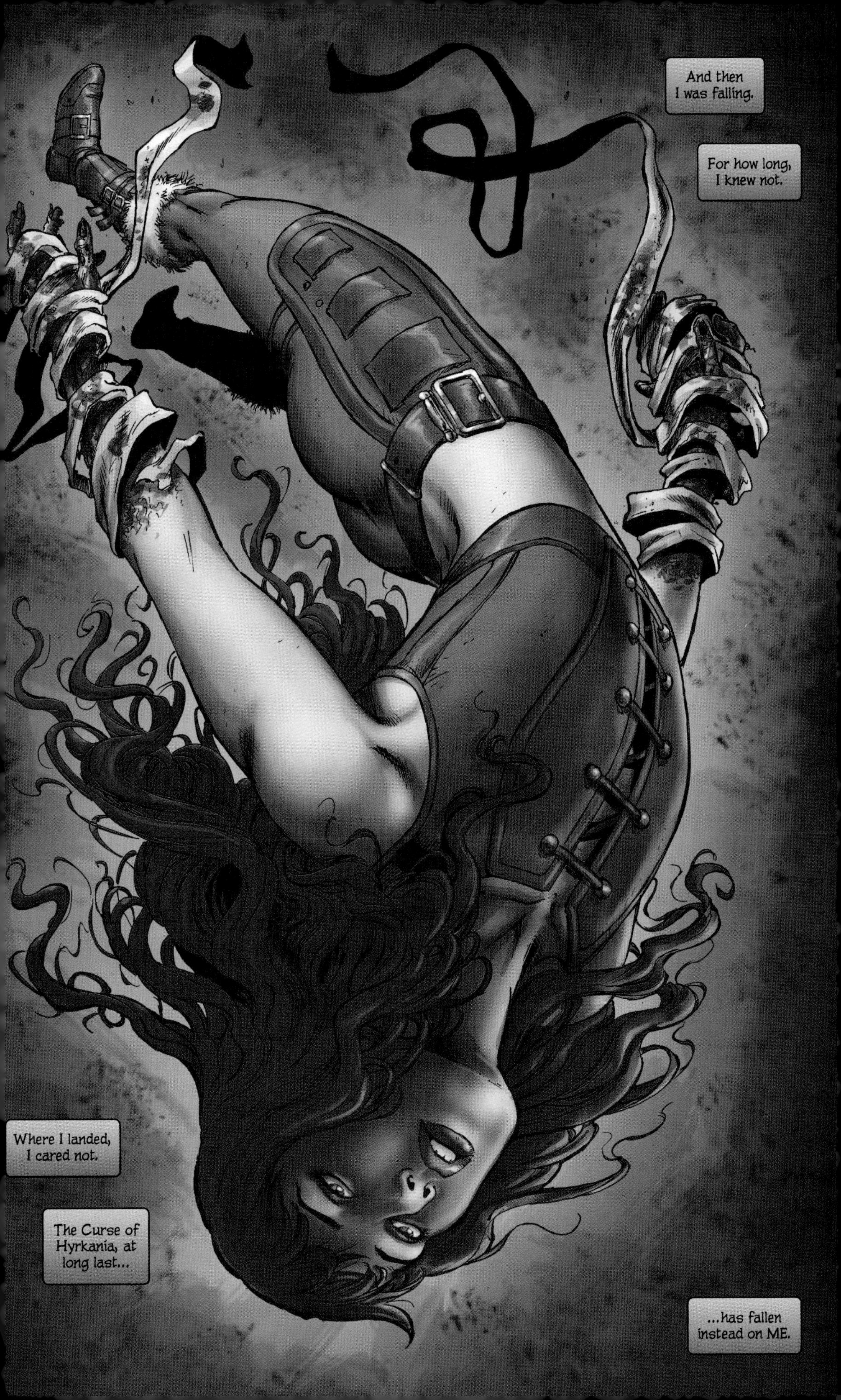

And then I was falling.
For how long, I knew not.
Where I landed, I cared not.
The Curse of Hyrkania, at long last...
...has fallen instead on ME.

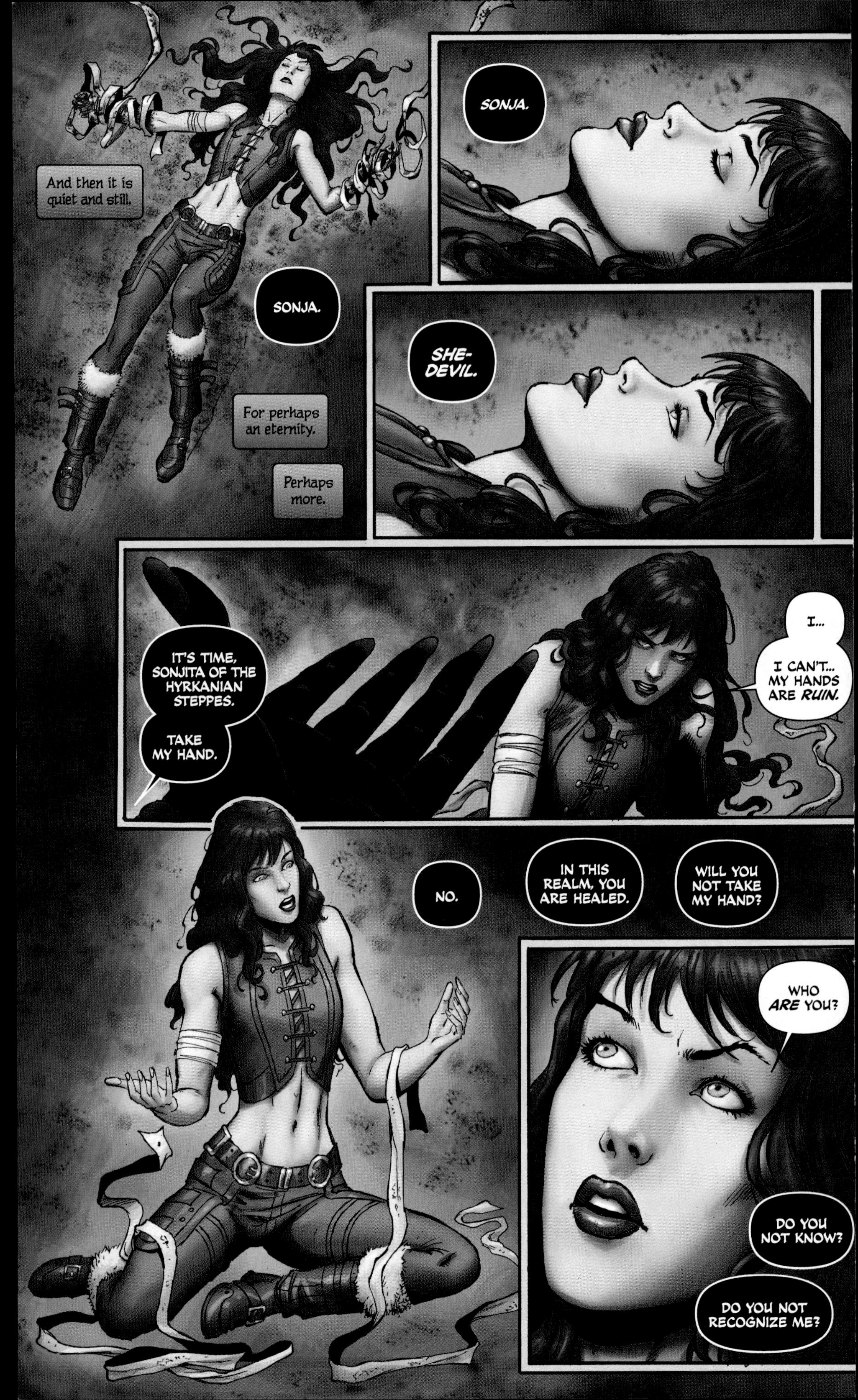

And then it is quiet and still.
SONJA.
SONJA.
SHE-DEVIL.
For perhaps an eternity.
Perhaps more.
IT'S TIME, SONJITA OF THE HYRKANIAN STEPPES.
TAKE MY HAND.
I...
I CAN'T... MY HANDS ARE *RUIN*.
NO.
IN THIS REALM, YOU ARE HEALED.
WILL YOU NOT TAKE MY HAND?
WHO *ARE* YOU?
DO YOU NOT KNOW?
DO YOU NOT RECOGNIZE ME?

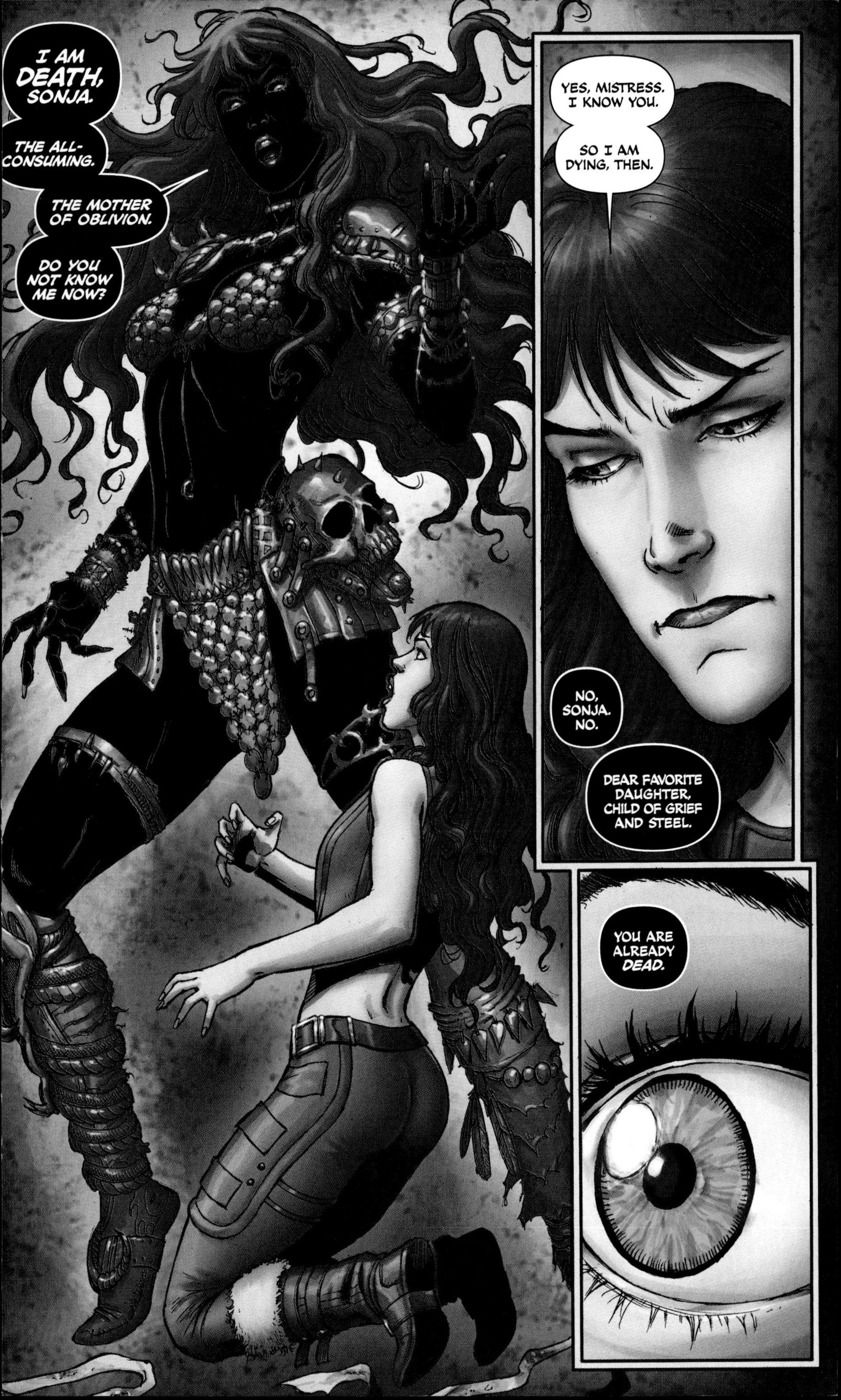
I AM DEATH, SONJA.
THE ALL-CONSUMING.
THE MOTHER OF OBLIVION.
DO YOU NOT KNOW ME NOW?
YES, MISTRESS. I KNOW YOU.
SO I AM DYING, THEN.
NO, SONJA. NO.
DEAR FAVORITE DAUGHTER, CHILD OF GRIEF AND STEEL.
YOU ARE ALREADY DEAD.

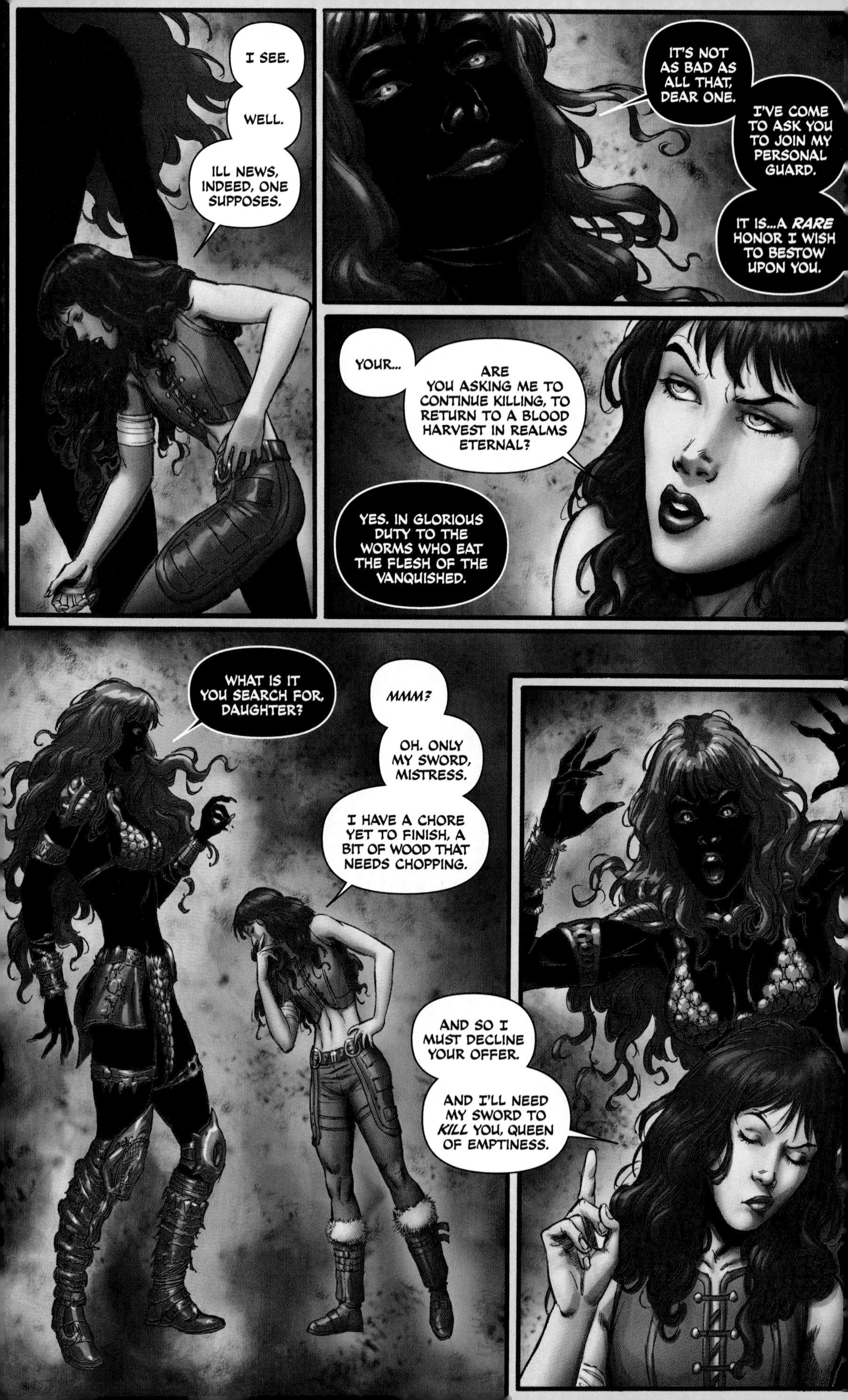
I SEE.
WELL.
ILL NEWS, INDEED, ONE SUPPOSES.
IT'S NOT AS BAD AS ALL THAT, DEAR ONE.
I'VE COME TO ASK YOU TO JOIN MY PERSONAL GUARD.
IT IS...A *RARE* HONOR I WISH TO BESTOW UPON YOU.
YOUR...
ARE YOU ASKING ME TO CONTINUE KILLING, TO RETURN TO A BLOOD HARVEST IN REALMS ETERNAL?
YES. IN GLORIOUS DUTY TO THE WORMS WHO EAT THE FLESH OF THE VANQUISHED.
WHAT IS IT YOU SEARCH FOR, DAUGHTER?
MMM?
OH. ONLY MY SWORD, MISTRESS.
I HAVE A CHORE YET TO FINISH, A BIT OF WOOD THAT NEEDS CHOPPING.
AND SO I MUST DECLINE YOUR OFFER.
AND I'LL NEED MY SWORD TO *KILL* YOU, QUEEN OF EMPTINESS.

SHE'S FIGHTING.

SHE SHOULD BE LONG DEAD. HER WOUNDS ARE *BEYOND* MY HEALING ARTS.

BUT SHE'S *FIGHTING.* TO THE *END.*

FATHER*!*

THERE'S A FIERCE COMPANY AT THE DOOR OF THE BAR.

THEY...THEY SAY THEY'RE HERE FOR THE DEVIL. FOR *SONJA!*

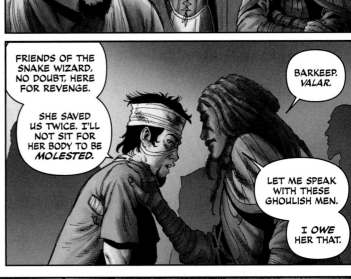

FRIENDS OF THE SNAKE WIZARD, NO DOUBT, HERE FOR REVENGE.

SHE SAVED US TWICE. I'LL NOT SIT FOR HER BODY TO BE *MOLESTED.*

BARKEEP. *VALAR.*

LET ME SPEAK WITH THESE GHOULISH MEN.

I *OWE* HER THAT.

MY NAME IS *HAVAN,* TRESPASSERS. THE *FIRE MAKER.*

AND YOU'LL NOT *HAVE* OUR LADY.

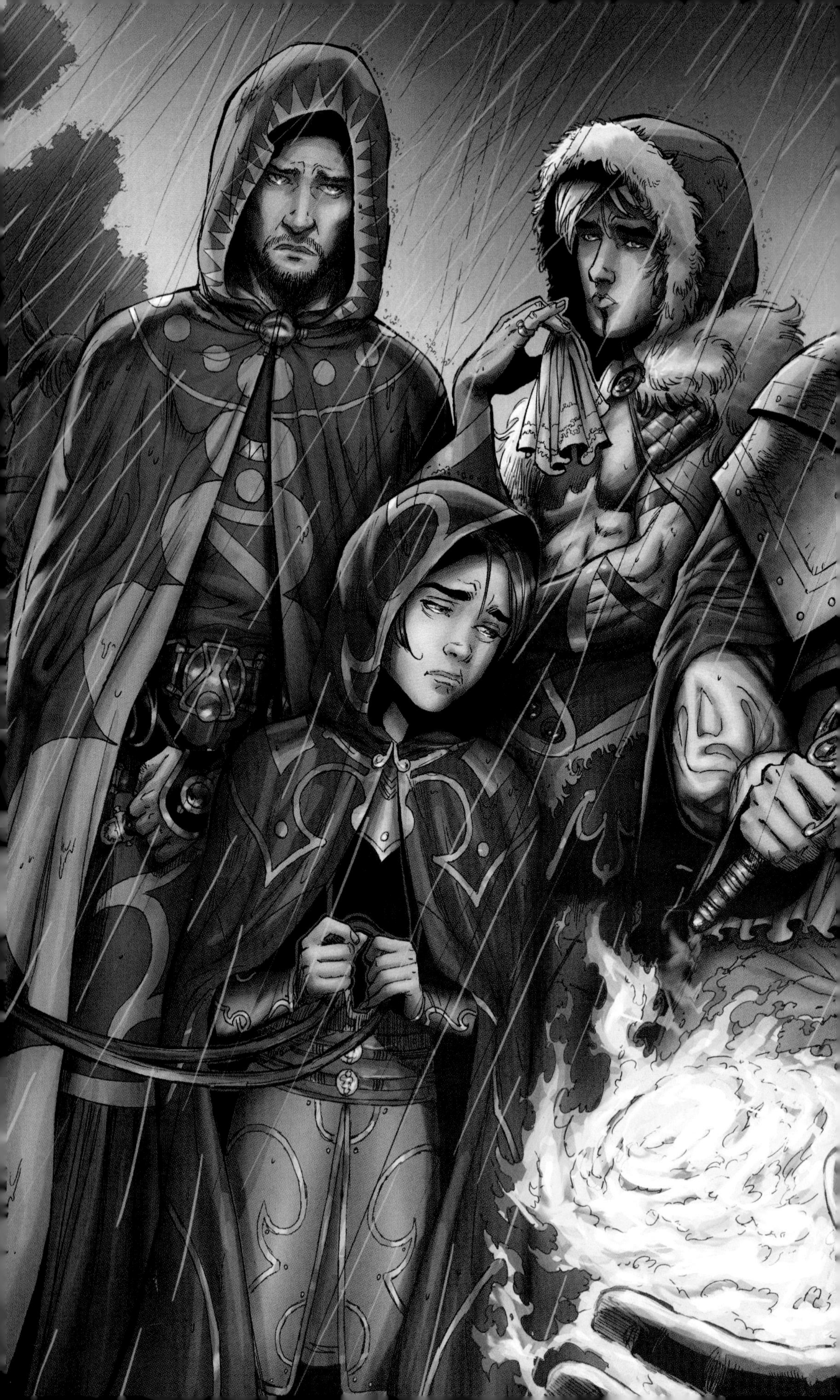

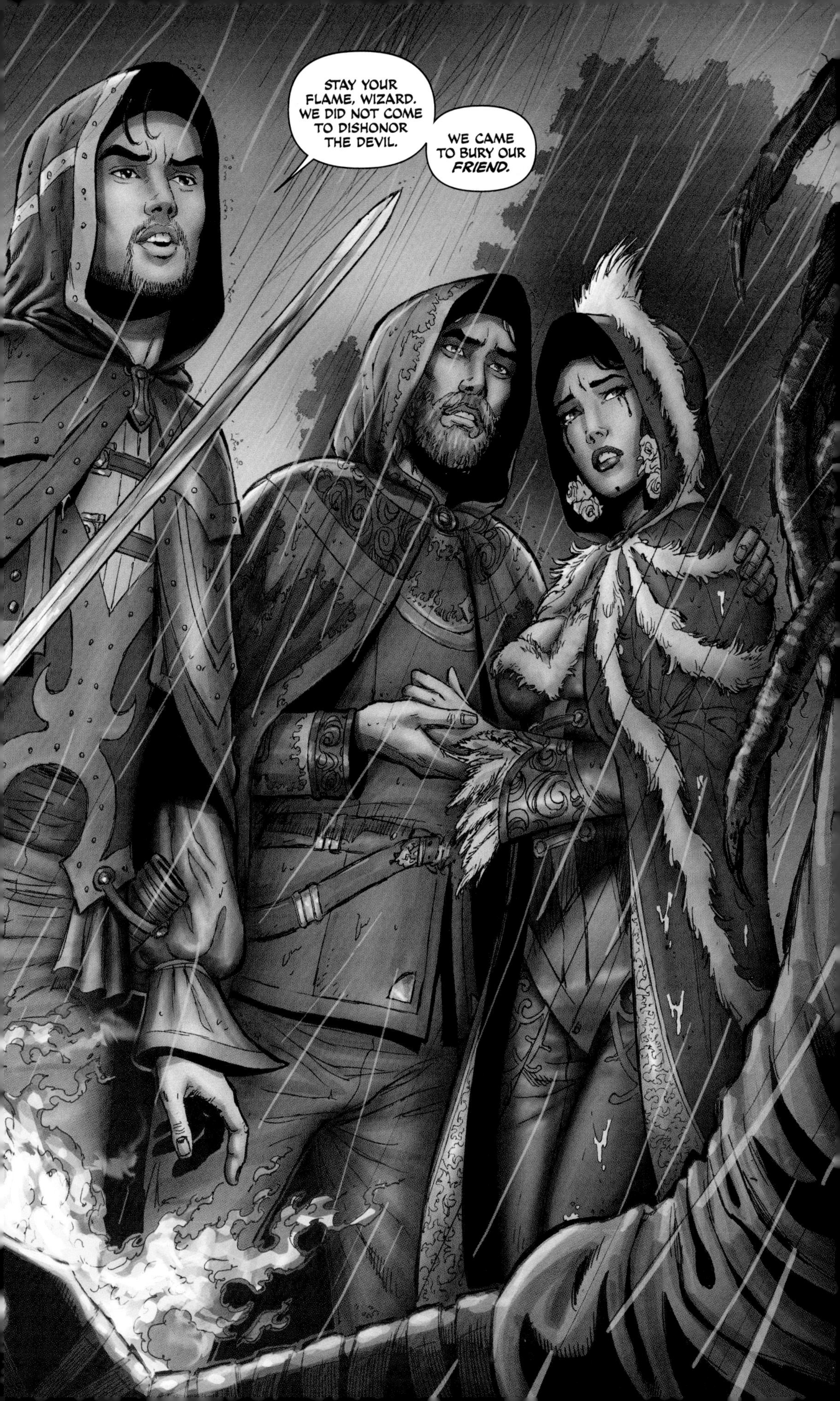
STAY YOUR FLAME, WIZARD. WE DID NOT COME TO DISHONOR THE DEVIL.
WE CAME TO BURY OUR *FRIEND.*

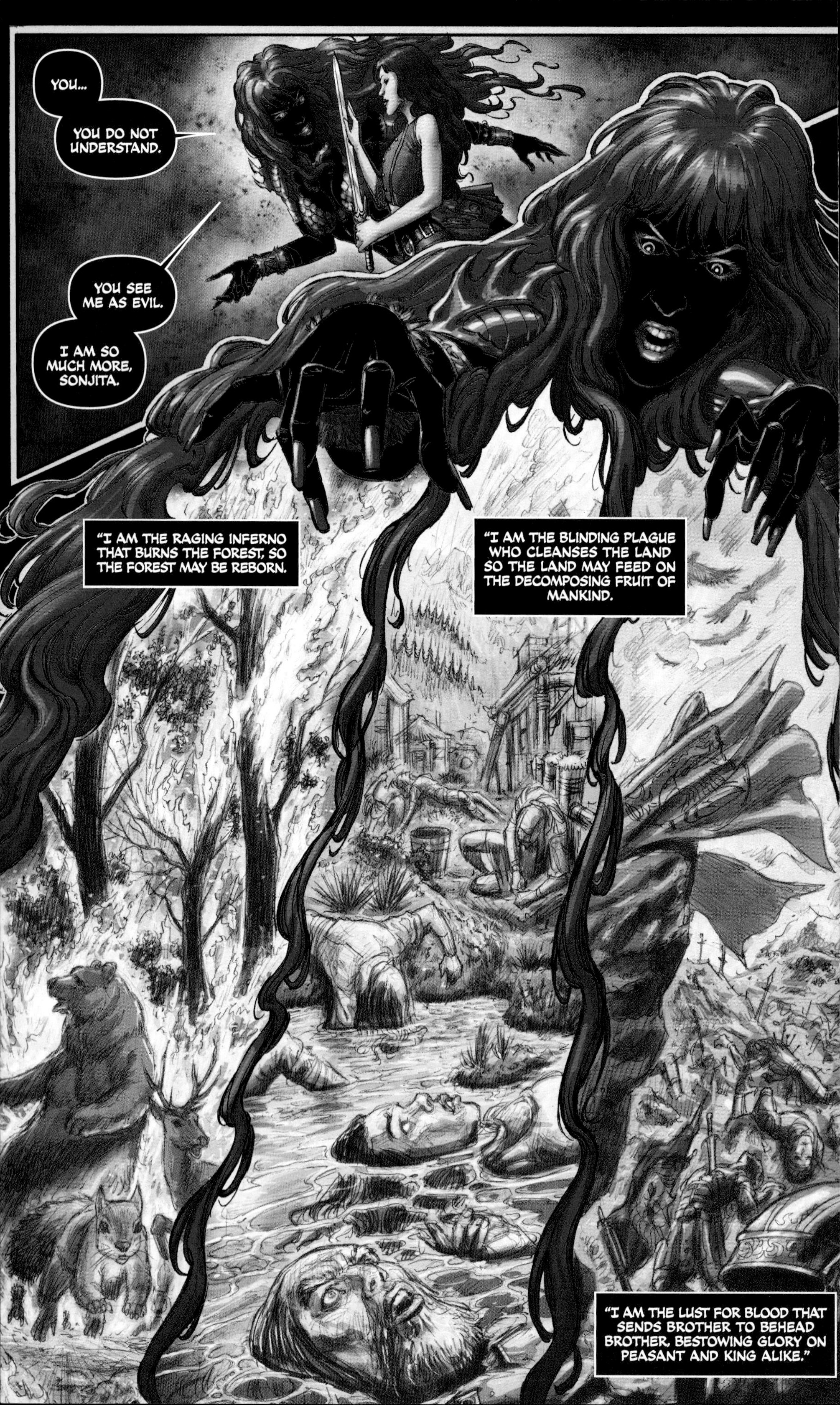
YOU...
YOU DO NOT UNDERSTAND.
YOU SEE ME AS EVIL.
I AM SO MUCH MORE, SONJITA.
"I AM THE RAGING INFERNO THAT BURNS THE FOREST, SO THE FOREST MAY BE REBORN.
"I AM THE BLINDING PLAGUE WHO CLEANSES THE LAND SO THE LAND MAY FEED ON THE DECOMPOSING FRUIT OF MANKIND.
"I AM THE LUST FOR BLOOD THAT SENDS BROTHER TO BEHEAD BROTHER, BESTOWING GLORY ON PEASANT AND KING ALIKE."

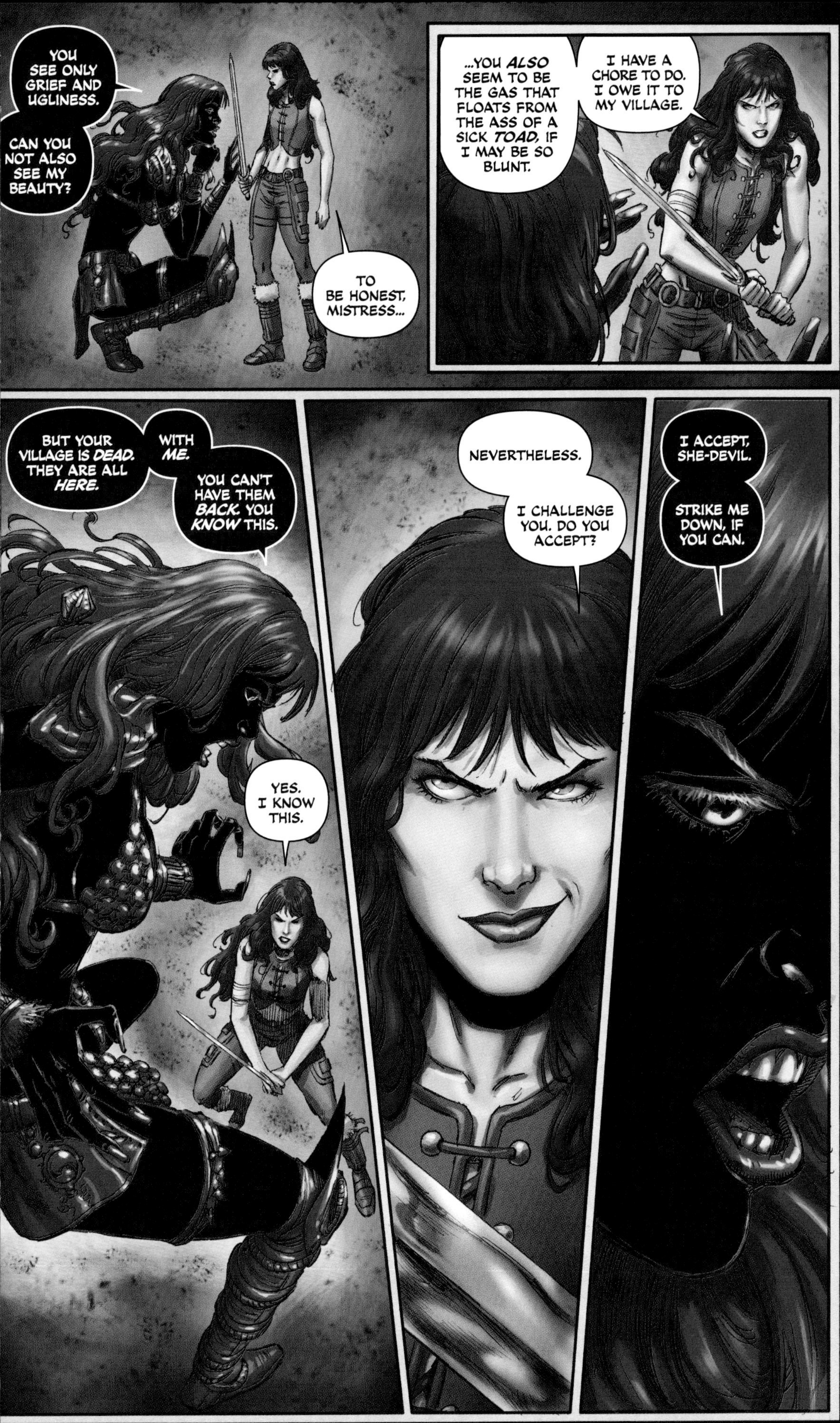
YOU SEE ONLY GRIEF AND UGLINESS.
CAN YOU NOT ALSO SEE MY BEAUTY?
TO BE HONEST, MISTRESS...
...YOU ALSO SEEM TO BE THE GAS THAT FLOATS FROM THE ASS OF A SICK TOAD, IF I MAY BE SO BLUNT.
I HAVE A CHORE TO DO. I OWE IT TO MY VILLAGE.
BUT YOUR VILLAGE IS DEAD. THEY ARE ALL HERE.
WITH ME.
YOU CAN'T HAVE THEM BACK. YOU KNOW THIS.
YES. I KNOW THIS.
NEVERTHELESS.
I CHALLENGE YOU. DO YOU ACCEPT?
I ACCEPT, SHE-DEVIL.
STRIKE ME DOWN, IF YOU CAN.

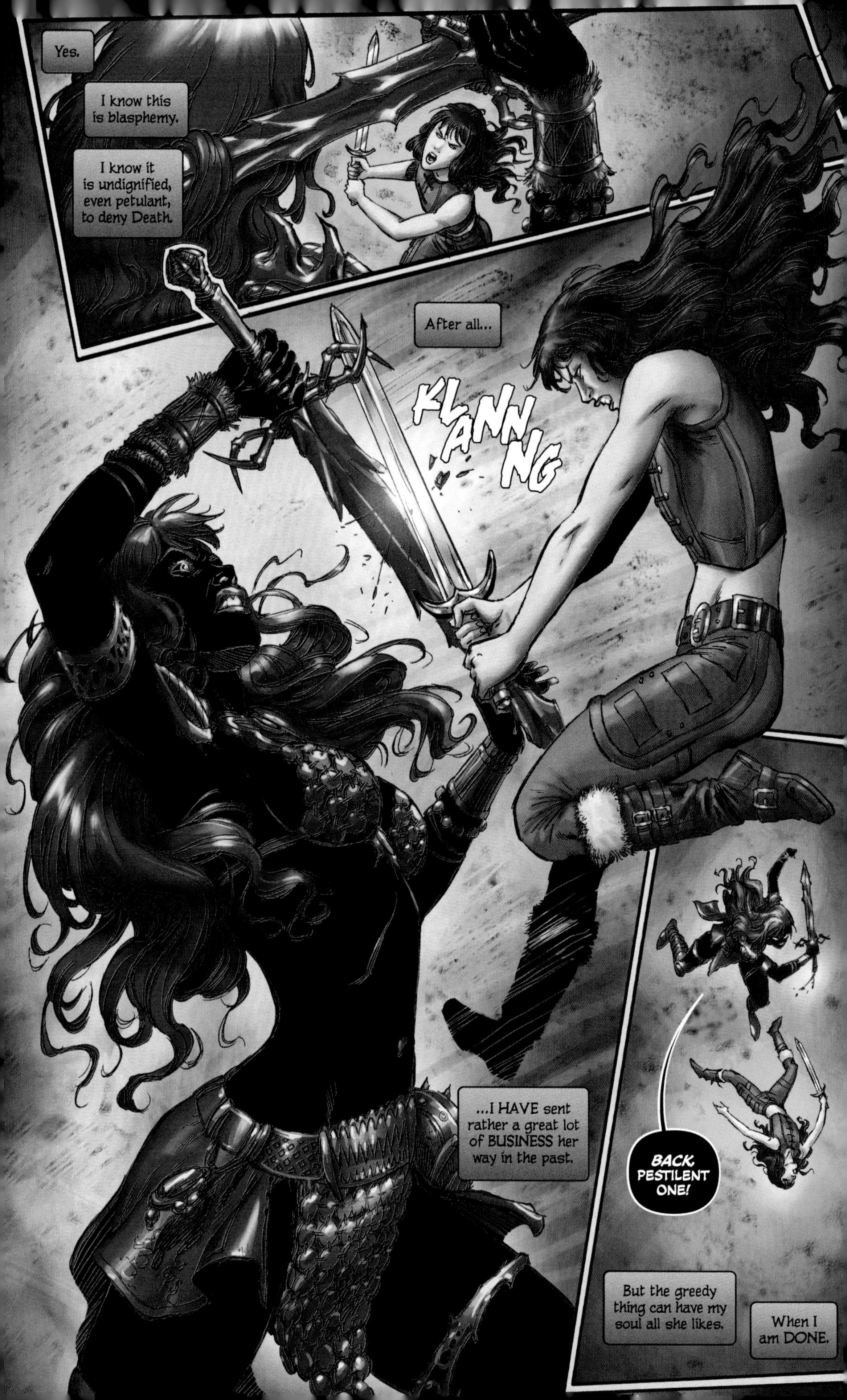
Yes.
I know this is blasphemy.
I know it is undignified, even petulant, to deny Death.
After all...
KLANNANNG
...I HAVE sent rather a great lot of BUSINESS her way in the past.
BACK, PESTILENT ONE!
But the greedy thing can have my soul all she likes.
When I am DONE.

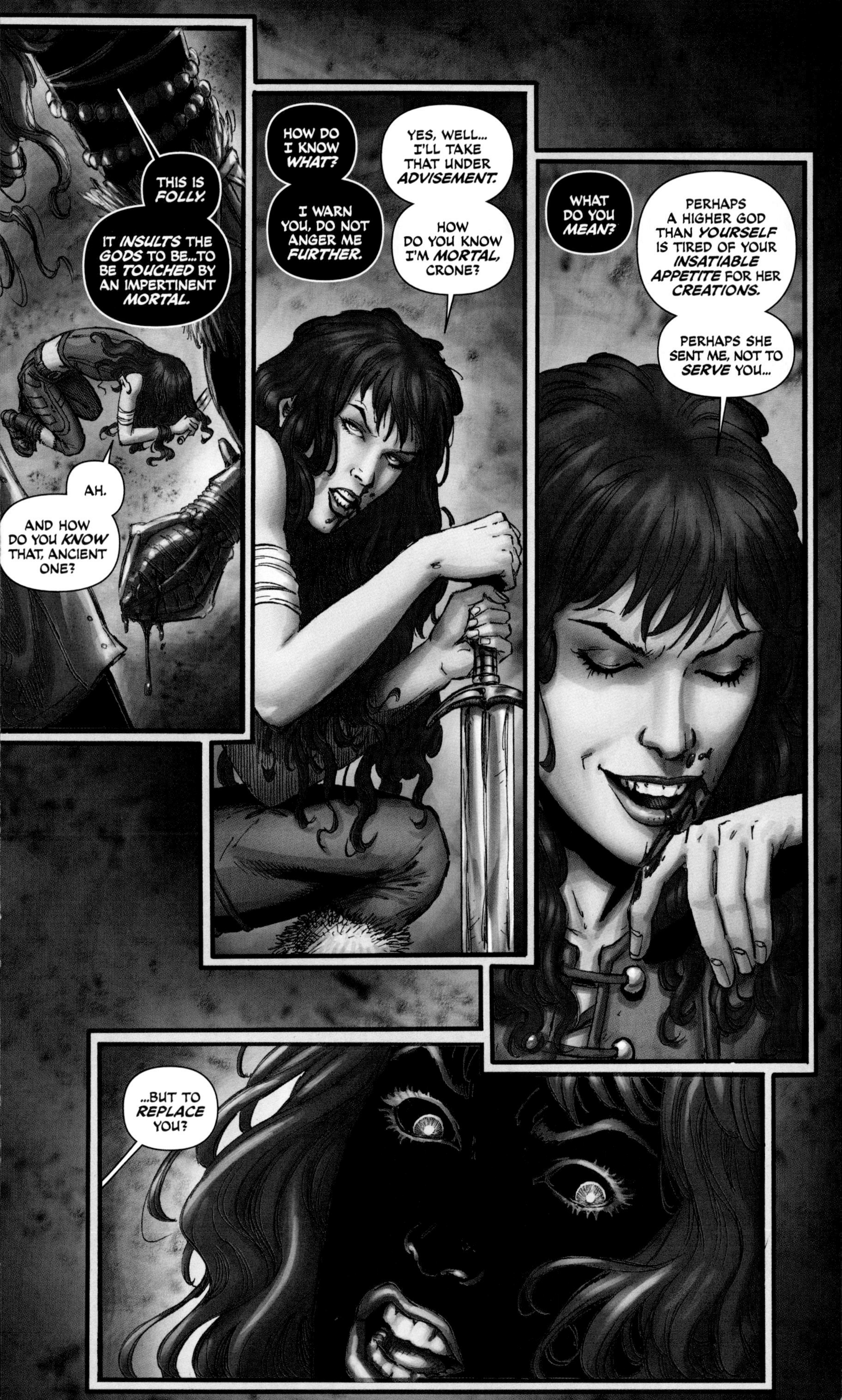
THIS IS *FOLLY.*
IT *INSULTS* THE *GODS* TO BE...TO BE *TOUCHED* BY AN IMPERTINENT *MORTAL.*
AH.
AND HOW DO YOU *KNOW* THAT, ANCIENT ONE?
HOW DO I KNOW *WHAT?*
I WARN YOU, DO NOT ANGER ME *FURTHER.*
YES, WELL... I'LL TAKE THAT UNDER *ADVISEMENT.*
HOW DO YOU KNOW I'M *MORTAL,* CRONE?
WHAT DO YOU *MEAN?*
PERHAPS A HIGHER GOD THAN *YOURSELF* IS TIRED OF YOUR *INSATIABLE APPETITE* FOR HER *CREATIONS.*
PERHAPS SHE SENT ME, NOT TO *SERVE* YOU...
...BUT TO *REPLACE* YOU?

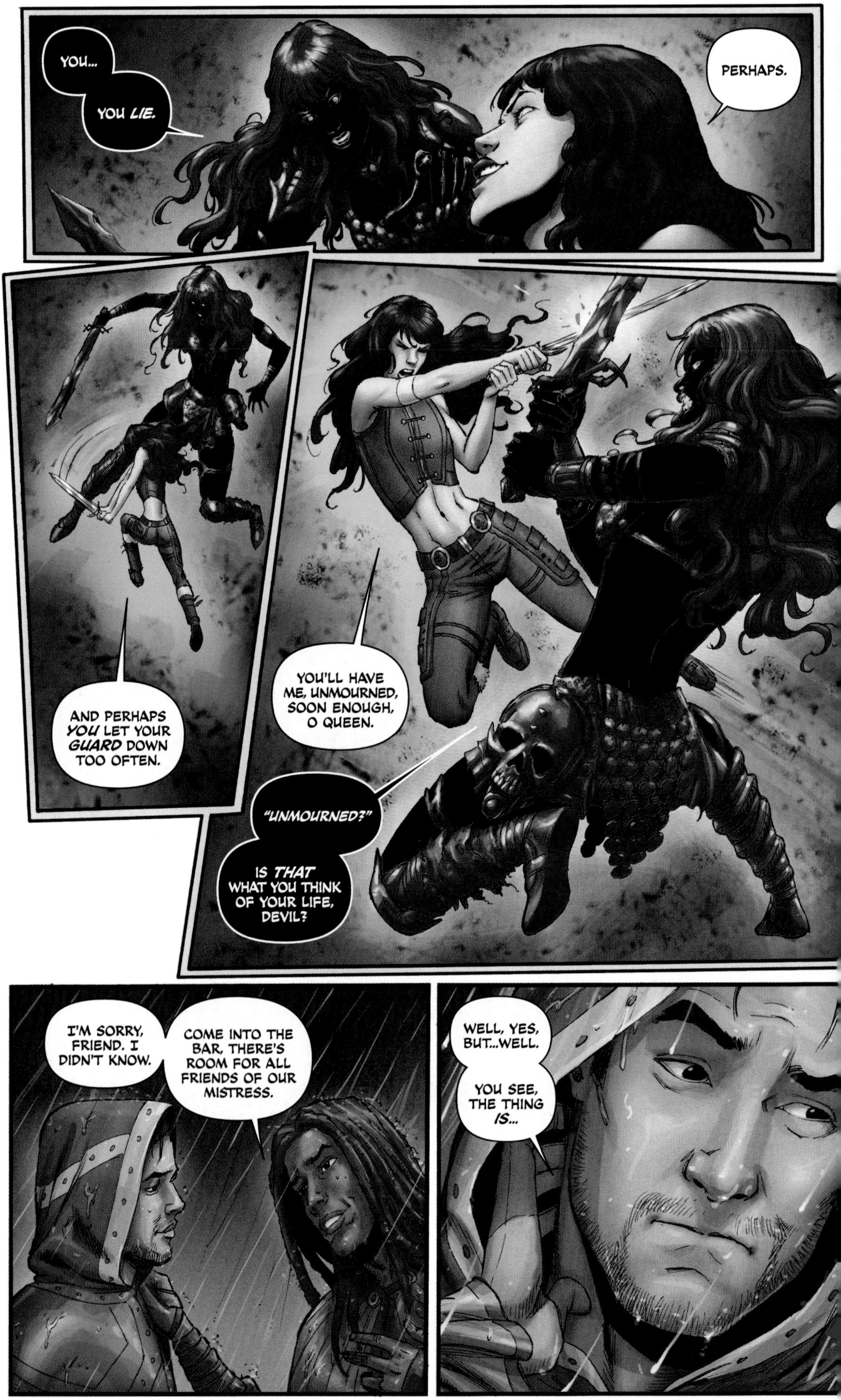
YOU...
YOU *LIE.*
PERHAPS.
AND PERHAPS *YOU* LET YOUR *GUARD* DOWN TOO OFTEN.
YOU'LL HAVE ME, UNMOURNED, SOON ENOUGH, O QUEEN.
"UNMOURNED?"
IS *THAT* WHAT YOU THINK OF YOUR LIFE, DEVIL?
I'M SORRY, FRIEND. I DIDN'T KNOW.
COME INTO THE BAR, THERE'S ROOM FOR ALL FRIENDS OF OUR MISTRESS.
WELL, YES, BUT...WELL.
YOU SEE, THE THING *IS...*

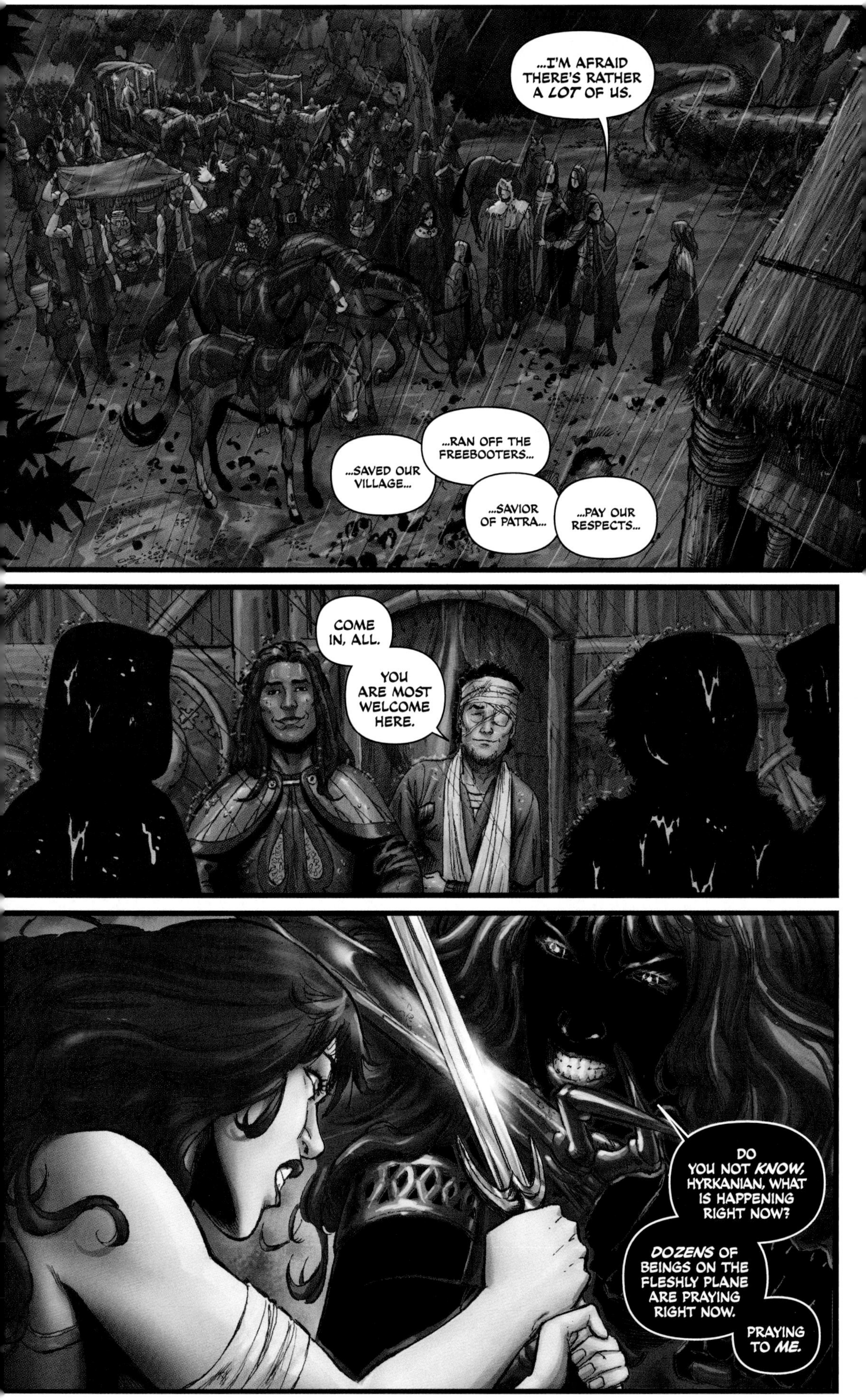
...I'M AFRAID THERE'S RATHER A *LOT* OF US.
...SAVED OUR VILLAGE...
...RAN OFF THE FREEBOOTERS...
...SAVIOR OF PATRA...
...PAY OUR RESPECTS...
COME IN, ALL.
YOU ARE MOST WELCOME HERE.
DO YOU NOT *KNOW,* HYRKANIAN, WHAT IS HAPPENING RIGHT NOW?
DOZENS OF BEINGS ON THE FLESHLY PLANE ARE PRAYING RIGHT NOW.
PRAYING TO *ME.*

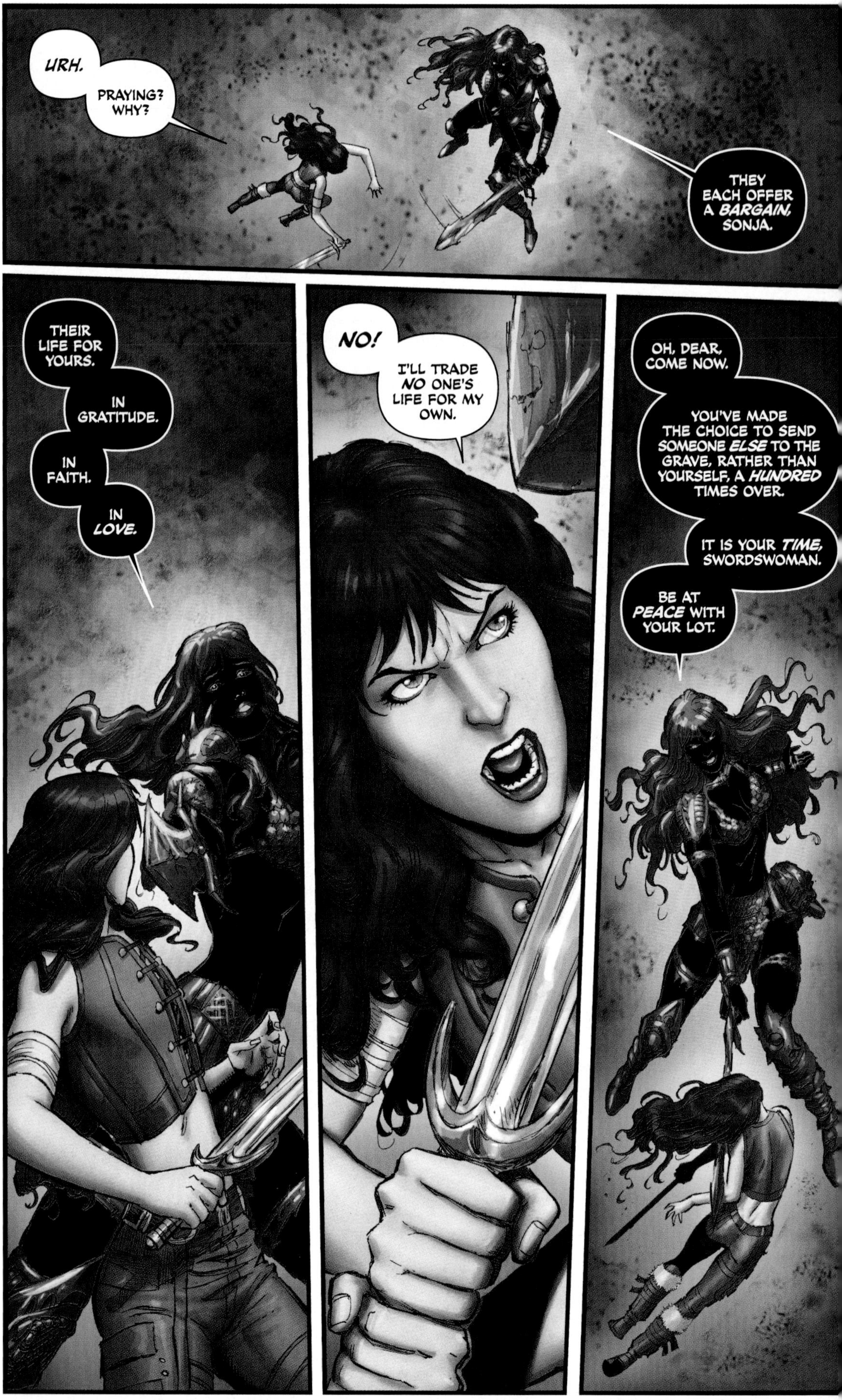
URH.
PRAYING? WHY?
THEY EACH OFFER A BARGAIN, SONJA.
THEIR LIFE FOR YOURS.
IN GRATITUDE.
IN FAITH.
IN LOVE.
NO!
I'LL TRADE NO ONE'S LIFE FOR MY OWN.
OH, DEAR, COME NOW.
YOU'VE MADE THE CHOICE TO SEND SOMEONE ELSE TO THE GRAVE, RATHER THAN YOURSELF, A HUNDRED TIMES OVER.
IT IS YOUR TIME, SWORDSWOMAN.
BE AT PEACE WITH YOUR LOT.

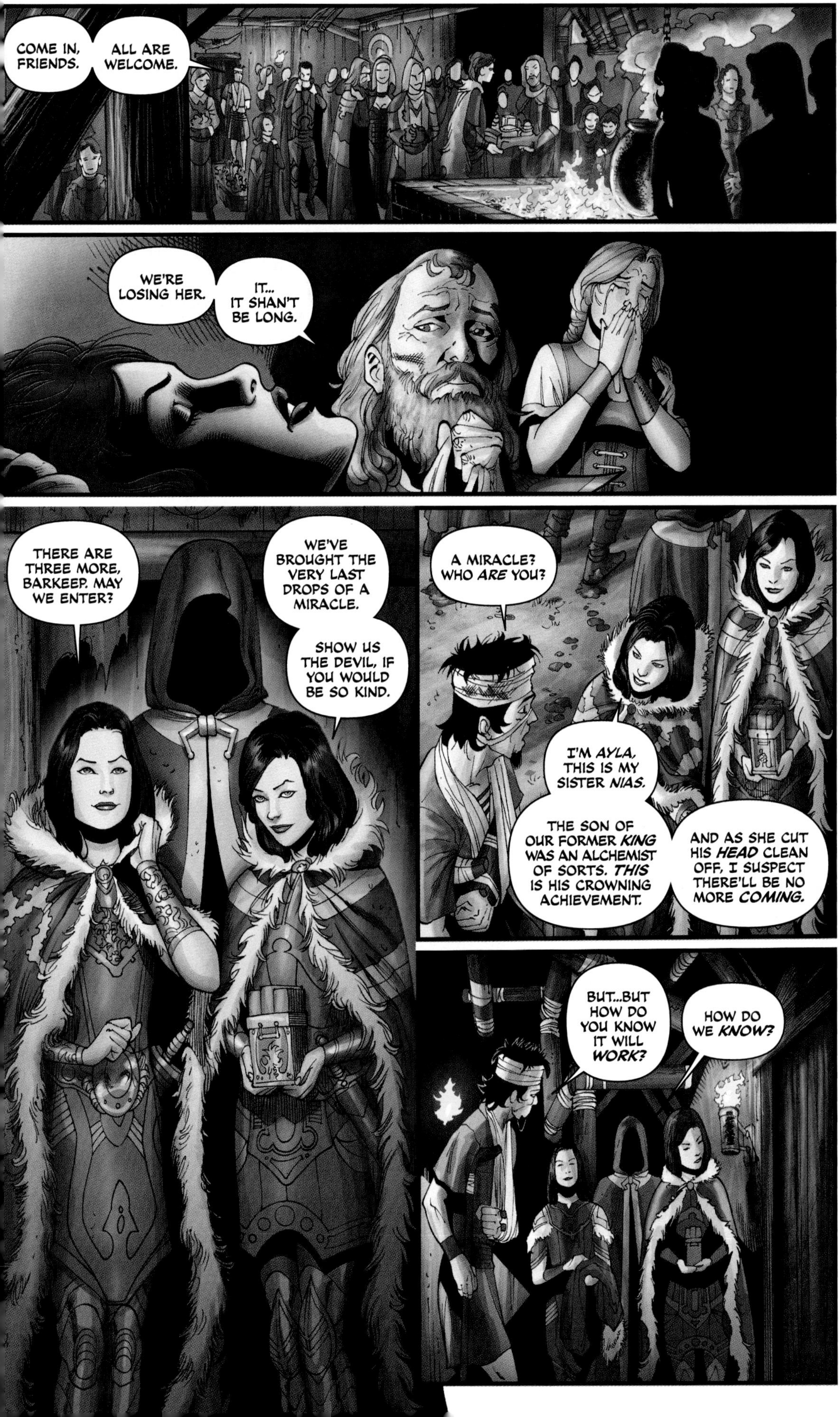
COME IN, FRIENDS.
ALL ARE WELCOME.
WE'RE LOSING HER.
IT... IT SHAN'T BE LONG.
THERE ARE THREE MORE, BARKEEP. MAY WE ENTER?
WE'VE BROUGHT THE VERY LAST DROPS OF A MIRACLE.
SHOW US THE DEVIL, IF YOU WOULD BE SO KIND.
A MIRACLE? WHO *ARE* YOU?
I'M *AYLA*, THIS IS MY SISTER *NIAS*.
THE SON OF OUR FORMER *KING* WAS AN ALCHEMIST OF SORTS. *THIS* IS HIS CROWNING ACHIEVEMENT.
AND AS SHE CUT HIS *HEAD* CLEAN OFF, I SUSPECT THERE'LL BE NO MORE *COMING*.
BUT...BUT HOW DO YOU KNOW IT WILL *WORK*?
HOW DO WE *KNOW*?

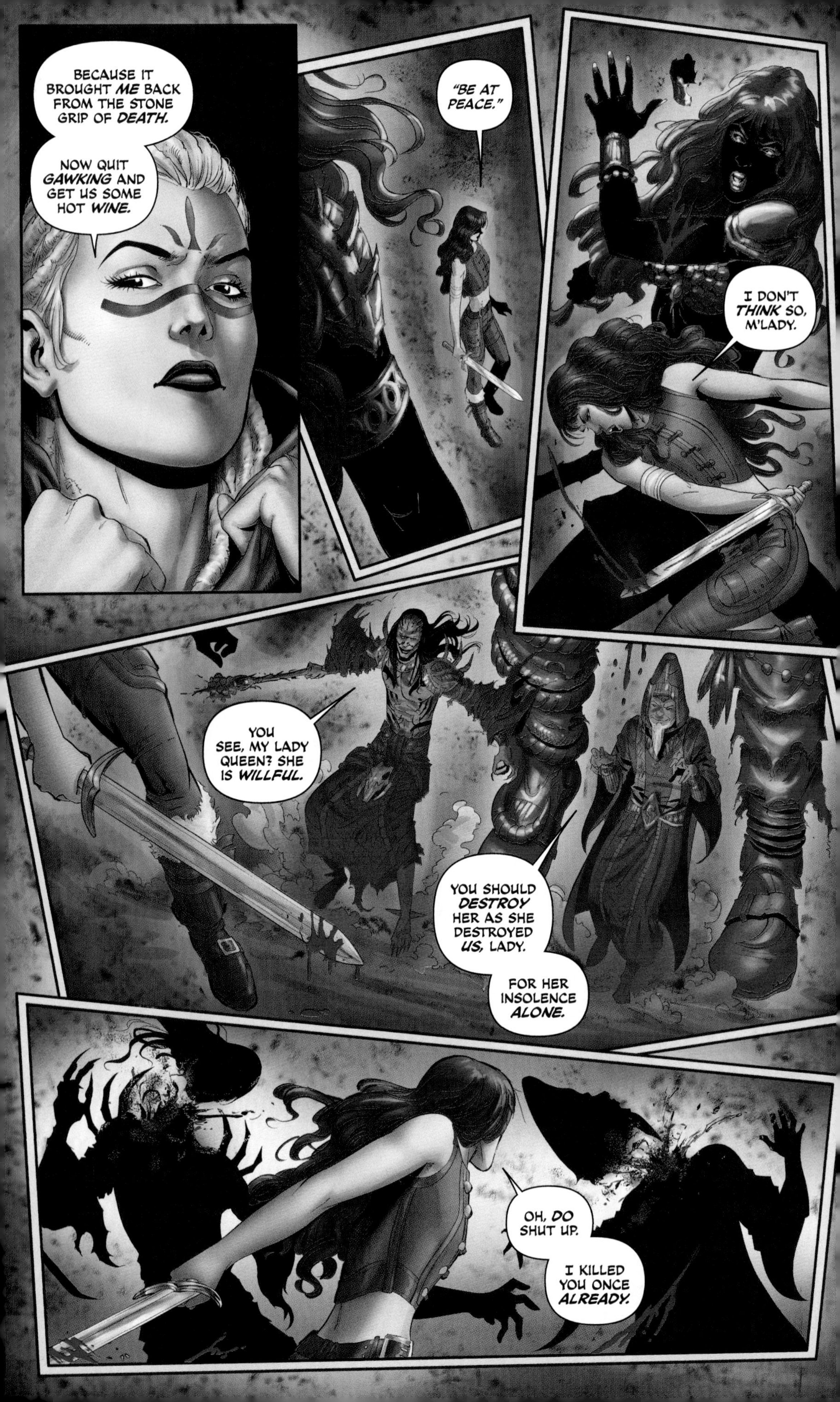

BECAUSE IT BROUGHT *ME* BACK FROM THE STONE GRIP OF *DEATH.*
NOW QUIT *GAWKING* AND GET US SOME HOT *WINE.*
"BE AT PEACE."
I DON'T *THINK* SO, M'LADY.
YOU SEE, MY LADY QUEEN? SHE IS *WILLFUL.*
YOU SHOULD *DESTROY* HER AS SHE DESTROYED *US,* LADY.
FOR HER INSOLENCE *ALONE.*
OH, *DO* SHUT UP.
I KILLED YOU ONCE *ALREADY.*

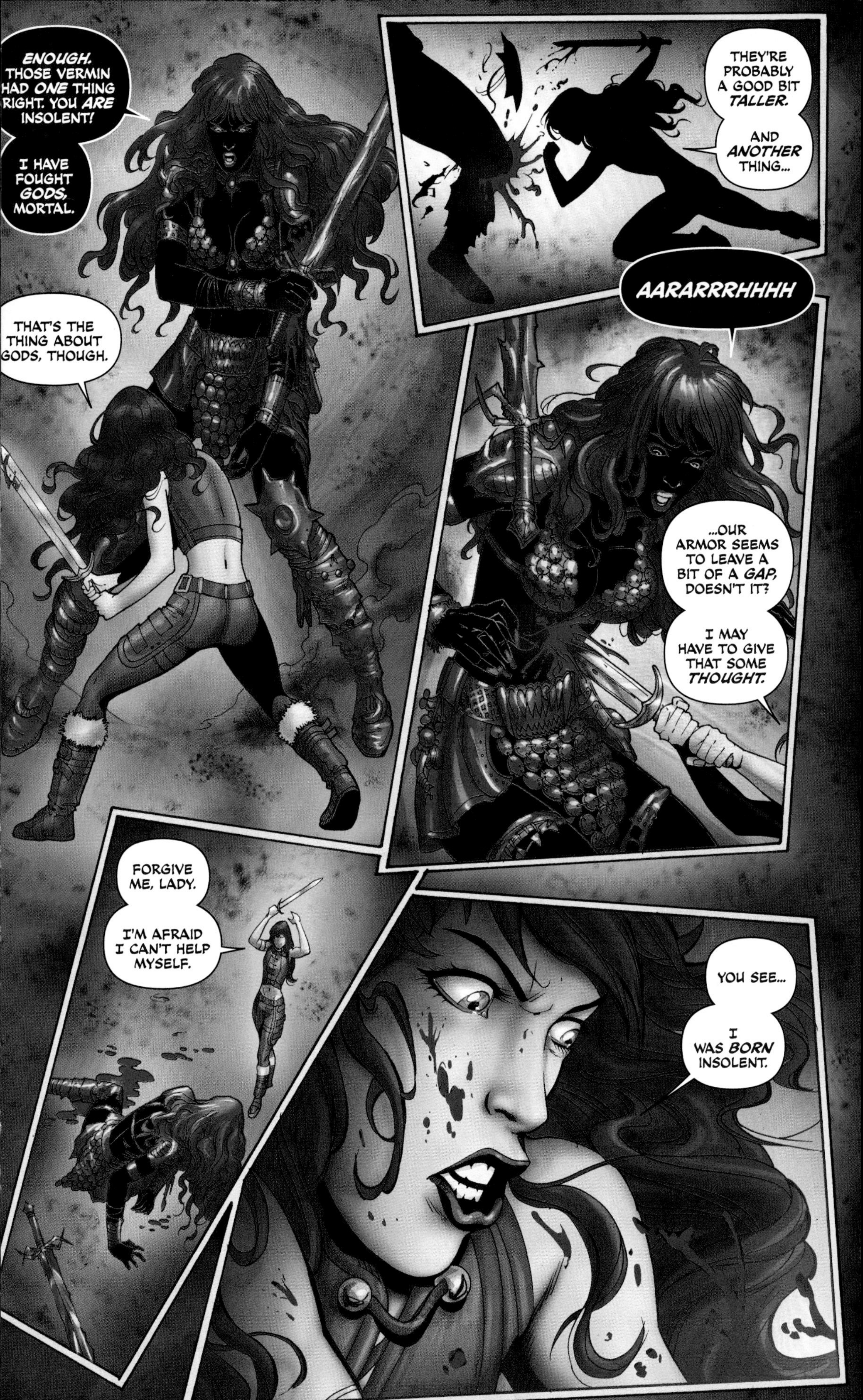
ENOUGH. THOSE VERMIN HAD ONE THING RIGHT. YOU ARE INSOLENT!
I HAVE FOUGHT GODS, MORTAL.
THAT'S THE THING ABOUT GODS, THOUGH.
THEY'RE PROBABLY A GOOD BIT TALLER.
AND ANOTHER THING...
AARARRRHHHH
...OUR ARMOR SEEMS TO LEAVE A BIT OF A GAP, DOESN'T IT?
I MAY HAVE TO GIVE THAT SOME THOUGHT.
FORGIVE ME, LADY.
I'M AFRAID I CAN'T HELP MYSELF.
YOU SEE...
I WAS BORN INSOLENT.

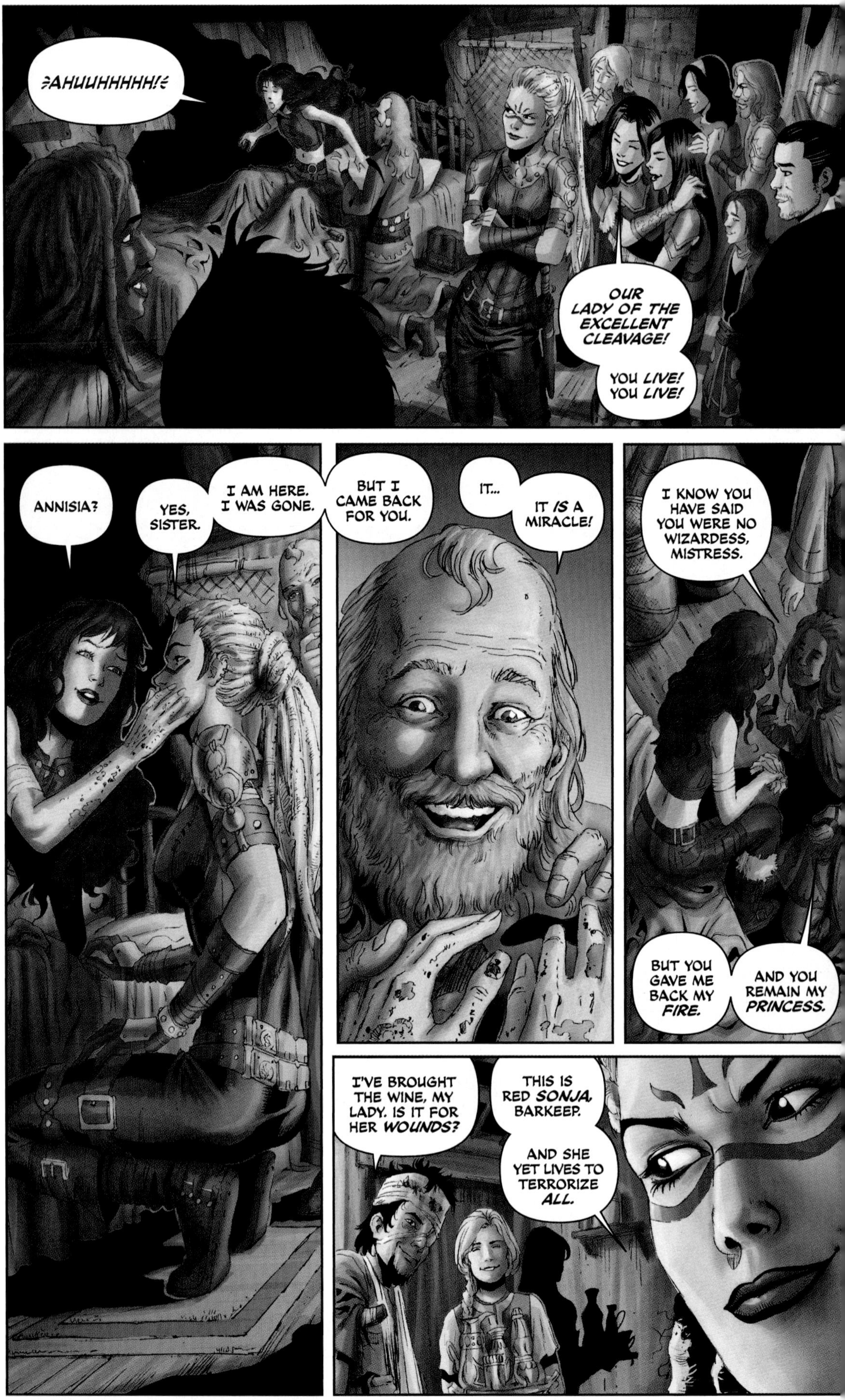

≥AHUUHHHHH!≤
OUR LADY OF THE EXCELLENT CLEAVAGE!
YOU LIVE! YOU LIVE!
ANNISIA?
YES, SISTER.
I AM HERE. I WAS GONE.
BUT I CAME BACK FOR YOU.
IT...
IT IS A MIRACLE!
I KNOW YOU HAVE SAID YOU WERE NO WIZARDESS, MISTRESS.
BUT YOU GAVE ME BACK MY FIRE.
AND YOU REMAIN MY PRINCESS.
I'VE BROUGHT THE WINE, MY LADY. IS IT FOR HER WOUNDS?
THIS IS RED SONJA, BARKEEP.
AND SHE YET LIVES TO TERRORIZE ALL.

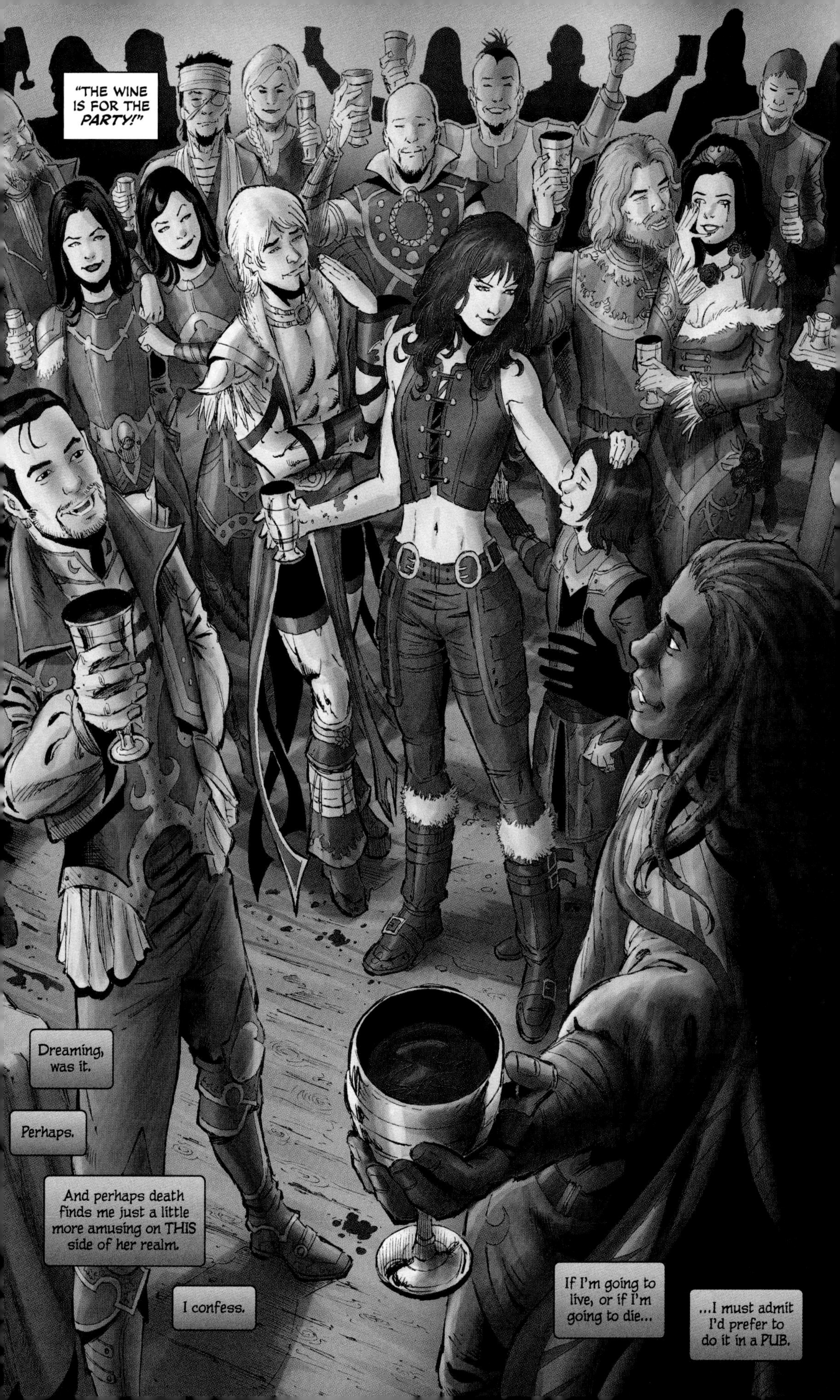
"THE WINE IS FOR THE *PARTY!*"
Dreaming, was it.
Perhaps.
And perhaps death finds me just a little more amusing on THIS side of her realm.
I confess.
If I'm going to live, or if I'm going to die...
...I must admit I'd prefer to do it in a PUB.

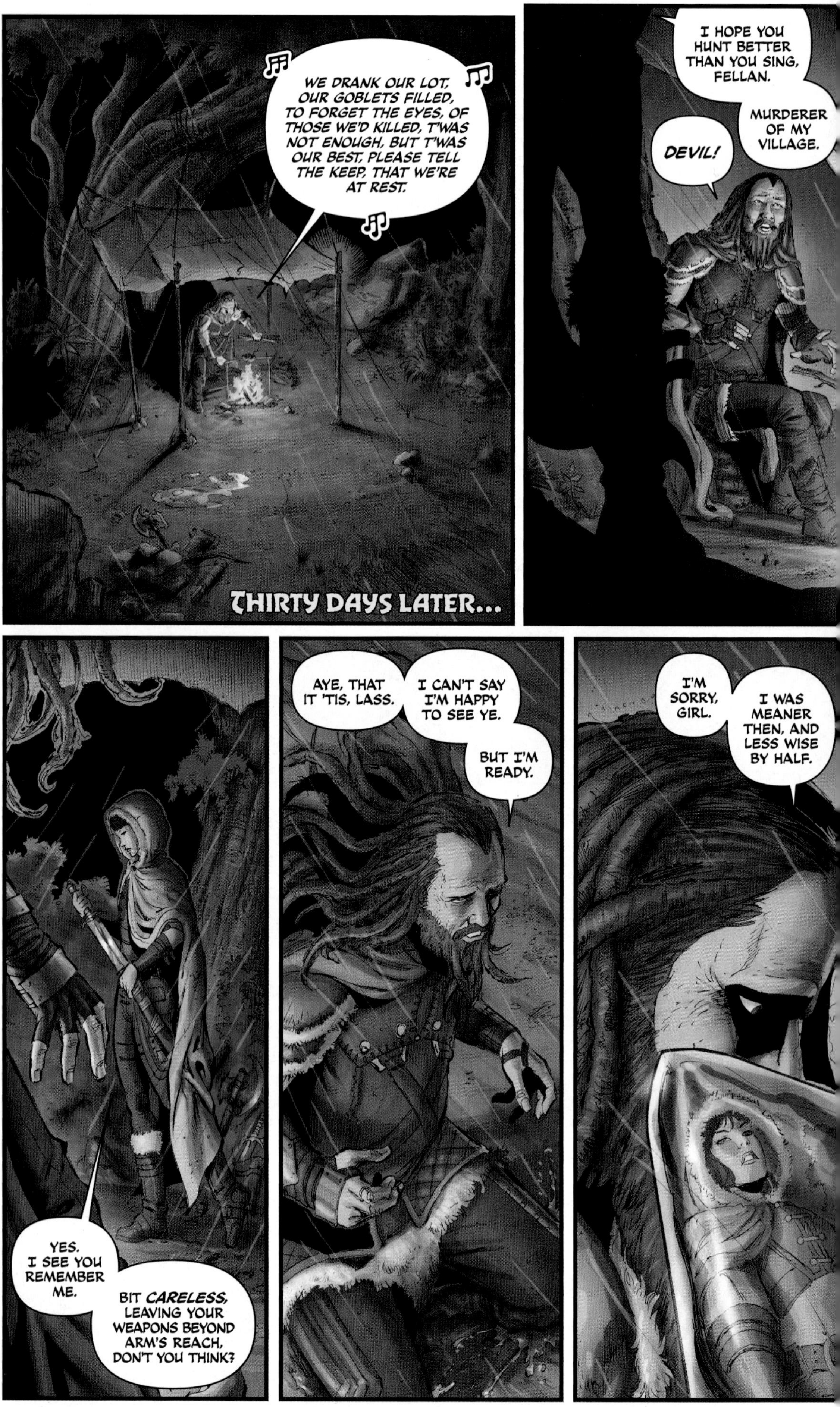
WE DRANK OUR LOT, OUR GOBLETS FILLED, TO FORGET THE EYES, OF THOSE WE'D KILLED, T'WAS NOT ENOUGH, BUT T'WAS OUR BEST, PLEASE TELL THE KEEP, THAT WE'RE AT REST.
THIRTY DAYS LATER...
I HOPE YOU HUNT BETTER THAN YOU SING, FELLAN.
MURDERER OF MY VILLAGE.
DEVIL!
YES. I SEE YOU REMEMBER ME.
BIT CARELESS, LEAVING YOUR WEAPONS BEYOND ARM'S REACH, DON'T YOU THINK?
AYE, THAT IT 'TIS, LASS.
I CAN'T SAY I'M HAPPY TO SEE YE.
BUT I'M READY.
I'M SORRY, GIRL.
I WAS MEANER THEN, AND LESS WISE BY HALF.

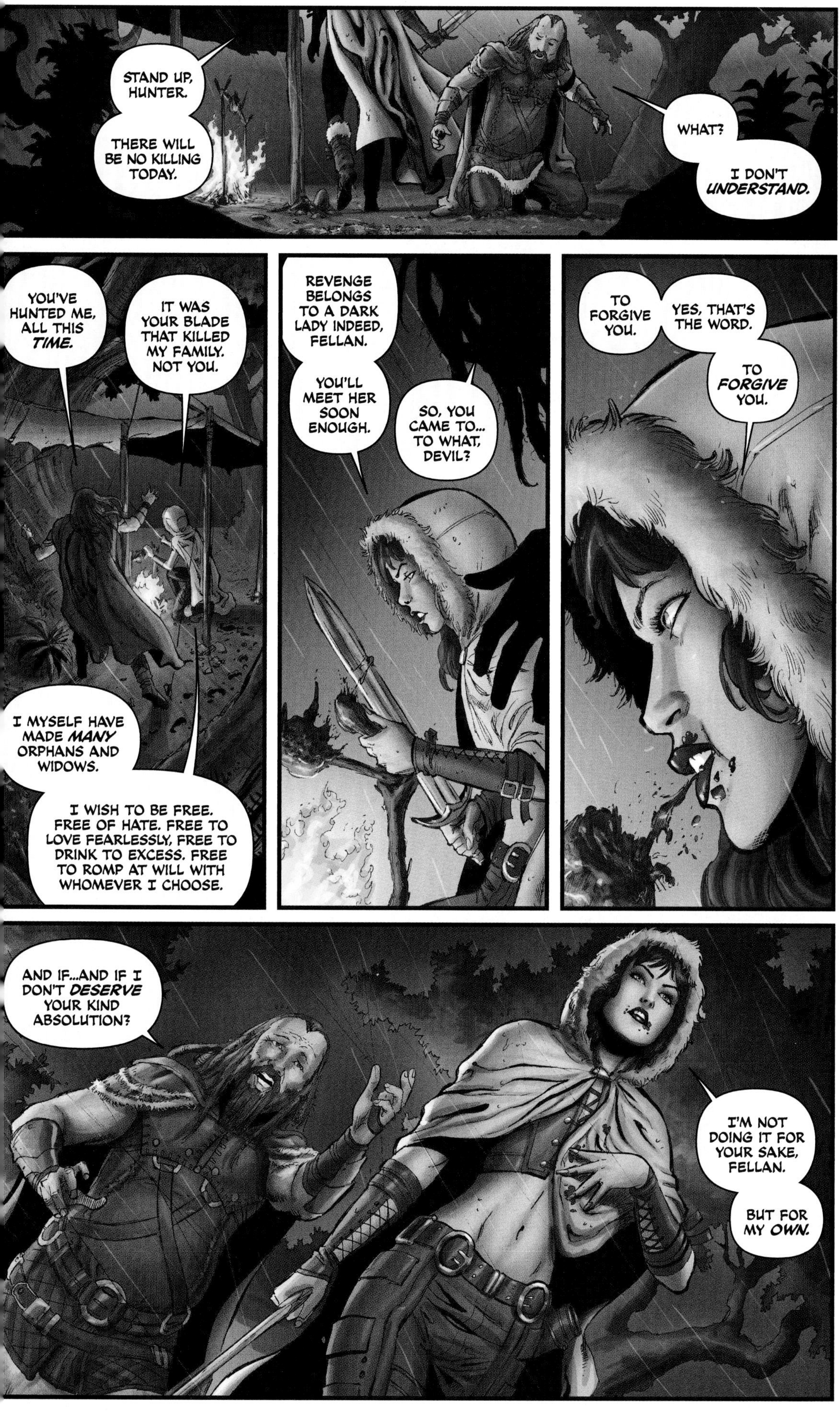
STAND UP, HUNTER.
THERE WILL BE NO KILLING TODAY.
WHAT?
I DON'T *UNDERSTAND.*
YOU'VE HUNTED ME, ALL THIS *TIME.*
IT WAS YOUR BLADE THAT KILLED MY FAMILY. NOT YOU.
I MYSELF HAVE MADE *MANY* ORPHANS AND WIDOWS.
I WISH TO BE FREE. FREE OF HATE. FREE TO LOVE FEARLESSLY, FREE TO DRINK TO EXCESS. FREE TO ROMP AT WILL WITH WHOMEVER I CHOOSE.
REVENGE BELONGS TO A DARK LADY INDEED, FELLAN.
YOU'LL MEET HER SOON ENOUGH.
SO, YOU CAME TO... TO WHAT, DEVIL?
TO FORGIVE YOU.
YES, THAT'S THE WORD.
TO *FORGIVE* YOU.
AND IF...AND IF I DON'T *DESERVE* YOUR KIND ABSOLUTION?
I'M NOT DOING IT FOR YOUR SAKE, FELLAN.
BUT FOR MY *OWN.*

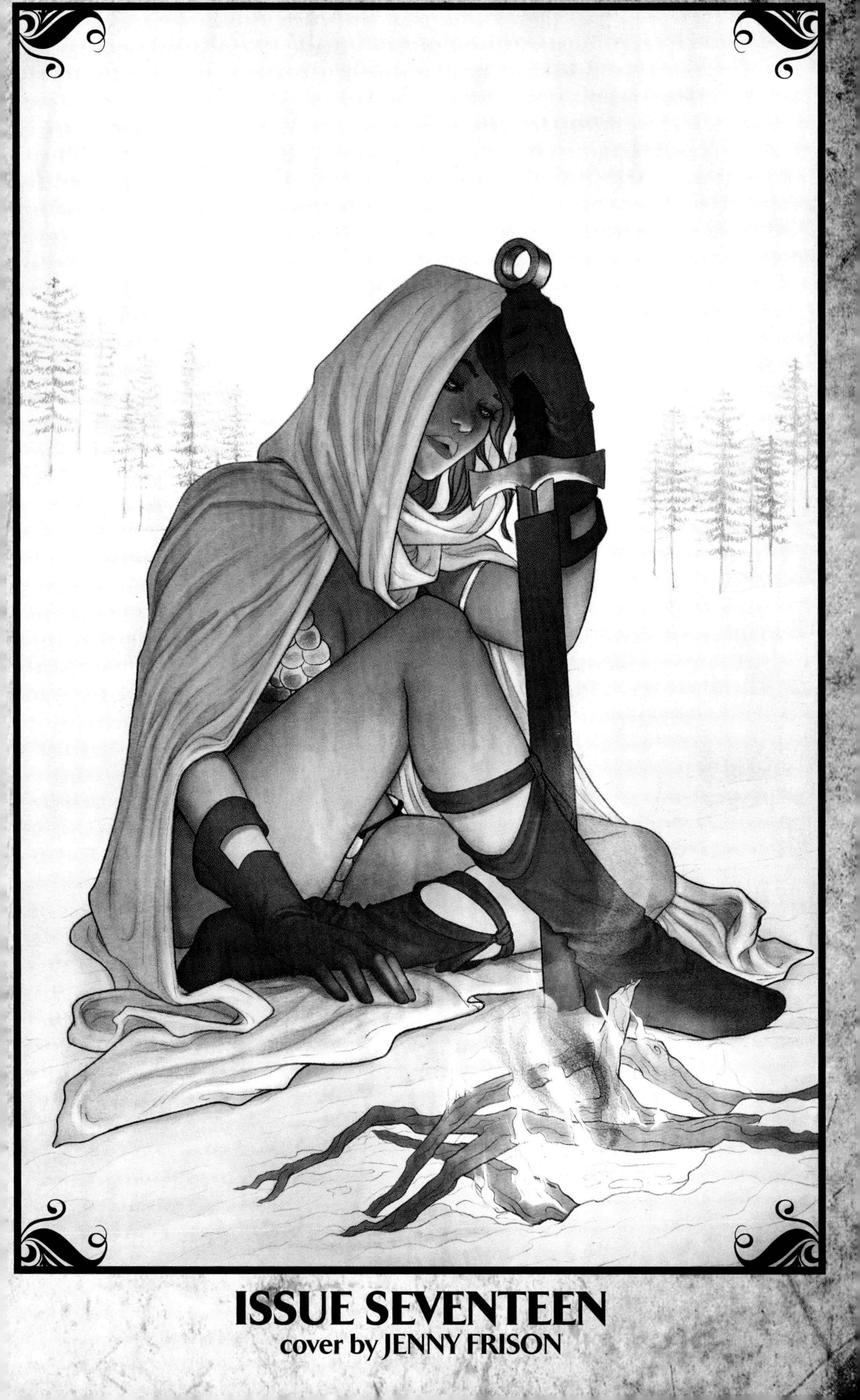

ISSUE SEVENTEEN
cover by JENNY FRISON

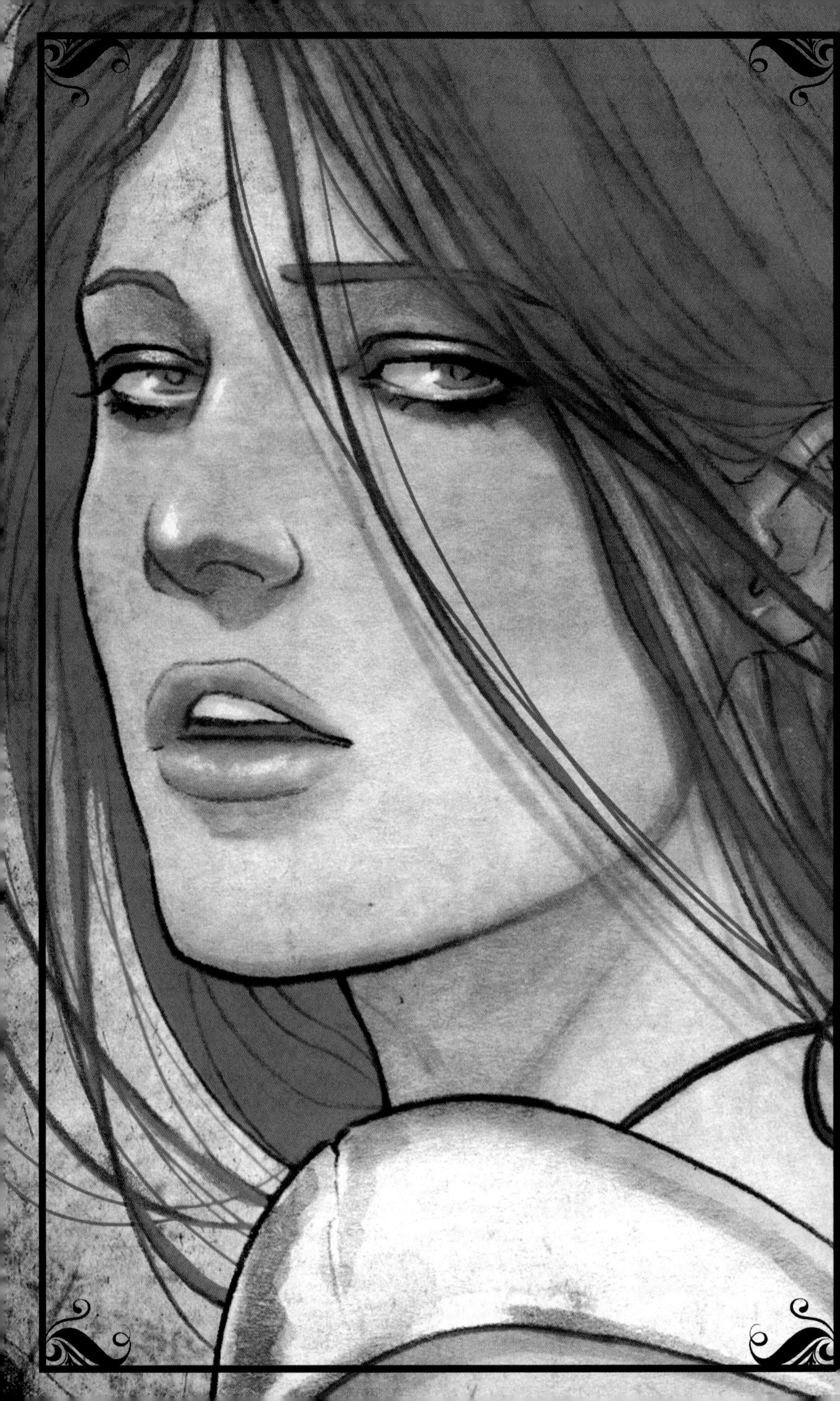

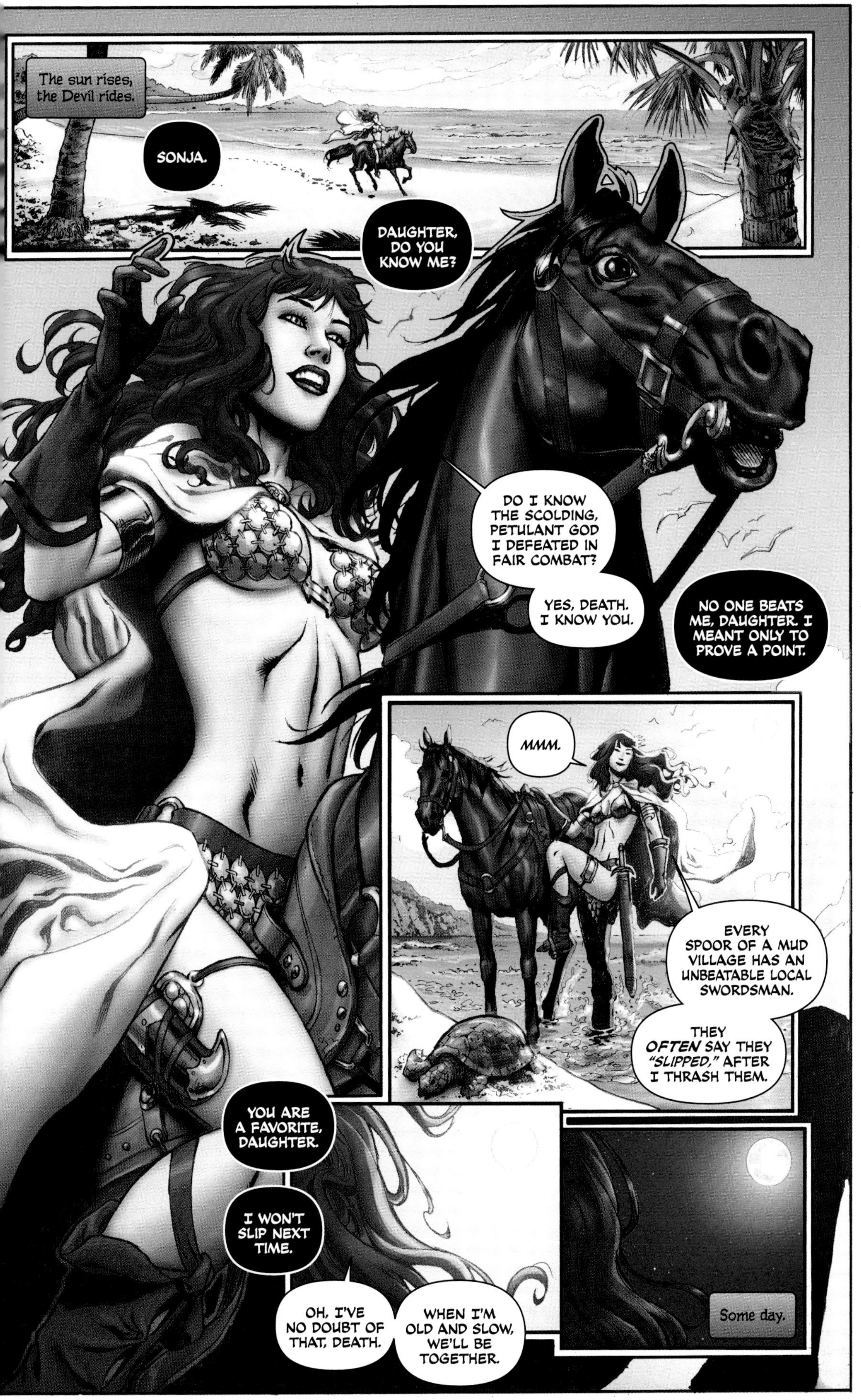
The sun rises, the Devil rides.
SONJA.
DAUGHTER, DO YOU KNOW ME?
DO I KNOW THE SCOLDING, PETULANT GOD I DEFEATED IN FAIR COMBAT?
YES, DEATH. I KNOW YOU.
NO ONE BEATS ME, DAUGHTER. I MEANT ONLY TO PROVE A POINT.
MMM.
EVERY SPOOR OF A MUD VILLAGE HAS AN UNBEATABLE LOCAL SWORDSMAN.
THEY OFTEN SAY THEY "SLIPPED," AFTER I THRASH THEM.
YOU ARE A FAVORITE, DAUGHTER.
I WON'T SLIP NEXT TIME.
OH, I'VE NO DOUBT OF THAT, DEATH.
WHEN I'M OLD AND SLOW, WE'LL BE TOGETHER.
Some day.

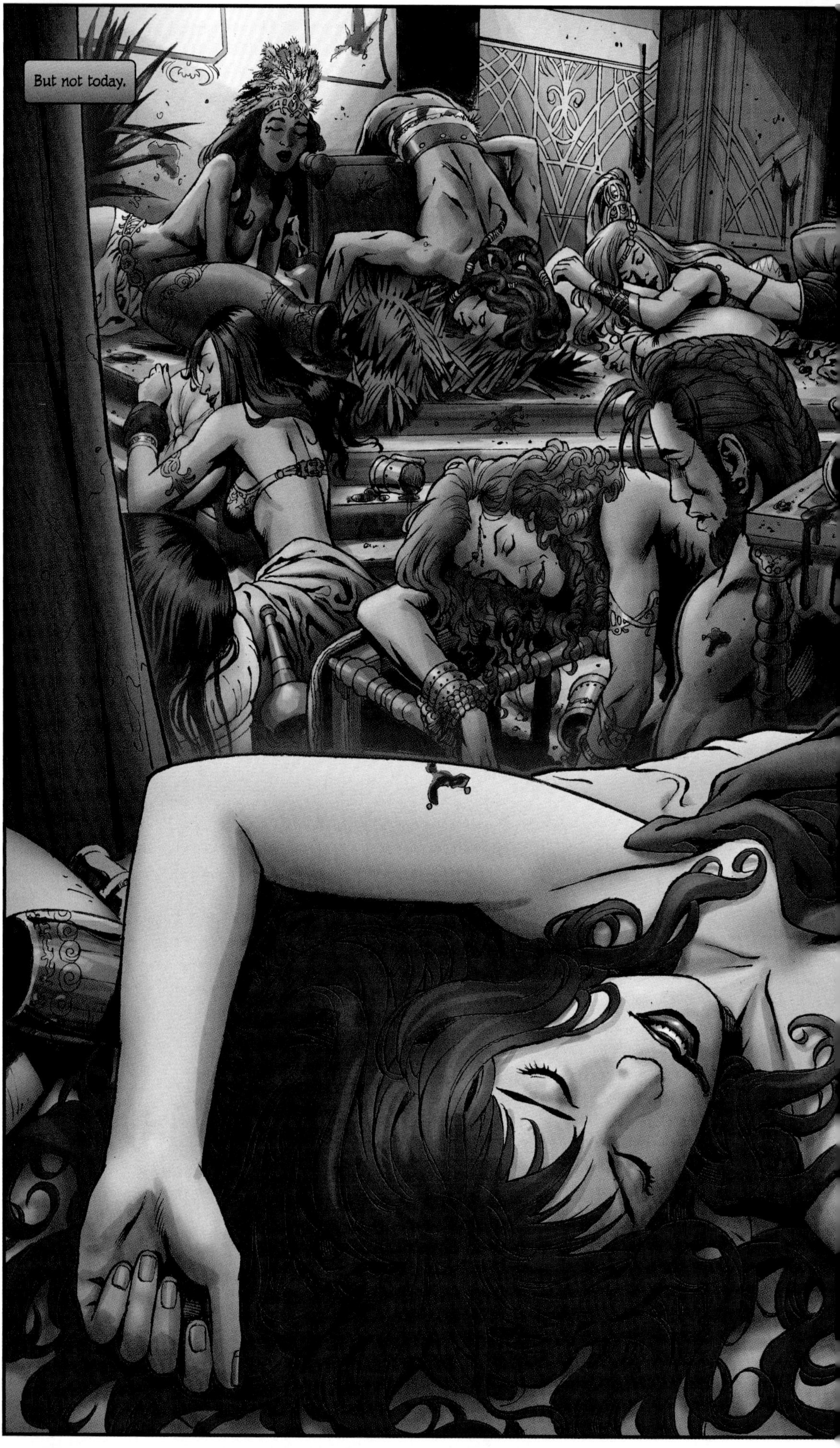
But not today.

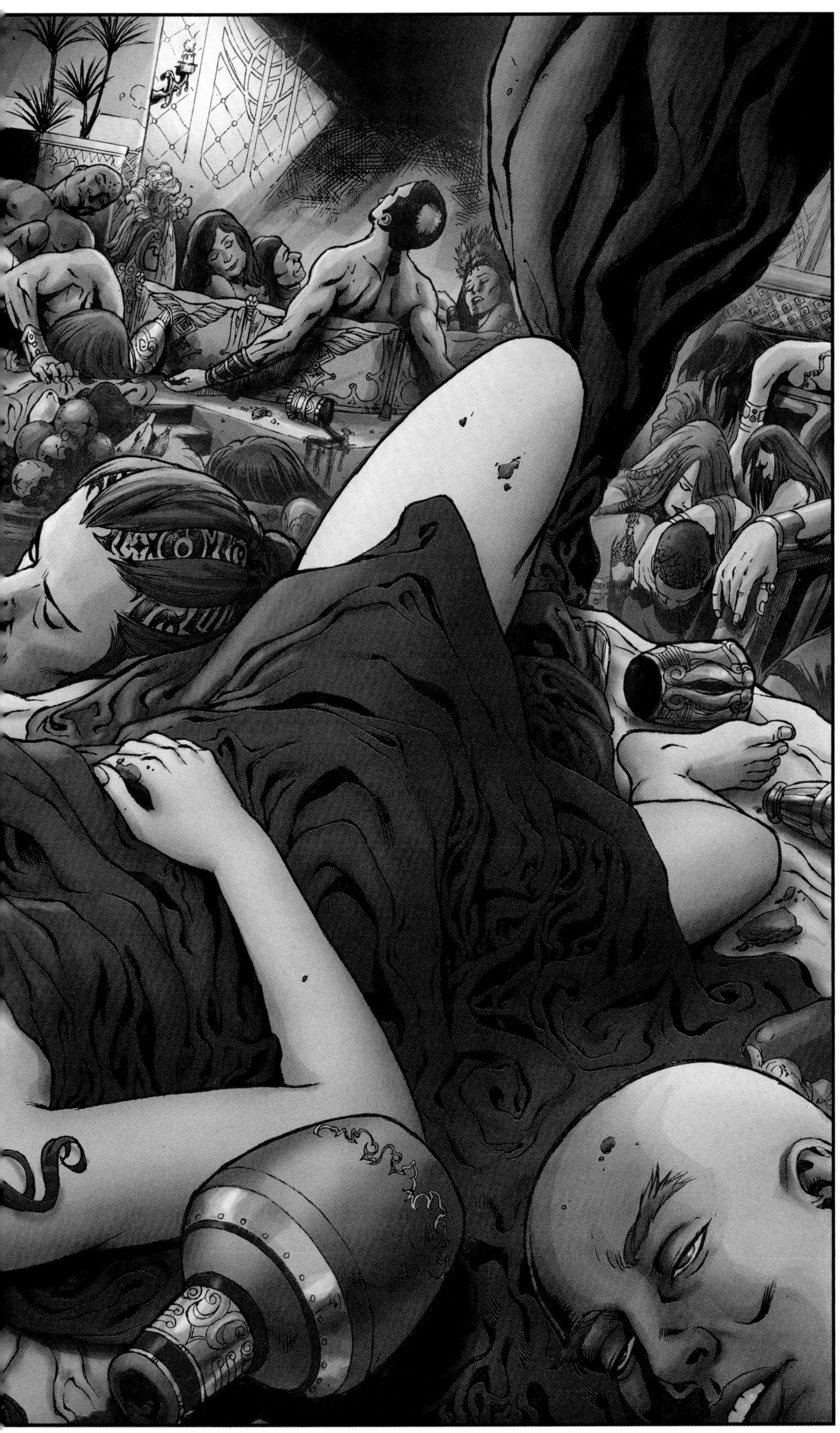

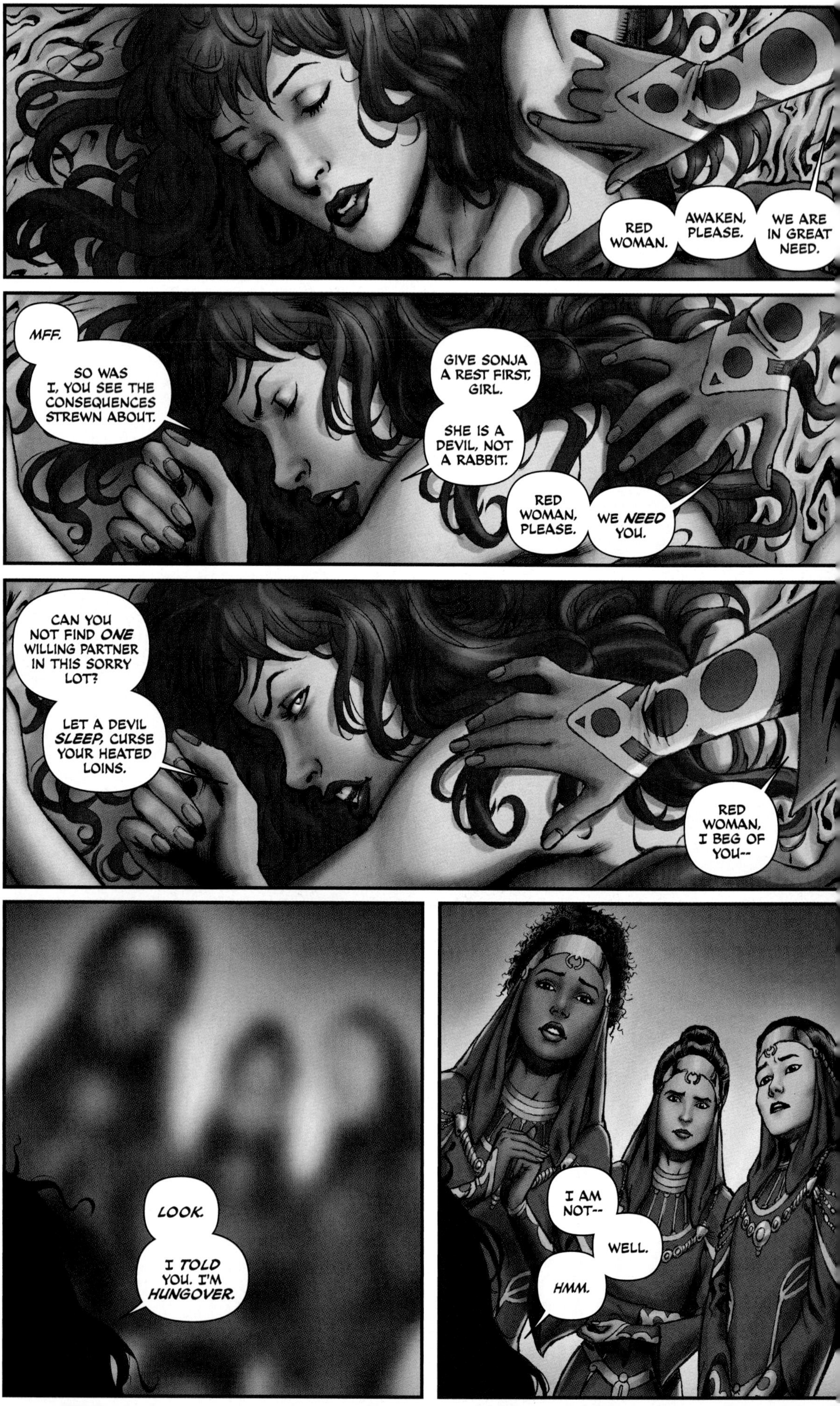
RED WOMAN.
AWAKEN, PLEASE.
WE ARE IN GREAT NEED.
MFF.
SO WAS I, YOU SEE THE CONSEQUENCES STREWN ABOUT.
GIVE SONJA A REST FIRST, GIRL.
SHE IS A DEVIL, NOT A RABBIT.
RED WOMAN, PLEASE.
WE NEED YOU.
CAN YOU NOT FIND ONE WILLING PARTNER IN THIS SORRY LOT?
LET A DEVIL SLEEP, CURSE YOUR HEATED LOINS.
RED WOMAN, I BEG OF YOU--
LOOK.
I TOLD YOU. I'M HUNGOVER.
I AM NOT--
WELL.
HMM.

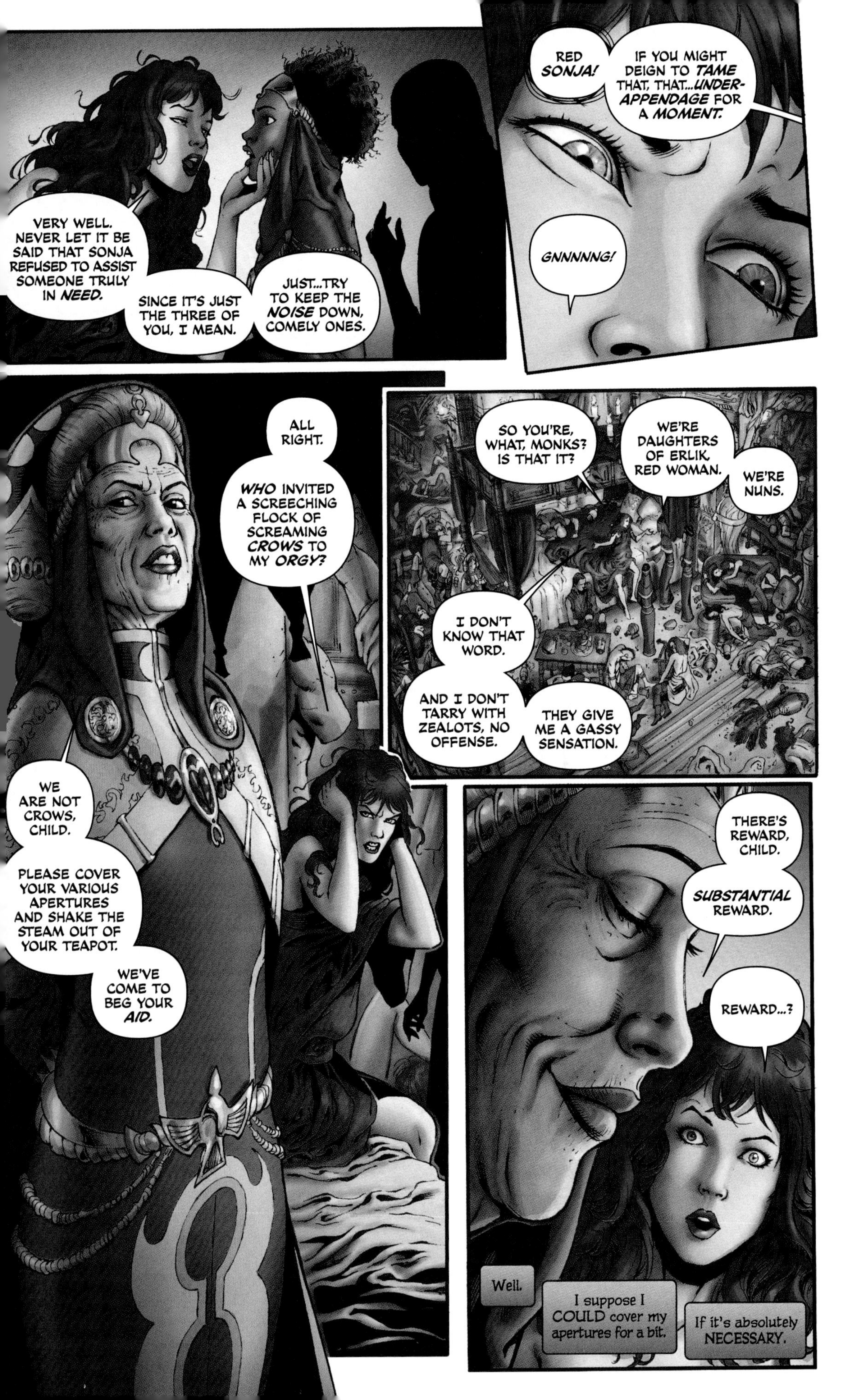
VERY WELL. NEVER LET IT BE SAID THAT SONJA REFUSED TO ASSIST SOMEONE TRULY IN NEED.
SINCE IT'S JUST THE THREE OF YOU, I MEAN.
JUST...TRY TO KEEP THE NOISE DOWN, COMELY ONES.
RED SONJA!
IF YOU MIGHT DEIGN TO TAME THAT, THAT...UNDER-APPENDAGE FOR A MOMENT.
GNNNNNG!
ALL RIGHT.
WHO INVITED A SCREECHING FLOCK OF SCREAMING CROWS TO MY ORGY?
WE ARE NOT CROWS, CHILD.
PLEASE COVER YOUR VARIOUS APERTURES AND SHAKE THE STEAM OUT OF YOUR TEAPOT.
WE'VE COME TO BEG YOUR AID.
SO YOU'RE, WHAT, MONKS? IS THAT IT?
WE'RE DAUGHTERS OF ERLIK, RED WOMAN.
WE'RE NUNS.
I DON'T KNOW THAT WORD.
AND I DON'T TARRY WITH ZEALOTS, NO OFFENSE.
THEY GIVE ME A GASSY SENSATION.
THERE'S REWARD, CHILD.
SUBSTANTIAL REWARD.
REWARD...?
Well.
I suppose I COULD cover my apertures for a bit.
If it's absolutely NECESSARY.

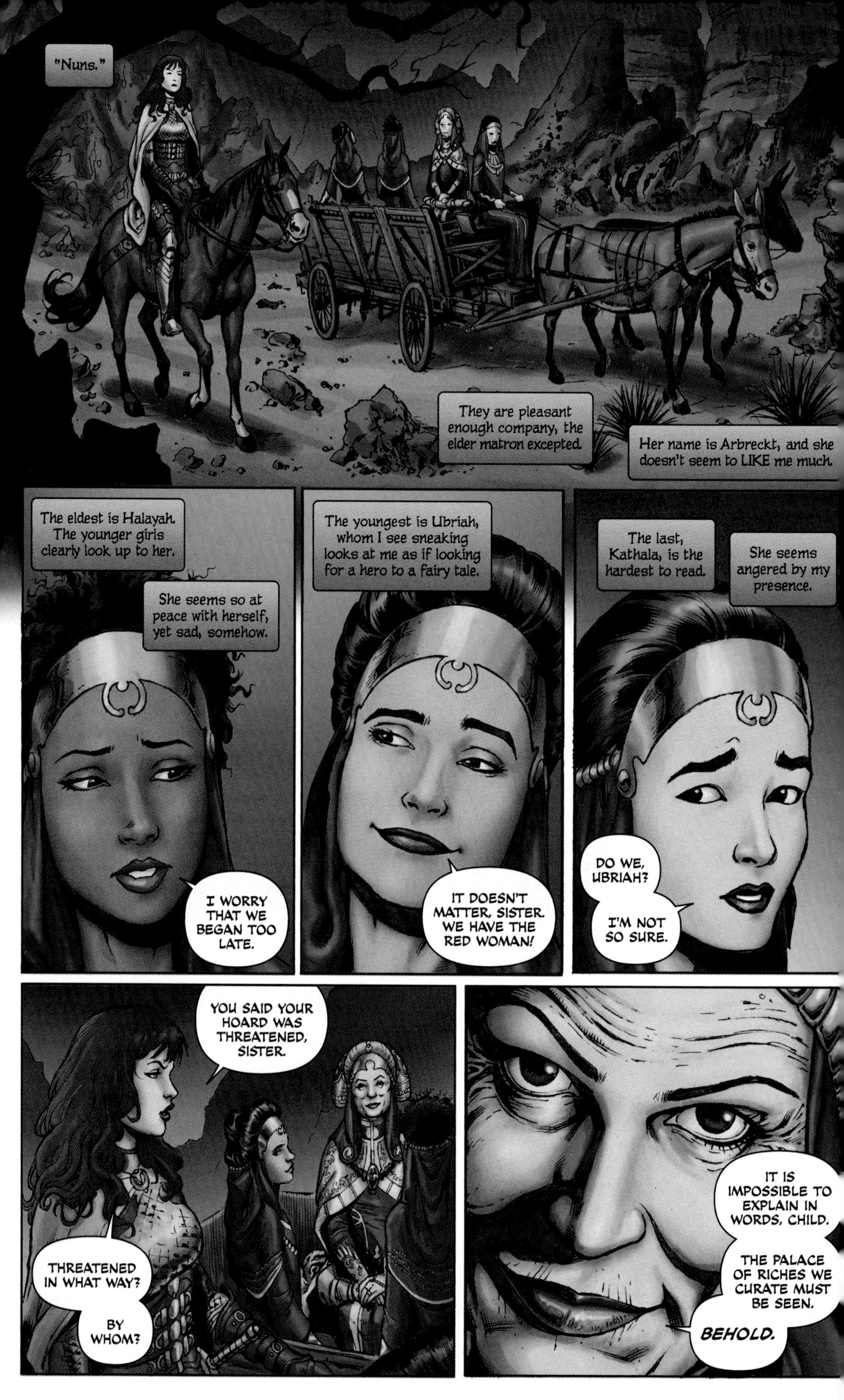
"Nuns."
They are pleasant enough company, the elder matron excepted.
Her name is Arbreckt, and she doesn't seem to LIKE me much.
The eldest is Halayah. The younger girls clearly look up to her.
She seems so at peace with herself, yet sad, somehow.
I WORRY THAT WE BEGAN TOO LATE.
The youngest is Ubriah, whom I see sneaking looks at me as if looking for a hero to a fairy tale.
IT DOESN'T MATTER, SISTER. WE HAVE THE RED WOMAN!
The last, Kathala, is the hardest to read.
She seems angered by my presence.
DO WE, UBRIAH?
I'M NOT SO SURE.
YOU SAID YOUR HOARD WAS THREATENED, SISTER.
THREATENED IN WHAT WAY?
BY WHOM?
IT IS IMPOSSIBLE TO EXPLAIN IN WORDS, CHILD.
THE PALACE OF RICHES WE CURATE MUST BE SEEN.
BEHOLD.

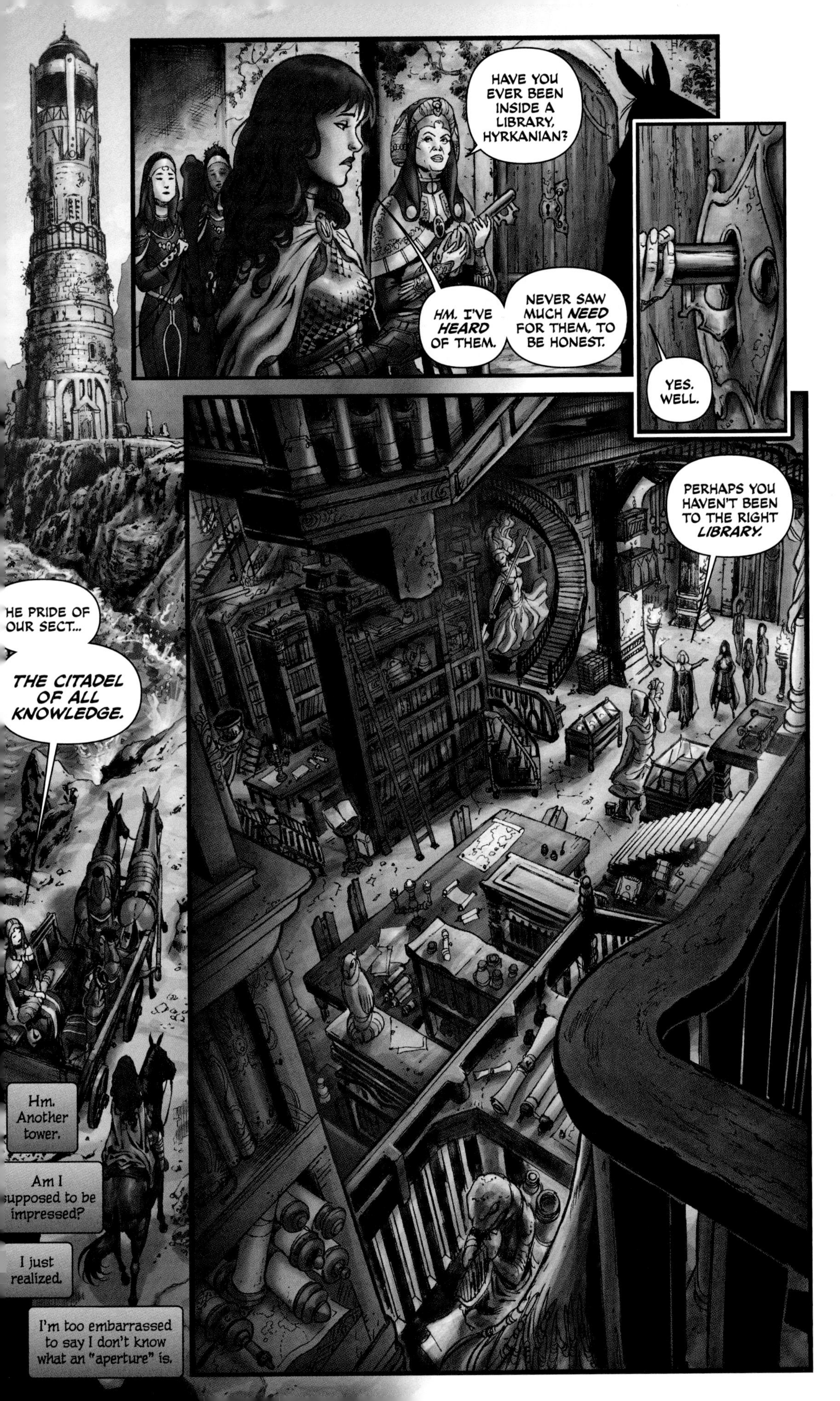

HAVE YOU EVER BEEN INSIDE A LIBRARY, HYRKANIAN?
HM. I'VE HEARD OF THEM.
NEVER SAW MUCH NEED FOR THEM, TO BE HONEST.
YES. WELL.
HE PRIDE OF OUR SECT...
THE CITADEL OF ALL KNOWLEDGE.
Hm. Another tower.
Am I supposed to be impressed?
I just realized.
I'm too embarrassed to say I don't know what an "aperture" is.
PERHAPS YOU HAVEN'T BEEN TO THE RIGHT LIBRARY.

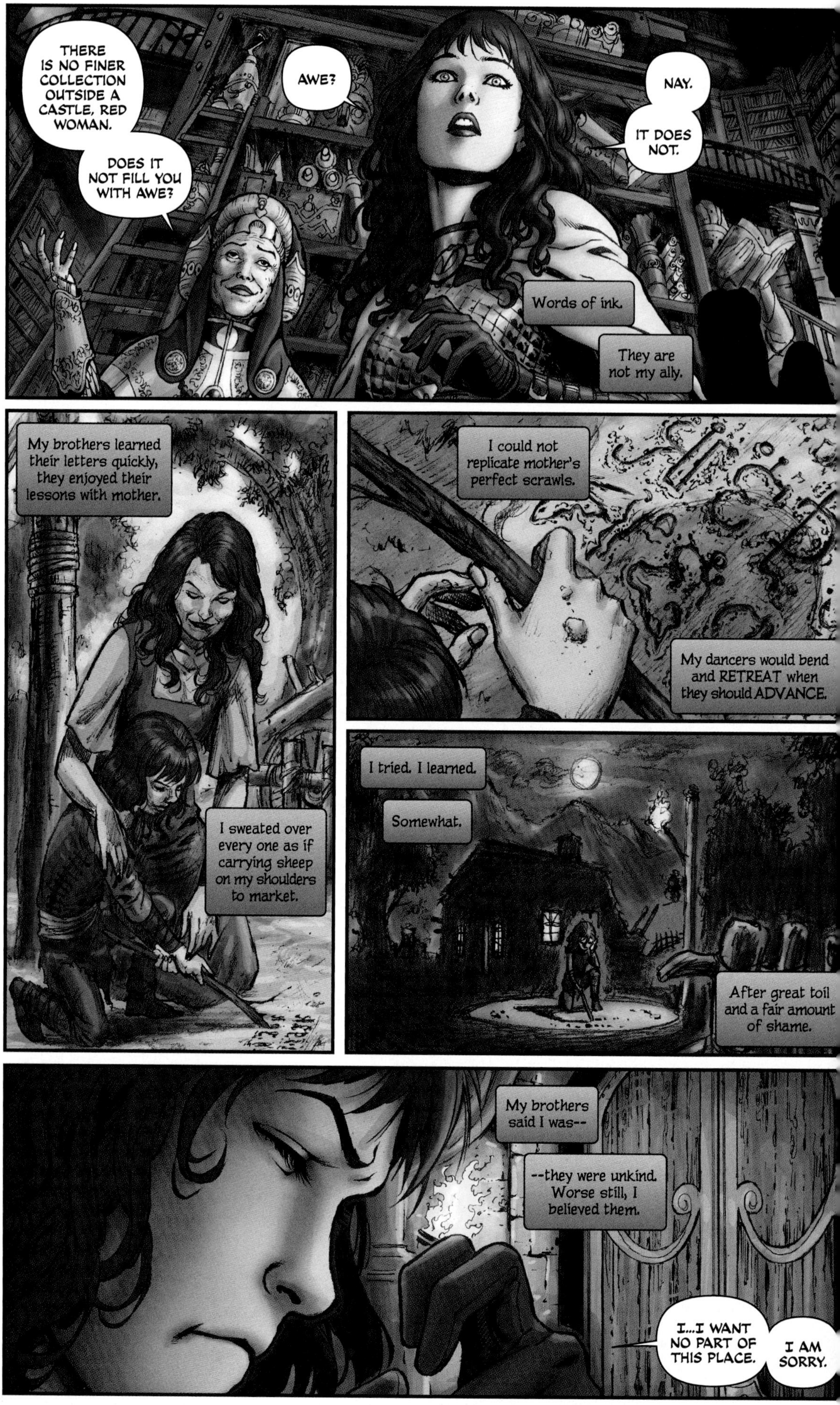
THERE IS NO FINER COLLECTION OUTSIDE A CASTLE, RED WOMAN.
DOES IT NOT FILL YOU WITH AWE?
AWE?
NAY.
IT DOES NOT.
Words of ink.
They are not my ally.
My brothers learned their letters quickly, they enjoyed their lessons with mother.
I sweated over every one as if carrying sheep on my shoulders to market.
I could not replicate mother's perfect scrawls.
My dancers would bend and RETREAT when they should ADVANCE.
I tried. I learned.
Somewhat.
After great toil and a fair amount of shame.
My brothers said I was--
--they were unkind. Worse still, I believed them.
I...I WANT NO PART OF THIS PLACE.
I AM SORRY.

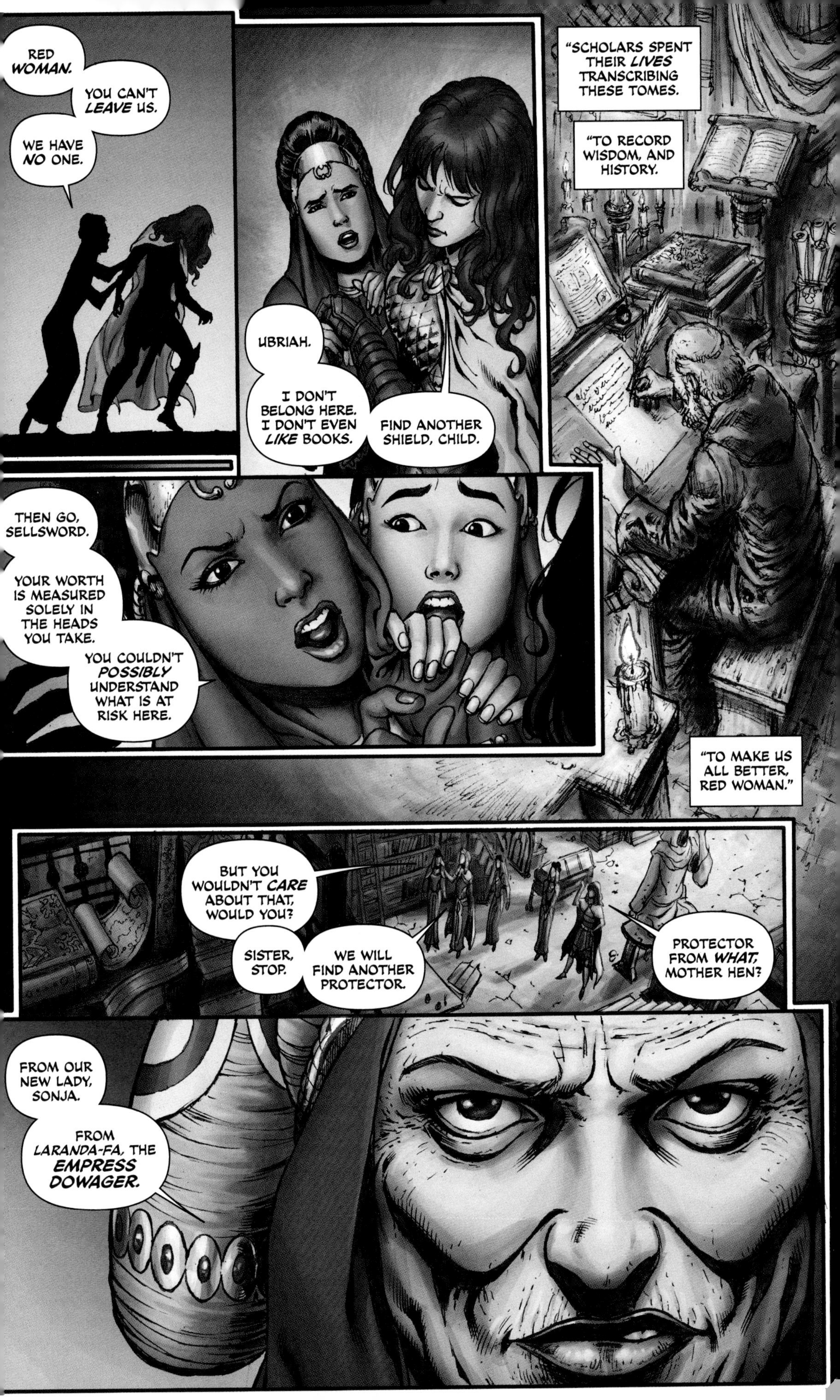

RED WOMAN.
YOU CAN'T LEAVE US.
WE HAVE NO ONE.
UBRIAH.
I DON'T BELONG HERE. I DON'T EVEN LIKE BOOKS.
FIND ANOTHER SHIELD, CHILD.
"SCHOLARS SPENT THEIR LIVES TRANSCRIBING THESE TOMES.
"TO RECORD WISDOM, AND HISTORY.
THEN GO, SELLSWORD.
YOUR WORTH IS MEASURED SOLELY IN THE HEADS YOU TAKE.
YOU COULDN'T POSSIBLY UNDERSTAND WHAT IS AT RISK HERE.
"TO MAKE US ALL BETTER, RED WOMAN."
BUT YOU WOULDN'T CARE ABOUT THAT, WOULD YOU?
SISTER, STOP.
WE WILL FIND ANOTHER PROTECTOR.
PROTECTOR FROM WHAT, MOTHER HEN?
FROM OUR NEW LADY, SONJA.
FROM LARANDA-FA, THE EMPRESS DOWAGER.

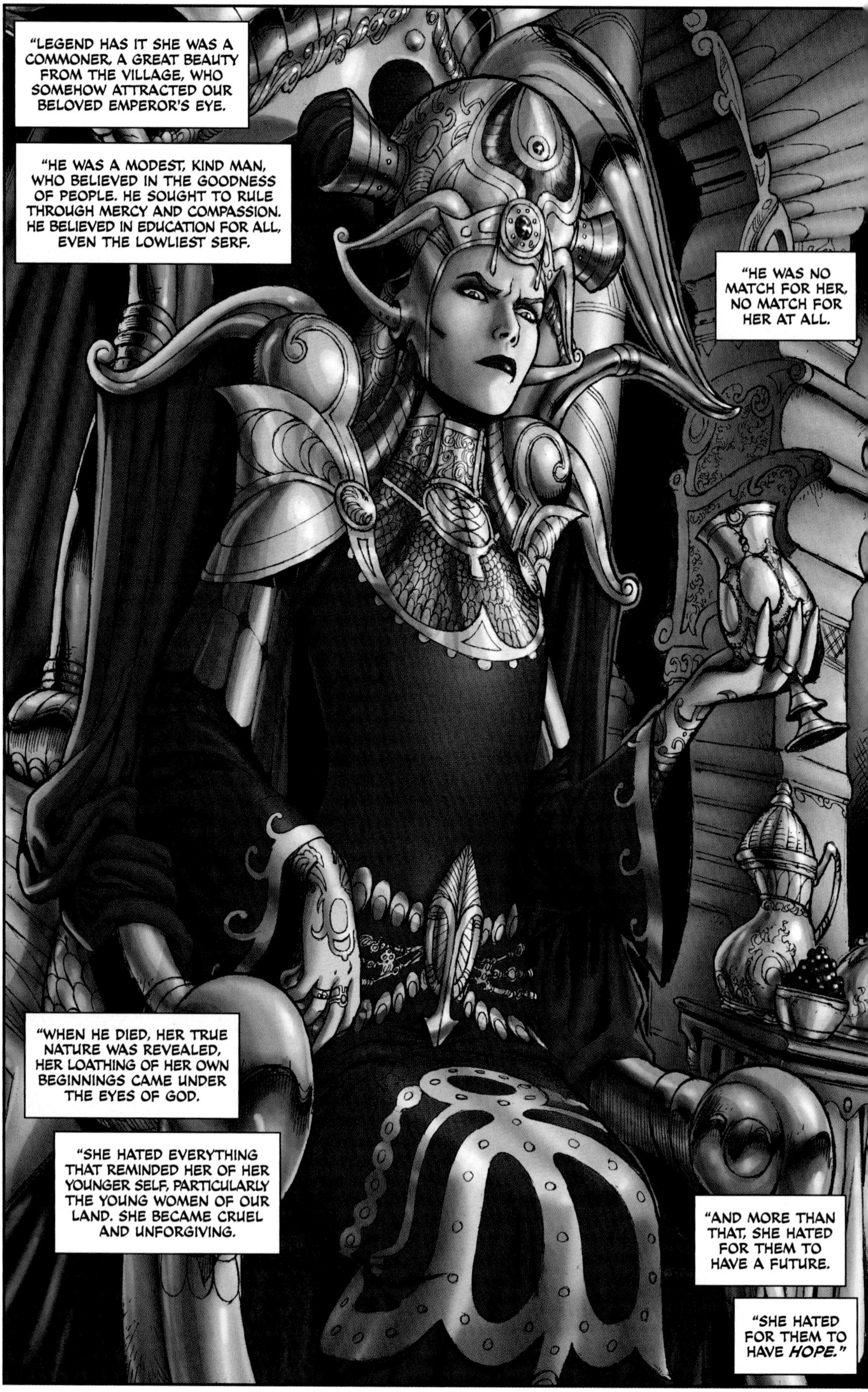
"LEGEND HAS IT SHE WAS A COMMONER, A GREAT BEAUTY FROM THE VILLAGE, WHO SOMEHOW ATTRACTED OUR BELOVED EMPEROR'S EYE.
"HE WAS A MODEST, KIND MAN, WHO BELIEVED IN THE GOODNESS OF PEOPLE. HE SOUGHT TO RULE THROUGH MERCY AND COMPASSION. HE BELIEVED IN EDUCATION FOR ALL, EVEN THE LOWLIEST SERF.
"HE WAS NO MATCH FOR HER, NO MATCH FOR HER AT ALL.
"WHEN HE DIED, HER TRUE NATURE WAS REVEALED, HER LOATHING OF HER OWN BEGINNINGS CAME UNDER THE EYES OF GOD.
"SHE HATED EVERYTHING THAT REMINDED HER OF HER YOUNGER SELF, PARTICULARLY THE YOUNG WOMEN OF OUR LAND. SHE BECAME CRUEL AND UNFORGIVING.
"AND MORE THAN THAT, SHE HATED FOR THEM TO HAVE A FUTURE.
"SHE HATED FOR THEM TO HAVE *HOPE.*"

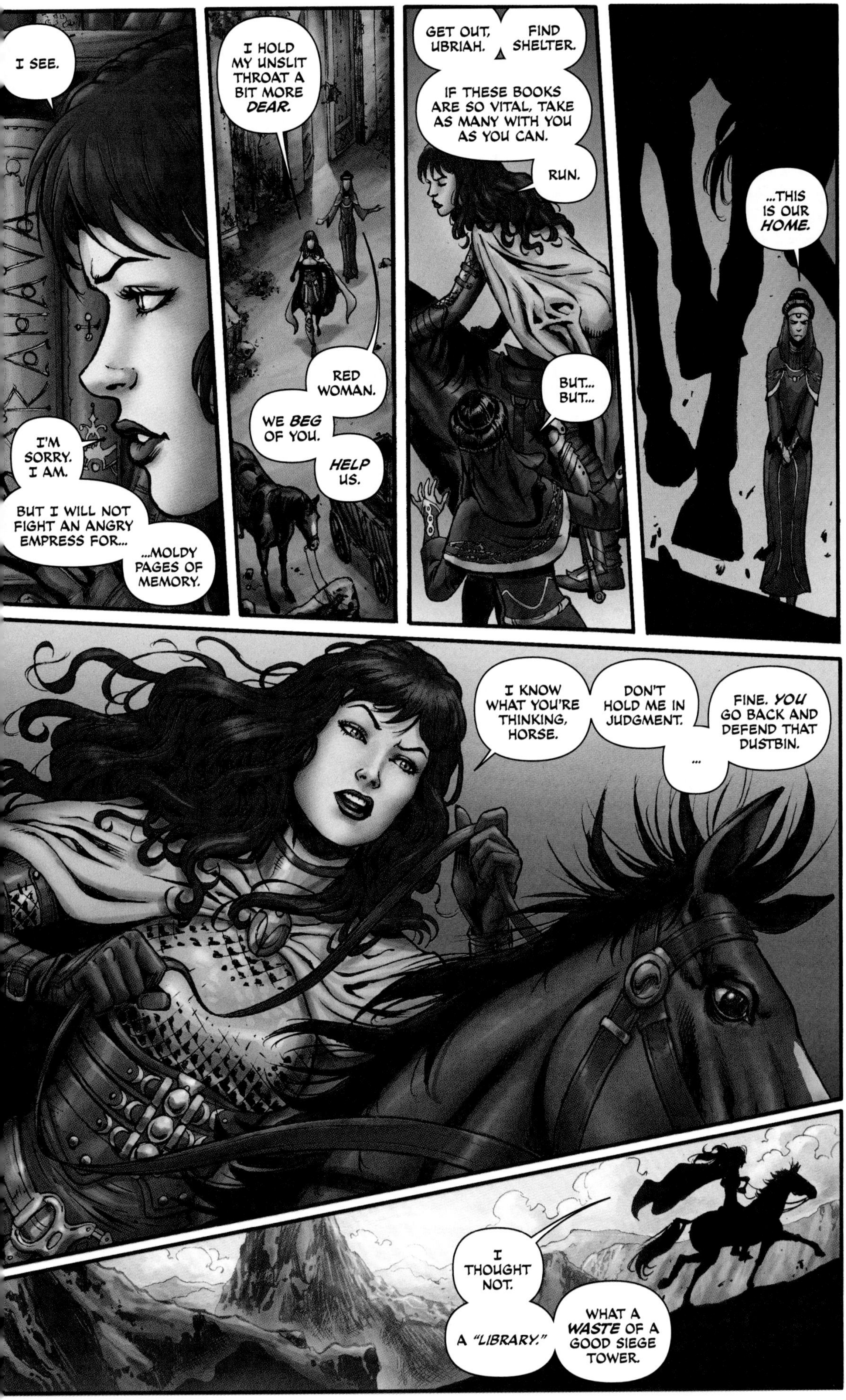
I SEE.
I'M SORRY. I AM.
BUT I WILL NOT FIGHT AN ANGRY EMPRESS FOR...
...MOLDY PAGES OF MEMORY.
I HOLD MY UNSLIT THROAT A BIT MORE *DEAR.*
RED WOMAN.
WE *BEG* OF YOU.
HELP US.
GET OUT, UBRIAH.
FIND SHELTER.
IF THESE BOOKS ARE SO VITAL, TAKE AS MANY WITH YOU AS YOU CAN.
RUN.
BUT... BUT...
...THIS IS OUR *HOME.*
I KNOW WHAT YOU'RE THINKING, HORSE.
DON'T HOLD ME IN JUDGMENT.
...
FINE. *YOU* GO BACK AND DEFEND THAT DUSTBIN.
I THOUGHT NOT.
A *"LIBRARY."*
WHAT A *WASTE* OF A GOOD SIEGE TOWER.

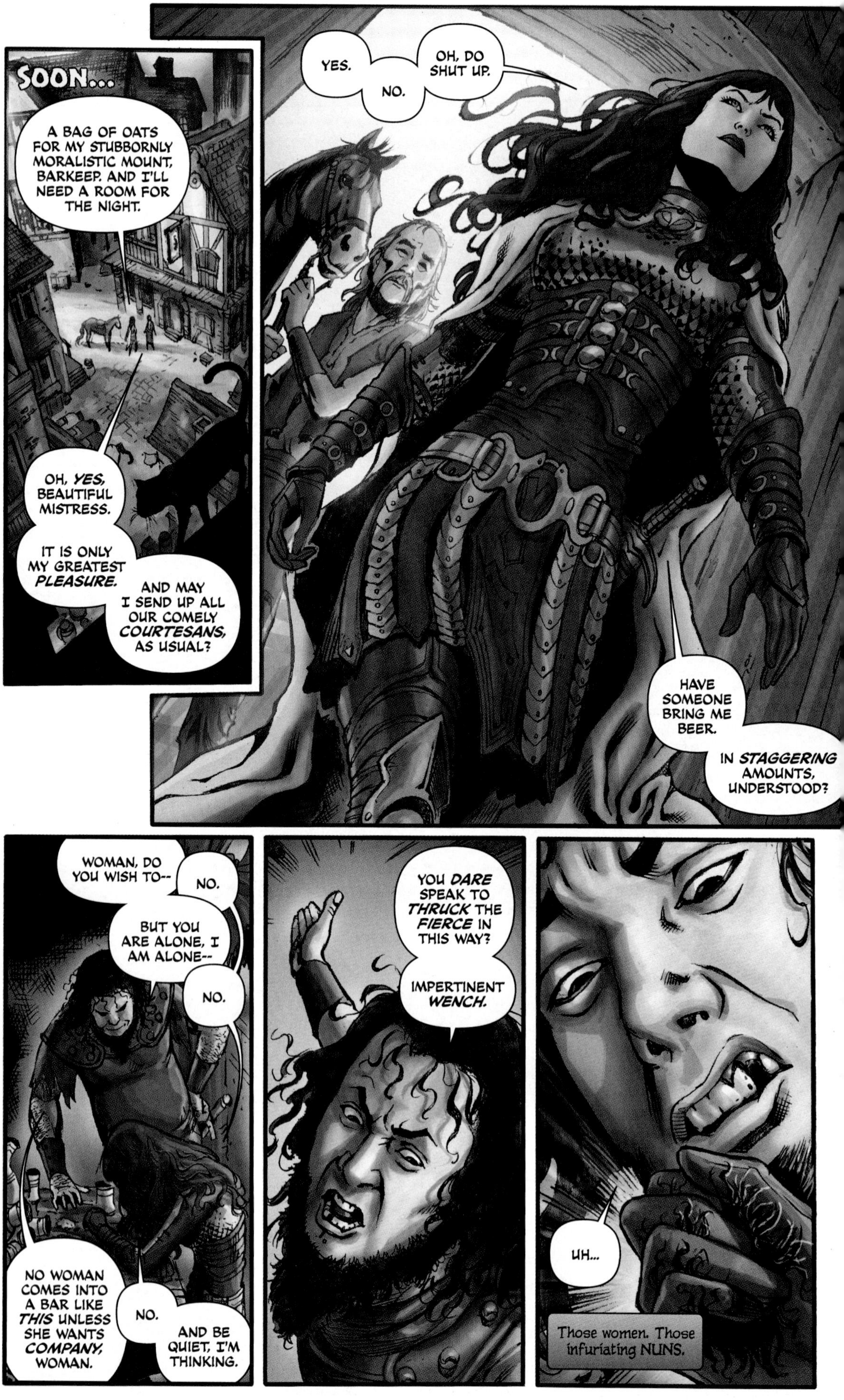
SOON...
A BAG OF OATS FOR MY STUBBORNLY MORALISTIC MOUNT, BARKEEP. AND I'LL NEED A ROOM FOR THE NIGHT.
OH, YES, BEAUTIFUL MISTRESS.
IT IS ONLY MY GREATEST PLEASURE.
AND MAY I SEND UP ALL OUR COMELY COURTESANS, AS USUAL?
YES.
NO.
OH, DO SHUT UP.
HAVE SOMEONE BRING ME BEER.
IN STAGGERING AMOUNTS, UNDERSTOOD?
WOMAN, DO YOU WISH TO--
NO.
BUT YOU ARE ALONE, I AM ALONE--
NO.
NO WOMAN COMES INTO A BAR LIKE THIS UNLESS SHE WANTS COMPANY, WOMAN.
NO.
AND BE QUIET, I'M THINKING.
YOU DARE SPEAK TO THRUCK THE FIERCE IN THIS WAY?
IMPERTINENT WENCH.
UH...
Those women. Those infuriating NUNS.

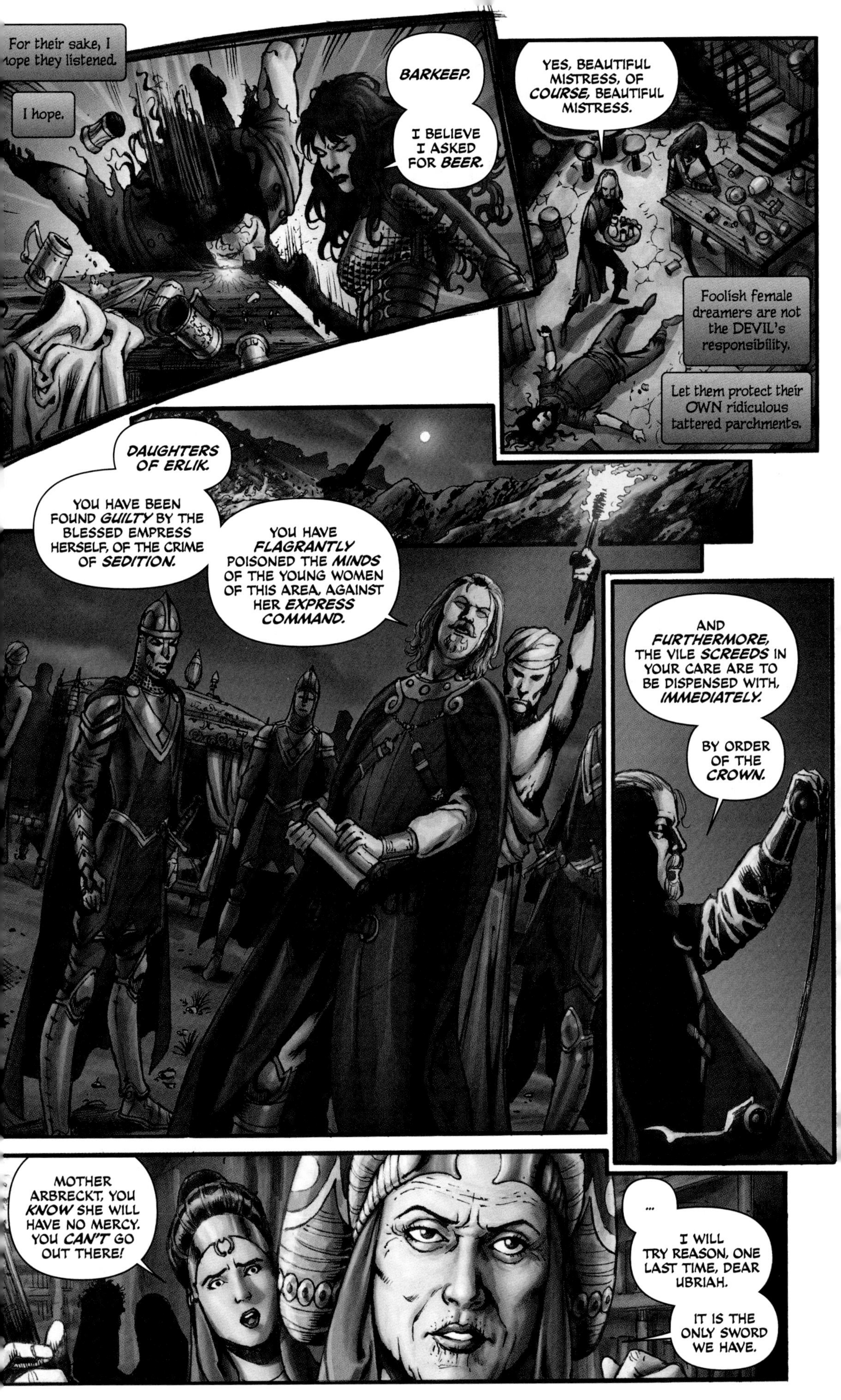
For their sake, I hope they listened.
I hope.
BARKEEP.
I BELIEVE I ASKED FOR BEER.
YES, BEAUTIFUL MISTRESS, OF COURSE, BEAUTIFUL MISTRESS.
Foolish female dreamers are not the DEVIL's responsibility.
Let them protect their OWN ridiculous tattered parchments.
DAUGHTERS OF ERLIK.
YOU HAVE BEEN FOUND GUILTY BY THE BLESSED EMPRESS HERSELF, OF THE CRIME OF SEDITION.
YOU HAVE FLAGRANTLY POISONED THE MINDS OF THE YOUNG WOMEN OF THIS AREA, AGAINST HER EXPRESS COMMAND.
AND FURTHERMORE, THE VILE SCREEDS IN YOUR CARE ARE TO BE DISPENSED WITH, IMMEDIATELY.
BY ORDER OF THE CROWN.
MOTHER ARBRECKT, YOU KNOW SHE WILL HAVE NO MERCY. YOU CAN'T GO OUT THERE!
...
I WILL TRY REASON, ONE LAST TIME, DEAR UBRIAH.
IT IS THE ONLY SWORD WE HAVE.

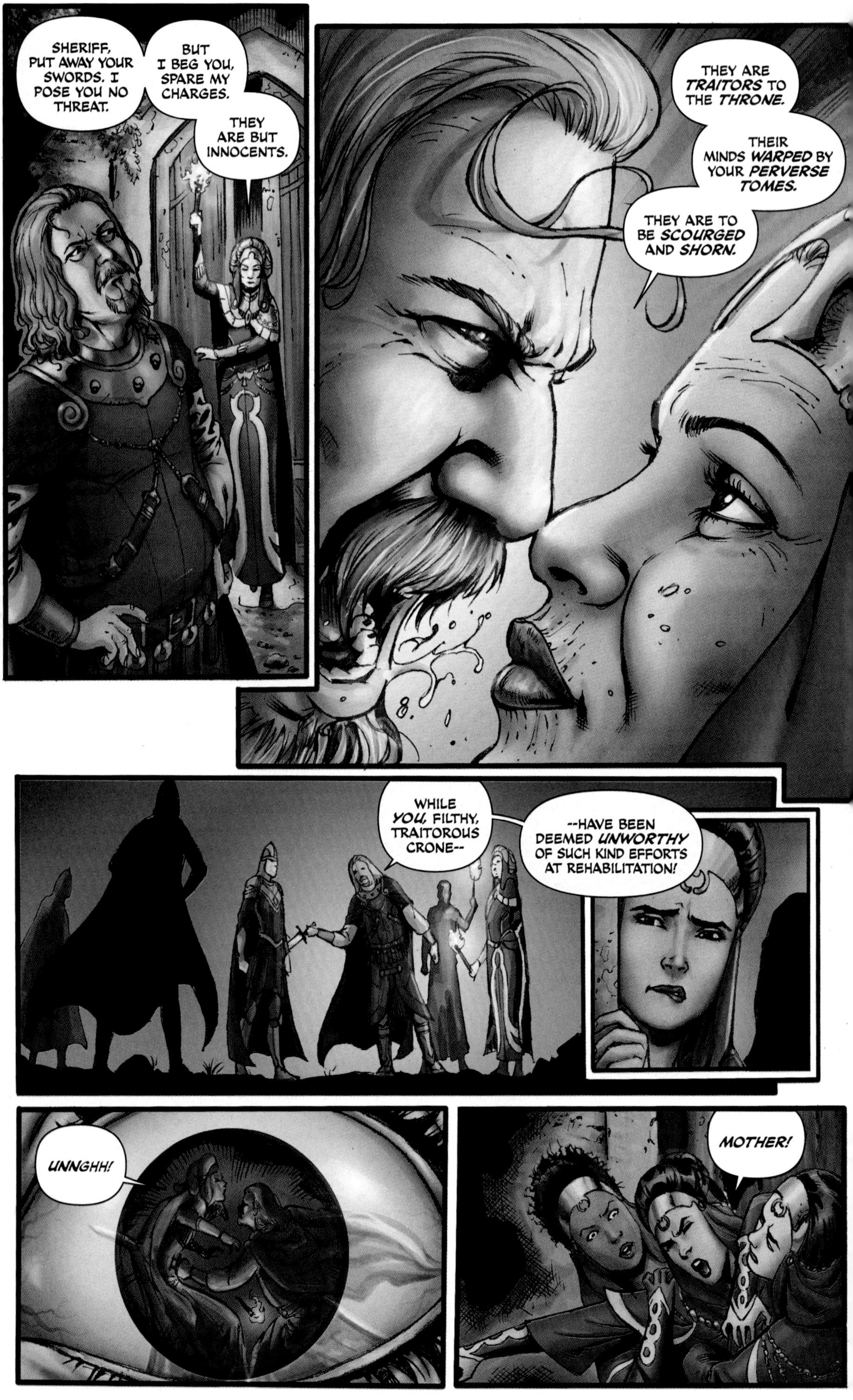
SHERIFF, PUT AWAY YOUR SWORDS. I POSE YOU NO THREAT.
BUT I BEG YOU, SPARE MY CHARGES.
THEY ARE BUT INNOCENTS.
THEY ARE TRAITORS TO THE THRONE.
THEIR MINDS WARPED BY YOUR PERVERSE TOMES.
THEY ARE TO BE SCOURGED AND SHORN.
WHILE YOU, FILTHY, TRAITOROUS CRONE--
--HAVE BEEN DEEMED UNWORTHY OF SUCH KIND EFFORTS AT REHABILITATION!
UNNGHH!
MOTHER!

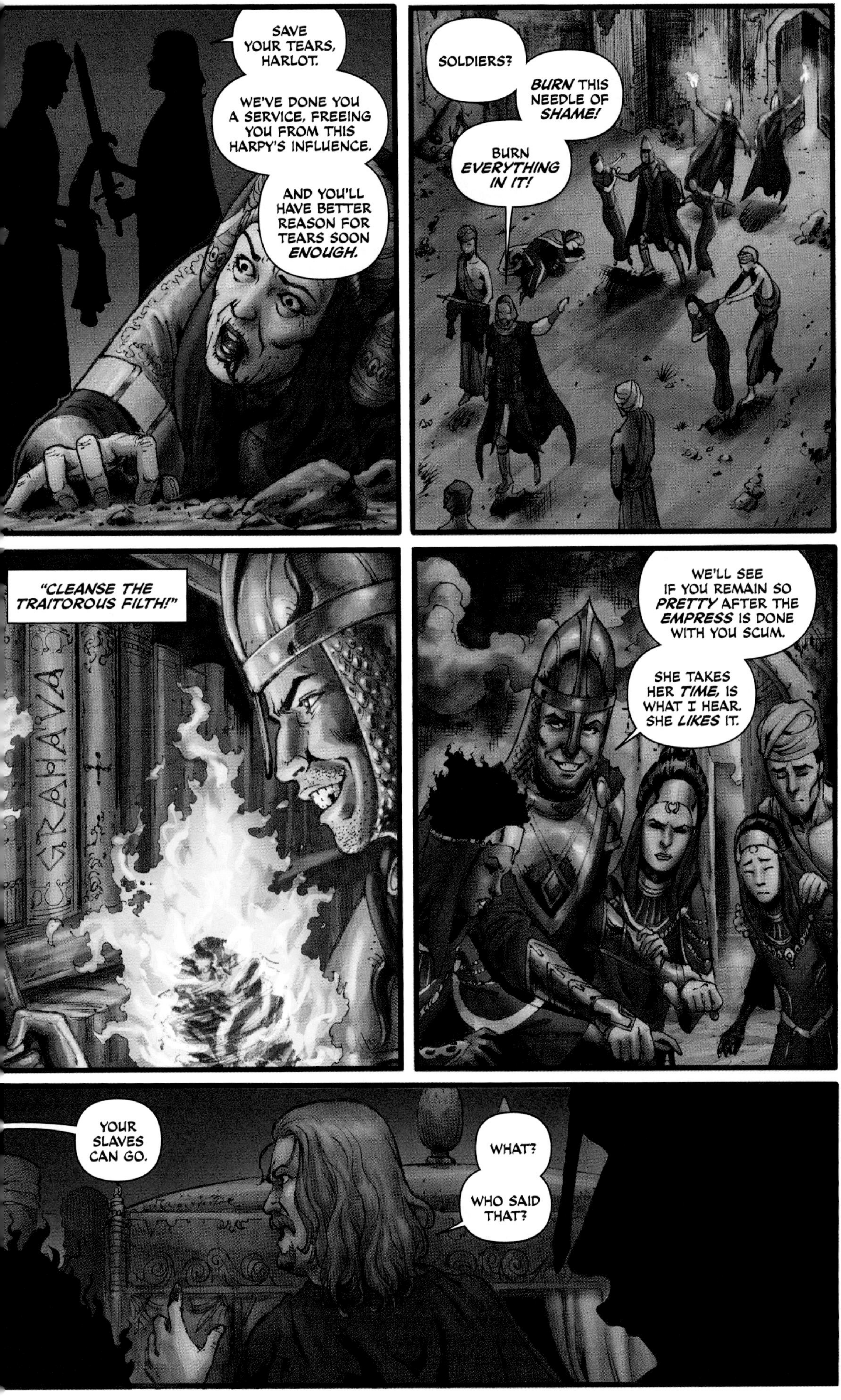
SAVE YOUR TEARS, HARLOT.
WE'VE DONE YOU A SERVICE, FREEING YOU FROM THIS HARPY'S INFLUENCE.
AND YOU'LL HAVE BETTER REASON FOR TEARS SOON *ENOUGH.*
SOLDIERS?
BURN THIS NEEDLE OF *SHAME!*
BURN *EVERYTHING IN IT!*
"CLEANSE THE TRAITOROUS FILTH!"
GRAHAVA
WE'LL SEE IF YOU REMAIN SO *PRETTY* AFTER THE *EMPRESS* IS DONE WITH YOU SCUM.
SHE TAKES HER *TIME,* IS WHAT I HEAR. SHE *LIKES* IT.
YOUR SLAVES CAN GO.
WHAT?
WHO SAID THAT?

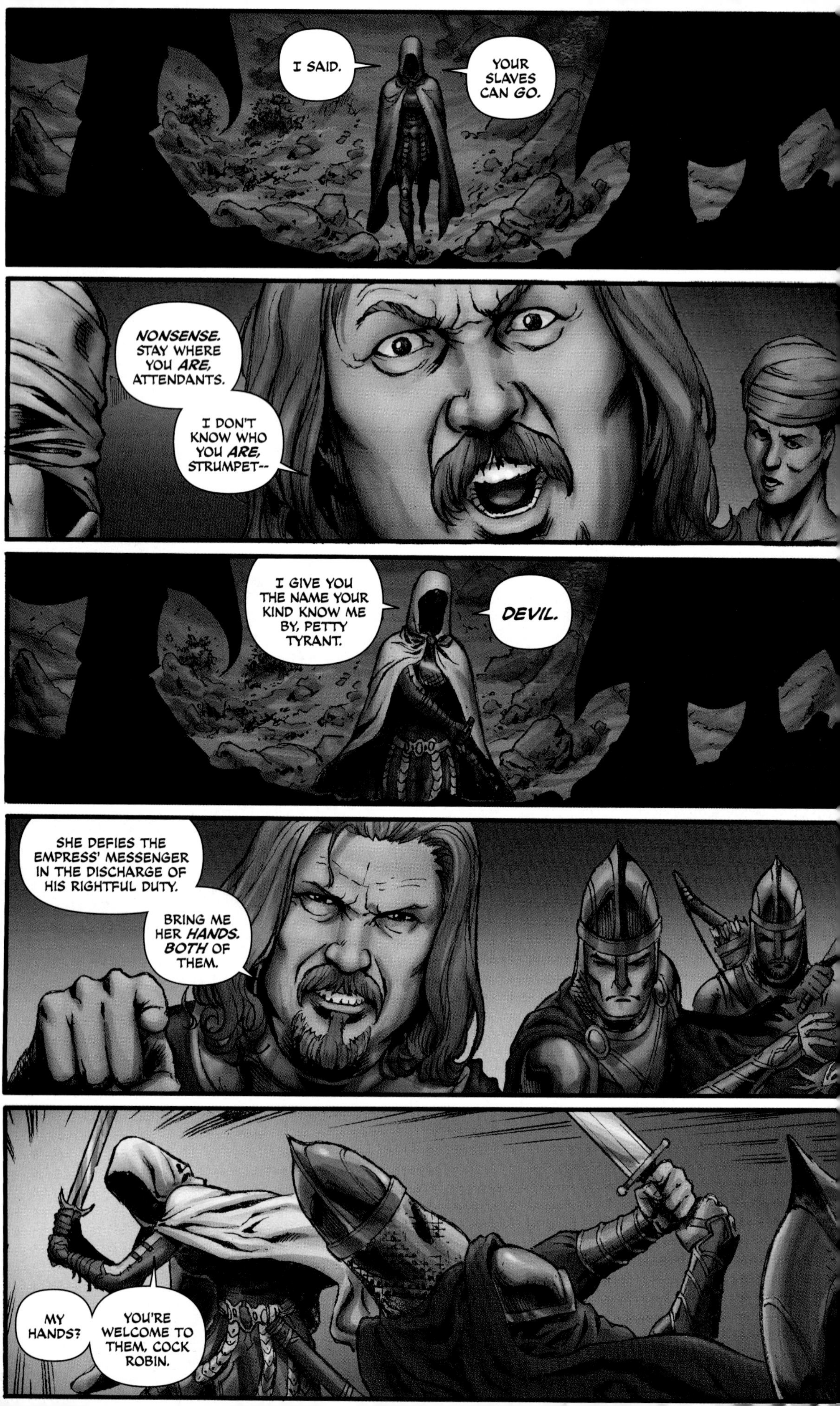
I SAID.
YOUR SLAVES CAN *GO.*
NONSENSE. STAY WHERE YOU *ARE,* ATTENDANTS.
I DON'T KNOW WHO YOU *ARE,* STRUMPET--
I GIVE YOU THE NAME YOUR KIND KNOW ME BY, PETTY TYRANT.
DEVIL.
SHE DEFIES THE EMPRESS' MESSENGER IN THE DISCHARGE OF HIS RIGHTFUL DUTY.
BRING ME HER *HANDS. BOTH* OF THEM.
MY HANDS?
YOU'RE WELCOME TO THEM, COCK ROBIN.

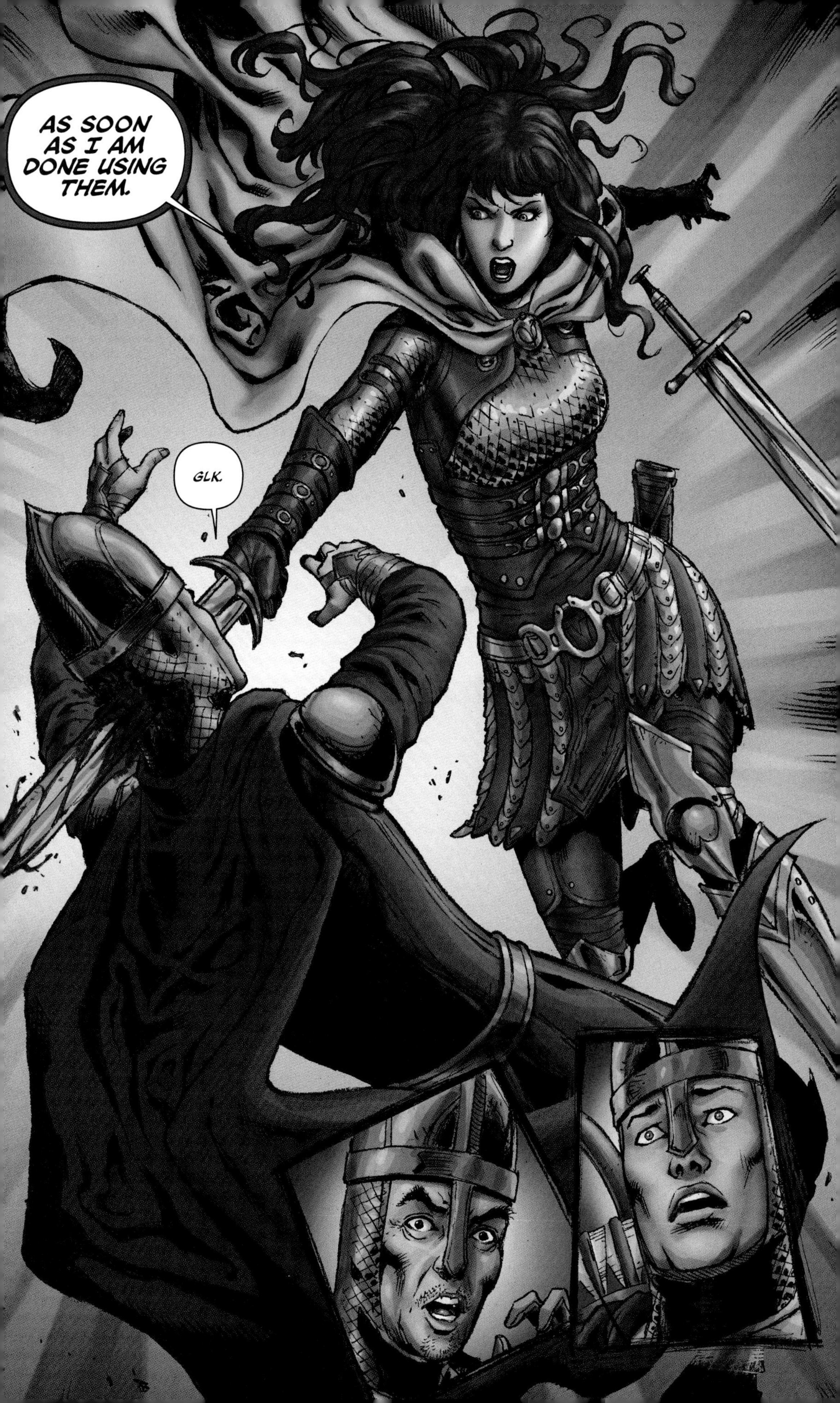
AS SOON AS I AM DONE USING THEM.
GLK.

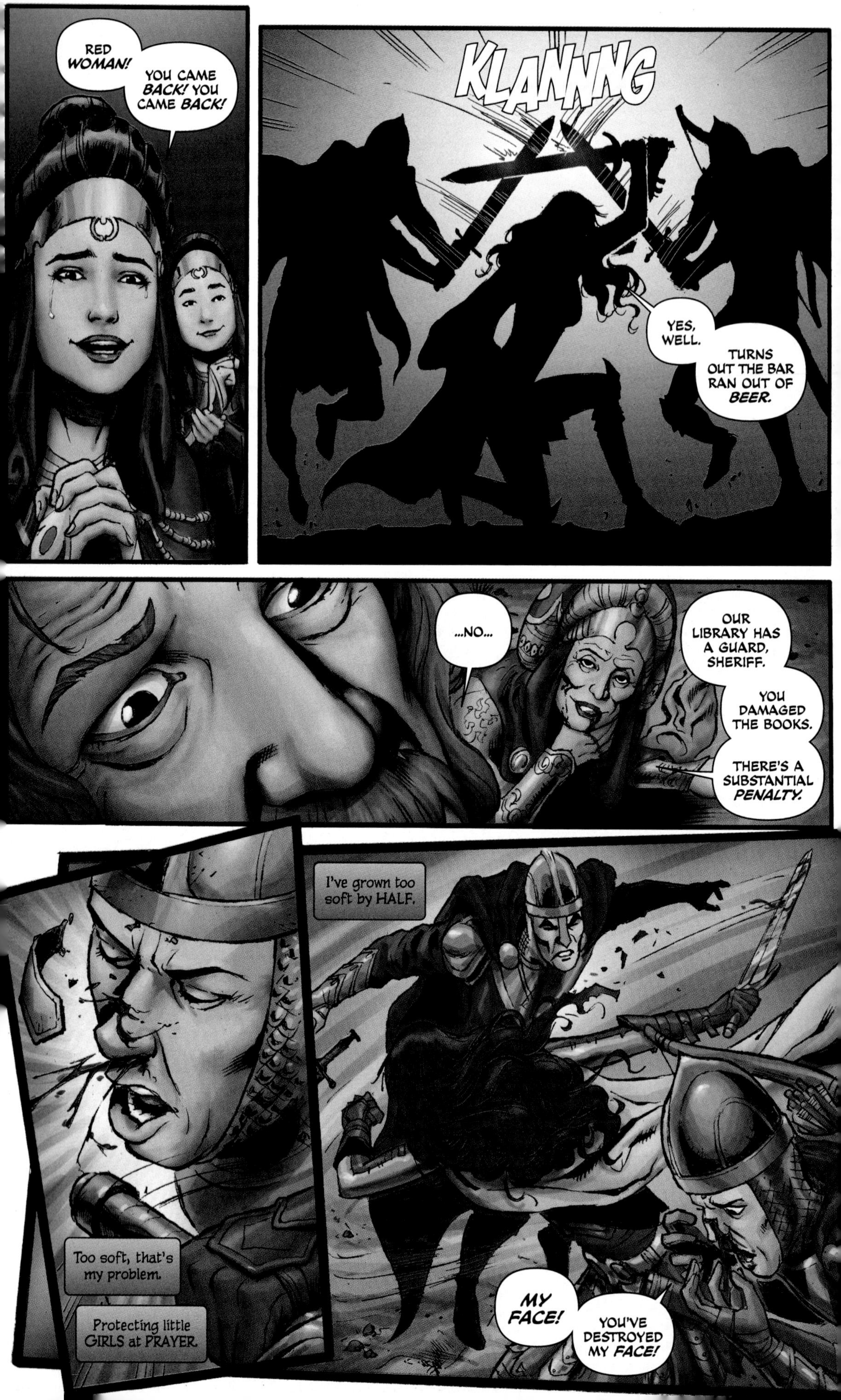
RED WOMAN!
YOU CAME BACK! YOU CAME BACK!
KLANNNG
YES, WELL.
TURNS OUT THE BAR RAN OUT OF BEER.
...NO...
OUR LIBRARY HAS A GUARD, SHERIFF.
YOU DAMAGED THE BOOKS.
THERE'S A SUBSTANTIAL PENALTY.
Too soft, that's my problem.
Protecting little GIRLS at PRAYER.
I've grown too soft by HALF.
MY FACE!
YOU'VE DESTROYED MY FACE!

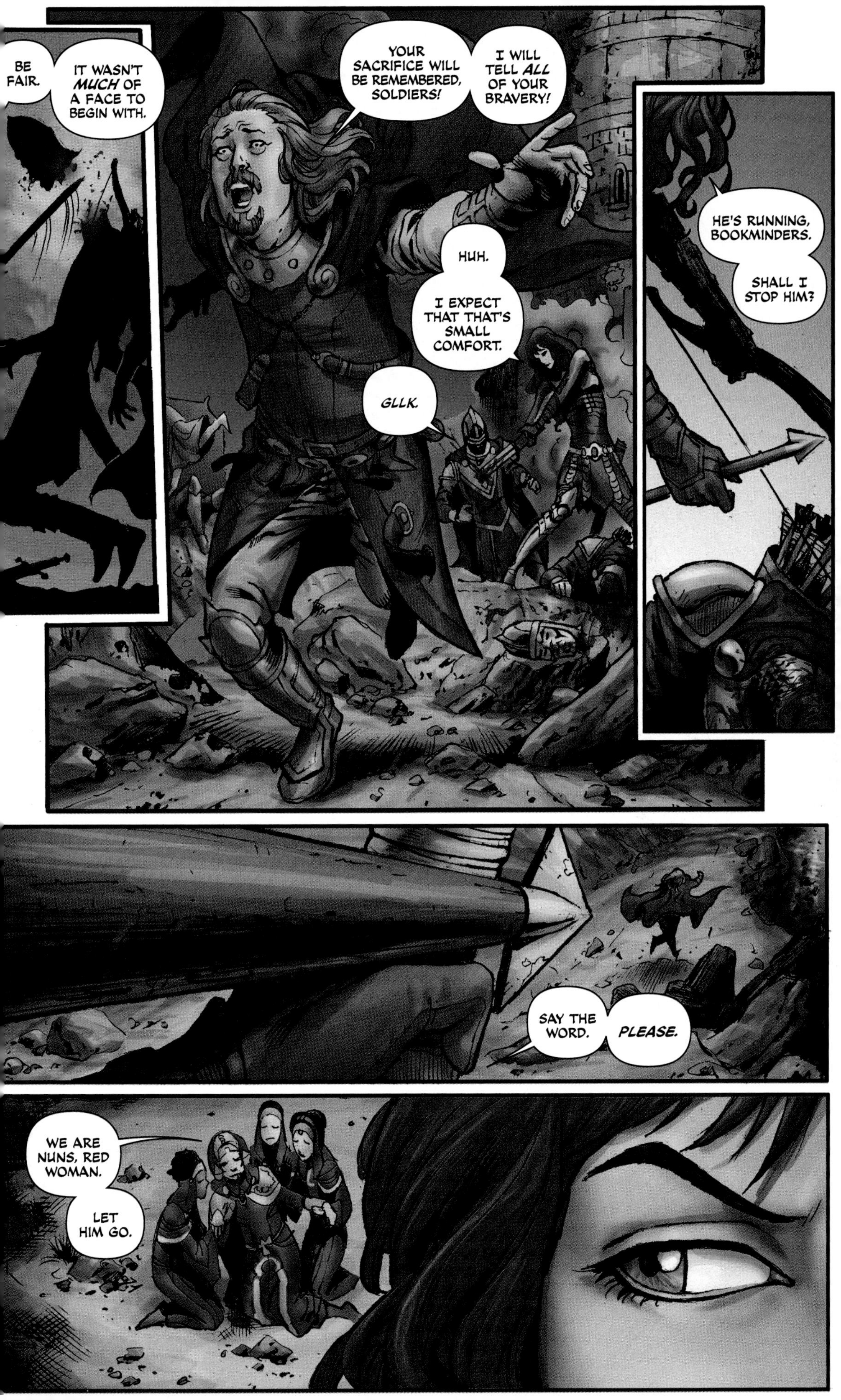

BE FAIR.
IT WASN'T *MUCH* OF A FACE TO BEGIN WITH.
YOUR SACRIFICE WILL BE REMEMBERED, SOLDIERS!
I WILL TELL *ALL* OF YOUR BRAVERY!
HUH.
I EXPECT THAT THAT'S SMALL COMFORT.
GLLK.
HE'S RUNNING, BOOKMINDERS.
SHALL I STOP HIM?
SAY THE WORD.
PLEASE.
WE ARE NUNS, RED WOMAN.
LET HIM GO.

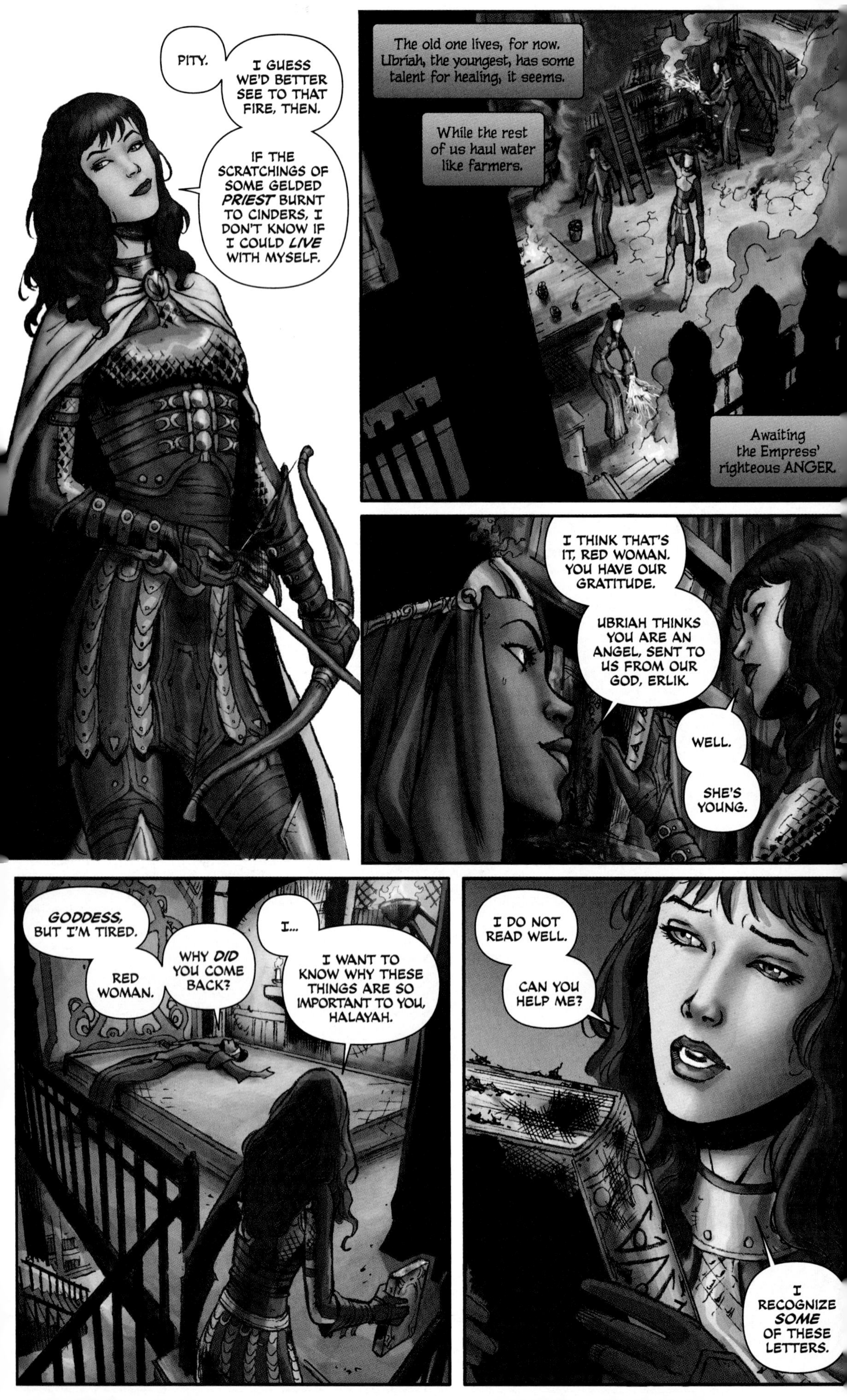

PITY.
I GUESS WE'D BETTER SEE TO THAT FIRE, THEN.
IF THE SCRATCHINGS OF SOME GELDED *PRIEST* BURNT TO CINDERS, I DON'T KNOW IF I COULD *LIVE* WITH MYSELF.
The old one lives, for now. Ubriah, the youngest, has some talent for healing, it seems.
While the rest of us haul water like farmers.
Awaiting the Empress' righteous ANGER.
I THINK THAT'S IT, RED WOMAN. YOU HAVE OUR GRATITUDE.
UBRIAH THINKS YOU ARE AN ANGEL, SENT TO US FROM OUR GOD, ERLIK.
WELL.
SHE'S YOUNG.
GODDESS, BUT I'M TIRED.
RED WOMAN.
WHY *DID* YOU COME BACK?
I...
I WANT TO KNOW WHY THESE THINGS ARE SO IMPORTANT TO YOU, HALAYAH.
I DO NOT READ WELL.
CAN YOU HELP ME?
I RECOGNIZE *SOME* OF THESE LETTERS.

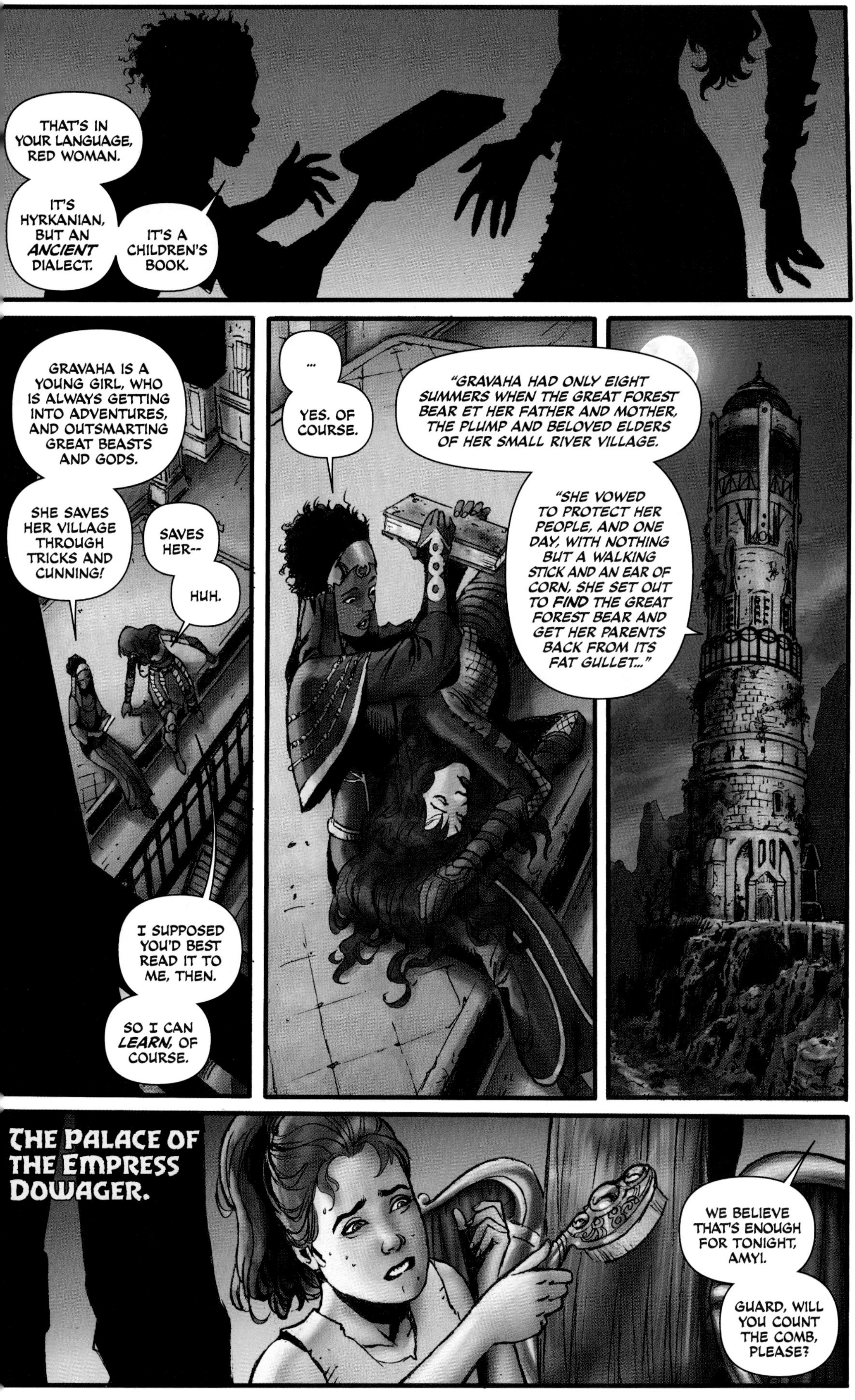
THAT'S IN YOUR LANGUAGE, RED WOMAN.
IT'S HYRKANIAN, BUT AN *ANCIENT* DIALECT.
IT'S A CHILDREN'S BOOK.
GRAVAHA IS A YOUNG GIRL, WHO IS ALWAYS GETTING INTO ADVENTURES, AND OUTSMARTING GREAT BEASTS AND GODS.
SHE SAVES HER VILLAGE THROUGH TRICKS AND CUNNING!
SAVES HER--
HUH.
I SUPPOSED YOU'D BEST READ IT TO ME, THEN.
SO I CAN *LEARN*, OF COURSE.
...
YES. OF COURSE.
"GRAVAHA HAD ONLY EIGHT SUMMERS WHEN THE GREAT FOREST BEAR ET HER FATHER AND MOTHER, THE PLUMP AND BELOVED ELDERS OF HER SMALL RIVER VILLAGE.
"SHE VOWED TO PROTECT HER PEOPLE, AND ONE DAY, WITH NOTHING BUT A WALKING STICK AND AN EAR OF CORN, SHE SET OUT TO *FIND* THE GREAT FOREST BEAR AND GET HER PARENTS BACK FROM ITS FAT GULLET..."
THE PALACE OF THE EMPRESS DOWAGER.
WE BELIEVE THAT'S ENOUGH FOR TONIGHT, AMYI.
GUARD, WILL YOU COUNT THE COMB, PLEASE?

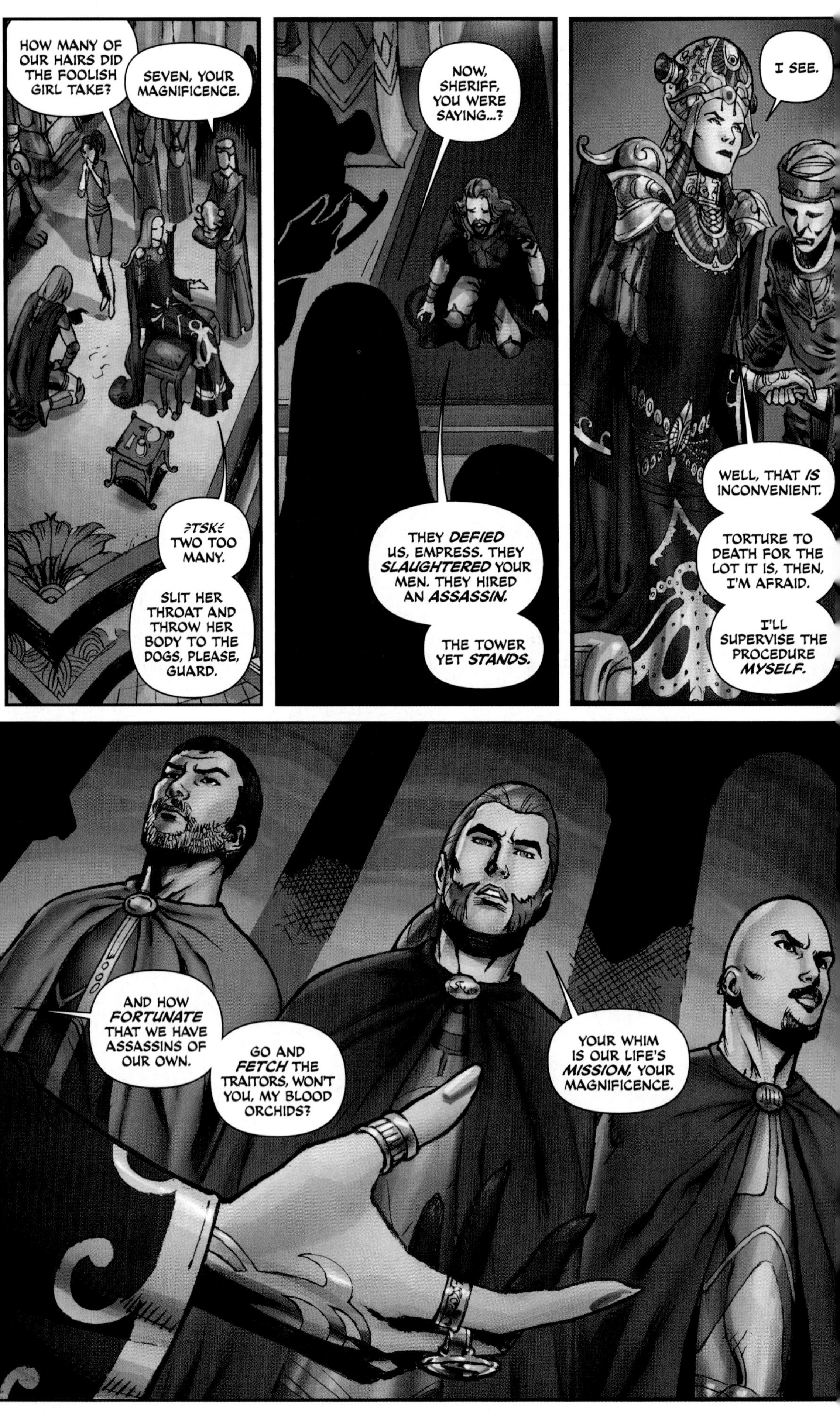
HOW MANY OF OUR HAIRS DID THE FOOLISH GIRL TAKE?
SEVEN, YOUR MAGNIFICENCE.
⸗TSK⸗ TWO TOO MANY.
SLIT HER THROAT AND THROW HER BODY TO THE DOGS, PLEASE, GUARD.
NOW, SHERIFF, YOU WERE SAYING...?
THEY *DEFIED* US, EMPRESS. THEY *SLAUGHTERED* YOUR MEN. THEY HIRED AN *ASSASSIN.*
THE TOWER YET *STANDS.*
I SEE.
WELL, THAT *IS* INCONVENIENT.
TORTURE TO DEATH FOR THE LOT IT IS, THEN, I'M AFRAID.
I'LL SUPERVISE THE PROCEDURE *MYSELF.*
AND HOW *FORTUNATE* THAT WE HAVE ASSASSINS OF OUR OWN.
GO AND *FETCH* THE TRAITORS, WON'T YOU, MY BLOOD ORCHIDS?
YOUR WHIM IS OUR LIFE'S *MISSION,* YOUR MAGNIFICENCE.

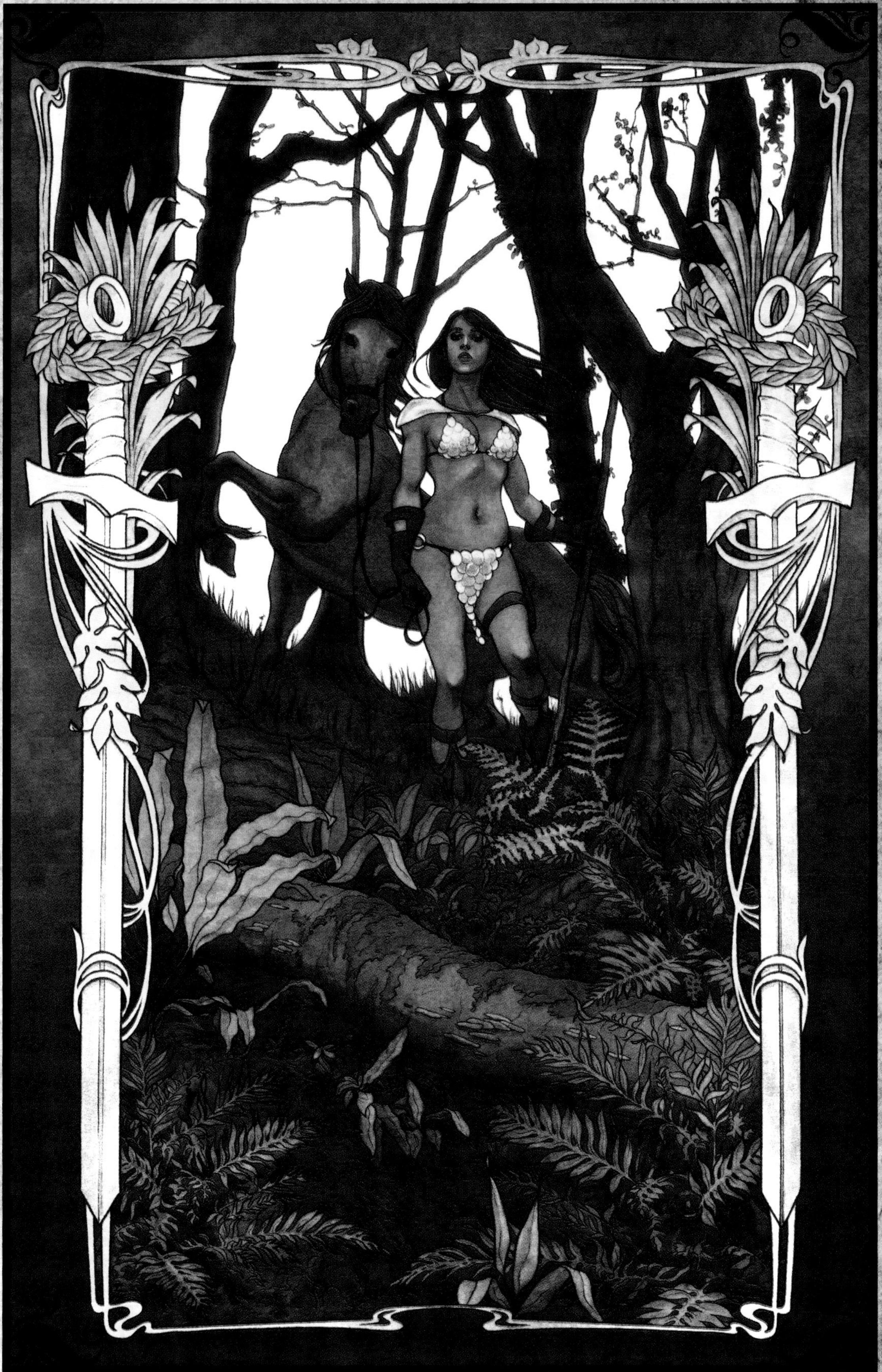

ISSUE EIGHTEEN
cover by JENNY FRISON

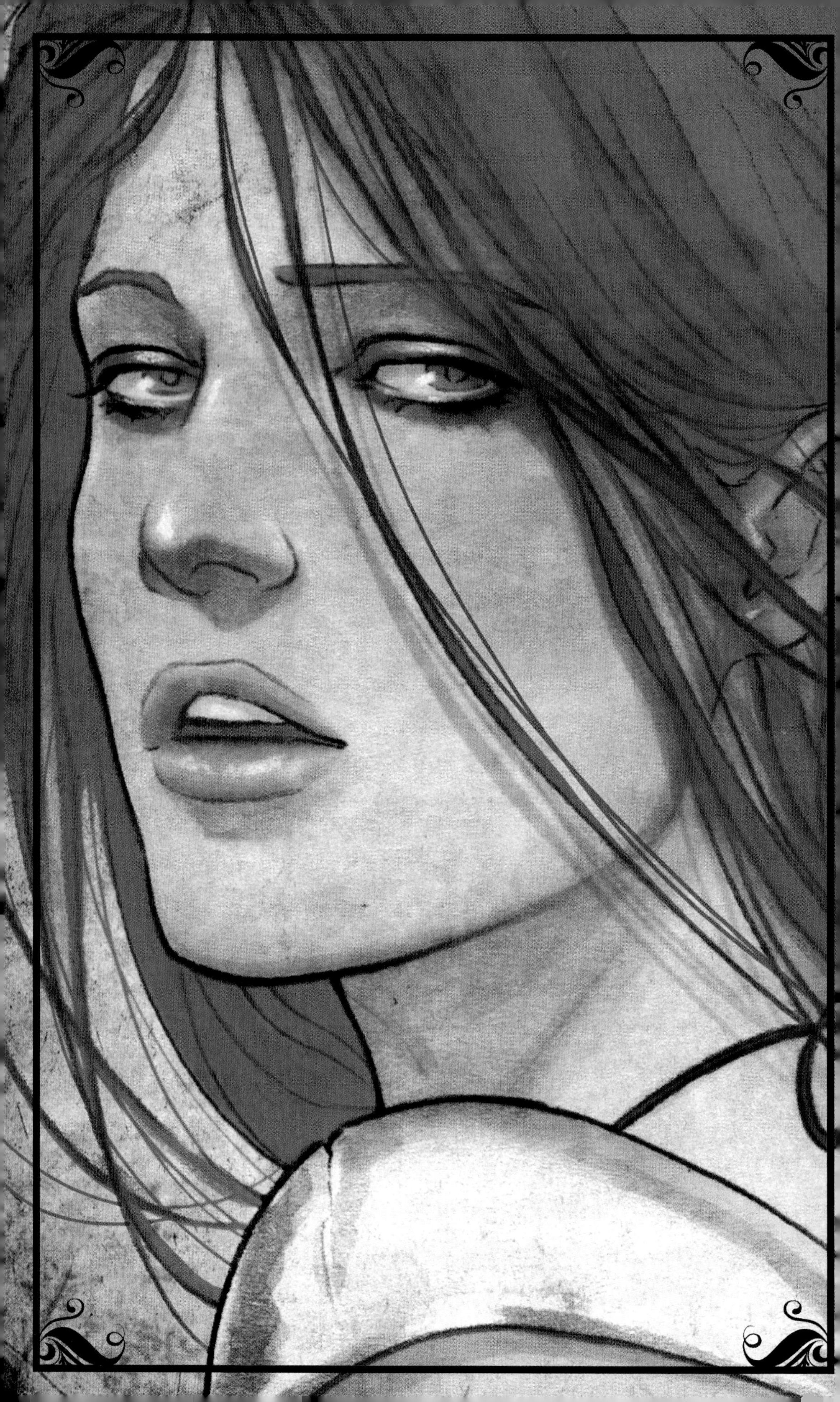

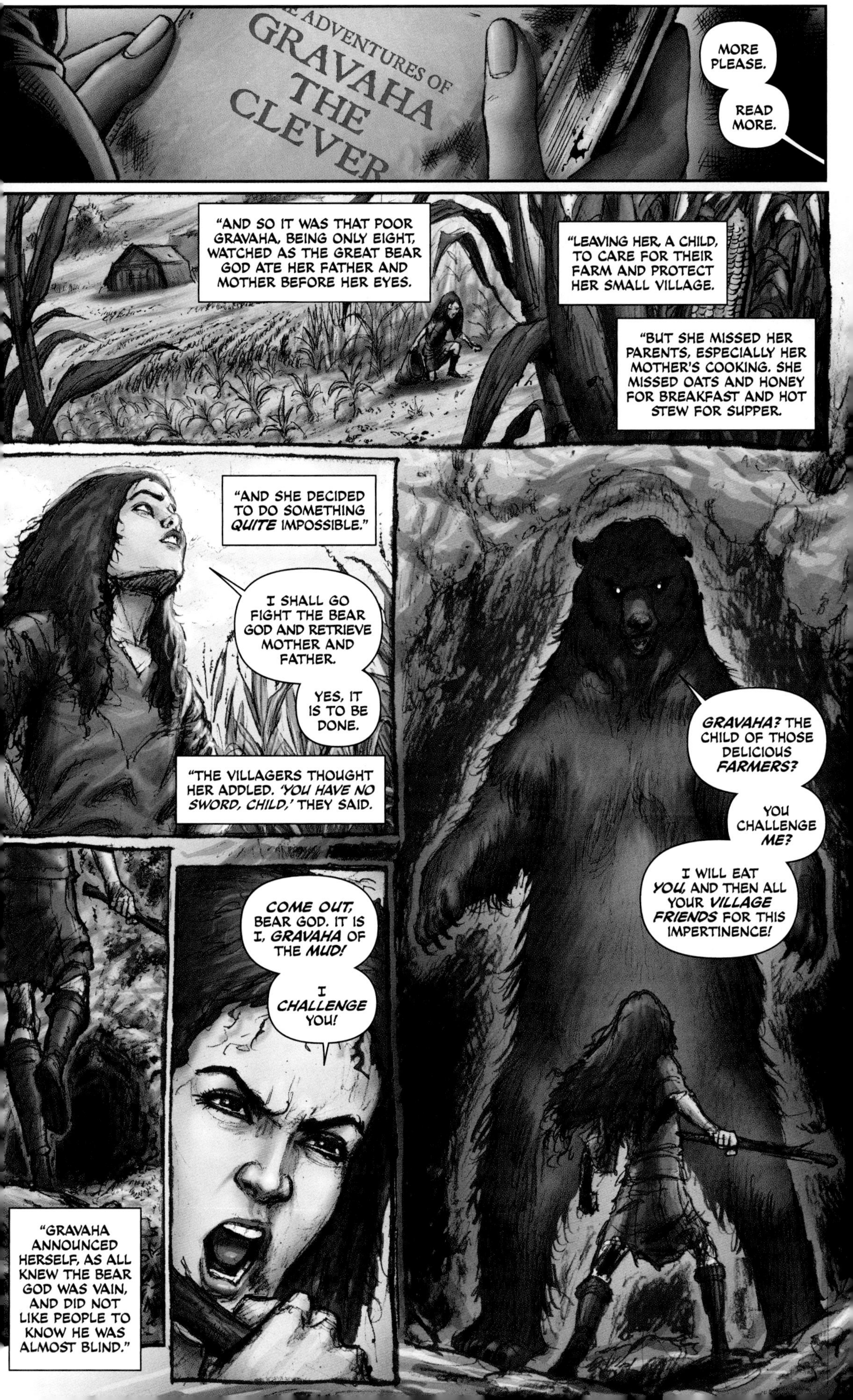
THE ADVENTURES OF GRAVAHA THE CLEVER
MORE PLEASE.
READ MORE.
"AND SO IT WAS THAT POOR GRAVAHA, BEING ONLY EIGHT, WATCHED AS THE GREAT BEAR GOD ATE HER FATHER AND MOTHER BEFORE HER EYES.
"LEAVING HER, A CHILD, TO CARE FOR THEIR FARM AND PROTECT HER SMALL VILLAGE.
"BUT SHE MISSED HER PARENTS, ESPECIALLY HER MOTHER'S COOKING. SHE MISSED OATS AND HONEY FOR BREAKFAST AND HOT STEW FOR SUPPER.
"AND SHE DECIDED TO DO SOMETHING *QUITE* IMPOSSIBLE."
I SHALL GO FIGHT THE BEAR GOD AND RETRIEVE MOTHER AND FATHER.
YES, IT IS TO BE DONE.
"THE VILLAGERS THOUGHT HER ADDLED. *'YOU HAVE NO SWORD, CHILD,'* THEY SAID.
COME OUT, BEAR GOD. IT IS I, *GRAVAHA* OF THE *MUD!*
I *CHALLENGE* YOU!
"GRAVAHA ANNOUNCED HERSELF, AS ALL KNEW THE BEAR GOD WAS VAIN, AND DID NOT LIKE PEOPLE TO KNOW HE WAS ALMOST BLIND."
GRAVAHA? THE CHILD OF THOSE DELICIOUS *FARMERS?*
YOU CHALLENGE *ME?*
I WILL EAT *YOU,* AND THEN ALL YOUR *VILLAGE FRIENDS* FOR THIS IMPERTINENCE!

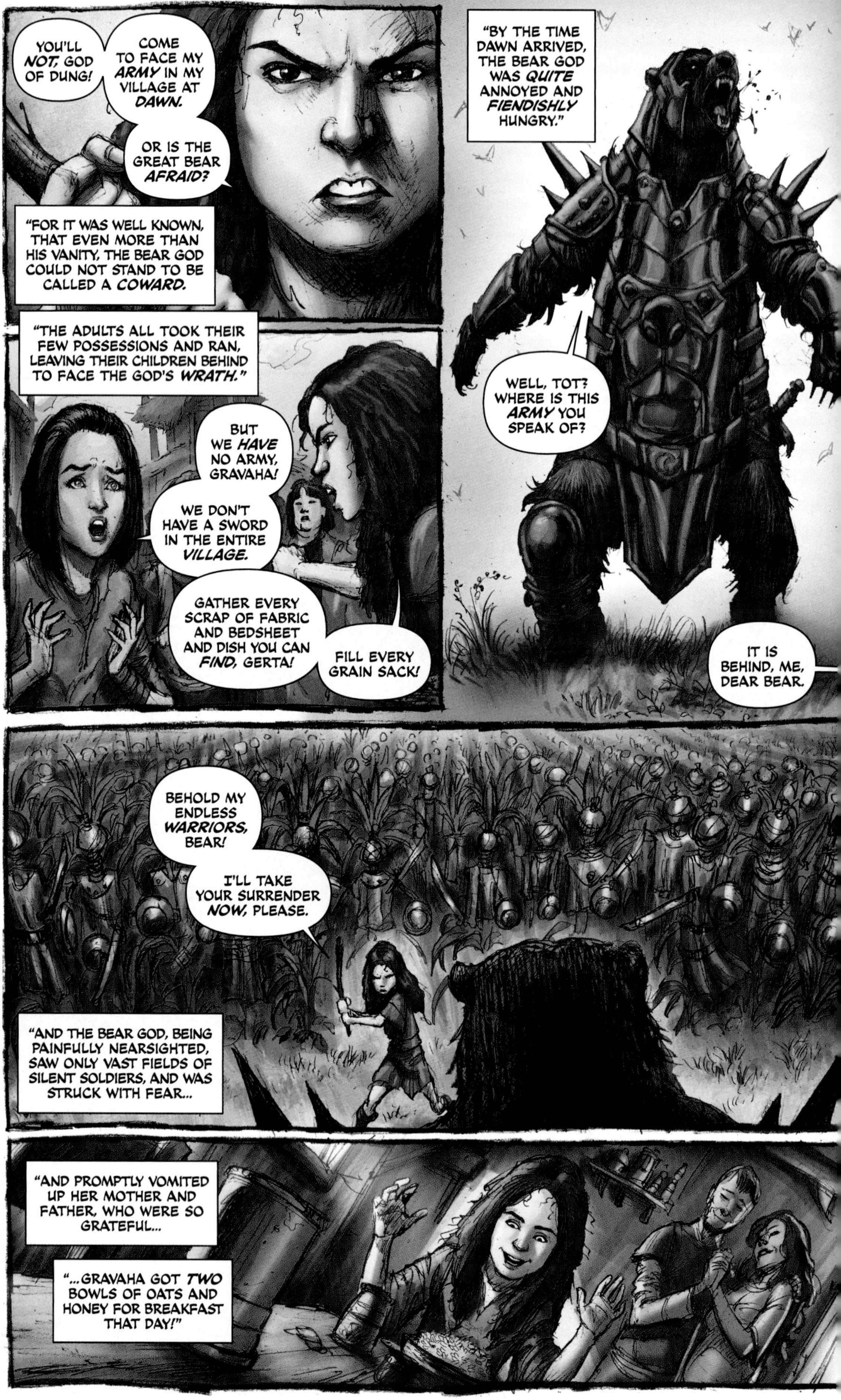
YOU'LL NOT, GOD OF DUNG!
COME TO FACE MY ARMY IN MY VILLAGE AT DAWN.
OR IS THE GREAT BEAR AFRAID?
"FOR IT WAS WELL KNOWN, THAT EVEN MORE THAN HIS VANITY, THE BEAR GOD COULD NOT STAND TO BE CALLED A COWARD.
"THE ADULTS ALL TOOK THEIR FEW POSSESSIONS AND RAN, LEAVING THEIR CHILDREN BEHIND TO FACE THE GOD'S WRATH."
BUT WE HAVE NO ARMY, GRAVAHA!
WE DON'T HAVE A SWORD IN THE ENTIRE VILLAGE.
GATHER EVERY SCRAP OF FABRIC AND BEDSHEET AND DISH YOU CAN FIND, GERTA!
FILL EVERY GRAIN SACK!
"BY THE TIME DAWN ARRIVED, THE BEAR GOD WAS QUITE ANNOYED AND FIENDISHLY HUNGRY."
WELL, TOT? WHERE IS THIS ARMY YOU SPEAK OF?
IT IS BEHIND, ME, DEAR BEAR.
BEHOLD MY ENDLESS WARRIORS, BEAR!
I'LL TAKE YOUR SURRENDER NOW, PLEASE.
"AND THE BEAR GOD, BEING PAINFULLY NEARSIGHTED, SAW ONLY VAST FIELDS OF SILENT SOLDIERS, AND WAS STRUCK WITH FEAR...
"AND PROMPTLY VOMITED UP HER MOTHER AND FATHER, WHO WERE SO GRATEFUL...
"...GRAVAHA GOT TWO BOWLS OF OATS AND HONEY FOR BREAKFAST THAT DAY!"

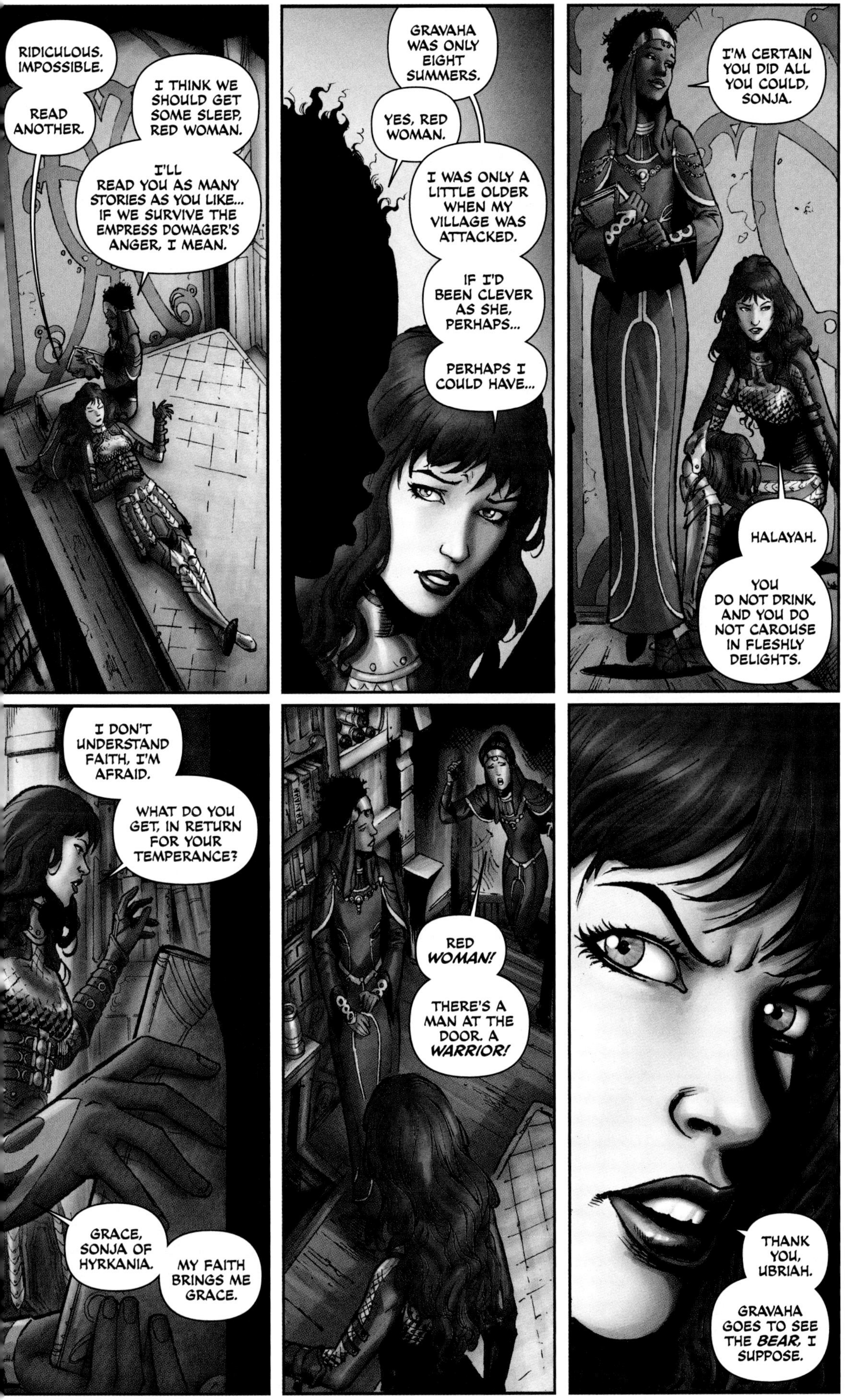
RIDICULOUS. IMPOSSIBLE.
READ ANOTHER.
I THINK WE SHOULD GET SOME SLEEP, RED WOMAN.
I'LL READ YOU AS MANY STORIES AS YOU LIKE... IF WE SURVIVE THE EMPRESS DOWAGER'S ANGER, I MEAN.
GRAVAHA WAS ONLY EIGHT SUMMERS.
YES, RED WOMAN.
I WAS ONLY A LITTLE OLDER WHEN MY VILLAGE WAS ATTACKED.
IF I'D BEEN CLEVER AS SHE, PERHAPS...
PERHAPS I COULD HAVE...
I'M CERTAIN YOU DID ALL YOU COULD, SONJA.
HALAYAH.
YOU DO NOT DRINK, AND YOU DO NOT CAROUSE IN FLESHLY DELIGHTS.
I DON'T UNDERSTAND FAITH, I'M AFRAID.
WHAT DO YOU GET, IN RETURN FOR YOUR TEMPERANCE?
GRACE, SONJA OF HYRKANIA.
MY FAITH BRINGS ME GRACE.
RED *WOMAN!*
THERE'S A MAN AT THE DOOR. A *WARRIOR!*
THANK YOU, UBRIAH.
GRAVAHA GOES TO SEE THE *BEAR*, I SUPPOSE.

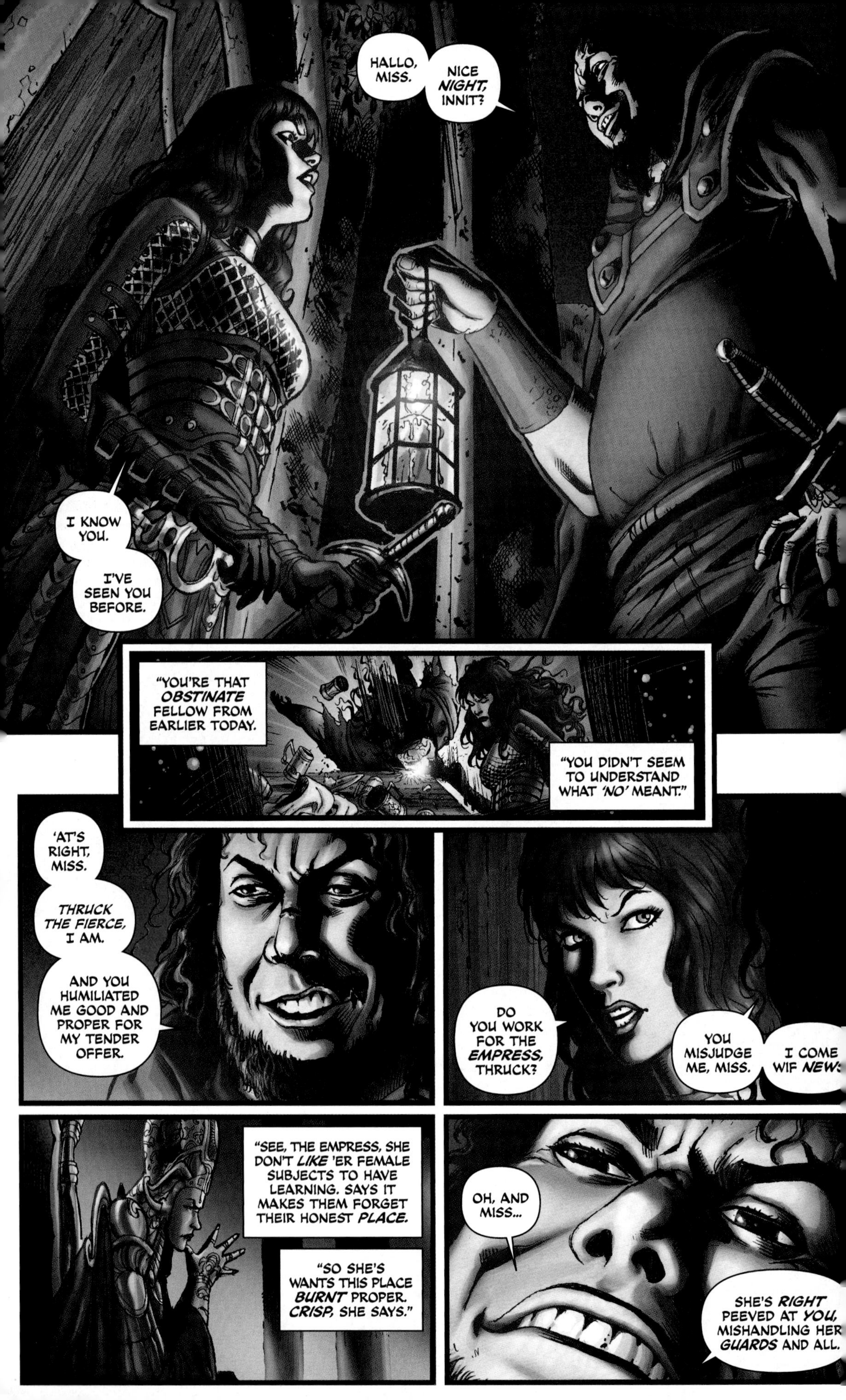
HALLO, MISS.
NICE *NIGHT,* INNIT?
I KNOW YOU.
I'VE SEEN YOU BEFORE.
"YOU'RE THAT *OBSTINATE* FELLOW FROM EARLIER TODAY.
"YOU DIDN'T SEEM TO UNDERSTAND WHAT *'NO'* MEANT."
'AT'S RIGHT, MISS.
THRUCK THE FIERCE, I AM.
AND YOU HUMILIATED ME GOOD AND PROPER FOR MY TENDER OFFER.
DO YOU WORK FOR THE *EMPRESS,* THRUCK?
YOU MISJUDGE ME, MISS.
I COME WIF *NEWS*
"SEE, THE EMPRESS, SHE DON'T *LIKE* 'ER FEMALE SUBJECTS TO HAVE LEARNING. SAYS IT MAKES THEM FORGET THEIR HONEST *PLACE.*
"SO SHE'S WANTS THIS PLACE *BURNT* PROPER. *CRISP,* SHE SAYS."
OH, AND MISS...
SHE'S *RIGHT* PEEVED AT *YOU,* MISHANDLING HER *GUARDS* AND ALL.

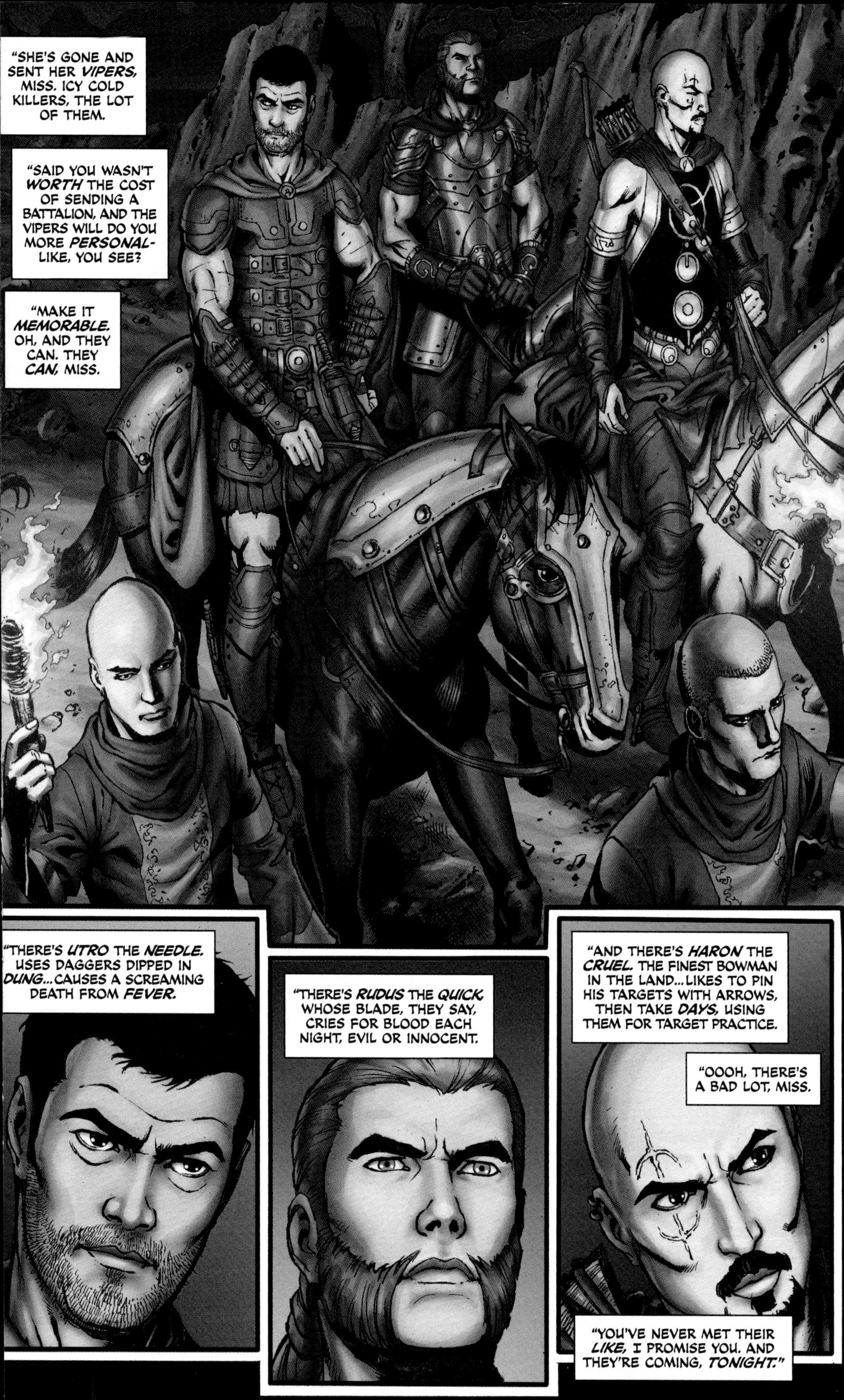
"SHE'S GONE AND SENT HER VIPERS, MISS. ICY COLD KILLERS, THE LOT OF THEM.
"SAID YOU WASN'T WORTH THE COST OF SENDING A BATTALION, AND THE VIPERS WILL DO YOU MORE PERSONAL-LIKE, YOU SEE?
"MAKE IT MEMORABLE. OH, AND THEY CAN. THEY CAN, MISS.
"THERE'S UTRO THE NEEDLE. USES DAGGERS DIPPED IN DUNG...CAUSES A SCREAMING DEATH FROM FEVER.
"THERE'S RUDUS THE QUICK, WHOSE BLADE, THEY SAY, CRIES FOR BLOOD EACH NIGHT, EVIL OR INNOCENT.
"AND THERE'S HARON THE CRUEL. THE FINEST BOWMAN IN THE LAND...LIKES TO PIN HIS TARGETS WITH ARROWS, THEN TAKE DAYS, USING THEM FOR TARGET PRACTICE.
"OOOH, THERE'S A BAD LOT, MISS.
"YOU'VE NEVER MET THEIR LIKE, I PROMISE YOU. AND THEY'RE COMING, TONIGHT."

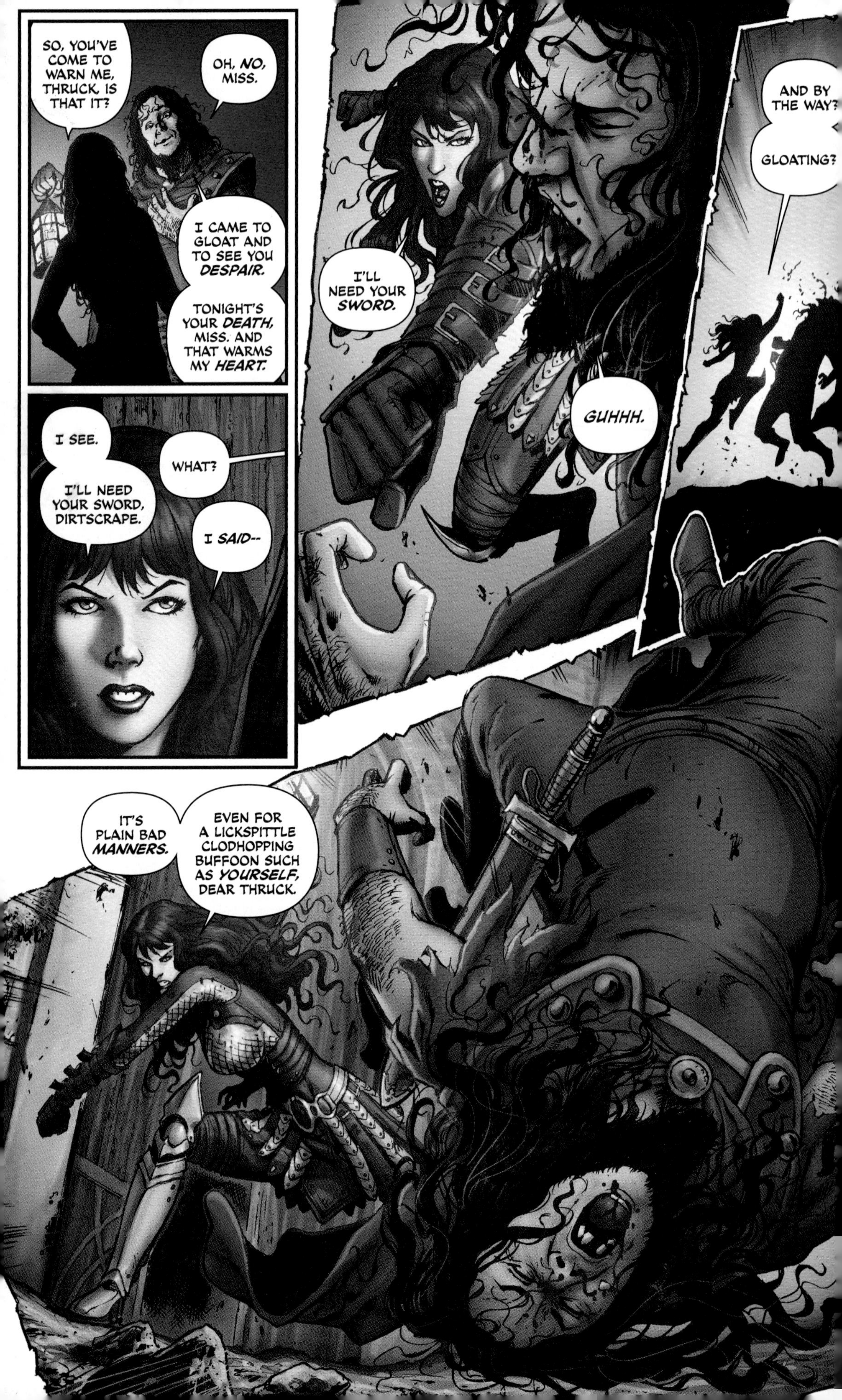
SO, YOU'VE COME TO WARN ME, THRUCK, IS THAT IT?
OH, *NO,* MISS.
I CAME TO GLOAT AND TO SEE YOU *DESPAIR.*
TONIGHT'S YOUR *DEATH,* MISS. AND THAT WARMS MY *HEART.*
I SEE.
WHAT?
I'LL NEED YOUR SWORD, DIRTSCRAPE.
I *SAID--*
I'LL NEED YOUR *SWORD.*
GUHHH.
AND BY THE WAY?
GLOATING?
IT'S PLAIN BAD *MANNERS.*
EVEN FOR A LICKSPITTLE CLODHOPPING BUFFOON SUCH AS *YOURSELF,* DEAR THRUCK.

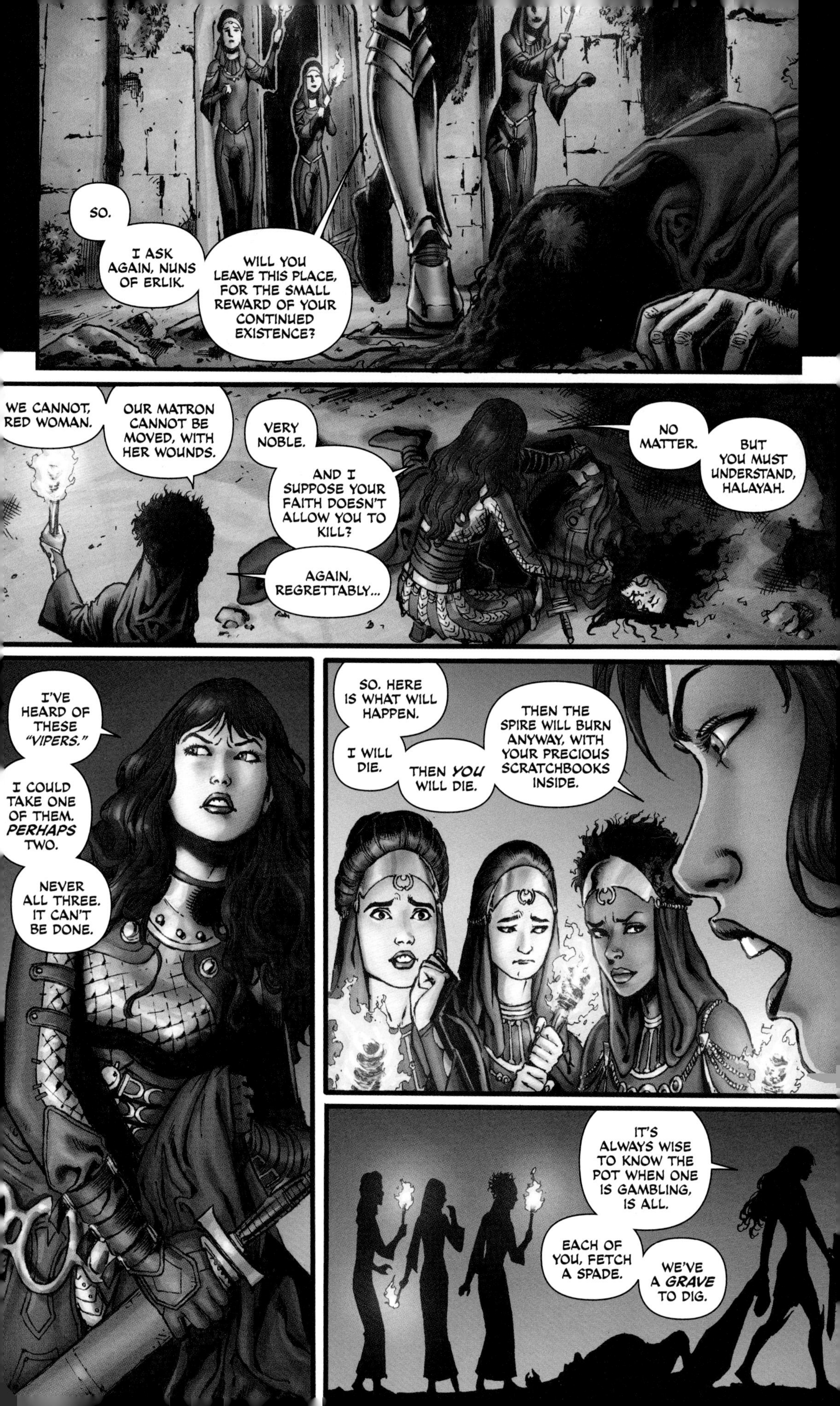
SO.
I ASK AGAIN, NUNS OF ERLIK.
WILL YOU LEAVE THIS PLACE, FOR THE SMALL REWARD OF YOUR CONTINUED EXISTENCE?
WE CANNOT, RED WOMAN.
OUR MATRON CANNOT BE MOVED, WITH HER WOUNDS.
VERY NOBLE.
AND I SUPPOSE YOUR FAITH DOESN'T ALLOW YOU TO KILL?
AGAIN, REGRETTABLY...
NO MATTER.
BUT YOU MUST UNDERSTAND, HALAYAH.
I'VE HEARD OF THESE *"VIPERS."*
I COULD TAKE ONE OF THEM. ***PERHAPS*** TWO.
NEVER ALL THREE. IT CAN'T BE DONE.
SO. HERE IS WHAT WILL HAPPEN.
I WILL DIE.
THEN *YOU* WILL DIE.
THEN THE SPIRE WILL BURN ANYWAY, WITH YOUR PRECIOUS SCRATCHBOOKS INSIDE.
IT'S ALWAYS WISE TO KNOW THE POT WHEN ONE IS GAMBLING, IS ALL.
EACH OF YOU, FETCH A SPADE.
WE'VE A ***GRAVE*** TO DIG.

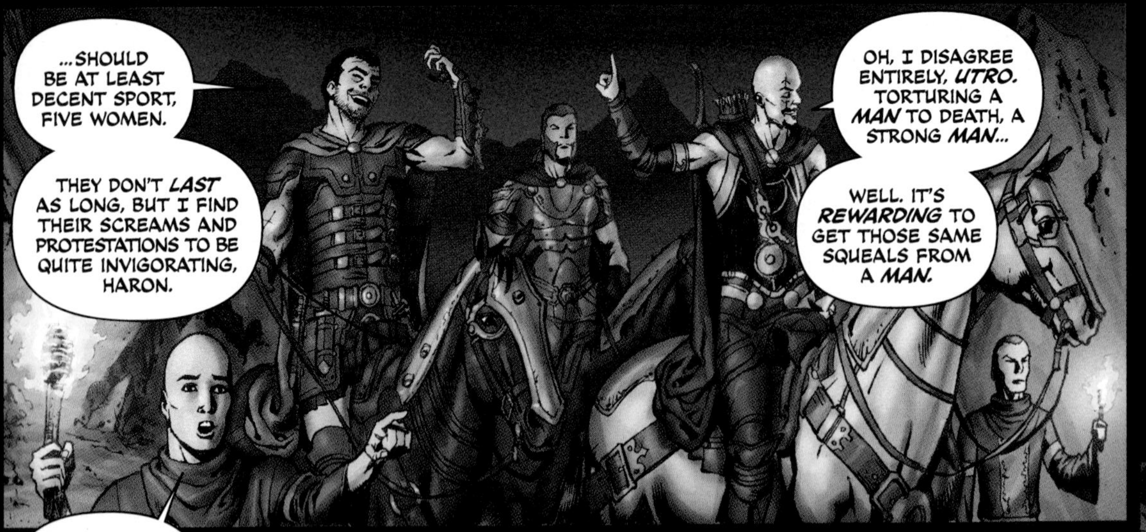
...SHOULD BE AT LEAST DECENT SPORT, FIVE WOMEN.
THEY DON'T LAST AS LONG, BUT I FIND THEIR SCREAMS AND PROTESTATIONS TO BE QUITE INVIGORATING, HARON.
OH, I DISAGREE ENTIRELY, UTRO. TORTURING A MAN TO DEATH, A STRONG MAN...
WELL. IT'S REWARDING TO GET THOSE SAME SQUEALS FROM A MAN.
BEGGING YOUR PARDON, SIR...BUT THERE'S THE SPIRE. THE LIBRARY!

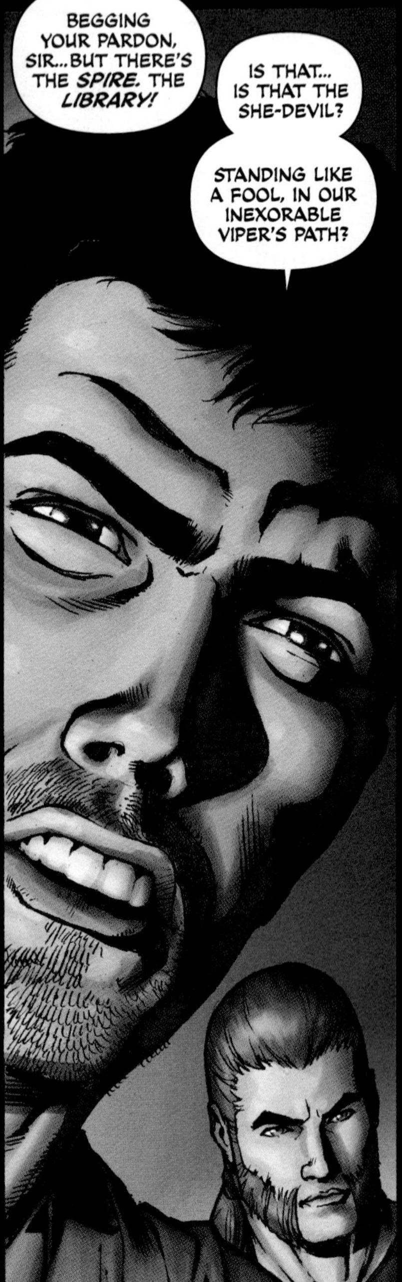
IS THAT... IS THAT THE SHE-DEVIL?
STANDING LIKE A FOOL, IN OUR INEXORABLE VIPER'S PATH?

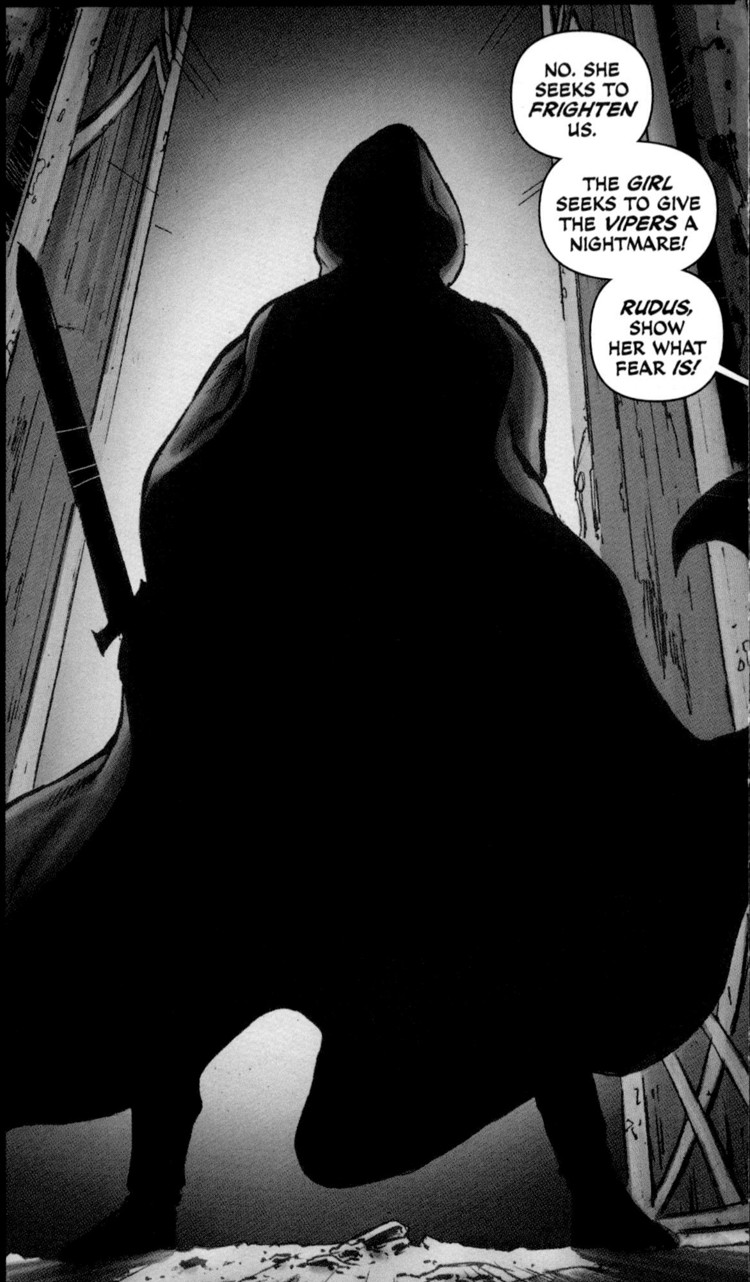
NO. SHE SEEKS TO FRIGHTEN US.
THE GIRL SEEKS TO GIVE THE VIPERS A NIGHTMARE!
RUDUS, SHOW HER WHAT FEAR IS!

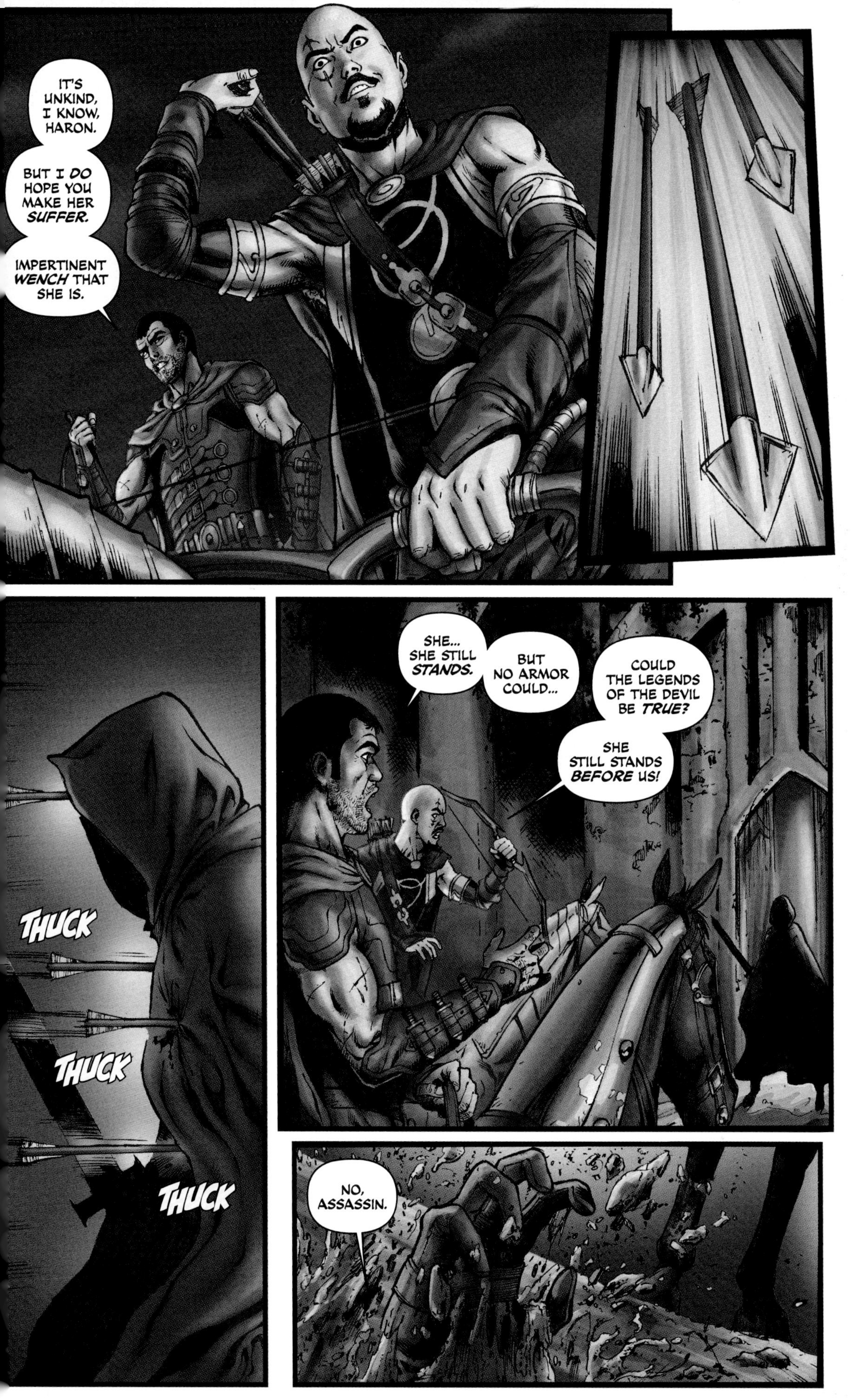

IT'S UNKIND, I KNOW, HARON.
BUT I *DO* HOPE YOU MAKE HER ***SUFFER.***
IMPERTINENT *WENCH* THAT SHE IS.
THUCK
THUCK
THUCK
SHE... SHE STILL *STANDS.*
BUT NO ARMOR COULD...
COULD THE LEGENDS OF THE DEVIL BE *TRUE?*
SHE STILL STANDS *BEFORE* US!
NO, ASSASSIN.

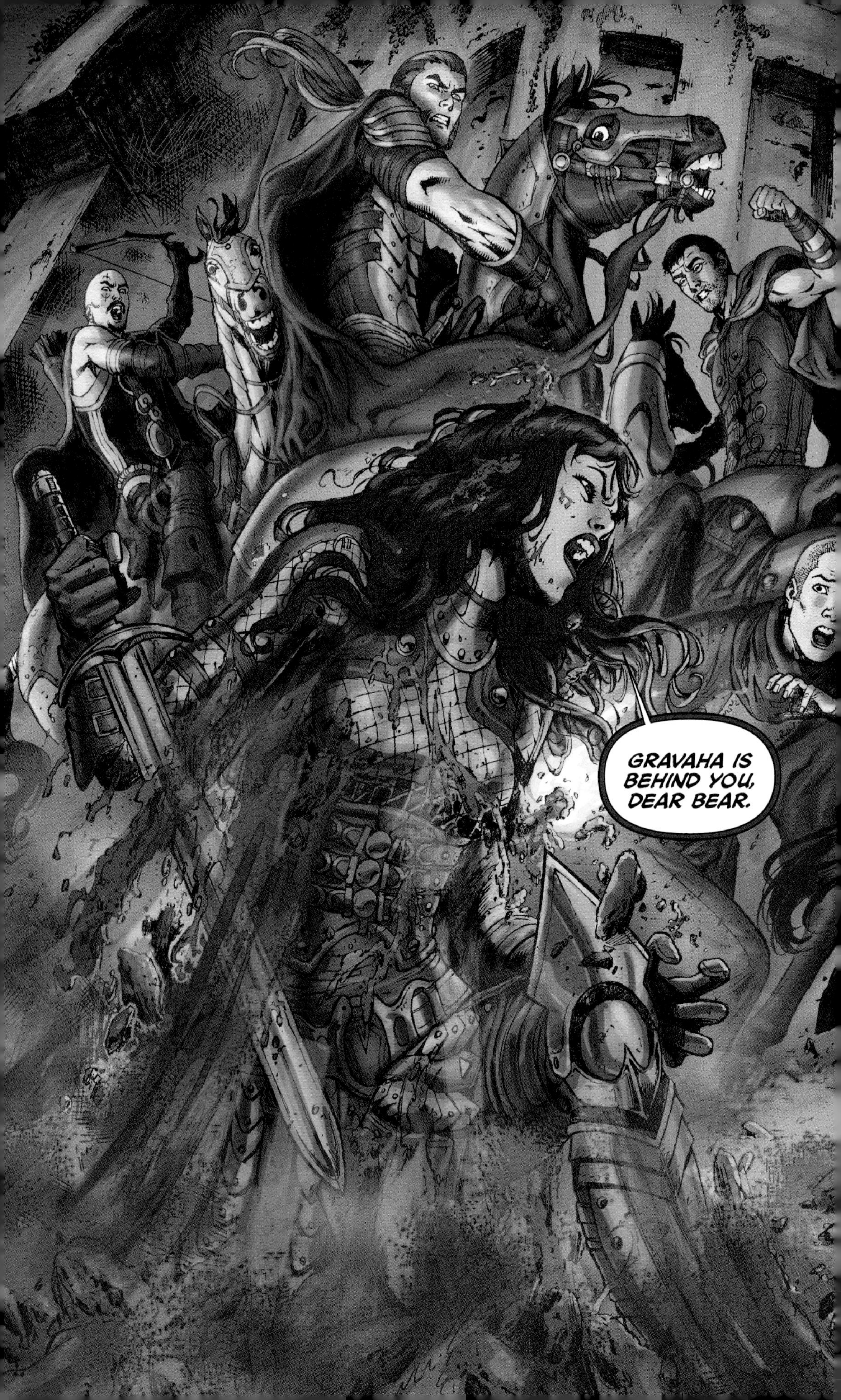
GRAVAHA IS BEHIND YOU, DEAR BEAR.

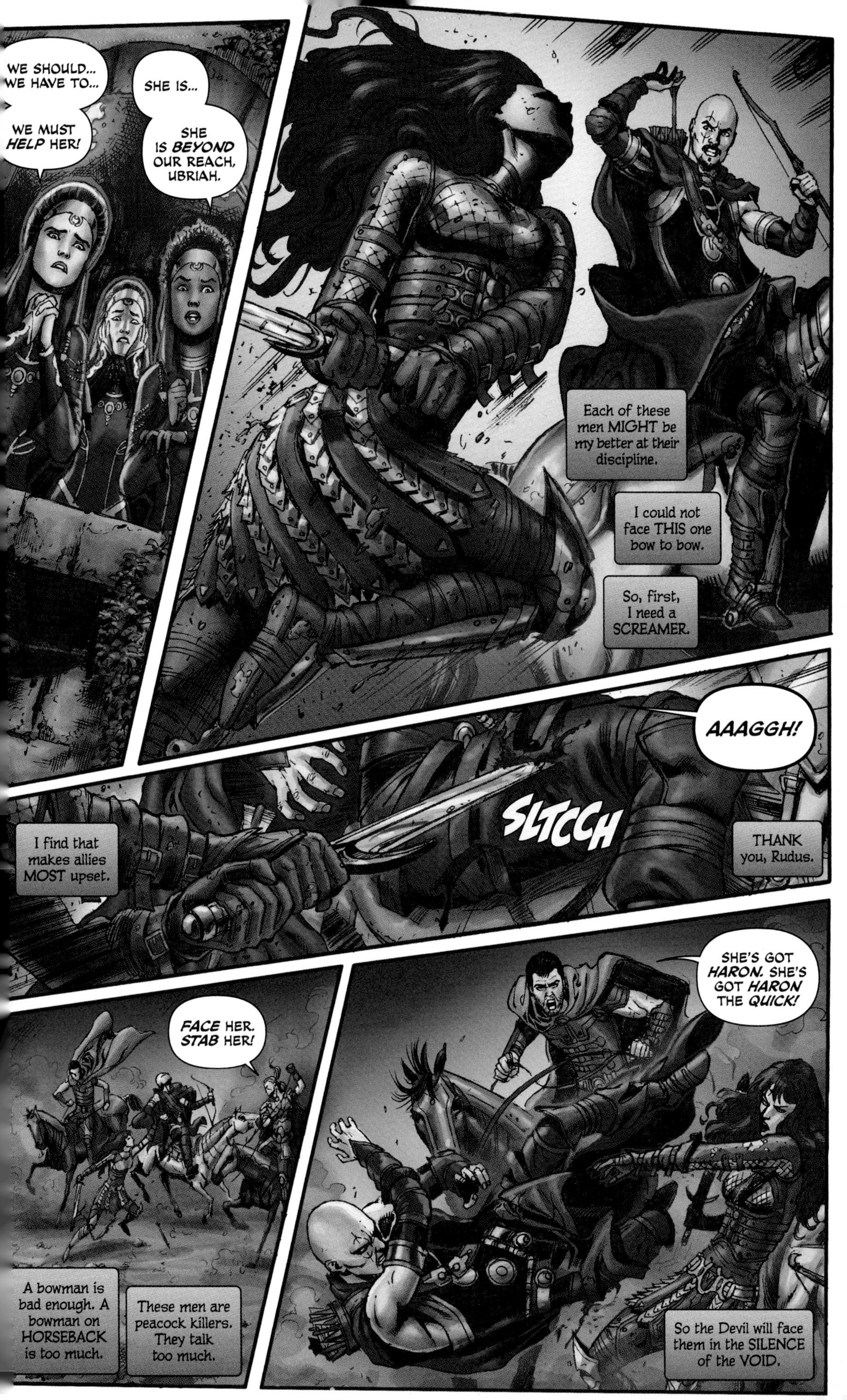

WE SHOULD... WE HAVE TO...
WE MUST *HELP* HER!
SHE IS...
SHE IS *BEYOND* OUR REACH, UBRIAH.
Each of these men MIGHT be my better at their discipline.
I could not face THIS one bow to bow.
So, first, I need a SCREAMER.
AAAGGH!
I find that makes allies MOST upset.
SLTCCH
THANK you, Rudus.
FACE HER. *STAB* HER!
A bowman is bad enough. A bowman on HORSEBACK is too much.
These men are peacock killers. They talk too much.
SHE'S GOT *HARON.* SHE'S GOT *HARON* THE *QUICK!*
So the Devil will face them in the SILENCE of the VOID.

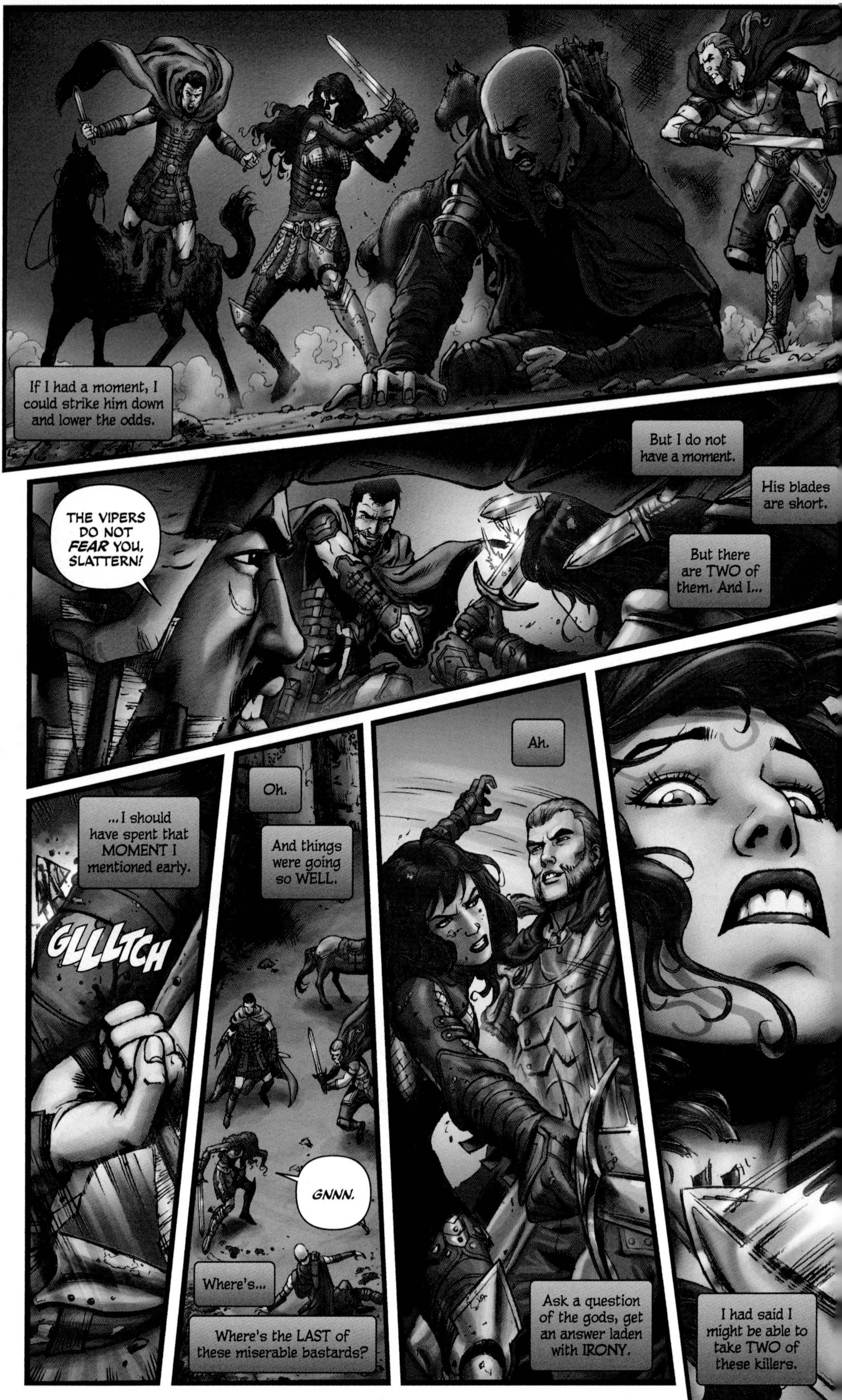

If I had a moment, I could strike him down and lower the odds.
But I do not have a moment.
His blades are short.
But there are TWO of them. And I...
THE VIPERS DO NOT FEAR YOU, SLATTERN!
...I should have spent that MOMENT I mentioned early.
GLLLTCH
Oh.
And things were going so WELL.
GNNN.
Where's...
Where's the LAST of these miserable bastards?
Ah.
Ask a question of the gods, get an answer laden with IRONY.
I had said I might be able to take TWO of these killers.

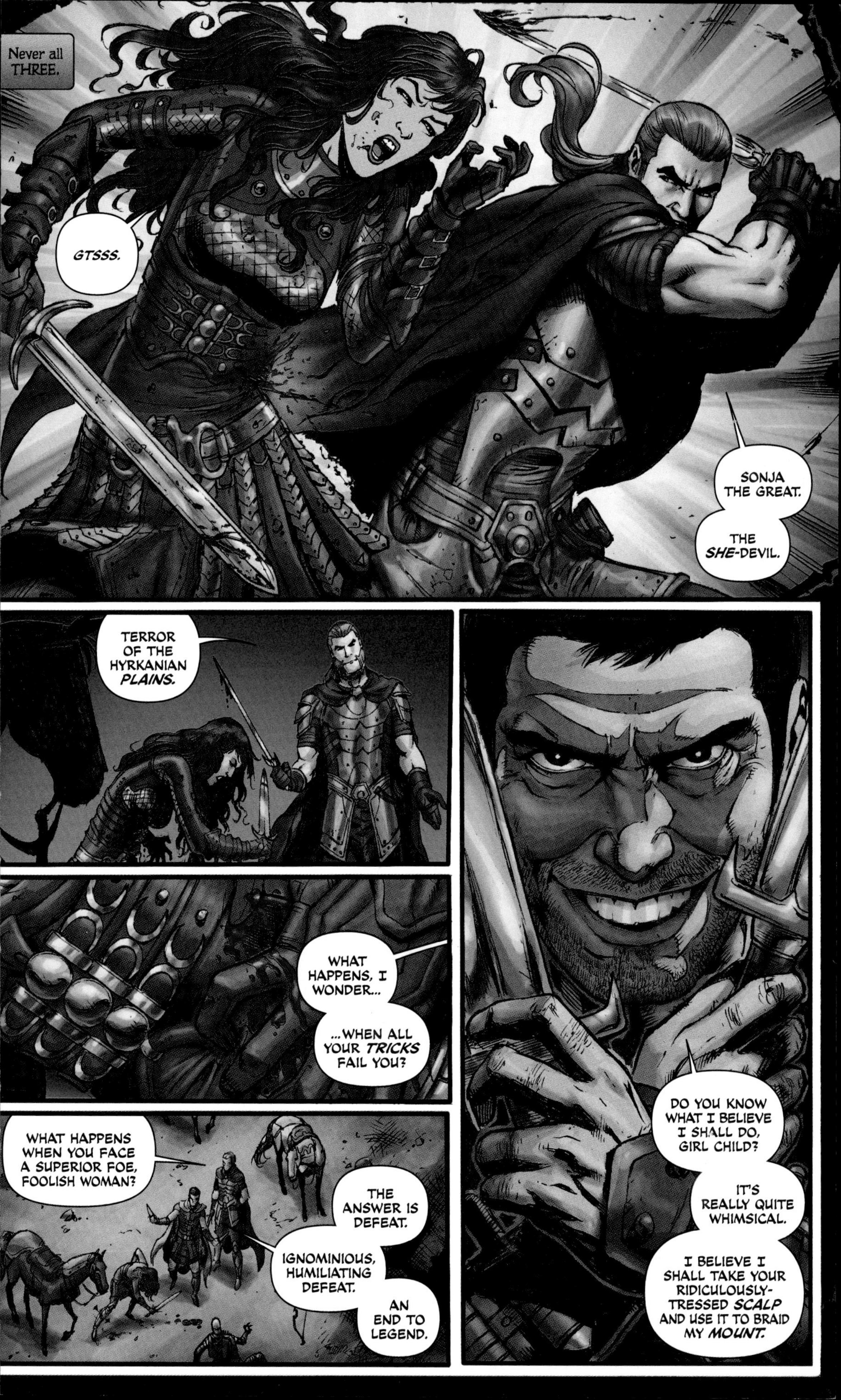
Never all THREE.
GTSSS.
SONJA THE GREAT.
THE SHE-DEVIL.
TERROR OF THE HYRKANIAN PLAINS.
WHAT HAPPENS, I WONDER...
...WHEN ALL YOUR TRICKS FAIL YOU?
WHAT HAPPENS WHEN YOU FACE A SUPERIOR FOE, FOOLISH WOMAN?
THE ANSWER IS DEFEAT.
IGNOMINIOUS, HUMILIATING DEFEAT.
AN END TO LEGEND.
DO YOU KNOW WHAT I BELIEVE I SHALL DO, GIRL CHILD?
IT'S REALLY QUITE WHIMSICAL.
I BELIEVE I SHALL TAKE YOUR RIDICULOUSLY-TRESSED SCALP AND USE IT TO BRAID MY MOUNT.

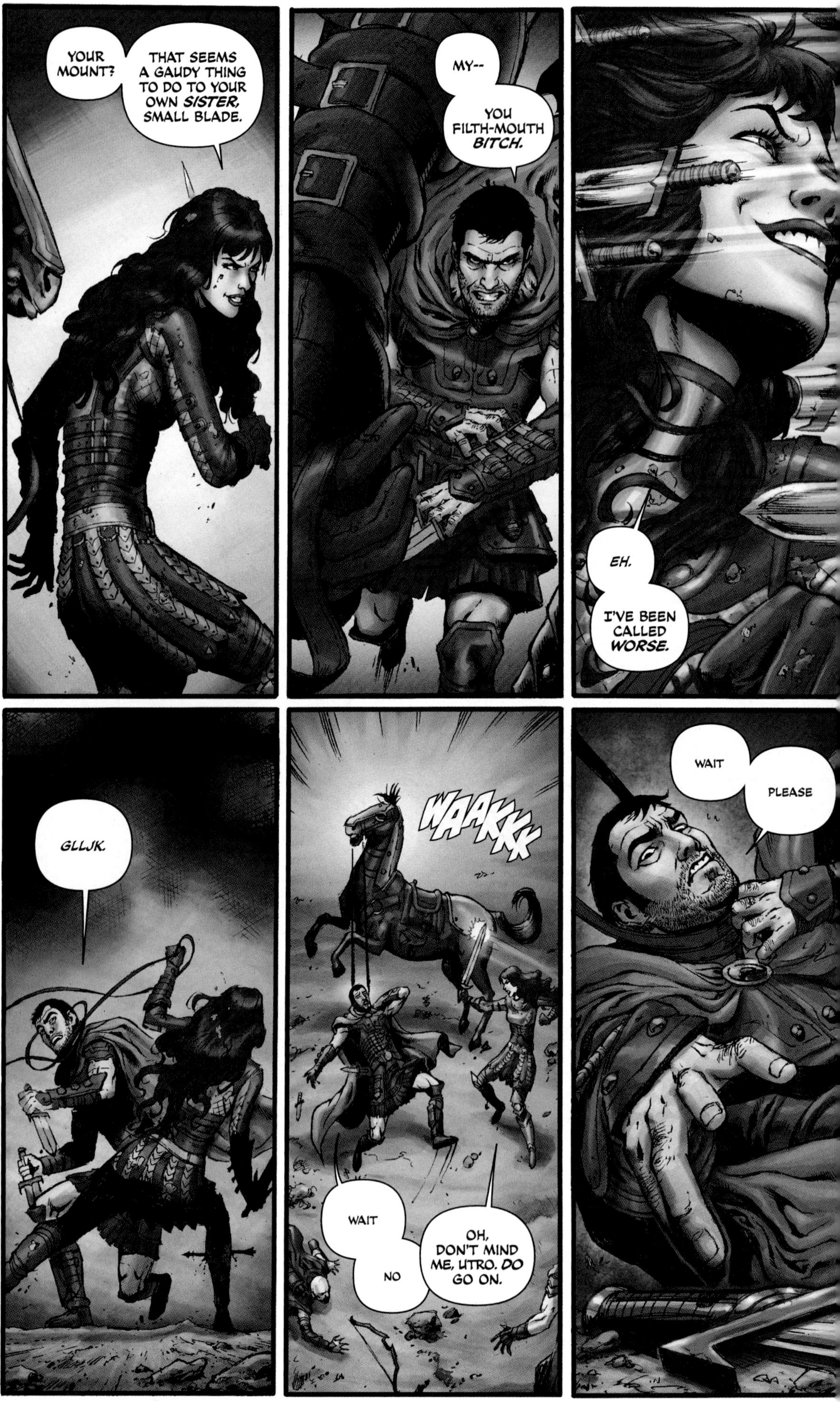

YOUR MOUNT?
THAT SEEMS A GAUDY THING TO DO TO YOUR OWN *SISTER,* SMALL BLADE.
MY--
YOU FILTH-MOUTH *BITCH.*
EH.
I'VE BEEN CALLED *WORSE.*
GLLJK.
WAAKKK
WAIT
NO
OH, DON'T MIND ME, UTRO. *DO* GO ON.
WAIT
PLEASE

I BELIEVE YOU WERE SAYING SOMETHING DISPARAGING ABOUT MY *HAIR?*

Damn.

The ARCHER.

THUCK

DO YOU REALLY THINK THE WORLD WOULD TOLERATE YOUR SHAMELESS CAPERING *FOREVER?*

A *WOMAN,* OF ALL THINGS?

DID YOU THINK WE WOULD *ALLOW* THAT TO *FESTER?*

TO BE HONEST, PINPRICK...

I HADN'T GIVEN IT MUCH *THOUGHT.*

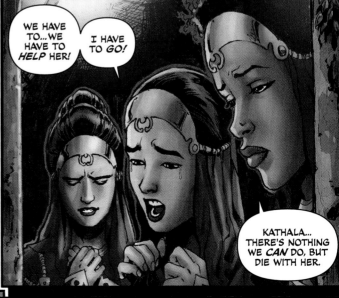

WE HAVE TO...WE HAVE TO *HELP* HER!

I HAVE TO *GO!*

KATHALA... THERE'S NOTHING WE *CAN* DO, BUT DIE WITH HER.

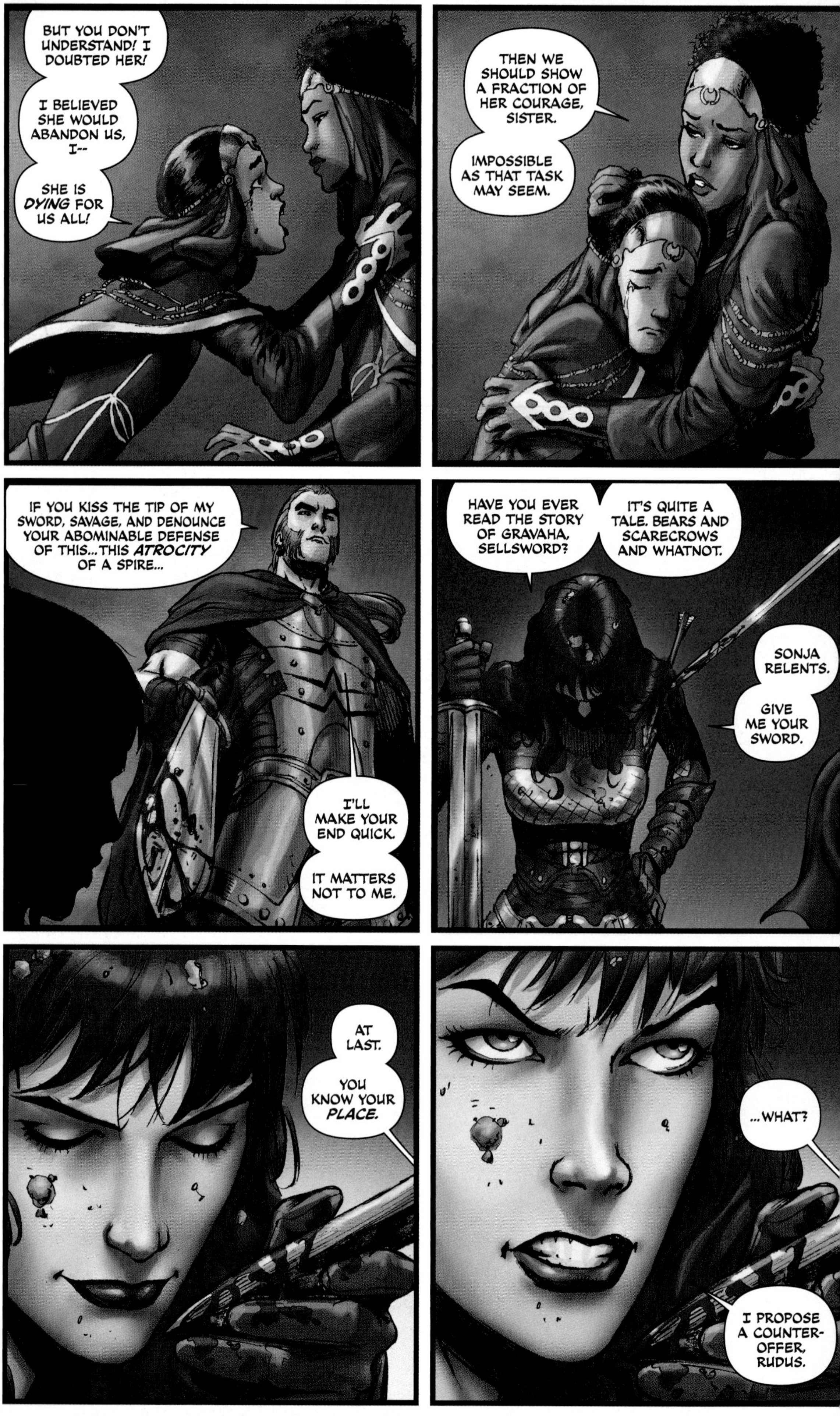
BUT YOU DON'T UNDERSTAND! I DOUBTED HER!
I BELIEVED SHE WOULD ABANDON US, I--
SHE IS DYING FOR US ALL!
THEN WE SHOULD SHOW A FRACTION OF HER COURAGE, SISTER.
IMPOSSIBLE AS THAT TASK MAY SEEM.
IF YOU KISS THE TIP OF MY SWORD, SAVAGE, AND DENOUNCE YOUR ABOMINABLE DEFENSE OF THIS...THIS ATROCITY OF A SPIRE...
I'LL MAKE YOUR END QUICK.
IT MATTERS NOT TO ME.
HAVE YOU EVER READ THE STORY OF GRAVAHA, SELLSWORD?
IT'S QUITE A TALE. BEARS AND SCARECROWS AND WHATNOT.
SONJA RELENTS.
GIVE ME YOUR SWORD.
AT LAST.
YOU KNOW YOUR PLACE.
...WHAT?
I PROPOSE A COUNTER-OFFER, RUDUS.

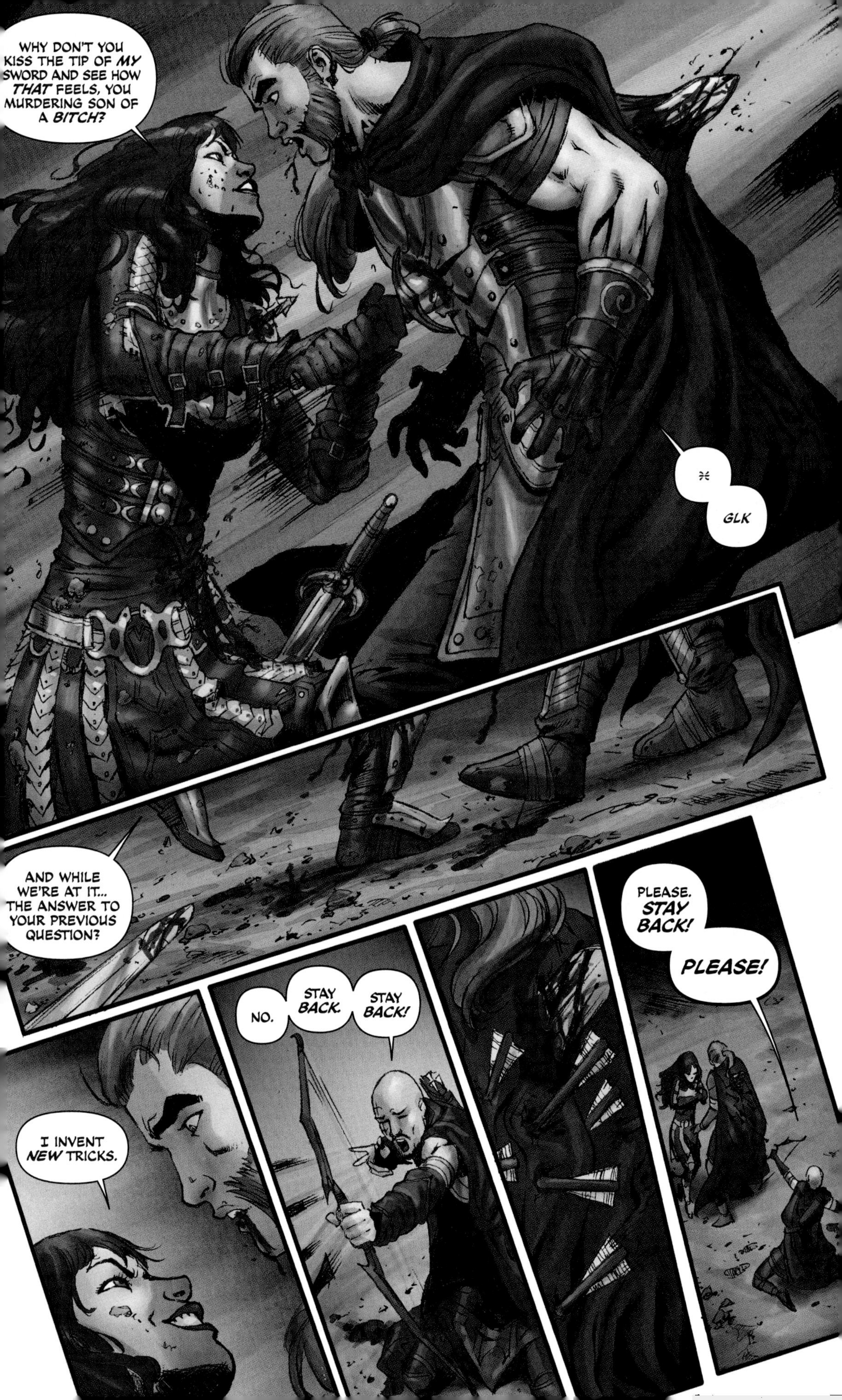
WHY DON'T YOU KISS THE TIP OF *MY* SWORD AND SEE HOW *THAT* FEELS, YOU MURDERING SON OF A *BITCH?*
GLK
AND WHILE WE'RE AT IT... THE ANSWER TO YOUR PREVIOUS QUESTION?
I INVENT *NEW* TRICKS.
NO.
STAY *BACK.*
STAY *BACK!*
PLEASE. *STAY BACK!*
PLEASE!

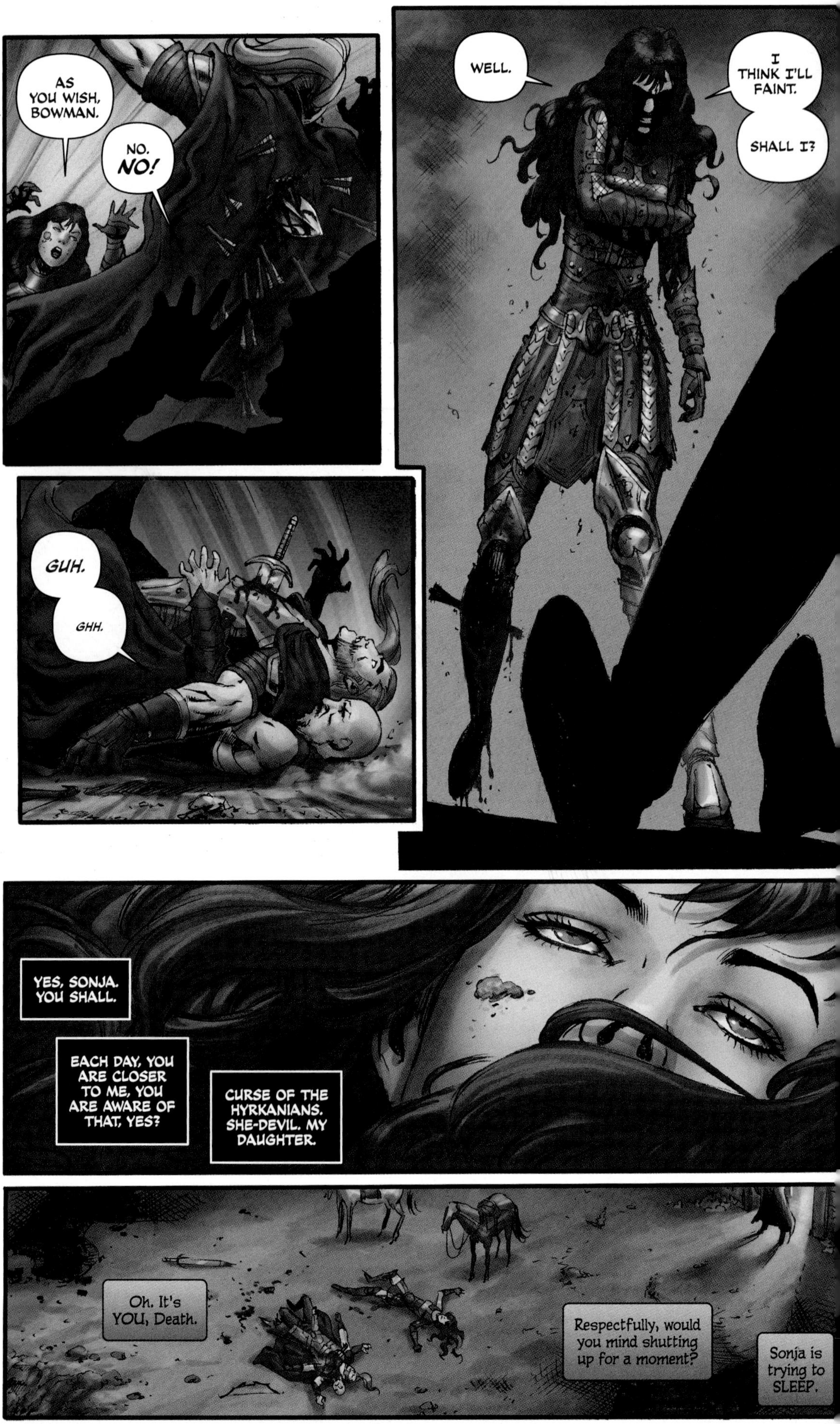
AS YOU WISH, BOWMAN.
NO. NO!
GUH.
GHH.
WELL.
I THINK I'LL FAINT.
SHALL I?
YES, SONJA. YOU SHALL.
EACH DAY, YOU ARE CLOSER TO ME, YOU ARE AWARE OF THAT, YES?
CURSE OF THE HYRKANIANS. SHE-DEVIL. MY DAUGHTER.
Oh. It's YOU, Death.
Respectfully, would you mind shutting up for a moment?
Sonja is trying to SLEEP.

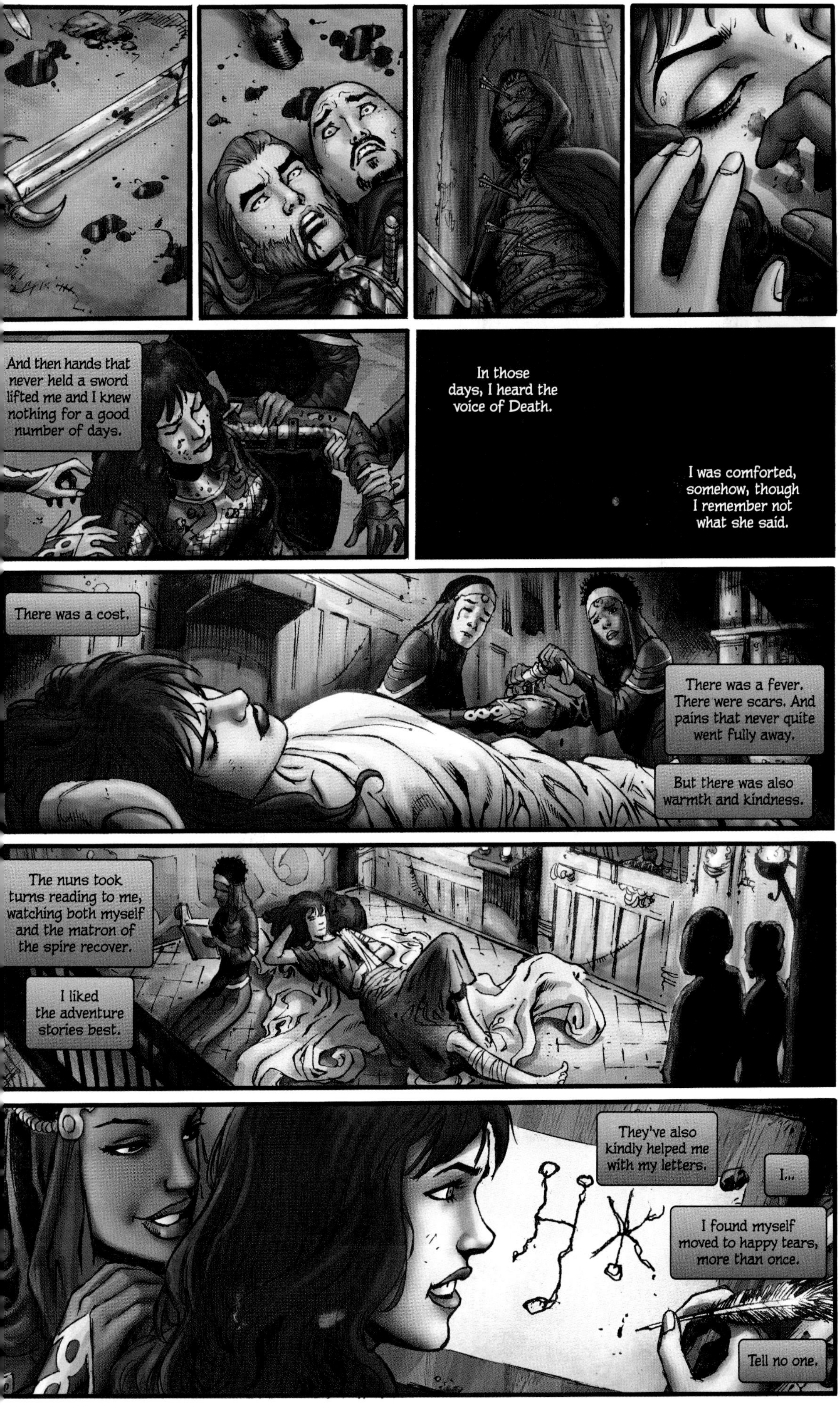
And then hands that never held a sword lifted me and I knew nothing for a good number of days.
In those days, I heard the voice of Death.
I was comforted, somehow, though I remember not what she said.
There was a cost.
There was a fever. There were scars. And pains that never quite went fully away.
But there was also warmth and kindness.
The nuns took turns reading to me, watching both myself and the matron of the spire recover.
I liked the adventure stories best.
They've also kindly helped me with my letters.
I...
I found myself moved to happy tears, more than once.
Tell no one.

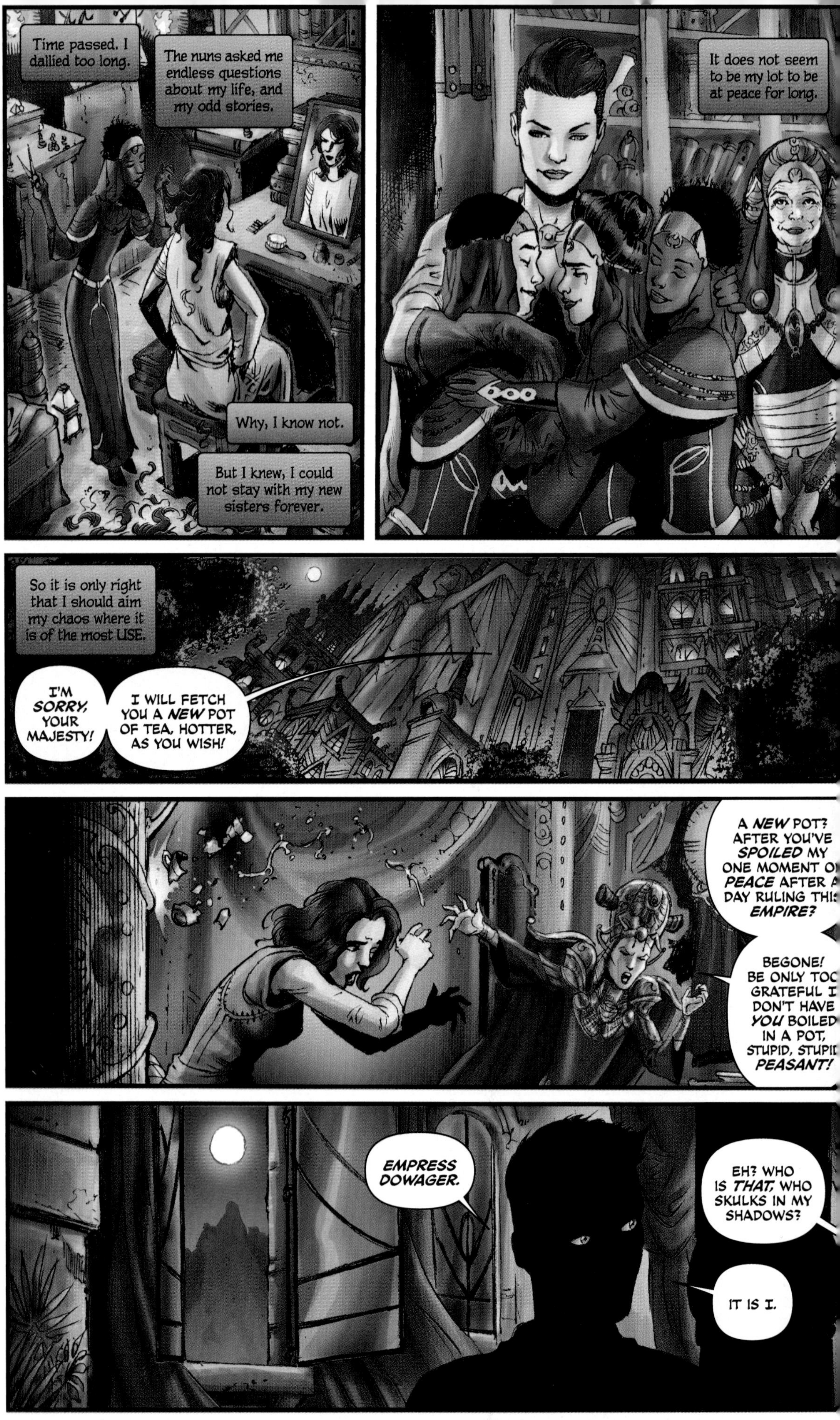
Time passed. I dallied too long.
The nuns asked me endless questions about my life, and my odd stories.
Why, I know not.
But I knew, I could not stay with my new sisters forever.
It does not seem to be my lot to be at peace for long.
So it is only right that I should aim my chaos where it is of the most USE.
I'M SORRY, YOUR MAJESTY!
I WILL FETCH YOU A NEW POT OF TEA, HOTTER, AS YOU WISH!
A NEW POT? AFTER YOU'VE SPOILED MY ONE MOMENT O PEACE AFTER A DAY RULING THI EMPIRE?
BEGONE! BE ONLY TOO GRATEFUL I DON'T HAVE YOU BOILED IN A POT, STUPID, STUPI PEASANT!
EMPRESS DOWAGER.
EH? WHO IS THAT, WHO SKULKS IN MY SHADOWS?
IT IS I.

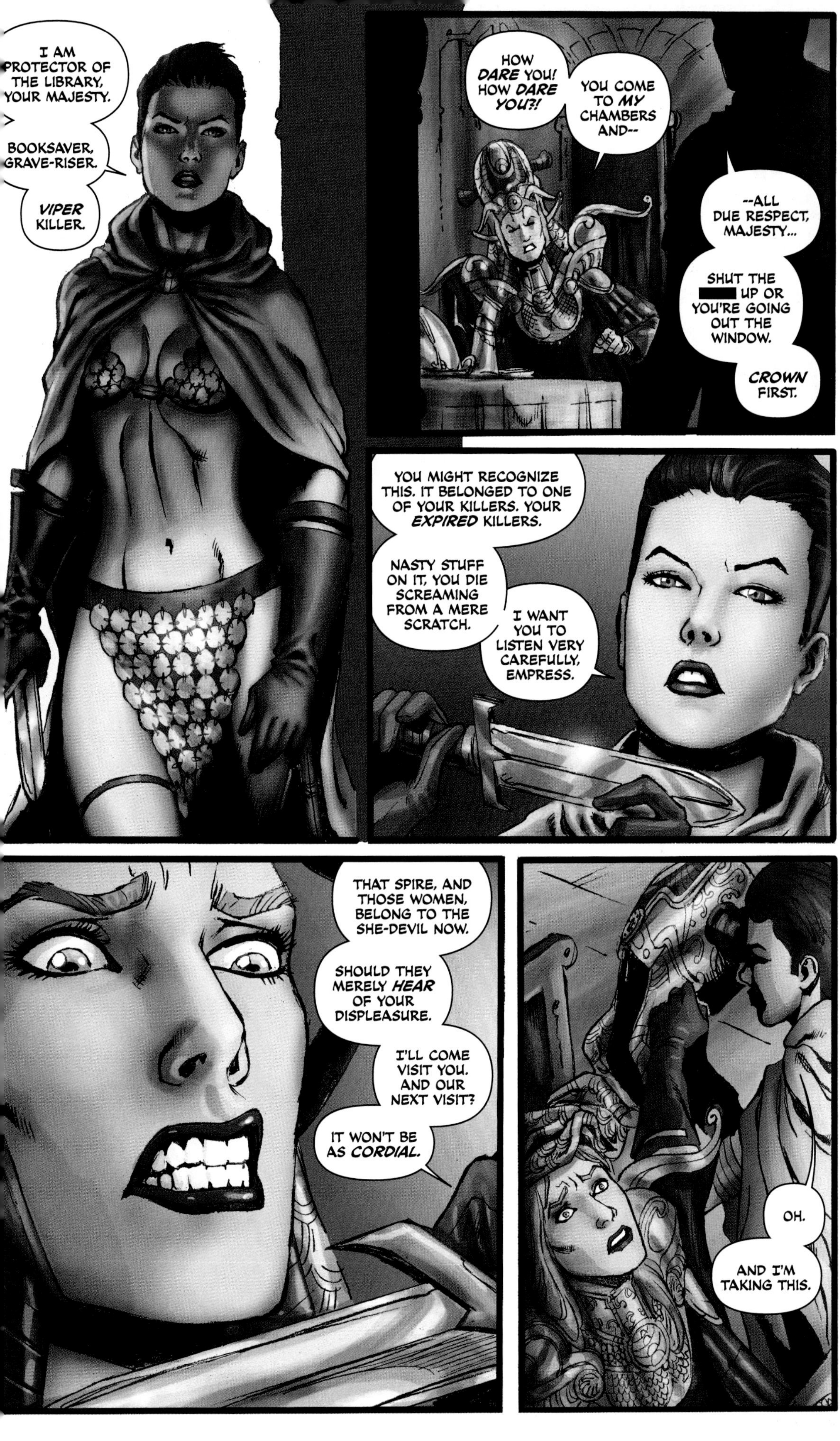
I AM PROTECTOR OF THE LIBRARY, YOUR MAJESTY.
BOOKSAVER, GRAVE-RISER.
VIPER KILLER.
HOW DARE YOU! HOW DARE YOU?!
YOU COME TO MY CHAMBERS AND--
--ALL DUE RESPECT, MAJESTY...
SHUT THE [redacted] UP OR YOU'RE GOING OUT THE WINDOW.
CROWN FIRST.
YOU MIGHT RECOGNIZE THIS. IT BELONGED TO ONE OF YOUR KILLERS. YOUR EXPIRED KILLERS.
NASTY STUFF ON IT, YOU DIE SCREAMING FROM A MERE SCRATCH.
I WANT YOU TO LISTEN VERY CAREFULLY, EMPRESS.
THAT SPIRE, AND THOSE WOMEN, BELONG TO THE SHE-DEVIL NOW.
SHOULD THEY MERELY HEAR OF YOUR DISPLEASURE.
I'LL COME VISIT YOU. AND OUR NEXT VISIT?
IT WON'T BE AS CORDIAL.
OH.
AND I'M TAKING THIS.

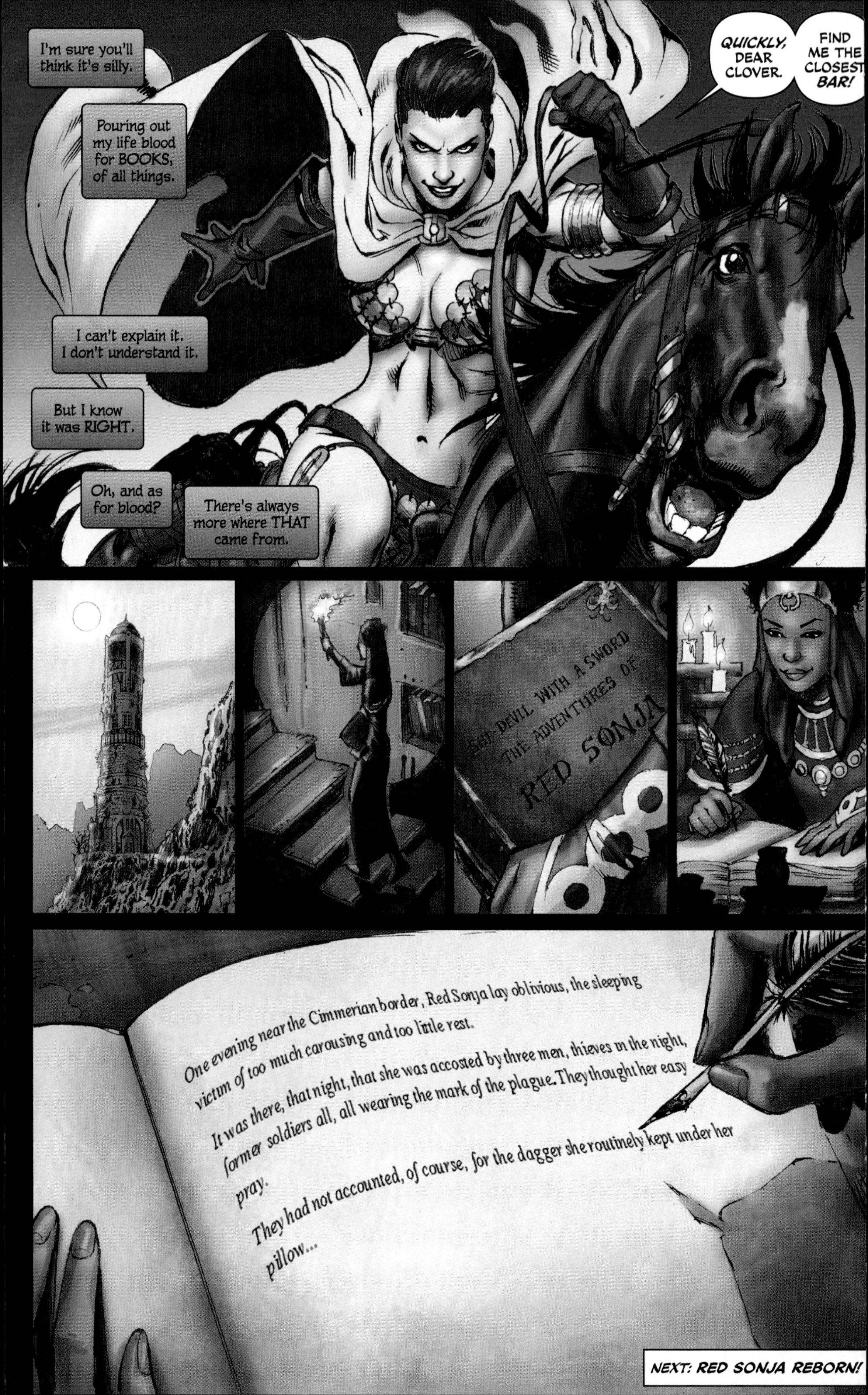
I'm sure you'll think it's silly.
Pouring out my life blood for BOOKS, of all things.
QUICKLY, DEAR CLOVER.
FIND ME THE CLOSEST BAR!
I can't explain it. I don't understand it.
But I know it was RIGHT.
Oh, and as for blood?
There's always more where THAT came from.
SHE-DEVIL WITH A SWORD
THE ADVENTURES OF
RED SONJA
One evening near the Cimmerian border, Red Sonja lay oblivious, the sleeping victim of too much carousing and too little rest.
It was there, that night, that she was accosted by three men, thieves in the night, former soldiers all, all wearing the mark of the plague. They thought her easy pray.
They had not accounted, of course, for the dagger she routinely kept under her pillow...
NEXT: RED SONJA REBORN!

BONUS MATERIAL

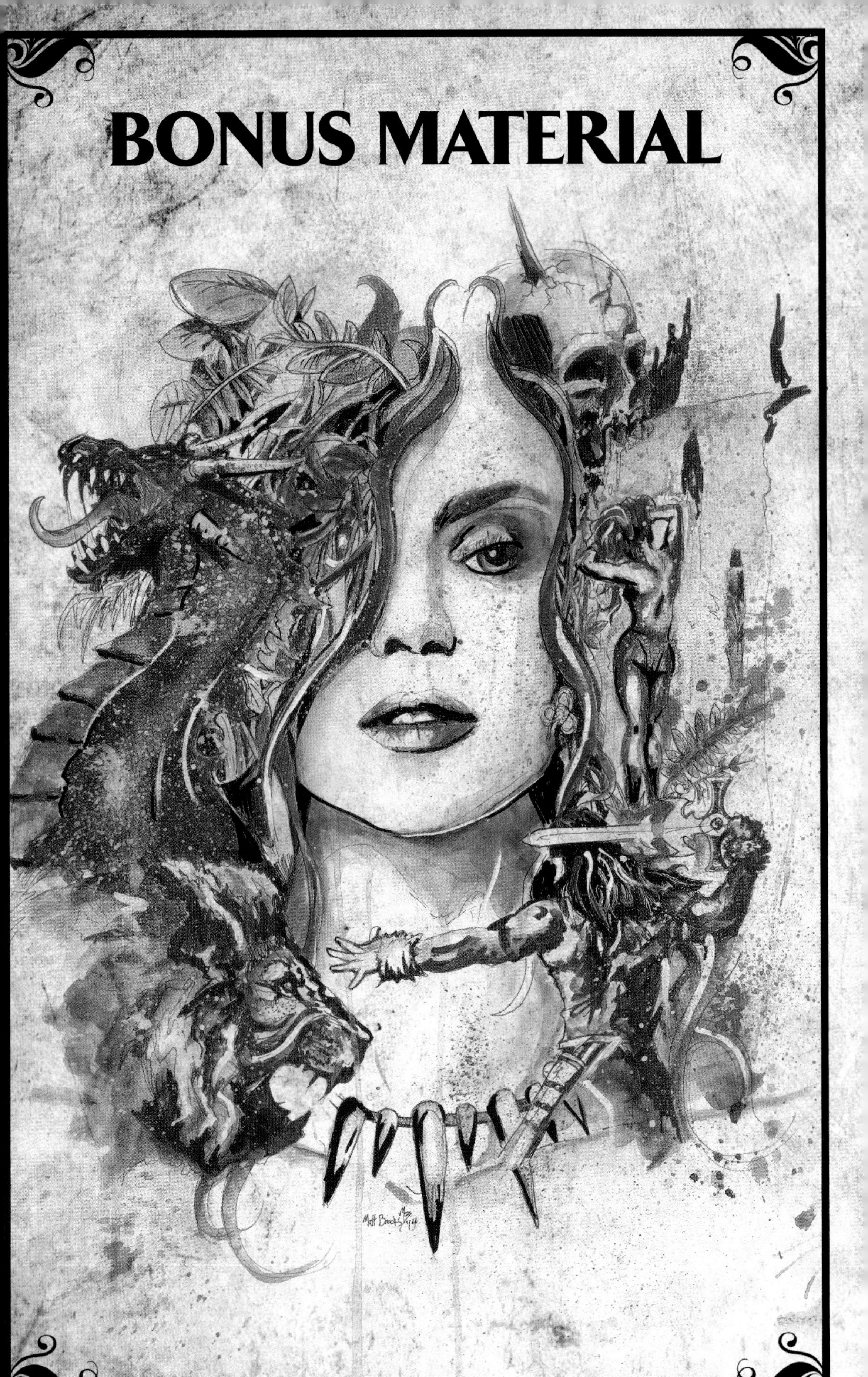

RED SONJA

(*) TITLE

RED SONJA #18 HYRKANIAN NOON
BY GAIL SIMONE

Walter, it's our last issue together, at least for now.

Thank you for being one of the best creative partners I have ever had. You make me proud to have worked on this book.

This is an excerpt, full script coming this weekend. Thank you for everything, you are the BEST.

<u>PAGE ONE:</u>

PANEL ONE: This is a row across the top of the page, showing the title of the book being read to Sonja, it is an ancient book, with formal lettering, saying

THE ADVENTURES OF GRAVAHA THE CLEVER

PANEL TWO: A young peasant girl, Gravaha, she's got red hair in pigtails, barbarian pigtails, and she's clearly poor, barefooted and wearing just a sack dress, patched and stitched poorly. She's working in the fields, planting seeds, in front of a shack of a barn or hovel. We see a row of endless corn behind her (that's important).

> CAP: "And so it was that poor Gravaha, being only eight, watched as the great bear god ate her father and mother before her eyes.

> CAP: "Leaving her, a child, to care for their farm and protect her small village."

PANEL THREE: She stands up straight, looking up at the sun.

> CAP: "But she missed her parents, especially her mother's cooking. She missed oats and honey for breakfast and hot stew for supper."

> CAP: "And she decided to do something QUITE impossible."

> GRAVAHA: I shall go fight the bear god and retrieve mother and father.

> GRAVAHA: Yes, it is to be done.

PANEL FOUR: Gravaha, standing in front of a dark cave, small and meek. She's holding a stick like a sword, completely uselessly.

> CAP: "The villagers thought her addled. 'You have no sword, child,' they said.

> CAP: "'You'll be reunited in the bear's GULLET,' they said.

> CAP: "Gravaha announced herself, as all knew the bear god was vain, and did not like people to know he was almost blind.

> GRAVAHA: COME OUT, bear god. It is I, GRAVAHA of the MUD!

> GRAVAHA: I CHALLENGE you!

PANEL FIVE: Bigger panel, if possible, showing a large bear, coming out of the cave, the bear is fearsome and strong, but can't see anything. Maybe we see tiny Gravaha looking up at this monster to compare their sizes.

> BEAR: GRAVAHA? The child of those delicious FARMERS?

> BEAR: You challenge ME?

> BEAR: I will eat YOU, and then all your VILLAGE FRIENDS for this impertinence!

page 2

page 3

PAGE TWO:

PANEL ONE: Gravaha holds the stick up.

> GRAVAHA: You'll NOT, god of dung!
>
> GRAVAHA: Come to face my ARMY in my village at DAWN.
>
> GRAVAHA: Or is the great bear AFRAID?
>
> CAP: "For it was well known, that even more than his vanity, the bear god could not stand to be called a COWARD."

PANEL TWO: Gravaha, in her village, talking to a host of other peasant children, all in rags.

> CAP: "The adults all took their few possessions and ran, leaving their children behind to face the god's WRATH.
>
> GIRL: But we HAVE no army, Gravaha! We don't have a sword in the entire VILLAGE.
>
> GRAVAHA: Gather every scrap of fabric and bedsheet and dish you can FIND, Gerta!
>
> GRAVAHA: Fill every grain sack, Wattle!

PANEL THREE: The bear god, in full battle armor, comes up the road, ready for war, angry and shouting and snarling.

> CAP: "By the time dawn arrived, the bear god was QUITE annoyed and FIENDISHLY hungry.
>
> BEAR: Well, tot? Where is this ARMY you speak of?
>
> GRAVAHA (off-panel): It is behind, me, dear bear.

PANEL FOUR: We see a vast, vast row of corn plants, and each one has a rag thrown over it, to look (to the nearsighted bear) like a person. Many have a dish as a shield, several have a stick as a sword. Most of them have a sack for a head. They are a multitude of corn warriors, but the bear doesn't know they aren't real. He can't see them. Gravaha stands in front.

> GRAVAHA: Behold my endless WARRIORS, bear!

GRAVAHA: I'll take your surrender NOW, please.

CAP: "And the bear god, being painfully nearsighted, saw only vast fields of silent soldiers, and was struck with fear..."

PANEL FIVE: Gravaha, at her table, having a big bowl of oats and honey, her proud, silly parents behind her, smiling.

CAP: "And promptly vomited up her mother and father, who were so grateful...

CAP: "...Gravaha got TWO bowls of oats and honey for breakfast that day!"

PAGE THREE:

PANEL ONE: Sonja, laying on the bench as in last issue, her head in Halaya's lap (in an innocent, non-sexual way, obviously), as the young woman reads the book. Sonja looks puzzled.

SONJA: Ridiculous. Impossible.

SONJA: Read another.

HALAYAH: I think we should get some sleep, Red Woman.

HALAYAH: I'll read you as many stories as you like...if we survive the Empress Dowager's anger, I mean.

PANEL TWO: Sonja sits up, staring at Halayah.

SONJA: Gravaha was only eight Summers.

HALAYAH: Yes, Red Woman.

SONJA: I was only a little older when my village was attacked.

SONJA: If I'd been clever as she, perhaps...

SONJA: Perhaps I could have...

PANEL THREE: Halayah gets up to put the book away.

HALAYAH: I'm certain you did all you could, Sonja.

SONJA: Halayah.

SONJA: You do not drink, and you do not carouse in fleshly delights.

HALAYAH: I do not.

PANEL FOUR: Sonja stands up, the question is very important to her, as she has some fear of religion due to her background. She idly touches the books on a bookshelf, not looking at Halayah during this very personal question.

SONJA: I don't understand faith, I'm afraid.

SONJA: What do you get, in return for your temperance?

HALAYAH: Grace, Sonja of Hyrkania.

HALAYAH: My faith brings me grace.

PANEL FIVE: Ubriah bursts into the room, in a panic. She's the youngest, and the most emotional of the nuns.

UBRIAH: Red WOMAN!

UBRIAH: There's a man at the door. A WARRIOR!

PANEL SIX: Sonja's face, grim. She knows it's all starting.

SONJA: Thank you, Ubriah.

SONJA: Gravaha goes to see the BEAR, I suppose.

page 4   page 5   page 6

PAGE FOUR:

PANEL ONE: Sonja, opens the Citadel's door, to see a hulking warrior at the doorstep, holding a lantern in the dark. She looks a bit surprised. She has one hand on her sword hilt, but has not drawn it, yet. The warrior is THRUCK the FIERCE, the thug from the tavern last issue. He has a sword as well, also not drawn.

THRUCK: Hallo, miss.

THRUCK: Nice NIGHT, innit?

SONJA: I know you.

SONJA: I've seen you before.

PANEL TWO: Flashback, her smashing the man's chin into the bar table while drunk.

CAP: "You're that OBSTINATE fellow from earlier today.

CAP: "You didn't seem to understand what 'no' meant."

PANEL THREE: Thruck smiles up at her, seemingly jaunty, but there's something dark there, as well.

THRUCK: 'At's right, miss.

THRUCK: Thruck the Fierce, I am.

THRUCK: And you humiliated me good and proper for my tender offer.

PANEL FOUR: Sonja's face, suspicious.

      SONJA: Do you work for the EMPRESS, Thruck?

      THRUCK: You misjudge me, miss.

      THRUCK: I come wif NEWS.

PANEL FIVE: We see the Empress, imperious on her golden throne, looking very displeased and contemptuous.

      CAP: "See, the Empress, she don't LIKE 'er female subjects to have learning. Says it makes them forget their honest PLACE.

      CAP: "So she's wants this place BURNT proper. CRISP, she says."

PANEL SIX: His smile, close up.

      THRUCK: Oh, and miss..

      THRUCK: She's RIGHT peeved at YOU, mishandling her GUARDS and all."

PAGE FIVE:

Full page panel, the three assassins from last issue, each calmly riding a horse. They look grim, calm. They have only one function in live...to bring death to those their clients pay to meet them.

They ride horses, they have a runner on each side holding a torch in the darkness. They are calm, above all else, and dead-eyed, like bringing four nuns to be tortured to death is just a job to them.

As ominous as possible, please, Walter. These are scary men, stone cold killers. :)

Also, please have them in the same left-to-right order as the last panel of last issue, okay?

      CAP: "She's gone and sent her VIPERS, miss. Icy cold killers, the lot of them.

      CAP: "Said you wasn't WORTH the cost of sending a battalion, and the Vipers will do you more PERSONAL-like, you see?

      CAP: "Make it MEMORABLE. "Oh, and they can. They CAN, miss.

      CAP (under the man on the left): There's UTRO the NEEDLE. Uses daggers dipped in DUNG...causes a screaming death from FEVER.

      CAP (under the middle man): "There's RUDUS the QUICK, whose blade, they say, cries for blood each night, evil or innocent.

      CAP (under right man): And there's HARON the CRUEL. The finest bowman in the land...likes to pin his targets with arrows, then take DAYS, using them for target practice.

      CAP: "Oooh, there's a bad lot, miss.

      CAP: "You've never met their LIKE, I promise you. And they're coming, TONIGHT.

PAGE SIX:

PANEL ONE: Sonja looks at the man, skeptically.

SONJA: So, you've come to warn me, Thruck, is that it?

THRUCK: Oh, NO, miss.

THRUCK: I came to gloat and to see you DESPAIR.

THRUCK: Tonight's your DEATH, miss. And that warms my HEART.

PANEL TWO: Sonja's face is blank.

SONJA: I see.

SONJA: I'll need your sword, dirtscrape.

THRUCK: What?

SONJA: I SAID—

PANEL THREE: She SMASHES him in the face, brutally, with her fist.

SONJA: I'll need your SWORD.

THRUCK: GUHHH.

PANEL FOUR: She hits him AGAIN with an uppercut, a brutal one, rocking his head backwards.

SONJA: And by the way?

SONJA: Gloating?

PANEL FIVE: She hits him one last time. A right cross across his face, knocking him out.

SONJA: It's plain bad MANNERS.

SONJA: Even for a lickspittle clodhopping buffoon such as YOURSELF, dear Thruck.

PAGE SEVEN:

PANEL ONE: The three young nuns come out to see what the fuss is about. They are carrying torches. Thruck lies unconscious on the ground, as Sonja regards him, unemotionally. She is not facing the nuns.

SONJA: So.

SONJA: I ask again, nuns of Erlik.

SONJA: Will you leave this place, for the small reward of your continued existence?

HALAYAH: We cannot, Red Woman.

HALAYAH: Our matron cannot be moved, with her wounds.

PANEL TWO: Sonja reaches down to steal Thruck's sword and cloack, or is kneeling to do so.

SONJA: Very noble.

SONJA: And I suppose your faith doesn't allow you to kill?

HALAYAH: Again, regrettably…

SONJA: No matter.

SONJA: But you must understand, Halayah.

PANEL THREE: Sonja stands up and faces them.

SONJA: I've heard of these "Vipers."

SONJA: I could take one of them. PERHAPS two.

SONJA: Never all three. It can't be done.

PANEL FOUR: The nuns look at her, in a bit of despair, but resolute.

SONJA: So. Here is what will happen.

SONJA: I will die.

SONJA; Then YOU will die.

SONJA: Then the spire will burn anyway, with your precious scratchbooks inside.

PANEL FIVE: Sonja walks away from them, slightly.

SONJA: It's always wise to know the pot when one is gambling, is all.

SONJA: Each of you, fetch a spade.

SONJA: We've a GRAVE to dig.

page 7

page 8

PAGE EIGHT:

PANEL ONE: The Vipers, riding their horses casually, their squires going along with torches. Rudus and Utro are talking to each other, while Haron looks somber and grim.

RUDUS: …should be at least decent sport, five women.

RUDUS: They don't LAST as long, but I find their screams and protestations to be quite invigorating, Utro.

UTRO: Oh, I disagree entirely, RUDUS.

UTRO: Torturing a MAN to death, a strong MAN…

UTRO: Well. It's REWARDING to get those same squeals from a MAN.

SQUIRE: Begging your pardon, sir…but there's the SPIRE. The LIBRARY!

PANEL TWO: They stop, squinting in the darkness, looking at something we can't see, off panel.

UTRO: Is that…is that the She-Devil?

UTRO: Standing like a fool, in our inexorable Viper's path?

PANEL THREE: Bigger panel, we see Sonja (it's not really Sonja, it's a dummy, but it LOOKS like Sonja, it's her boots, Thruck's sword and cloak, and it's standing in front of the Spire door. The torch light from behind the dummy makes it look like Sonja stands, cloaked, hood over her head, silent and ready to fight. The reader should not know this isn't Sonja, she has to look badass and scary here, like Batman, just standing in the path of these killers, between them and their prize, the Spire.

HARON (off): No. She seeks to FRIGHTEN us.

HARON (off): The GIRL seeks to give the VIPERS a nightmare!

HARON: RUDUS, show her what fear IS!

page 9   page 10   page 11

PAGE NINE:

PANEL ONE: Haron brings up his bow, as Utro smiles, grimly.

UTRO: It's unkind, I know, Haron.

UTRO: But I DO hope you make her SUFFER.

UTRO: Impertinent WENCH that she is.

PANEL TWO: The bow lets fly an arrow.

PANEL THREE: Several of the arrows find their mark on the dummy, through the cloak.

FX (arrows): thuck thuck thuck!

PANEL FOUR: The Vipers gasp in astonishment.

UTRO: She...she still STANDS.

UTRO: But no armor could...

HARON: Could the legends of the Devil be TRUE?

HARON: She still stands BEFORE us!

PANEL FIVE: Out of the dirt behind the men, we see Sonja's hand crawling up out of the dirt...she's buried herself in the path.

SONJA: No, Assassin.

PAGE TEN:

FULL PAGE PANEL, Sonja coming up out of the ground, dirt falling from her hair and body, holding her own sword up high, she is absolutely terrifying. She doesn't look her usual self, she looks wild with fury and covered in dirt and pebbles and twigs. The horses are bucking, wide-eyed.

Even the Vipers react with surprise, but the horses and squires are absolutely horrified by this creature that leaps up out of the ground like a dead body returned. It's a scene of sheer, terror-induced CHAOS.

SONJA: GRAVAHA IS BEHIND YOU, DEAR BEAR.

PAGE ELEVEN:

PANEL ONE: The three nuns, in wide-eyed astonishment, as they watch from the tower.

UBRIAH: We should...we have to...

UBRIAH: We must HELP her!

HALAYAH: She is...

HALAYAH: She is BEYOND our reach, Ubriah.

PANEL TWO: Sonja, holding her sword overhead with both hands, charges Haron, who is notching another arrow.

SONJA CAP: Each of these men MIGHT be my better at their discipline.

SONJA CAP: I could not face THIS one bow to bow.

SONJA CAP: So, first, I need a SCREAMER.

PANEL THREE: She stabs through his leg while he's still on the horse.

FX: slitcch

RUDUS: AAAAAAHGGHHH!

SONJA CAP: I find that makes allies MOST upset.

SONJA CAP: THANK you, Rudus.

PANEL FOUR: She reaches up to grab Haron's arm, while the others are circling on their horses to face her.

RUDUS: FACE her. STAB her!

SONJA CAP: A bowman is bad enough. A bowman on HORSEBACK is too much.

SONJA CAP: These men are peacock killers. They talk too much.

PANEL FIVE: She YANKS him off the horse, his face astonished, as the horse is panicking.

SONJA CAP: So the Devil will face them in the SILENCE of the VOID.

RUDUS: She's got HARON. She's got HARON the QUICK!

page 12   page 13   page 14

PAGE TWELVE:

PANEL ONE: HARON falls at her feet as she spins around, her sword still bloody from wounding him.

SONJA CAP: If I had a moment, I could strike him down and lower the odds.

PANEL TWO: Utro comes at her with both daggers up, she barely gets her sword up in time to block. We see Rudus dismounting himself from his steed.

UTRO: The Vipers do not FEAR you, slattern!

SONJA CAP: But I do not have a moment.

PANEL THREE: Sonja, pushed back, her back to Haron, who is on the ground behind her, angrily grabbing an arrow from his quiver. She is pushed back by Utro's fierce attack.

SONJA CAP: His blades are short.

SONJA CAP: But there are TWO of them. And I...

PANEL FOUR: HARON, on the ground behind her, shoves an arrow through Sonja's calf, painfully.

SONJA CAP: ...I should have spent that MOMENT I mentioned early.

FX (arrow): gllltch

SONJA: Gnnn.

PANEL FIVE: Sonja stumbles back, noticeably favoring her good leg, the arrow still puncturing her other, and bleeding badly.

SONJA CAP: Oh.

SONJA CAP: And things were going so WELL.

PAGE THIRTEEN:

PANEL ONE: Sonja allows herself one moment to duck her head and squint in pain.

SONJA CAP: Where's...

SONJA CAP: Where's the LAST of these miserable bastards?

PANEL TWO: Rudus, the swordsman, rushes at her, she barely parries in time.

SONJA CAP: Ah.

SONJA CAP: Ask a question of the gods, get an answer laden with IRONY.

FX: KLLAANNG

PANEL THREE: She stabs at him, he parries, and sidesteps, adroitly.

SONJA CAP: I had said I might be able to take TWO of these killers.

PANEL FOUR: Sonja BARELY moves her head backwards in time to avoid a horizontal swing of Rudus' blade, meant to decapitate her.

SONJA CAP: I may have been optimistic, it appears.

PAGE FOURTEEN:

PANEL ONE: He stabs her in the side, right through her armor, she grimaces in agony. She has a horse behind her, one of the Vipers' horses, we see its reins hanging down.

SONJA CAP: Gtsss.

PANEL TWO: Rudus holds his blade up, bloody with her crimson. He's smiling.

RUDUS: Sonja the Great.

RUDUS: The SHE-Devil.

RUDUS: Terror of the Hyrkanian PLAINS.

PANEL THREE: Sonja, holding her side (close up) as blood is flowing out over her fingers, she's holding the wound.

RUDUS (off-panel): What happens, I wonder...

RUDUS (off-panel): ...when all your TRICKS fail you?

PANEL FOUR: Utro steps in front of Rudus, politely.

RUDUS: What happens when you face a superior foe, foolish woman?

UTRO: The answer is defeat, Haron.

UTRO: Ignominious, humiliating defeat.

UTRO: An end to legend.

PANEL FIVE: Utro, holding up his knives...smiling.

UTRO: Do you know what I believe I shall do, girl child?

UTRO: It's really quite whimsical.

UTRO: I believe I shall take your ridiculously-tressed SCALP and use it to braid my MOUNT.

PAGE FIFTEEN:

PANEL ONE: Sonja reaches behind her, grabbing the reins of the horse...she's smiling, darkly.

SONJA: Your mount?

SONJA: That seems a gaudy thing to do to your own SISTER, small blade.

PANEL TWO: Utro, infuriated, leaps at her with both knives raised. She's still holding the reins of the horse in one hand.

UTRO: My—

UTRO: You filth-mouth BITCH.

SONJA: Eh.

SONJA: I've been called WORSE.

PANEL THREE: She ducks under his blades, smaller panel.

PANEL FOUR: She spins him around so that she is behind him, wrapping the reins around his neck,

UTRO: glljk.

PANEL FIVE: She SLAPS the ass of the horse, hard, with her sword (the flat side, obviously). The horse rears, as Utro helplessly clutches at his throat, the reins wrapped tightly. Utro has dropped both knives.

FX (horse butt): wwakkkk

UTRO: wait

UTRO: no

SONJA: Oh, don't mind me, Utro. DO go on.

PANEL SIX: Insert panel, him desperately reaching and pawing at the ground with one hand for his knives, which have fallen JUST out of reach.

UTRO: wait

UTRO: plse

page 15   page 16

PAGE SIXTEEN:

PANEL ONE: The horse takes off in a terrified gallop, dragging the wild, terrified, choking UTRO with it, his hands clutching with futility at the reins wrapped around his neck, choking him to death as he is being dragged by the horse.

      SONJA: I believe you were saying something disparaging about my HAIR?

PANEL TWO: Her smile is broken by an arrow that is fired into her shoulder, knocking her backwards with tremendous impact, a bit of blood flying from the wound through the air.

      FX (arrow): THUK.

      SONJA CAP: Damn.

      SONJA CAP: The ARCHER.

PANEL THREE: The archer, Haron, on one knee, in pain, but his face full of contempt, as he notches another arrow in his bow.

      HARON: Do you really think the world would tolerate your shameless capering FOREVER?

      HARON: A WOMAN, of all things?

      HARON: Did you think we would ALLOW that to FESTER?

PANEL FOUR: Sonja, on her knees. Bleeding from three wounds, hair disheveled, one hand on the ground, one hand on her sword, as Rudus stands near, sword pointed at her. She's obviously suffering.

      SONJA: To be honest, pinprick...

      SONJA: I hadn't given it much THOUGHT.

PANEL FIVE: Kathala, the middle nun, in tears, as they watch the spectacle. The others look on in pain and sadness.

      KATHALA: We have to...we have to HELP her!

      KATHALA: I have to GO!

HALAYAH: Kathala...there's nothing we CAN do, but die with her.

page 17   page 18   page 19

PAGE SEVENTEEN:

PANEL ONE: Kathala, weeping as she grabs Halayah by the arms.

KATHALA: But you don't understand! I doubted her!

KATHALA: I believed she would abandon us, I—

KATHALA: She is DYING for us ALL!

PANEL TWO: Halayah hugs the weeping nun to her chest.

HALAYAH: Then we should show a fraction of her courage, sister.

HALAYAH: Impossible as that task may seem.

PANEL THREE: Rudus lowers his sword towards Sonja, on her knees. He thinks she's beaten.

RUDUS: If you kiss the tip of my sword, savage, and denounce your abominable defense of this...this ATROCITY of a spire...

RUDUS: I'll make your end quick.

RUDUS: It matters not to me.

PANEL FOUR: Sonja, holding the wound in her side, hair in her face, in pain, not looking up at the man.

SONJA: Have you ever read the story of Gravaha, sellsword?

RUDUS: Eh?

SONJA: It's quite a tale. Bears and scarecrows and whatnot.

SONJA: Sonja relents.

SONJA: Give me your sword.

PANEL FIVE: He holds the tip of it towards her, she gently holds it with her free hand, head bowed, eyes down.

      RUDUS: At last.

      RUDUS: You know your PLACE.

PANEL SIX: Same pov exactly, same panel size and everything. But Sonja looks UP at him, smiling a dark, mean smile.

      RUDUS: ...What?

      SONJA: I propose a counter-offer, Rudus.

PAGE EIGHTEEN:

PANEL ONE: From the side, Sonja STABS her blade through Rudus' lower chest, hard enough that it comes out his back. His face is one of total shock, but hers is darkly gleeful. A bit of his blood splatters on her (again, not a gory amount, just a bit). The blade is clearly giving him a fatal blow. He is more stunned than angry, he can't believe a WOMAN got the best of him.

      SONJA: Why don't you kiss the tip of MY sword and see how THAT feels, you murdering son of a BITCH?

      RUDUS: —

      RUDUS: glk

PANEL TWO: She walks with Rudus, him walking backwards, stumbling, still in shock, and she's holding him up by her sword...she is using him as a human shield from the archer.

      SONJA: And while we're at it...the answer to your previous question?

PANEL THREE: Her face, smiling huge, staring right into his shocked, dying eyes.

      SONJA: I invent NEW tricks.

PANEL FOUR: The bowman on the ground is worried, shooting his arrows wildly.

      HARON: No.

      HARON: Stay BACK.

      HARON: Stay BACK!

PANEL FIVE: She is walking towards the bowman, using Rudus as her shield, as several arrows are sticking out of his back, along with her bloody sword. She's almost upon Haron, still on the ground.

      FX (arrow): THUK

      HARON: Please. STAY BACK!

      HARON: PLEASE!

PAGE NINETEEN:

PANEL ONE: We see Sonja shove Rudus, hard, letting go of her sword, which is still in his body, poking out the back. Rudus is clearly going to fall on Haron, with that blade coming out of his back and INTO the bowman.

SONJA: As you wish, bowman.

HARON: No. NO!

PANEL TWO: Rudus falls backwards onto Haron, whose eyes go wide in pain.

HARON: GUH.

HARON: ghh.

PANEL THREE: Sonja, standing. She's got an arrow in her shoulder, blood running down her side and her leg also has an arrow.

SONJA: Well.

SONJA: I think I'll faint.

SONJA: Shall I?

PANEL FOUR: She falls, partially onto the two dead men, face up.

DEATH CAP: Yes, Sonja. You shall.

DEATH CAP: Each day, you are closer to me, you are aware of that, yes?

DEATH CAP: Curse of the Hyrkanians. She-Devil. My daughter.

PANEL FIVE: Birds eye view of the fight, scattered horses and weapons, we see Sonja on her back in the dirt, near her freshly dead foes.

SONJA CAP: Oh. It's YOU, Death.

SONJA CAP: Respectfully, would you mind shutting up for a moment?

SONJA CAP: Sonja is trying to SLEEP.

PAGE NINETEEN: (editor's note: repeated "page nineteen" in original script)

PANEL ONE: The hands of the nuns (we don't see their faces), as they ever so gently, even reverently lift her almost-lifeless body from the dirt.

SONJA CAP: And then hands that never held a sword lifted me and I knew nothing for a good number of days.

PANEL TWO: Blackness, just a black panel.

SONJA CAP: In those days, I heard the voice of Death.

SONJA CAP: I was comforted, somehow, though I remember not what she said.

PANEL THREE: Halayah, wringing a wet towel from a basin held by Kathala, they are trying to bring down Sonja's fever. She's on a couch, sweat on her brow, her face is fevered and her eyes are closed. The girls are clearly concerned. Sonja is wearing only a blanket here.

SONJA CAP: There was a cost.

SONJA CAP: There was a fever. There were scars. And pains that never quite went fully away.

SONJA CAP: But there was also warmth and kindness.

PANEL FOUR: Sonja relaxing, wearing a toga-like drape, arms behind her head, as Halayah reads to her from a large book.

    SONJA CAP: The nuns took turns reading to me, watching both myself and the matron of the spire recover.

    SONJA CAP: I liked the adventure stories best.

PANEL FIVE: Kathala is helping Sonja write a Hyrkanian symbol on papyrus with a feather quill. Sonja's hand is still shaky with writing, but better. Kathala is happily praising Sonja, who looks happy herself.

    SONJA CAP: They've also kindly helped me with my letters.

    SONJA CAP: I...

    SONJA CAP: I found myself moved to happy tears, more than once.

    SONJA CAP: Tell no one.

PAGE TWENTY:

PANEL ONE: Sonja is looking in a mirror as Ubriah cuts her hair. She is wearing the toga, she has a bandage on her shoulder. Halayah is speaking to Sonja.

    SONJA CAP: Time passed. I dallied too long.

    SONJA CAP: The nuns asked me endless questions about my life, and my odd stories.

    SONJA CAP: Why, I know not.

    SONJA CAP: But I knew, I could not stay with my new sisters forever.

PANEL TWO: Sonja, now with shorter hair, some sort of cool warrior's haircut of your choosing, Walter (it's just for the end of this story, it won't be permanent), as she hugs the three tearful nuns. Albreckt, the older nun, watches with a smile.

    SONJA CAP: It does not seem to be lot to be at peace for long.

PANEL THREE: A rich castle, at night, it can be partially in the moon's silhouette.

    SONJA CAP: So it is only right that I should aim my chaos where it is of the most USE.

    VOICE (from castle): I'm SORRY, your majesty!

    VOICE (from castle): I will fetch you a NEW pot of tea, hotter, as you wish!

PANEL FOUR: The Empress Dowager THROWS her cup of tea at a young servant peasant's head, barely missing her, the cup SMASHING against the castle wall just inches from the terrified girl. The Empress is still wearing a crown.

    EMPRESS: A NEW pot? After you've SPOILED my one moment of PEACE after a day ruling this EMPIRE?

    EMPRESS: Begone! Be only too grateful I don't have YOU boiled in a pot, stupid, stupid PEASANT!

PANEL FIVE: In the shadows of the room, near a now open castle window, showing dark night outside, we see the silhouette of Sonja, only her eyes showing clearly. She's got her new haircut, and her classic costume on.

SONJA: EMPRESS DOWAGER.

EMPRESS: Eh? Who is THAT, who skulks in my shadows?

SONJA: It is I.

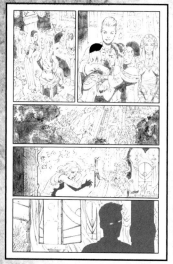

page 20   page 21   page 22

PAGE TWENTY-ONE:

PANEL ONE: Sonja steps forwards, grimly.

SONJA: I am protector of the library, your majesty.

SONJA: Booksaver, grave-riser.

SONJA: VIPER killer.

PANEL TWO: The Empress, nearly beside herself with rage.

EMPRESS: How DARE you! How DARE YOU?!

EMPRESS: You come to MY chambers and—

SONJA (off-panel): —All due respect, Majesty...

SONJA (off-panel): Shut the **** up or you're going out the window.

SONJA: CROWN first.

PANEL THREE: Sonja comes up to the Empress, holding one of Utro's knives, pointing it towards the Empress' neck.

SONJA: You might recognize this. It belonged to one of your killers. Your EXPIRED killers.

SONJA: Nasty stuff on it, you die screaming from a mere scratch.

SONJA: I want you to listen very carefully, Empress.

PANEL FOUR: She puts the blade under the empress' throat, she could slit her throat at any time. The Empress' eyes are wide with terror.

SONJA: That spire, and those women, belong to the She-Devil now.

SONJA: Should they merely HEAR of your displeasure.

SONJA: I'll come visit you. And our next visit..?

SONJA: It won't be as CORDIAL.

PANEL FIVE: Sonja removes the crown from the Empress' terrified head.

SONJA: Oh.

SONJA: And I'm taking this.

PAGE TWENTY-TWO:

PANEL ONE: Sonja, on her horse, cloak flowing, riding off into the night, laughing.

SONJA CAP: I'm sure you'll think it's silly.

SONJA CAP: Pouring out my life blood for BOOKS, of all things.

SONJA CAP: I can't explain it. I don't understand it.

SONJA CAP: But I know it was RIGHT.

PANEL TWO: Most of these panels are silent. This is an establishing shot of the spire, at night.

PANEL THREE: Halayah is walking up the stairs with a torch and a book, a large hardcover book.

PANEL FOUR: Focus on the book, the title is

SHE-DEVIL WITH A SWORD

The Adventures of

RED SONJA

PANEL FIVE: Halayah is at a writing desk, she has a feather pen and a bit of an inkpot (really just a wooden dish for ink). She's writing in the book.

We see a page-like caption, showing the writing in her own hand (please make this so it doesn't look just like a computer font, Simon! :)) The page is across the bottom of the page, and has the following writing on it.

"One evening near the Cimmerian border, Red Sonja lay oblivious, the sleeping victim of too much carousing and too little rest.

It was there, that night, that she was accosted by three men, thieves in the night, former soldiers all, all wearing the mark of the plague. They thought her easy pray.

They had not accounted, of course, for the dagger she routinely kept under her pillow..."

NEXT:

RED SONJA REBORN!

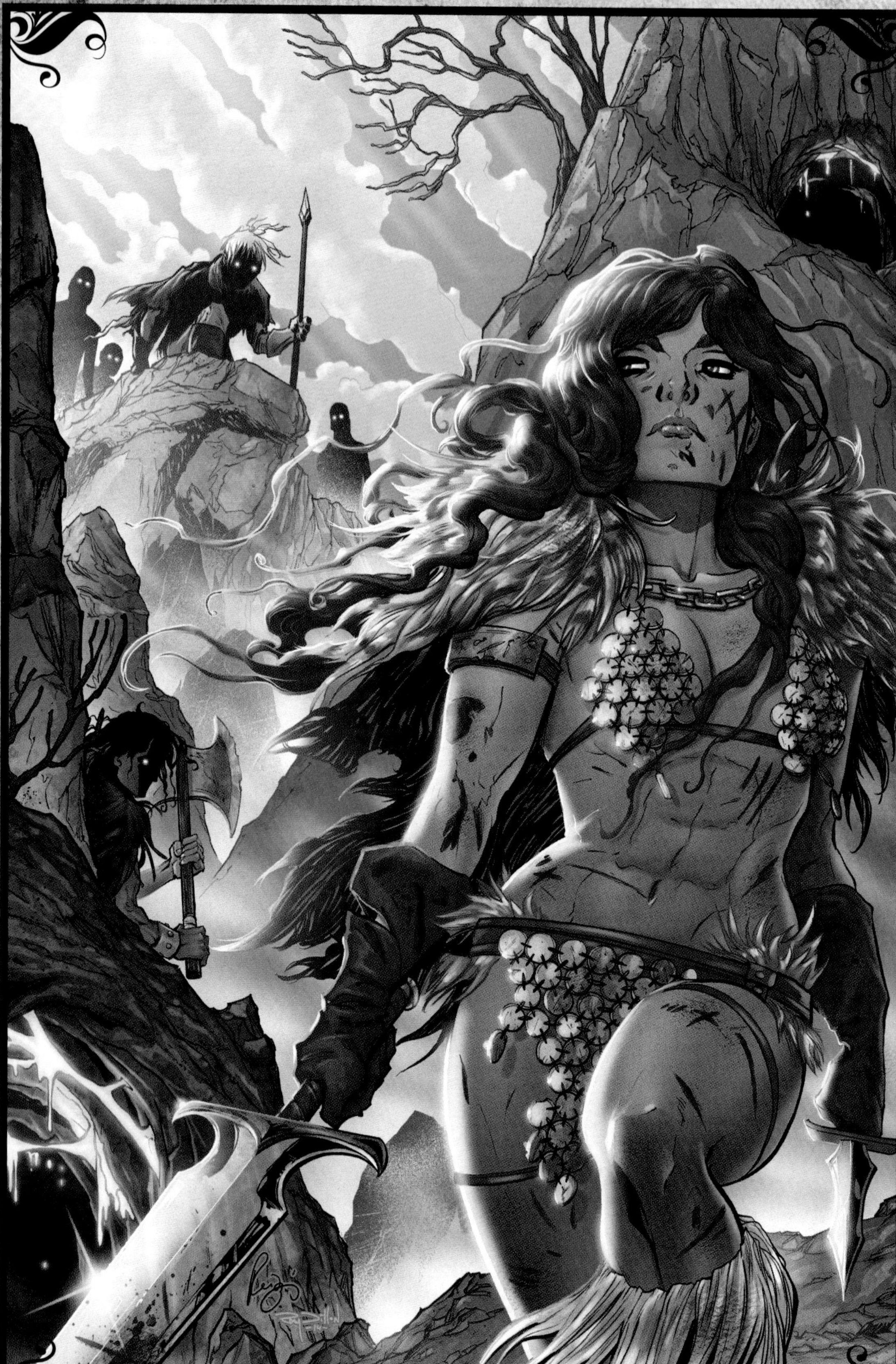

ISSUE THIRTEEN

cover by RENAE DE LIZ and RAY DILLON

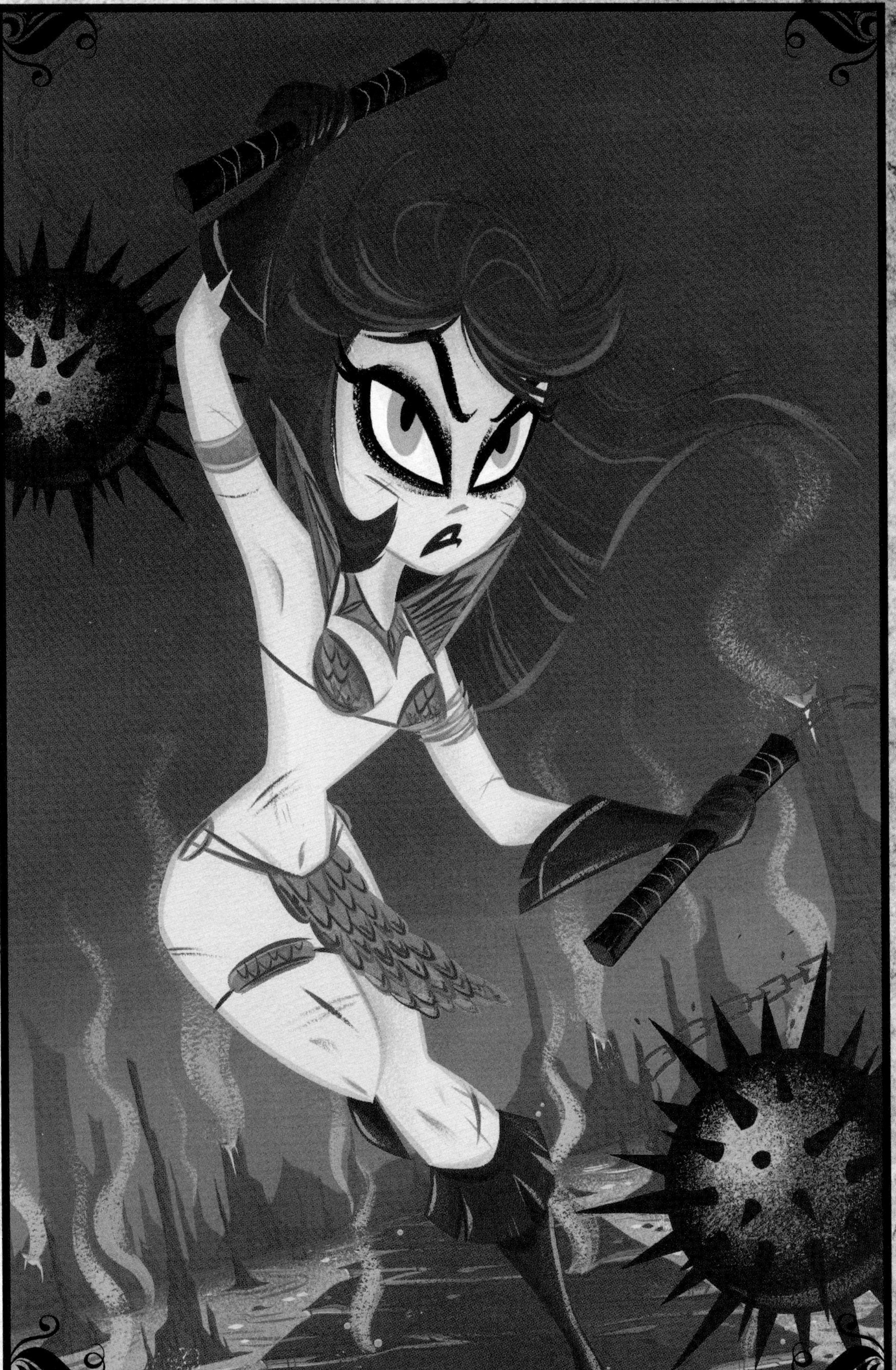

ISSUE THIRTEEN
cover by STEPHANIE BUSCEMA

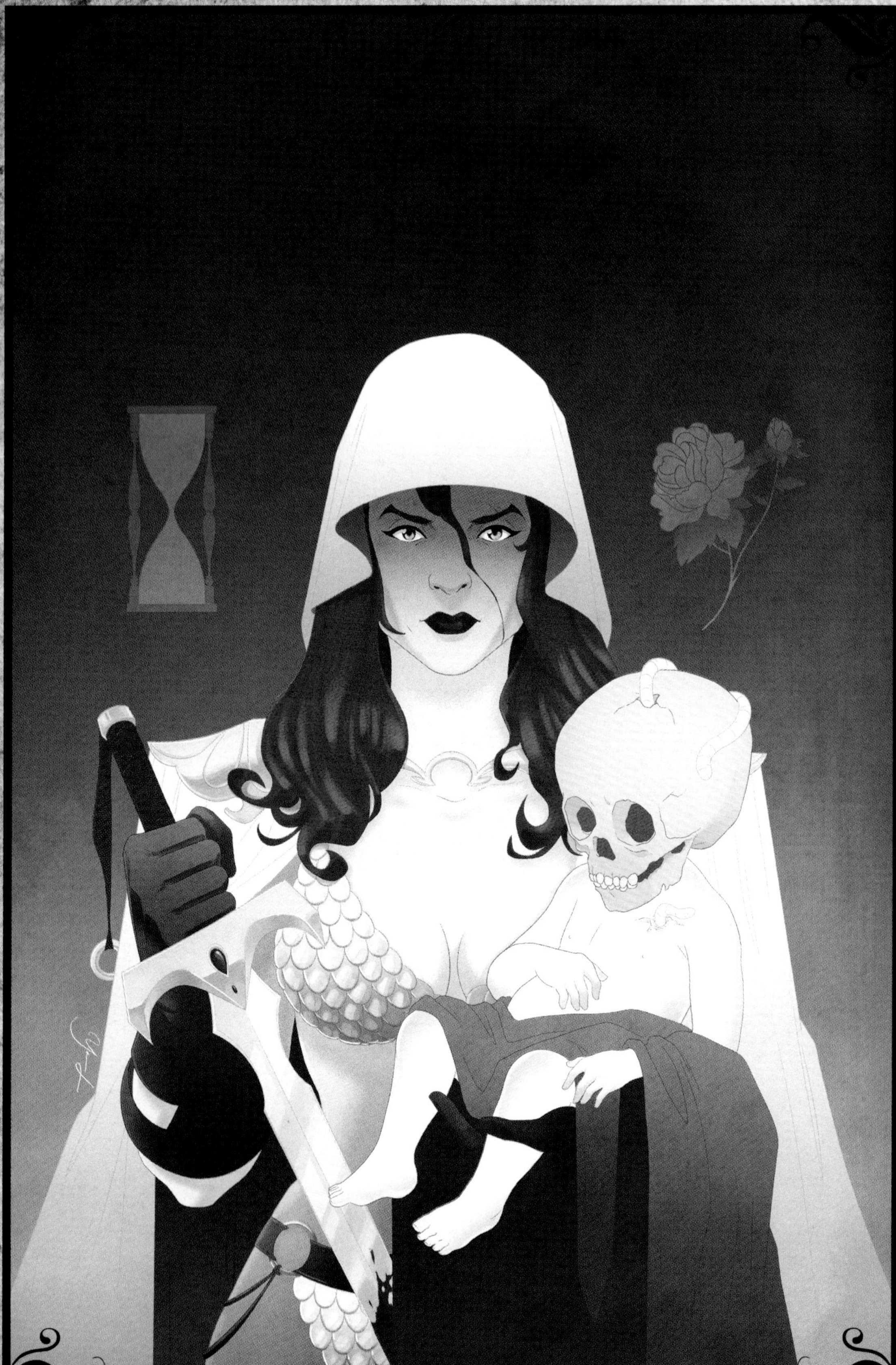

ISSUE FOURTEEN
cover by YASMIN LIANG

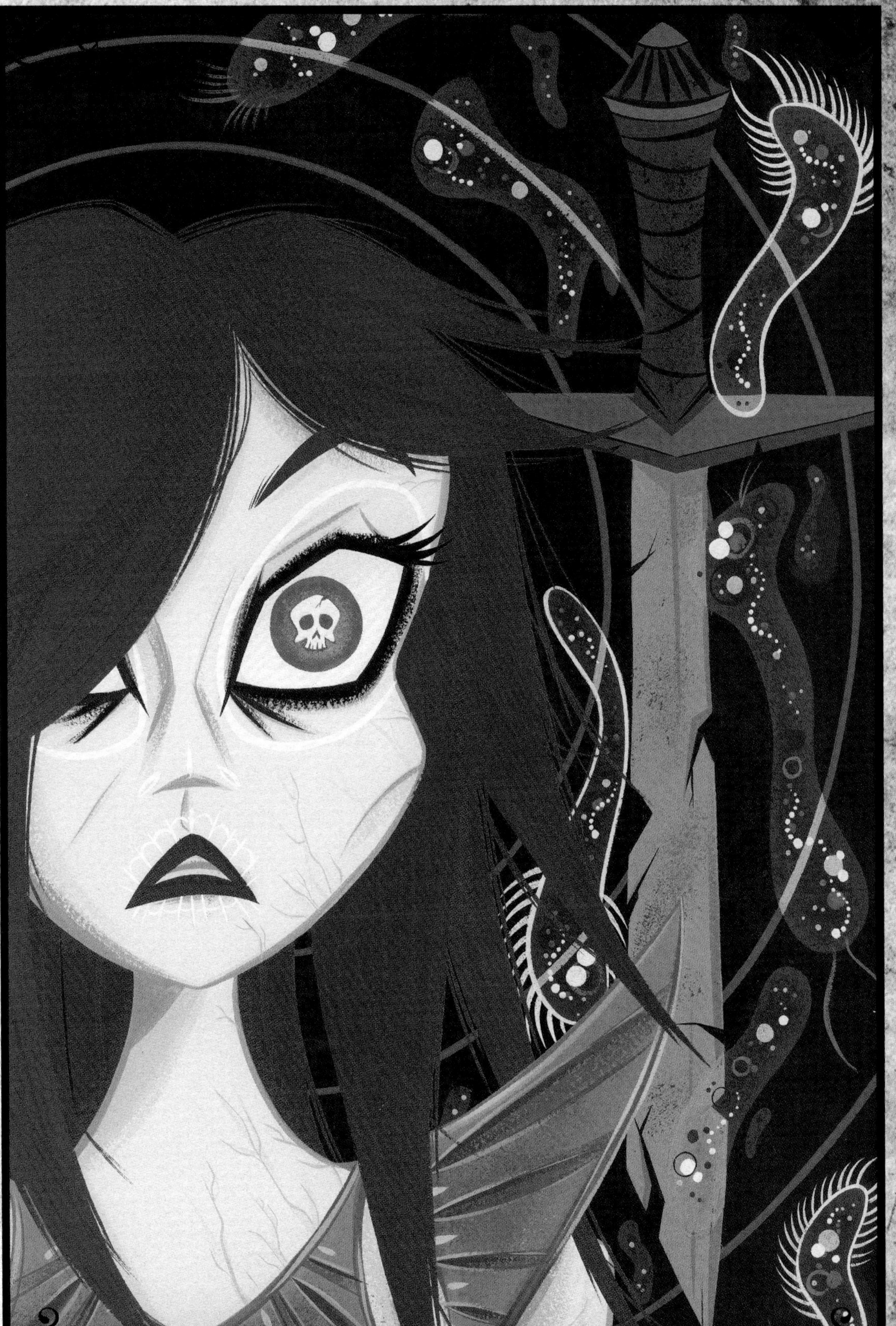

ISSUE FOURTEEN
cover by STEPHANIE BUSCEMA

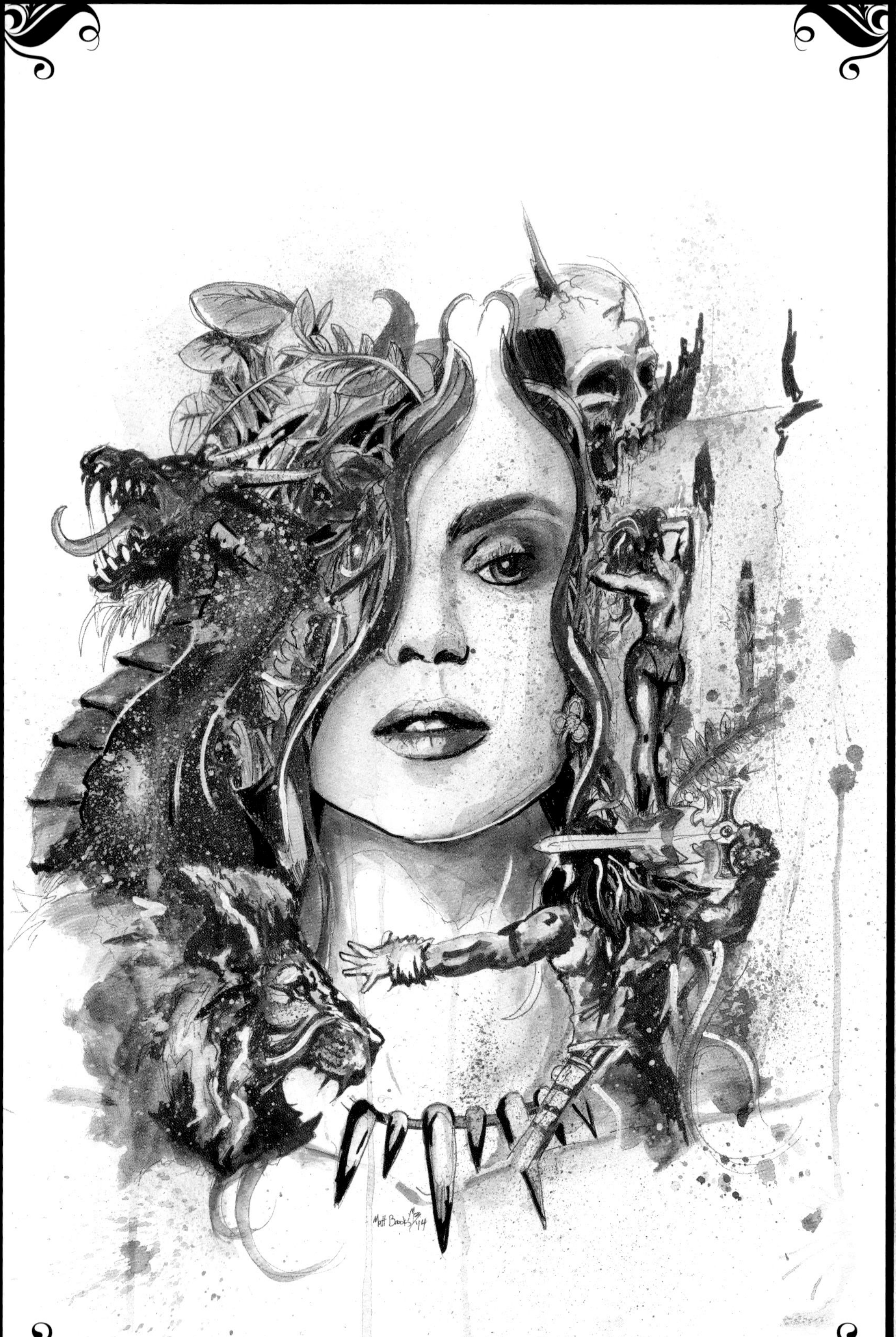
Matt Brooks '14

ISSUE FOURTEEN
cover by MATT BROOKS

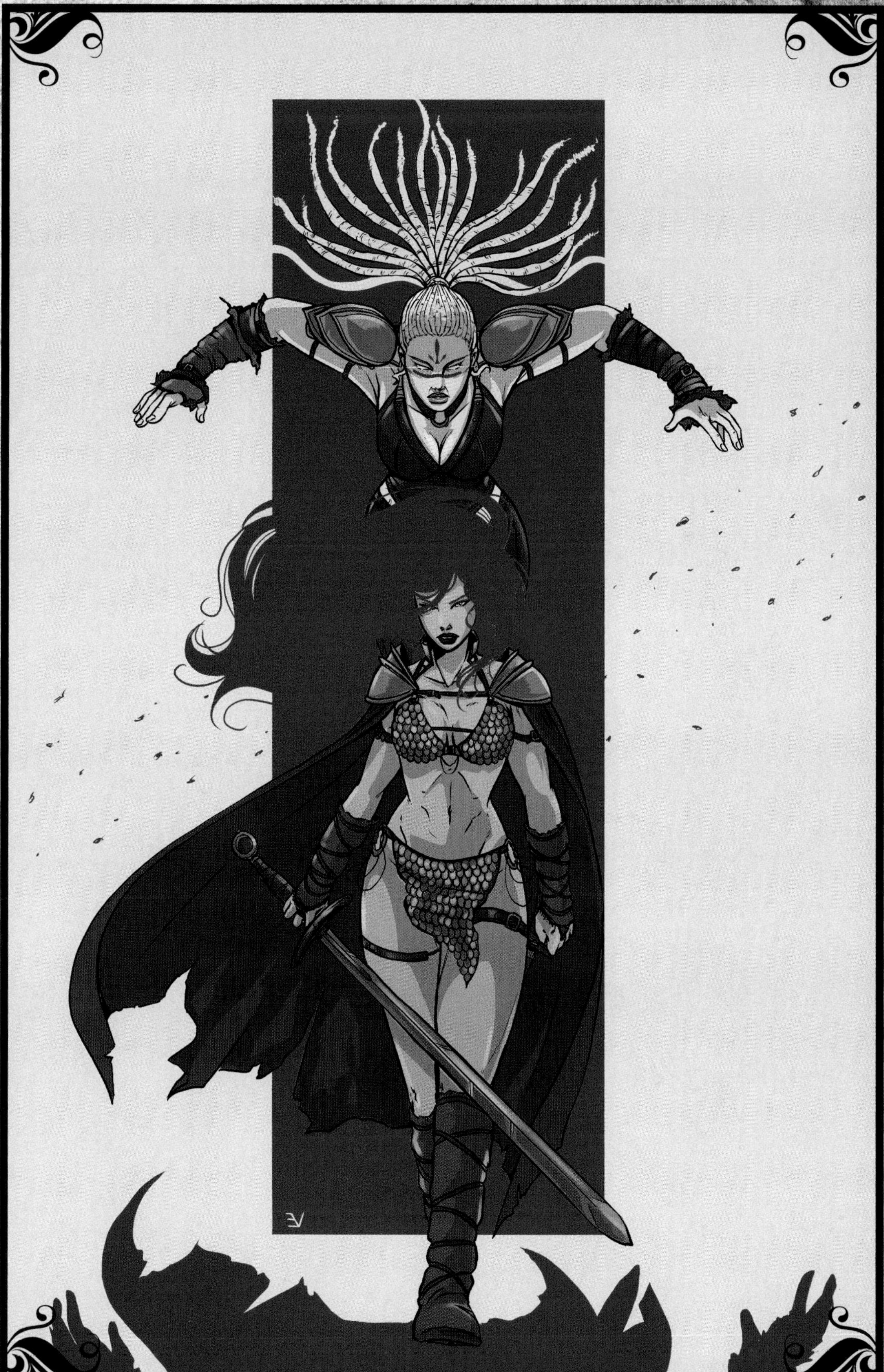

ISSUE FIFTEEN
cover by EMMA VIECELI

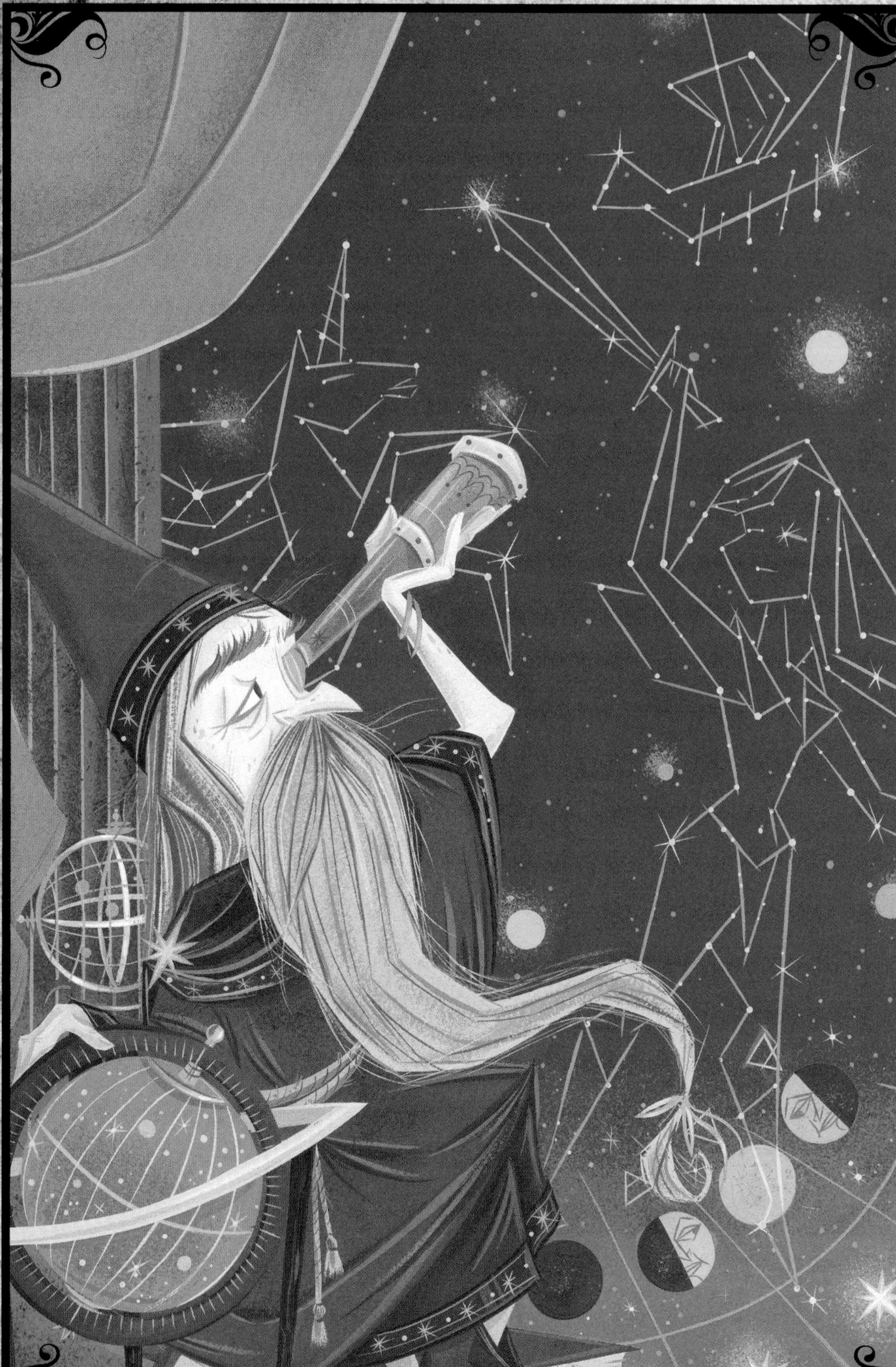

ISSUE FIFTEEN
cover by STEPHANIE BUSCEMA

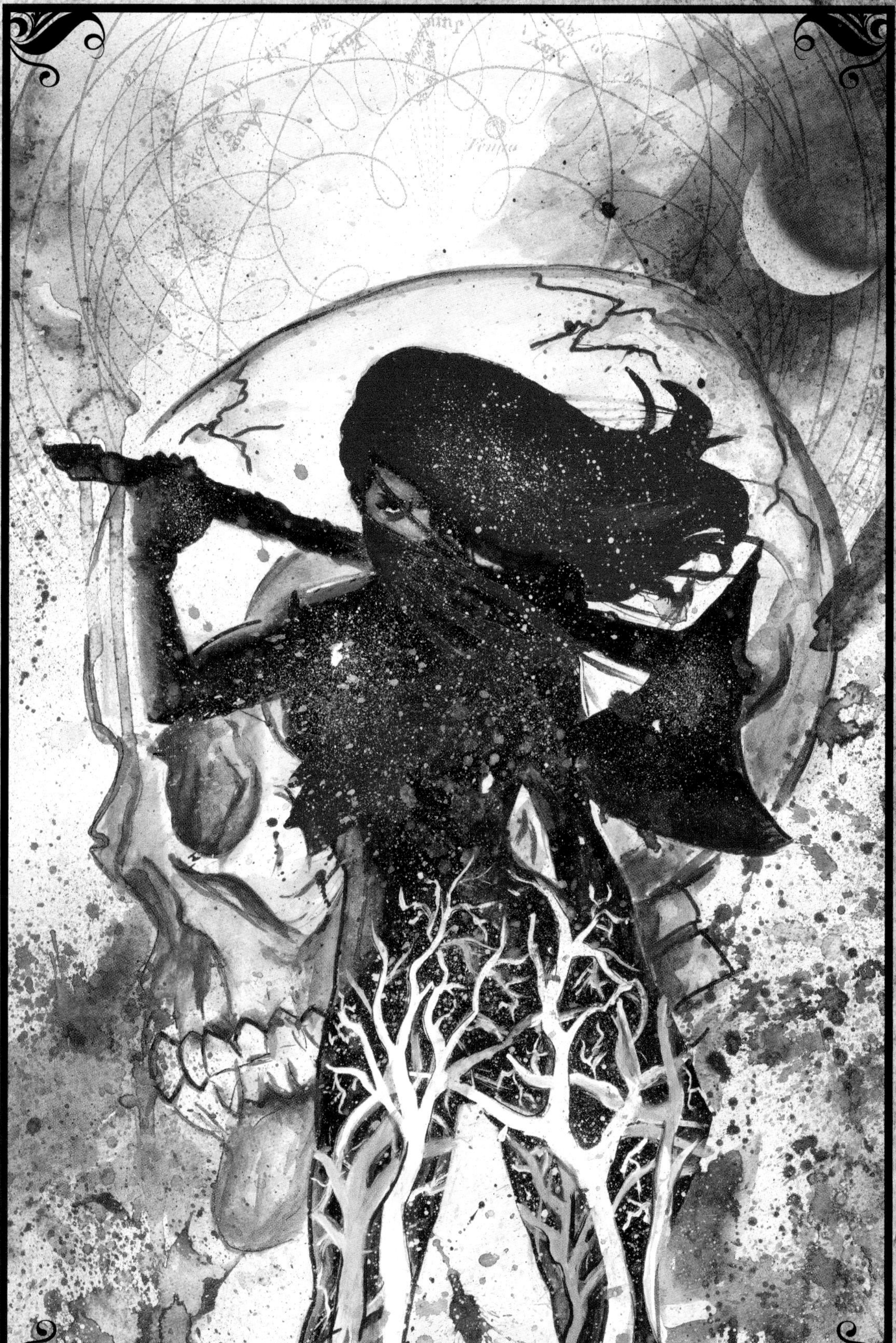

ISSUE FIFTEEN
cover by MATT BROOKS

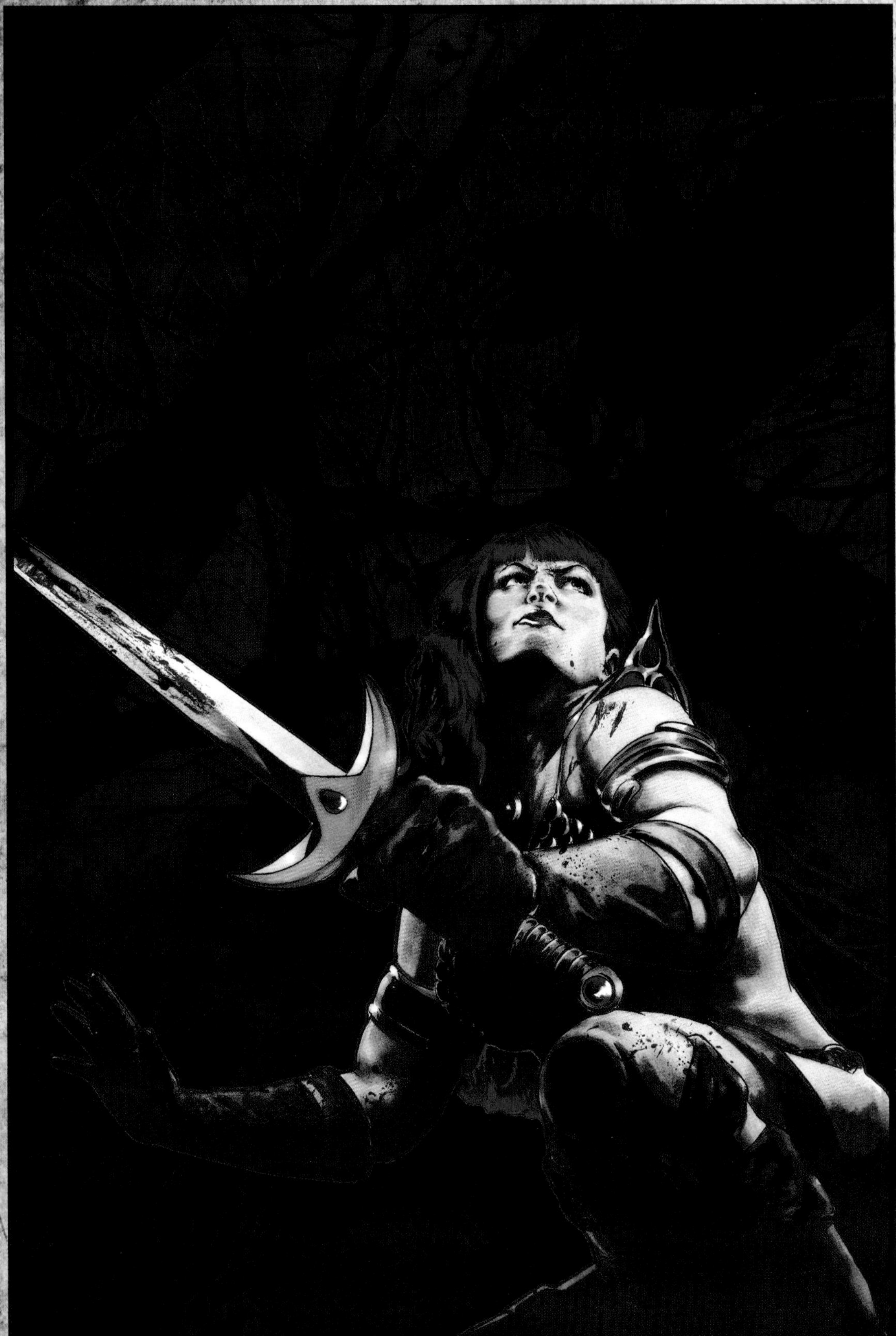

ISSUE SIXTEEN
cover by CAT STAGGS

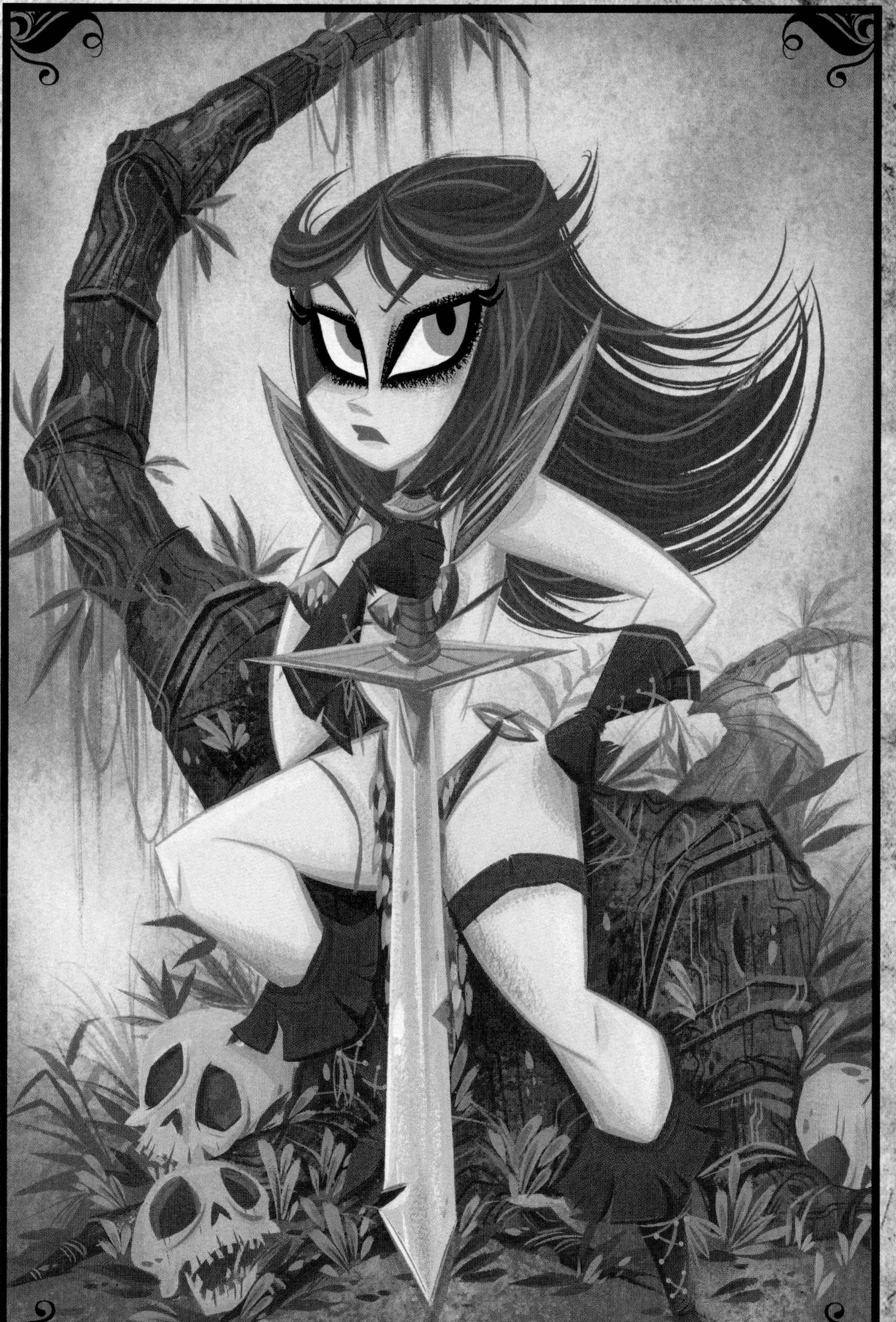

ISSUE SIXTEEN
cover by STEPHANIE BUSCEMA

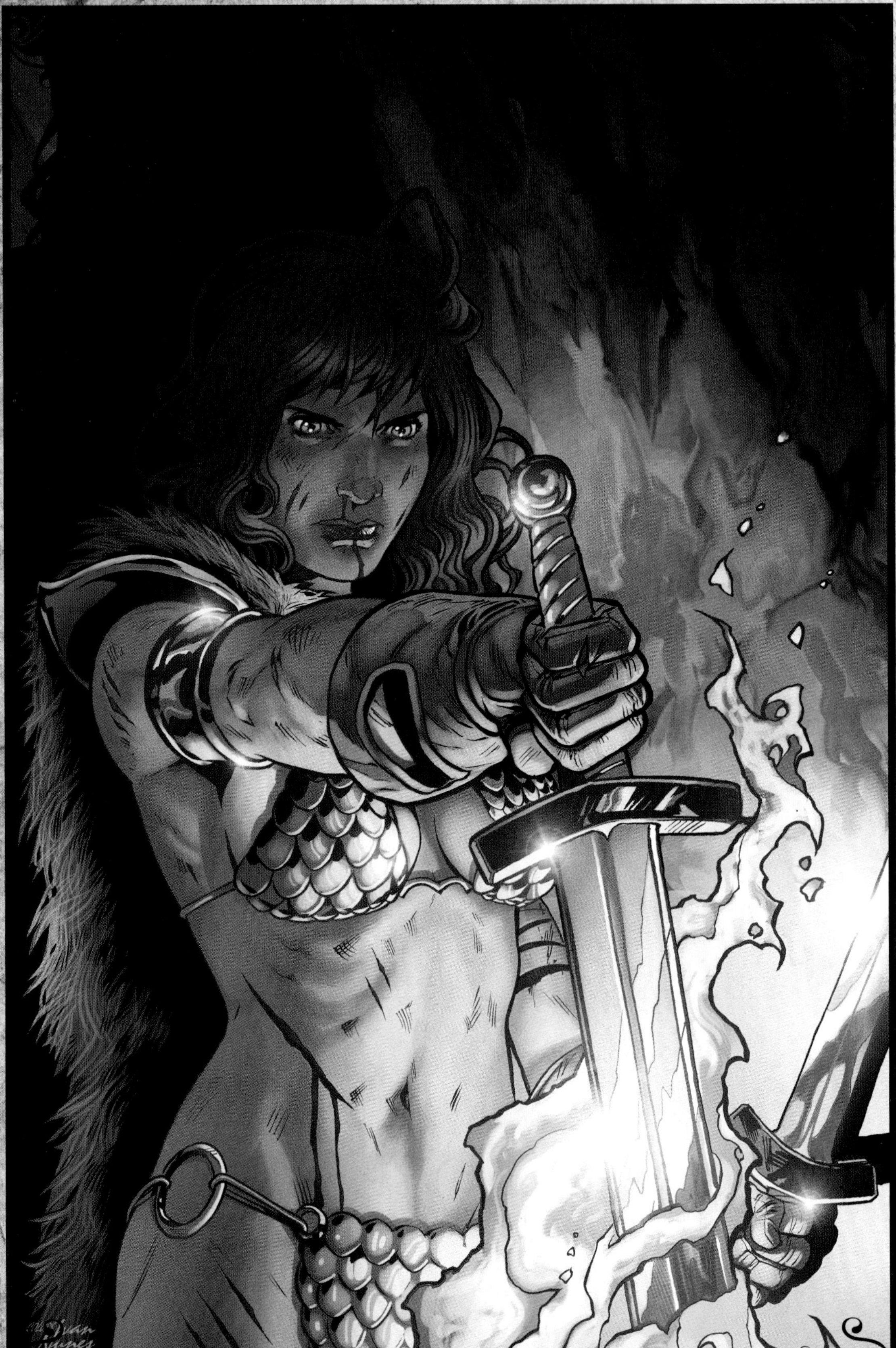

ISSUE SEVENTEEN
cover by REBEKAH ISAACS

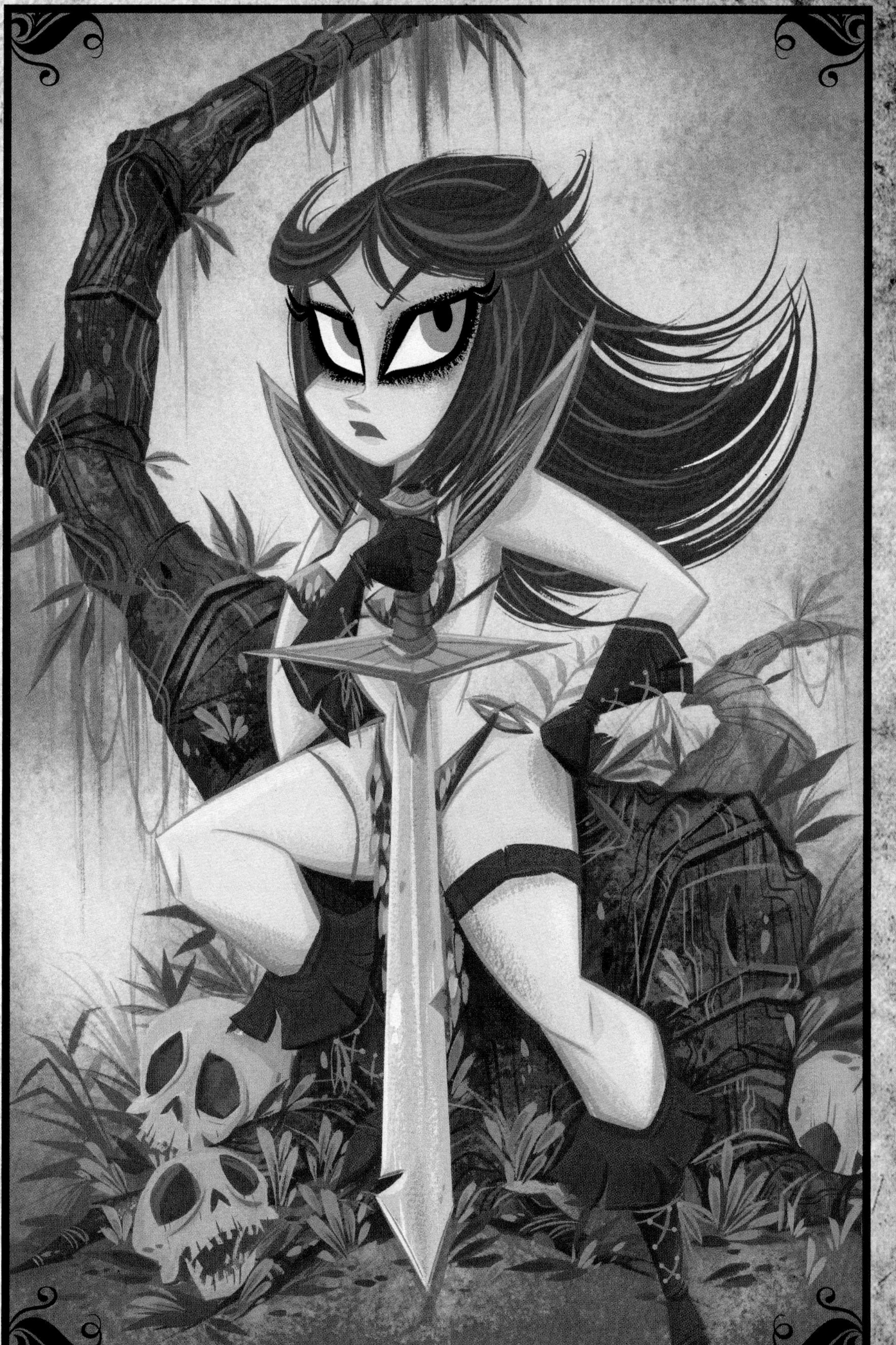

ISSUE SEVENTEEN
cover by STEPHANIE BUSCEMA

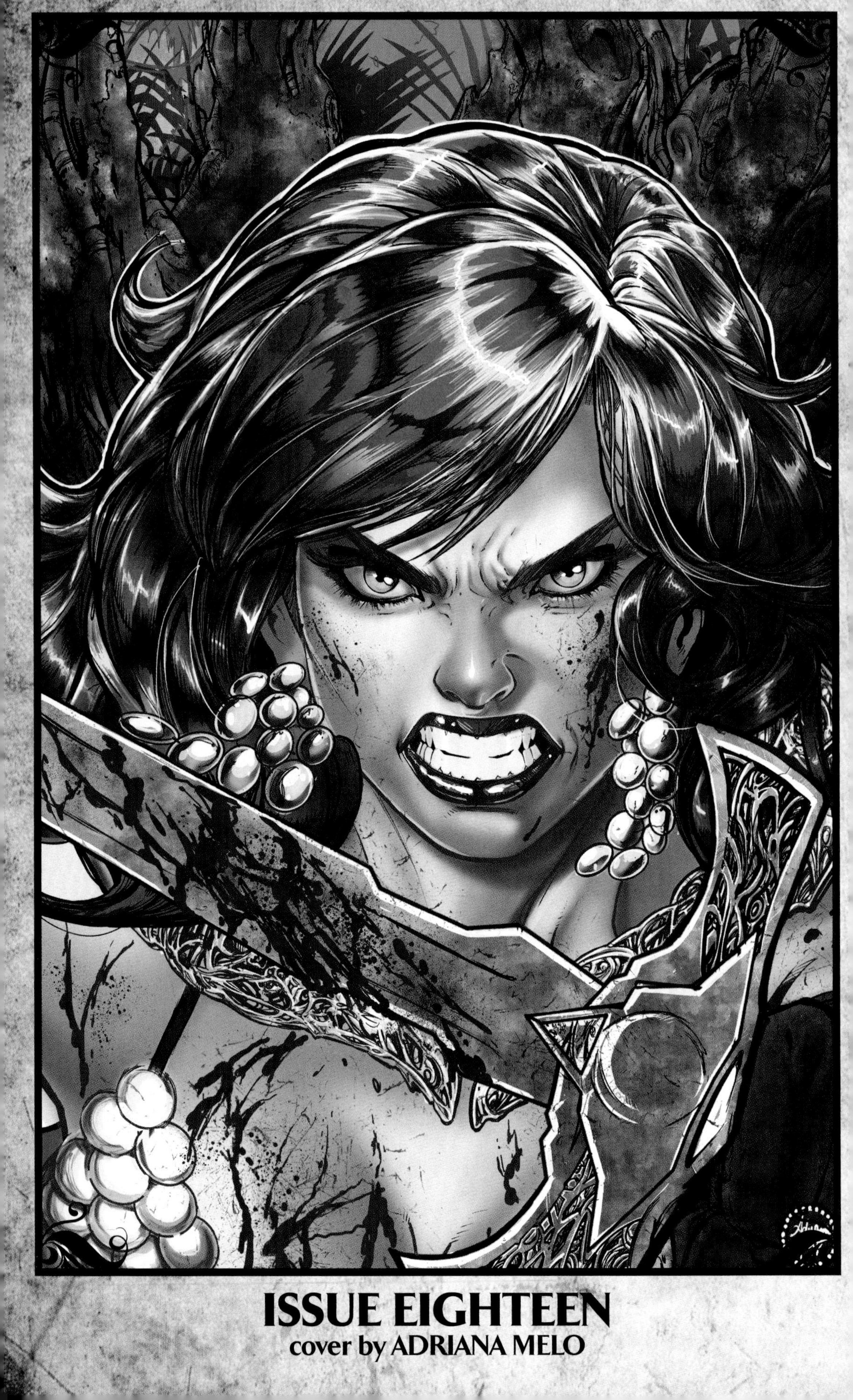

ISSUE EIGHTEEN
cover by ADRIANA MELO